Contemporary Ukraine

Contemporary Ukraine

Dynamics of
Post-Soviet
Transformation

Edited by
Taras Kuzio

M.E. Sharpe

Armonk, New York
London, England

Library of Congress Cataloging-in-Publication Data

Contemporary Ukraine: dynamics of post-soviet transformation /
edited by Taras Kuzio.
p. cm.
Papers presented at the conference held at the
University of Birmingham, June 13–15, 1996.
Includes bibliographical references and index.
ISBN 0-7656-0223-7 (cloth: alk. paper). —
ISBN 0-7656-0224-5 (pbk.:alk. paper)
1. Ukraine—History—1991– —Congresses.
I. Kuzio, Taras.
DK508.846.C66   1998
947.08′6—DC21   97-36023
CIP
Printed in the United States of America

The paper used in this publication meets the minimum requirements of
American National Standard for Information Sciences—
Permanence of Paper for Printed Library Materials,
ANSI Z 39.48-1984.

BM (c)   10   9   8   7   6   5   4   3   2   1
BM (p)   10   9   8   7   6   5   4   3   2   1

Contents

List of Tables, Figures, and Maps

Tables

Figures

Maps

About the Editor and Contributors

Taras Kuzio is a research fellow at the Centre for Russian and East European Studies, University of Birmingham, and formerly senior research fellow of the Council of Advisors to the Ukrainian parliament. His previous posts include research associate at the International Institute for Strategic Studies and executive director at the Ukraine Business Agency.

He was editor of *Ukraine Business Review* (1994–1996), editor of *Ukrainian Reporter* (1990–1992), and deputy editor of *Soviet Nationality Survey* (1983–1989). His books and monographs include *Ukraine: Perestroika to Independence,* with Andrew Wilson (1994), *Ukrainian Security Policy* (1995), *Ukraine Under Kuchma: Political Reform, Economic Transformation, and Security Policy in Independent Ukraine* (1997), and *Ukraine: State and Nation Building in Ukraine* (1998).

Dr. Roy Allison is director of the Russian and Eurasia Programme, Royal Institute of International Affairs.

Dr. Judy Batt is a senior lecturer at the Centre for Russian and East European Studies, University of Birmingham.

Dr. Sarah Birch is a lecturer in Ukrainian studies at the Department of Government, University of Essex.

Dr. Marko Bojcun is a senior lecturer at the University of North London.

Saul Estrin is associated with the Economics Department, London Business School.

Dr. Peter Ferdinand is director of the Centre for Studies in Democratization, University of Warwick.

Dr. Paul Hare is director of the Centre for Economic Reform and Transformation at Heriot-Watt University in Edinburgh.

Mohammed Ishaq is associated with the Centre for Economic Reform and Transformation at Heriot-Watt University in Edinburgh.

Louise Jackson was a research associate at the Centre for Russian and East European Studies, University of Birmingham.

Dr. Valeri Khmelko is associated with the Kyiv International Institute of Sociology, National University of the Kyiv-Mohyla Academy.

Dr. Neil Malcolm is director of the Russian and East European Research Centre, University of Wolverhampton.

Dr. Alexander Motyl is associate director of the Harriman Institute at Columbia University.

Marc Nordberg was associated with the Centre for Russian and East European Studies, University of Birmingham.

Mykola Riabchouk is deputy editor of *Vsesvit* and *Krytyka* in Kyiv.

Dr. James Sherr is a lecturer at Lincoln College, University of Oxford, and a fellow at the Conflict Studies Research Centre, Royal Military Academy in Sandhurst, UK.

Dr. Roman Solchanyk is associated with the RAND Corporation in Santa Monica, California.

Dr. John E. Tedstrom is senior economist and research leader for Russian, Ukrainian, and Eurasian affairs at the RAND Corporation in Washington, D.C.

Dr. Andrew Wilson is a lecturer at the School of Slavonic and East European Studies, University of London.

Kataryna Wolczuk is a lecturer at the Centre for Russian and East European Studies, University of Birmingham.

Preface

The conference "Soviet to Independent Ukraine: A Troubled Transformation" was held at the University of Birmingham 13–15 June 1996 with the financial assistance of the Foreign and Commonwealth Office and the Economic and Social Research Council. A keynote speaker was former President Leonid Kravchuk, and the conference was opened by Sergui Komisarenko, Ukraine's ambassador to the UK. The authors brought together in this volume have one common purpose—to discuss the difficult post-Soviet transformation in Ukraine and its attempt to construct a nation, build a state, democratize, and marketize. Studies on post-Soviet Ukraine that survey all of these four areas still remain scarce.[1] Three scholars (Alexander J. Motyl, Andrew Wilson, and this author) are the authors of the only other three surveys that cover certain aspects of Ukraine's post-Soviet transformations.[2]

Although this book deals with all four of Ukraine's transitions, it is more conveniently divided into five parts. Part A lays out the complicated legacies that Ukraine inherited from external domination and totalitarianism and their impact on nation and state building. Motyl remains critical of those Western scholars and policy advisers who advocated—and still advocate—radical transformation in the former USSR (in fact, only Estonia, alone of the fifteen Soviet successor states, introduced shock therapy policies). Motyl persuasively argues that Ukraine had little option but to attempt to undertake nation and state building prior to launching political and economic transformation. Without the former, which Motyl argues former President Leonid Kravchuk focused upon during his tenure in office, political and economic reform under his successor, Leonid Kuchma, could not have been launched. Motyl therefore believes that Kravchuk and Kuchma complement each other.

Roman Solchanyk discusses the various factors which will determine whether Ukraine's post-Soviet transition will continue to remain stable and enduring. In comparison to the late Kravchuk era, Ukraine is now regarded by the West as both a linchpin of European security and a relative oasis of stability. This is a consequence of three factors: first, under Kuchma

Ukraine showed its commitment to political and economic reform; second, there is growing disillusionment in and conflict between Russia and the West; finally, any comparison of Ukraine's transition to that of the remainder of the CIS member states shows to what degree Ukraine is ahead of the rest in its transformation process. Nevertheless, Solchanyk points to the difficulties that lie ahead. These include a hard-core communist lobby, weak and amorphous domestic centrist political parties and parliamentary factions, a deformed and evolving eastern-southern Ukrainian identity, and no full normalization of Ukrainian-Russian relations.

The chapter by Marc Nordberg surveys the development of new institutions to fill the quasi state that Ukraine inherited from the former USSR. It discusses in a comparative context the numerous difficulties inherent in state and institution building in a post-Soviet country such as Ukraine. The chapter shows how state and institution building is directly linked to both nation building, on the one hand, and political-economic transformation, on the other. Without a reformed state and new institutions it is difficult to see how nation building and economic and political change can be implemented at the macro and micro levels in Ukraine. The development of new institutions and a public administration geared toward democratic and market economic values are therefore essential for the success of Ukraine's nation and state building project.

Part B continues this discussion by focusing on the legacy of regionalism and its influence upon Ukraine's national identity (or identities, as Ukraine has not one but a number of political subcultures). Valeri Khmelko and Andrew Wilson draw heavily on opinion polling data supplied by the Kyiv-based International Institute of Sociology to show that the 1989 Soviet census exaggerated the number of Ukrainian-speakers. Instead of relying, as the Soviet census did, on 'native tongue' as an indicator of a person's primary language, Khmelko and Wilson use 'language of convenience.' In actual fact, as Riabchouk argues, no matter which definition we use it will be difficult—if not impossible—to determine the exact proportion of Ukrainian- and Russian-speakers in Ukraine. National identity is a fluid process; it would be strange indeed if the number of Ukrainian-speakers had not risen since 1992.[3] In addition, many Ukrainians use Ukrainian and Russian interchangeably. For example, is President Kuchma—who spoke only Russian prior to becoming president, after which he switched to Ukrainian—a Russophone or Ukrainophone? Nevertheless, language remains an important—but not the sole—marker of national identity in Ukraine. Khmelko and Wilson's chapter provides a revealing insight into the often contradictory, but also at times complementary, identities that Ukraine inherited from the former USSR.

Mykola Riabchouk discusses the weakness of civil society and national identity in Ukraine. As Riabchouk correctly points out, this has had a positive influence on Ukrainian nation and state building by moderating support for the radical right and forcing Ukraine to adopt an inclusive—not an exclusive—model of state building. Riabchouk also notes, though, that the weakness of civil society and national identity in Ukraine have drawbacks as well. The need to focus on nation and state building prevented Ukraine from fully launching its political and economic reforms in early 1992 (unlike, say, the Russian Federation). This, in turn, led to a serious domestic crisis, which itself threatened nation and state building during 1993–1994 by eroding support for the independent state in areas of Ukraine where national consciousness is weak.

Louise Jackson investigates the importance of regionalism and identities at the local level in eastern Ukraine. What immediately becomes apparent is that it is a mistake to assume that eastern Ukraine is one homogeneous unit (in the same manner that it would be wrong to assume that western Ukraine is such a unit). Jackson does not investigate regionalism in Zaporizhzhia using headlines once common in the Western media and governmental discourse ('civil war,' 'bankrupt,' 'disintegration,' 'pro-Russian') when discussing eastern Ukraine. Jackson argues that while regionalism remains a difficult hurdle to overcome for Ukraine's nation and state builders, it is not insurmountable nor a threat to its territorial integrity.

All three chapters in Part B raise many questions. Would not a federal system of territorial organization be better suited to Ukraine's regional differences? Or would federalism serve only to worsen Ukraine's regional divisions at a time of nation and state building? What are the roles of Ukraine's central and regional elites in nation and state building? Will Ukraine's minorities reject aspects of the perceived nationalizing state? Is a strong state, as Kuchma has consistently argued, not a prerequisite for successful nation building, democratization, and marketization? Can one not also be a supporter of Ukrainian nation and state building while being a Russian-speaker?

Parts C and D survey the difficulties Ukraine has encountered in undertaking democratization and marketization. Although Western scholars have often investigated political and economic reform in Ukraine while ignoring nation and state building, the two chapters by Kataryna Wolczuk and Sarah Birch show how difficult it is to divorce any of the four planks of Ukraine's post-Soviet transformation from the others. Wolczuk surveys the six-year period that led to the adoption by Ukraine of its first post-Soviet constitution in June 1996. Ukraine was the final Soviet successor state to adopt a new constitution, and the question is why. The lack of any post-Soviet constitution proved a great hindrance to President Kravchuk in implementing political or economic reform, particularly at the local level. Ukraine's inherited regional identities, lack of a unified political culture, incomplete modern nation, and weak national consciousness, outlined in earlier chapters, all forced the Ukrainian leadership to seek the center ground. Sarah Birch examines voting behavior in the 1994 parliamentary elections by investigating the role, if any, of regionalism, ethnicity, age, and education.[4] She concludes that all of these factors play a role to some degree, which again points to the interconnection between political reform and nation and state building.

Nevertheless, three overall conclusions emerge from Wolczuk's and Birch's chapters. First, regionalism and ethnicity, while important, cannot be regarded as dominant influences and must be taken into consideration together with other factors. Second, Ukrainian party politics and elections do not approximate those found in the West. It is therefore unclear if the tools of Western political science are always appropriate to study post-Soviet political and economic developments. Third, consensus politics may help Ukraine democratize in the medium-long run by encouraging coalition building, tolerance, and compromise. But in the short term the lack of a constitution meant that the Ukrainian state was rudderless at a time when it required determined leadership to push through its sequential systematic changes.

Part D provides a study of the often neglected economics of Ukraine's post-Soviet transformation process. As Neil Malcolm argues in his introduction, it would again be wrong to analyze Ukraine's economic policies and its domestic crises in isolation from the nationality, state, and political aspects of Ukraine's four transitions as outlined by Taras Kuzio. The chapter by Paul Hare, Mohammed Ishaq, and Saul Estrin and that by John Tedstrom fill an important gap in the literature devoted to Ukraine's economy, its interdependence with Russia and the Commonwealth of Independent States (CIS), the economic policies pursued, and the causes of its economic crisis. To what degree Ukraine could have launched the kind of radical economic reform pursued by the Russian Federation, Latvia, and Estonia is still a matter of debate, to which the authors in this collection contribute. Economists tend to argue that Ukraine should have focused less on nation and state building, including foreign affairs, and more on domestic economic questions. Political scientists with an interest in the fields of nationalism, ethnicity, and nation and state building, such as Motyl, tend to stress the importance of first grappling with the legacies of an inherited quasi state and incompletely developed nation. Both political scientists and economists, though, will undoubtedly support the case that insufficient attention may have been devoted to the economy in the Kravchuk era. The pursuit of populist policies in the Kravchuk era that led to hyperinflation, stagnation, and a dangerous drop in support for independence in eastern Ukraine might have been avoided and cannot be laid solely at the door of an overemphasis on nation and state building.

Part E includes two chapters devoted to Ukraine's security policies.[5] James Sherr and Taras Kuzio discuss the domestic sources of Ukrainian security policy. Kuzio focuses on the complex interconnections between the incomplete national identities of the three east Slavic states (Ukraine, Belarus, and the Russian Federation). A central argument of Kuzio's chapter is that Ukraine and the Russian Federation have been unable to study normalize their relations and establish a strategic partnership because of their inherited national identities. Both countries understand the concept of a strategic partnership in a different manner. Ukraine therefore has continued the push to 'rejoin Europe' that was begun under President Kravchuk. Sherr broadens this discussion of the domestic sources of Ukraine's security policy beyond national identity to include other factors and then places these within the context of Ukraine's relations with the West and the Russian Federation. The study of the domestic sources of Ukraine's foreign and defense policies is still at an early stage, and therefore the contributions by Kuzio and Sherr to the discussion of these issues are a welcome addition to the available secondary sources.

The conference ended with a discussion of the policy implications for Western governments and institutions of Ukraine's quadruple transition. While it was acknowledged that Ukraine had finally become a strategic ally of the West, it still remained unclear how the West perceived Ukraine—as part of a Russian sphere of influence within the Eurasian CIS or as a country with an equal chance of 'rejoining Europe.'

If Ukraine is a strategic asset to the West, its integration within Eurasia cannot be in the West's interests. Any integration within the CIS should be only on a voluntary basis, and the West should not agree to provide the Russian Federation with spheres of influence. Ukraine's profile should be expanded within Western structures. The West should have played a more assertive role in resolving points of dispute between Ukraine and the Russian Federation (for example, the Black Sea Fleet). Finally, the West should focus on the enhancement, strengthening, and enrichment of its relations with Ukraine. Ultimately, Ukraine should be treated as a fully independent country—not as an appendage of the Russian Federation nor as part of its declared sphere of influence. Ukraine's integration and cooperation with Central Europe should also be encouraged by the West.

Ukraine's energy security needs to be given priority. Ukraine's energy interdependence with the Russian Federation has ramifications beyond the realm of economics. While demanding that Ukraine close the Chornobyl nuclear plant, the West should provide financial assistance to alleviate Ukraine's domestic energy crisis.[6] Trade barriers, such as those imposed by the European Union on Ukrainian commodities, should be reduced or eliminated in order that a free trade area could be created between Ukraine and the European Union.

A broadly agreed-upon policy conclusion was that the West needed to support state building in Ukraine. Ukraine, like all of the non-Russian successor states to the former USSR, inherited a quasi state with weak institutions. It is in the interests of the West to ensure that these state institutions are given greater substance in order to be better able to unite the country, implement central policies at the local level, and ensure law and order.[7] Hand in hand with the support given to state building, the West should promote the development of democratization and marketization at all levels of Ukrainian society. Western assistance to Ukraine therefore should not ignore the development of the state, civil society, and the market economy at the local level.

The central theme running throughout this book points to an important conclusion: that Ukraine's four transitions of nation building, state building, democratization, and marketization cannot be discussed in isolation from one another. They are all intimately bound together, and it would be unwise for Western policy makers and scholars to ignore this crucial facet of Ukraine's post-Soviet transformation process.

Notes

1. See T. Kuzio, *Ukraine: State and Nation Building* (London and New York, Routledge, 1998).

2. A.J. Motyl, *Dilemmas of Independence: Ukraine after Totalitarianism* (New York: Council on Foreign Affairs, 1993); A. Wilson, *Ukrainian Nationalism in the 1990s: A Minority Faith* (Cambridge: Cambridge University Press, 1997); T. Kuzio, *Ukraine under Kuchma: Political Reform, Economic Transformation and Security Policy in Independent Ukraine* (London and New York: Macmillan and St. Martin's Press, 1997).

3. See T. Kuzio, "National Identity in Independent Ukraine: An Identity in Transition," *Nationalism and Ethnic Politics,* vol. 2. no. 4 (December 1996), pp. 582–608.

4. See M. Riabchouk, "Two Ukraines?" *East European Reporter,* vol. 5, no. 4 (July–August 1994), pp. 18–22, and S. Birch and Ihor Zinko, "The Dilemma of Regionalism," *Transition,* vol. 2, no. 22 (1 November 1996), pp. 22–25, 64.

5. See T. Kuzio, *Ukrainian Security Policy,* Washington Paper no. 167 (Washington, DC: Center for Strategic and International Studies and Praeger, 1995).

6. See two articles by Paul D'Anieri, "Interdependence and Sovereignty in the Ukrainian-Russian Relationship," *European Security,* vol. 4, no. 4 (Winter 1995), pp. 603–621, and "Dilemmas of Interdependence: Autonomy, Prosperity, and Sovereignty in Ukraine's Russia Policy," *Problems of Post-Communism,* January-February 1997, pp. 16–25.

7. See T. Kuzio, "Organised Crime and Corruption in Ukraine," *Jane's Intelligence Review,* vol. 9, no. 1 (January 1997), pp. 10–13.

Acknowledgments

The University of Birmingham gratefully acknowledges the financial assistance of the Foreign and Commonwealth Office and the Economic and Social Research Council–funded research project "The Political Economy of New States in Central-Eastern Europe and the Former Soviet Union" (Research Grant R000235650), which made the conference "Soviet to Independent Ukraine: A Troubled Transformation" possible. The editor also gratefully acknowledges the financial support of the Leverhulme Trust, which provided for the three-year research project on post-Soviet Ukrainian transition.

Ukraine: Territorial Administrative Structure

Referendum on Independence

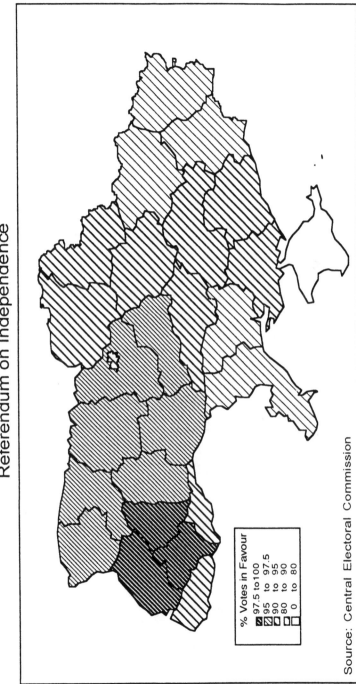

% Votes in Favour
97.5 to 100
95   to   97.5
90   to   95
80   to   90
0   to   80

Source: Central Electoral Commission

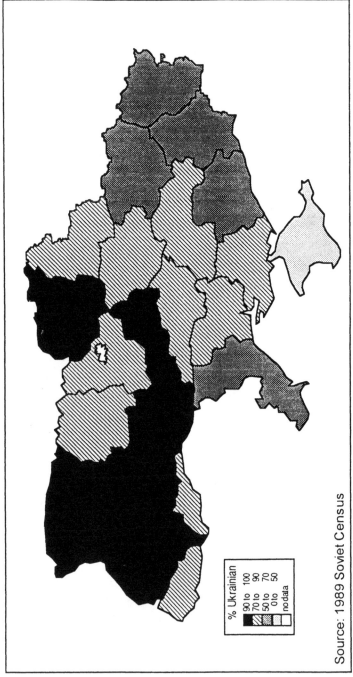

Ethnic Ukrainians

% Ukrainian
90 to 100
70 to 90
50 to 70
0 to 50
no data

Source: 1989 Soviet Census

Ukrainian as Native Language

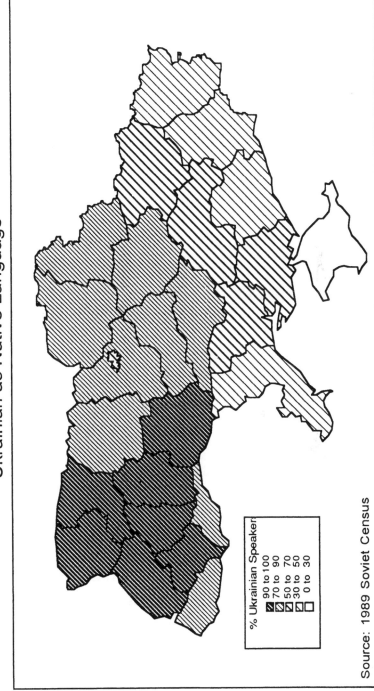

% Ukrainian Speakers
90 to 100
70 to 90
50 to 70
30 to 50
0 to 30

Source: 1989 Soviet Census

PART A

Nation and State Building

Introduction

Peter Ferdinand

Contrary to many predictions in 1991, and contrary to its experience in the Russian civil war of 1918–1920, when it was torn apart by the competing forces of the Bolsheviks, the Whites, and the Ukrainian nationalists, Ukraine has been a political success since the collapse of the Soviet Union. Indeed, it has been more successful than most of the other states of the former Soviet Union in facing the challenges of nation building and state building.

The following three chapters focus upon the achievements and problems in this area. Perhaps the greatest, and also the most surprising, success has come in nation building. Although much of the population speak Russian rather than Ukrainian, and although most Russians inside Russia still have difficulty in coming to terms with the existence of a separate Ukrainian state after over three hundred years of unity, the people of Ukraine have so far managed to build a new country in a spirit of tolerance and compromise.

As Alexander Motyl emphasizes in Chapter 1, Ukrainians owe a lot to the contributions of Presidents Kravchuk and Kuchma. Both of them have managed to compete for power without tearing the country apart. These two leaders helped to construct 'rules of the political game' that have kept the country together and committed to democracy, despite the facts that their political programs were quite different, that their core support came from different regions of the country, and that they had no prior political experience in making democracy work. They both promoted a sense of nationhood based on nonethnic criteria, and both accepted the continued use of Russian by those who wanted it. Also, as Motyl points out, both leaders have skillfully avoided pushing disputes with Russia too far, even though they recognized the utility of Russian hostility as a way of stimulating unity at home.

The only exception to this picture of success in nation building is Crimea. There Russians constitute a majority, and the region experienced strong secessionist currents with overt support from political actors in Moscow until the government in Kyiv intervened in 1995. Even here, however, the

1

Ukrainian government has avoided operating in too heavy-handed a fashion and has so far managed to contain the problem.

This has been eased by the fact that, as Roman Solchanyk emphasizes in Chapter 2, there is an asymmetry between the attitudes toward the Ukrainian state held by Russians in Russia, on one hand, and by Russians and Russian-speakers in Ukraine, on the other. Russians in Russia still often look forward to the restoration of some greater Russian state that would also incorporate Belarus.

According to opinion surveys in Ukraine, however, Russians and Russian-speakers there may not always feel Ukrainian, but very few of them feel positively Russian. Instead they retain a residual 'Soviet' identity where it is not Ukrainian. Thus their loyalty to the Ukrainian state may be greater than is often assumed, and Russian nationalists in Moscow and elsewhere will find it difficult to turn them against Kyiv unless circumstances deteriorate significantly within Ukraine.

The achievements of state building have been significant but less conclusive. Motyl points to the country's presence and profile abroad as well as to the creation of a national army, but both he and Marc Nordberg (in Chapter 3) stress persisting problems. These include the weakness of the central authorities, partly exacerbated by the small size of the central bureaucracy they inherited, and the weakening control of Kyiv over the country's provinces, coupled with the increasing power in the hands of the president and his close advisers. Ukraine has also so far made little progress in establishing an effective democratic party system.

Evidently building a new state apparatus and democracy takes time. Complete solutions will not come quickly. Motyl identifies one fundamental problem that may become worse rather than better, what he terms the 'Zaireization' of the regime: growing corruption in an increasingly parasitic state. More democracy could help to stem this. But concentration of power in the hands of the leadership is a temptation to further corruption, while the weakening of effective power in Kyiv could encourage lower-level officials to line their own pockets.

Thus both the consolidation of democracy and economic liberalization are vital for sustaining the momentum of reform. Combining and synchronizing them will be extremely difficult. Yet both are essential in the medium and long term. The risks to the state have been tackled successfully so far, but they will not simply go away. It is too early to tell whether Ukraine will weather them. But the fact that the country is past the transitional phase of state building and democratization and has now moved on to their consolidation does give encouragement.

— 1 —

State, Nation, and Elites in Independent Ukraine

Alexander Motyl

The Soviet Union's collapse produced an independent Ukraine, but collapse also saddled it with institutions and elites that precluded a rapid transition to democracy, civil society, rule of law, and the market. Like most other Soviet successor states, Ukraine was forced down the path of sequential and, hence, slow and evolutionary change. For better or for worse, as I argue in this chapter, that path had to begin with the nation and the state; constructing them was a logical possibility and a systemic priority.

Constrained by this structural legacy, Ukraine's first two presidents, although ostensibly espousing radically different agendas, had little choice but to devote most of their reformist zeal to nation building and state building.

As a result, Ukraine has moved down the path of sequential change. The same combination of institutions and elites that made moderately successful nation building and state building possible, however, may have also set limits on change and, in the worst-case scenario, could even propel Ukraine down the path of 'Zaireization.' Ukraine's transformation into a corrupt and impoverished state is not inevitable, but the very possibility of such a development should be cause for concern—above all for Ukraine, of course, but also for the West, which may have a vested interest in a long-term, strategic partnership with Kyiv.

The Soviet Legacy

The Soviet political system is best envisioned as consisting of two conceptually distinct parts: empire and totalitarian state. The USSR was an empire in which a Russian core exerted effective political control over non-Russian peripheries.[1] Centralized Russian organizations ruled both Russia and the republics, while non-Russian organizations vertically dependent on the center only administered them. The USSR was also a totalitarian state that exercised virtually total horizontal and vertical control over public life.[2] The linchpin of the system was the Communist Party. Its central organs in Moscow both ruled the empire and controlled the totalitarian state, while its non-Russian branches supervised the economy and polity at the level of the republics.

The non-Russian polities that emerged from the USSR in late 1991 bore the birthmarks of their Soviet past.[3] Thanks to empire, they lacked bona fide states, inheriting only administrative pieces of the Soviet Union's ruling organizations. Thanks to totalitarianism, they lacked market economies, civil societies, rule of law, and democracy as well as, in most cases, full-fledged nations. Finally, thanks to the suddenness of collapse, the non-Russian states inherited more or less intact former communist elites and more or less inexperienced anticommunist elites.

Like their counterparts in the other non-Russian polities, Ukraine's postimperial, post-totalitarian administrative agencies were woefully under-staffed and underfunded, their functionaries were undertrained, and their relations with one another were undefined. Not surprisingly, Ukraine's incipient state was immediately seized by former Communist Party functionaries who retained their positions of central, regional, and local dominance. Institutional legacies combined with elite realities to make the rapid, radical reform recommended by Western policy makers impossible.

Obstacles to Reform

The self-proclaimed task before all reformers of all successor states was to introduce democracy, rule of law, civil society, and the market. *Pace* John Mueller, each of these goals represents a cluster of institutions absent from the imperial-totalitarian system.[4] Democracy involves an effective division and balance of governmental powers, elite circulation by means of elections, and the aggregation of popular interests in parties. Rule of law entails regularized and transparent procedures for running state agencies and their relations with society. Civil society refers to a matrix of interconnected social institutions existing independently of the state. The market presupposes private property and a set of legal procedures for exchanging capital, land, and labor.[5]

It was hard enough for post-Soviet policy makers to construct all these institutional clusters in a setting of social disarray, political uncertainty, and economic collapse.[6] The task was doubly difficult for polities such as

Ukraine, where, following independence, former communists became fervent nationalists while retaining their influence within the government, economy, and society. Although some had an interest in economic and social change, most did not. Perhaps inevitably, change in Ukraine would be piecemeal and slow.

No less important, change would be sequential, as some desired ends were preconditions of others. Genuine democracy and civil society are as inconceivable without rule of law as rule of law is inconceivable without a state, a point also made by Stephen Holmes.[7] But not all ends are preconditions of others. States and nations can exist in the absence of markets, civil societies, and rule of law. Nor do states and nations presuppose each other. As a result, Ukraine had little choice but to go down the reform path that corresponded to the interests of its conservative elites and conformed to the logic of postcommunist systemic change.

However retrograde they seemed to Western free-marketeers, nation building and state building made sense in Ukraine's postimperial, post-totalitarian circumstances. First, building a nation and a state was *possible,* in terms both of Ukraine's postimperial, post-totalitarian legacy and of the self-aggrandizing, antireformist tendencies of much of its elite. Second, building a state was *necessary,* as the first step in the sequence of reform. Last but not least, building a nation was desirable, as popular cohesion and national consensus could facilitate the process of state building—but state building in the functional equivalent of an institutional wasteland, as the resultant entity could be captured by marauders and transformed into a tool of their own self-enrichment.[8]

Kravchuk and Kuchma

The structural constraints imposed on Ukraine by the Soviet Union's collapse translated into very few policy options for Ukrainian elites. Western advisers may have preferred that they embark on rapid, fundamental, and comprehensive change—or revolution—but moderate leaders with even a superficial understanding of post-Soviet Ukrainian realities would have appreciated that such a transformation was systematically impossible.[9] That Western advisers failed to see that their recommendations were tantamount to revolutionary voluntarism is unusual, inasmuch as revolutionary fervor has been alien to mainstream Western policy, but also understandable, in light of the degree to which free-market fever and the possibility of democratic enlargement have gripped the post–Cold War imagination.[10] Suffice it to say that most post-Soviet policy makers did well to resist the revolutionary temptation and pursue what Sir Karl Popper called "piecemeal social engineering."[11]

Leonid Kravchuk and Leonid Kuchma both fit the Popperian mode. Despite the latter's oftentimes radical rhetoric, Kravchuk and Kuchma have pursued quintessentially moderate, middle-of-the-road policies. Unlike their counterparts in Russia and Belarus, they have eschewed force and violence. Instead, they have tried to create coalitions and build consensus; they have done things slowly, hesitantly, even fitfully. In a word, they have muddled along, much to the consternation of Western radicals. And, in muddling along, they have been as successful as Ukraine's burdensome Soviet inheritance permitted them to be and as potentially unsuccessful as it threatened them with becoming.

Kuchma, naturally, prefers to depict his tenure in office as a radical departure from Kravchuk's—and, with respect to the economy, he has a point. Rather more striking, however, is the continuity between the two presidents. Despite quite similar Soviet backgrounds, and despite rather different public personae and platforms, the two have been equally committed to building a nation and a state.

Both Kravchuk and Kuchma were high-ranking Soviet Ukrainian officials. Nothing in their careers suggested that they would at some point salute the Ukrainian nationalist flag and swear allegiance to an independent Ukrainian state. It was Kravchuk who designed communist ideology for many years, producing the ideological rationale for Soviet power and the ideological justification for Ukraine's lack of independence. And it was Kuchma who directed the Pivdenmash rocket plant in Dnipropetrovs'k, producing the advanced technology that justified the Soviet Union's claims to superpower status. Kravchuk was elected president in December 1991 on an essentially state- and nation-building platform.

In contrast, Kuchma downplayed the importance of the nation and the state in his 1994 campaign, giving priority to the imperatives of economic reform and cooperation with Russia. In mid-1994, the apparent contrast between the two could not have been greater: Kravchuk was depicted as a Ukrainian nationalist, Kuchma as a Russified pragmatist. In particular, Kravchuk's supporters feared that Kuchma would sell the Ukrainian nation and state to Russia, while Kuchma's supporters expected him finally to dispense with what they criticized as Kravchuk's excessive concern with state and nation building.[12]

Just about everyone was proven wrong. Very quickly, Kuchma adopted almost all of Kravchuk's positions regarding the importance of the state, the desirability of a nation, and the potential danger of Russia. Kuchma did adopt a radical economic reform program in October 1994, but that step evinced far more continuity than talk of radical breakthroughs suggested. First, a move toward the market was systematically possible in light of the steps Kravchuk had already taken toward building a state. Second, market-oriented reforms proved to be an excellent policy club with which one elite, that supportive of Kuchma, could beat another, that around Kravchuk, in the presidential campaign. Third, the fact that the economic reform program was a product of Ukraine's systemic and elite dynamics meant that it would not be as radical as it was proclaimed to be.[13] And indeed, the two years following the announcement of the radical economic reform showed that while substantial progress was made, the transition suffered as many setbacks as victories and was anything but rapid. Economic reform, like nation building and state building, was inevitably subject to constraints and limitations and could not be revolutionary.

Nation Building and Its Limits

It is striking how quickly Kravchuk and Kuchma managed to converge on virtually identical approaches to nation building. First, both identified Russia as 'the other' against whom the inhabitants of Ukraine might define themselves as Ukrainian. Second, both promoted a sense of nationhood based on inclusive criteria. And third, although both publicly identified themselves with the Ukrainian nation as such, Kravchuk and Kuchma accepted the reality of Russian as the language spoken in most of Ukraine's cities, including Kyiv, and in much of Ukraine's media, while consistently pursuing policies that promoted, more or less equally, Ukrainian, Russian, and other languages and cultures.

Because the people inhabiting Ukraine possess a variety of ethnic characteristics, Kravchuk and Kuchma may have had no alternative to emphasizing civic and territorial loyalty and downplaying ethnic allegiance. But a 'civic' approach to nation building also had its limitations. It could succeed only if the target audience would develop a loyalty to a territory, a style of life, and/or a state. As a historical space and a geographical place, 'Ukraina' resonated with much of the population, but in different ways for different ethnic or regional segments. A Ukrainian lifestyle may traditionally have been, or have been perceived as being, more relaxed and prosperous, but since independence it could offer only poverty and despair due to the drastic contraction in the economy. And the postimperial, post-totalitarian Ukrainian state had little to recommend it as well.

By 1996, therefore, the Kravchuk-Kuchma strategy of building a nation produced mixed results. Popular commitment to Ukrainian independence was strongest in western Ukraine, the central provinces, and Kyiv, and weakest in the Donbas and the Crimea.[14] Ukrainian-language use was on the rise, but barely perceptibly, while the print media were more inclined to use Russian than before.[15] Clearly, if nation building involves the emergence of a coherent group of people committed to one language, one identity, and one state, then Ukraine still had a long way to go. If, on the other hand, the criteria are weakened and emphasis is placed on a willingness to live side by side, tolerate the dominant languages and cultures, and evince some degree of sentimental attachment to the land, then Ukraine was, arguably, no worse off than a variety of advanced industrial states.

State Building and Its Limits

Kravchuk and Kuchma proved equally committed to building a Ukrainian state. As heads of a postimperial, post-totalitarian entity with almost no marks of stateness, they had four immediate tasks: to insert Ukraine into a variety of international institutions, to maintain an army and control the borders, to construct an administrative apparatus, and to extend state power into the provinces.

In addition to the logical imperatives of sequential change, three conditions argued for the primacy of these dimensions of state building. Tensions with postimperial Russia, which broke out within days of the Ukrainian declaration of independence, were one such factor. Negotiations required negotiators with staffs; the potential for conflict required an army and generals to go with it; the necessity of delineating interests and boundaries required analysts and border guards.[16]

Ukraine's sudden entrance onto the world stage also necessitated a state, for reasons both of prestige and of effectiveness. Embassies had to be manned, representations and delegations had to be formed, and treaties had to be signed. In particular, Ukraine's possession of nuclear weapons, and Washington's fetishization of the issue, had the unintended effect of encouraging Kyiv to fetishize the state and its accouterments, such as weapons, militaries, and diplomatic fanfare.

Finally, the shapelessness of Ukraine's political institutions, and the importance to both Kravchuk and Kuchma of building a solid base for their personal power and prestige—if not policy—necessitated that their symbolic authority acquire organizational and institutional forms.[17] That meant staffs, advisers, effective chains of command, and all the other characteristics of governance that Ukraine, as a postimperial, post-totalitarian entity, lacked.

As with nation building, however, the Kravchuk-Kuchma record of state building was mixed. Ukraine's international presence—embassies, consulates, missions, delegations—was their major achievement. The progressive growth, rationalization, and technical improvement of the bureaucratic apparatus in Kyiv were also impressive. Border guards were assigned to

Ukraine's frontiers, and an army, however oversized and underfunded, was maintained. In a word, more or less effective state building was possible where the imperial-totalitarian institutional legacy was weakest.

Where that legacy was strong, state building left much to be desired. Kyiv's ability to extend effective command beyond the capital city remained almost as minimal in 1996 as in 1992, despite the 'treadmill of reforms' pursued by Kravchuk and Kuchma. It was no small task to project central power into the rest of the country by building an effective regional and local state apparatus on the ruins of the system of soviets and in the face of entrenched elite opposition or indifference.

Janus-Faced Elites

Paradoxically, the established elites, and the relationships they enjoyed with one another, made state building possible—after all, it was in their interest to consolidate political power—and ensured that the process would be tortuous. For some elites, such as those grouped about the president and parliament, state building directly augmented their authority. For most others, whether in the capital city or in the provinces, an effective state threatened to diminish their de facto powers. For all elites, however, state building meant the acquisition of new, or the redefinition of old, institutional roles and, hence, would necessarily involve protracted struggles and painful adjustments.

The central struggle within the capital involved the president and parliament, the Supreme Rada. As in most of the other successor states, their relationship was institutionally undefined. The result was deadlock and the inability to adopt meaningful reform measures. However, this failing was neither fatal, as the imperatives of sequencing ruled out premature marketization anyway, nor undesirable, as deadlock promoted institutionalization. Deadlock contributed to the emergence of stable and regularized procedures precisely because, with the 'rules of the game' undefined and unclear, deadlock itself functioned as a surrogate game, the central rules of which were the recognition by both sides of the existence and indispensability of the other to the game. Standoff implied some form of cooperation and some degree of moderation, thereby permitting the eventual formation of more complex rules of the game. Despite their verbal assertions of radical singularity, therefore, most of Ukraine's elites developed a commitment to consensus, even on controversial issues. Thus, the Supreme Rada overwhelmingly approved Kuchma's reform package in late 1994 and, for all its hemming and hawing, supported economic change in the years that followed.[18]

Creeping institutionalization culminated in the adoption by the Supreme Rada of a constitution on 28 June 1996. After five years of interminable debate, the draft presented to the parliament that spring seemed as doomed as its predecessors. Deputies disagreed violently on most of the substantive as well as symbolic issues. For example, the national democrats demanded that the document speak in the name of the 'Ukrainian people,' while the communists insisted on 'the people of Ukraine' (the formula that, ironically, had served both Kravchuk and Kuchma so well). Finally, on 26 June Kuchma decreed that, in light of the Supreme Rada's evident inability to agree on anything, he would submit the draft to a referendum.

His move proved a political masterstroke. Threatened with irrelevance, the parliamentarians spent all night debating the draft and—mirabile dictu—passed it with the requisite majority.[19] Ukraine adopted its constitution consensually, even if abetted by political arm-twisting. In marked contrast to Russia, violence was eschewed. The left and the right, like the Supreme Rada and the president, had to agree to disagree, and, in doing so, to recognize each other as genuine partners with real roles to play in the political system.

As an arena of struggle with little institutional identity, the protostate also became a vehicle for the circulation and self-promotion of regional elites. Between 1992 and 1994, west Ukrainians and Kyivites, with a substantial admixture of easterners, dominated the game, only to be supplanted by east Ukrainians from the Donbas in 1995 and 1996.[20] The central state's 'permeability' had several salutary consequences. One was to promote elite loyalty to the state, if only as a feeding ground. Another was to endow the elite with a corporate interest that worked against radicalization and polarization. A third was to give elites the opportunity to subordinate their ethnic inclinations (assuming, of course, that they had any) to career advancement and self-enrichment. In effect, institutional flabbiness co-opted the elites into the emergent state and nation. As Sherman Garnett suggests, the pursuit of self-interest may have proven to be the most potent source of state building and nation building in Ukraine.[21]

Creeping Zaireization?

And yet, for all the silver linings, elite control of the state did represent a dark cloud with one overwhelmingly negative consequence. While elite infighting could produce a certain dynamism that might result in genuine reform, the indisputable fact of elite parasitism could also mean that, first, systemic change would necessarily remain limited, even when the logic of reform no longer called for incremental steps; and, second, that the state might be incapable of reforming itself and thus remain a corrupt and inefficient organism feeding off a declining and ultimately doomed economy. In other words, elite parasitism could transform Ukraine into an east-central European version of former Zaire.

Volodymyr Polokhalo paints an especially dark picture of the Ukrainian polity:

> Making use of the passivity of society, the extreme weakness of democratic institutions, and state control over the mass media, the party of power now headed by a second president has built a complex but quite recognisable political pyramid. . . . This is the largest and most universal trust company exploiting popular credulity. The whole population are its investors in both the purely financial and economic sense as well as in terms of delegating their own will to power. The company is monopolistic and out of control; it has paid no dividends for almost five years, yet it functions legitimately. . . . The further distancing of power from the people, its being out of control, its defending itself from real competition and responsibility are all obvious. The Ukrainian paradigm of state-building today is but the manifestation of creating . . . a state for its own sake, outside society and above it.[22]

Polokhalo's analysis is persuasive, but only up to a point. While he accurately depicts the parasitic features of the state elite, he overstates their power (as his use of the term 'neo-totalitarian state' clearly suggests).[23] In reality, the Ukrainian *derzhava* is, still, at best a flabby protostate, one equally incapable of pushing through radical reforms and of acting in a genuinely authoritarian or neo-totalitarian manner.

The real danger facing Ukraine is not creeping totalitarianization, but creeping Zaireization, as corrupt elites feed off their state, their society, and their economy, ultimately driving them all to possible perdition. The attempted assassination on 16 July 1996, of then Prime Minister Pavlo Lazarenko—presumably the work of corrupt officials opposed to his reform program—indicates that this danger is not entirely abstract.[24]

Might civil society check state corruption and state power and guarantee nonstate vitality?[25] Unfortunately, if civil society is, as I suggested, premised on rule of law, then civil society must also be premised on the state, which is a logical precondition of rule of law. If so, then championing civil society, while intrinsically useful and normatively good, leads to a vicious circle as far as the parasitic state is concerned.

If civil society is not the answer to the problem of the parasitic state, what, then, could prevent Ukraine's possible Zaireization? Ukrainians like to think that their population, well-educated, 'European,' and ostensibly hardworking, will save the day. Alas, there is no reason to suppose that such qualities would make much of a difference with respect to the quality of the state. They may enhance the prosperity of individual households, but they do not begin to address the complex institutional issues that postimperial, post-totalitarian state building entails.

All is not lost, however, as the above analysis does suggest several ways in which the Ukrainian state might be saved from itself. The first is creeping institutionalization. Ukrainian elites may or may not know it, but, increasingly, they are getting entangled in the tentacles of growing democratization and rule of law. Flagrant corruption should become less possible with time. To be sure, the example of India also shows that even robust democracy and rule of law are insufficient to eliminate parasitism. Still, in imposing certain institutional constraints on the political process, democracy and rule of law can bring about some degree of compliance with nonparasitic norms.

Second, economic collapse, which is partly the result of the elites' inability and/or unwillingness to embark on reform, also represents a physical limit to its parasitism. There are, after all, only so many physical assets that one can steal in a formerly centralized economy. At some point, even thieves may want to put their booty to productive use at home. Here, too, however, there is no cause for excessive optimism. The experience of too many third-world states shows that long-term economic decline is perfectly compatible with bureaucratic corruption.

Third, the rapid growth of an underground economy and the concomitant emergence of nonstate organized crime may also act as a barrier to official parasitism. As one Ukrainian entrepreneur put it, "The Ukrainian mafia is the best guarantor of our statehood."[26] Corrupt bureaucrats have an interest in state control of significant segments of the economy, while private criminals would prefer the state to withdraw, possibly completely. But, once again, no panacea is at hand. Not only may the cure be worse than the disease, but there is no reason to think that organized crime could not establish a cozy cartel-like relationship with state officials, a pattern found even in such European states as Italy.

Will these three factors transform Ukraine into a 'normal' state? Probably, but if so, only in the medium to long term. In the foreseeable future it is hard to imagine Ukraine's not remaining mired in the same kind of systemic corruption and parasitism common to all the Soviet successor states. Polokhalo's fears may be excessive, but they are not unjustified. Zaireization will remain an unfortunate possibility for some time to come.

A Deus ex Machina?

It may be small comfort for Ukraine that the trend toward Zaireization is present in all the successor states, including Russia. In contrast to most of them, however, Ukraine may be saved by an external force that could compel its elites to engage in nonparasitic behavior and, thus, to save themselves and their state.

It is Ukraine's good fortune—after years of having been perceived as a 'nuisance state'—to be poised to become the West's geopolitical partner. That the West may be ready to shield Ukraine from possible Russian predation is the conventional wisdom; that the West might also save Ukraine from itself is perhaps less obvious, but no less true. How did this turn of events come about?

The coming of Kuchma improved Ukraine's image in the West. But, as noted above, Kuchma was not all that different a state and nation builder than Kravchuk, and it was, after all, Kravchuk who in early 1994 signed the Tripartite Accord on strategic nuclear weapons. Nor have Kuchma's economic policies been sufficiently impressive to explain the West's change of heart. Rather, the factor that decisively tilted the West in Ukraine's favor was exogenous—Russia. President Yeltsin's virtual abandonment of economic reform, the genocidal war in Chechnya, the reassertion of great-power rhetoric in Russia's relations with the West, the victory of the imperially minded communists in the December 1995 parliamentary elections, the growing influence of Aleksandr Lebed in the aftermath of the June 1996 presidential elections, and Moscow's insistence on the primacy of its interests in the former Soviet space effectively spelled the end of Russia's honeymoon with the West.[27]

As Russia's fortunes waned, Ukraine's rose. Geopolitics saw to that. With Russia looking like a threat to Western interests, and with Ukraine acting like a potentially stable and possibly prosperous pro-Western state, the latter was progressively transformed into a strategic asset.[28] Western presidents, ministers, and diplomats signaled their new thinking by making periodic pilgrimages to Kyiv, inviting their Ukrainian counterparts to substantive discussions in Western capitals, and visibly increasing their economic, technical, and political support. In turn, Kuchma responded by tilting Ukraine's foreign policy toward the West.[29] Ukraine was unlikely to join such Western institutions as NATO and the European Union in the immediate future, but its growing acceptance by the West would have a positive impact on state and nation building at home. Ukraine's security was enhanced, but, no less important, the prestige of the state could but rise, thereby facilitating Kyiv's efforts at building a 'civic' nation.

For the impact on Ukraine to be more than transitory, however, the West would have to make an explicit commitment to Ukrainian statehood and, possibly, even to its security, while making no less of a commitment to encouraging Ukraine's elites to act in a nonparasitic fashion. After all, one of the reasons for former Zaire's own Zaireization was its status as a sheltered outpost of Western interests. And, of course, Zaireization was not restricted to Zaire: Haiti, Honduras, Nicaragua, Nigeria, Egypt, and many other third-world countries that enjoyed Western protection fit the bill. But there are exceptions to the rule: Taiwan, South Korea, post–World War II Japan, and postwar Germany and Austria. The West can make a difference, if making a difference is in the West's strategic interest.

Will the West make a difference in the case of Ukraine? Until mid-1994, the answer appeared to be a resounding no. At present, as noted above, Ukraine may be becoming the strategic darling of the West. Will it retain this status? The answer may be yes, inasmuch as the prognosis for Russia and its relations with the West cannot be overly optimistic.[30] Willy-nilly, then, Ukraine could be on the verge of becoming a front-line vassal state of the West—perhaps even the South Korea of east-central Europe.

Notes

1. This understanding of empire reflects Michael W. Doyle's. See his *Empires* (Ithaca: Cornell University Press, 1986). See also Alexander J. Motyl, "Thinking about Empire: A Conceptual Inquiry with Some Implications for Theory," in Karen Barkey and Mark von Hagen, eds., *Imperial Collapse: Causes and Consequences* (Boulder, CO: Westview), pp. 19–29. I discuss Russian domination in *Sovietology, Rationality, Nationality* (New York: Columbia University Press, 1990), pp. 161–173, and *Will the Non-Russians Rebel? State, Ethnicity, and Stability in the USSR* (Ithaca: Cornell University Press, 1987), pp. 36–52. See also Roman Szporluk, "Reflections on Ukraine after 1994: The Dilemmas of Nationhood," *The Harriman Review,* vol. 7, nos. 7–9 (March-May 1994), pp. 1–9.

2. On totalitarianism as a type of regime, see Giovanni Sartori, "Totalitarianism, Model Mania and Learning from Error," *Journal of Theoretical Politics,* vol. 5, no. 1 (January 1993), pp. 5–22. On totalitarianism as a type of state, see Alexander J. Motyl, "The End of Sovietology: From Soviet Studies to Post-Soviet Studies," in A. Motyl, ed., *The Post-Soviet Nations. Perspectives on the Demise of the USSR* (New York: Columbia University Press, 1992), pp. 309–311.

3. Having enjoyed independence in the interwar period, Estonia, Latvia, and Lithuania are not comparable to the other post-Soviet states and, thus, do not figure in my analysis. Unlike Russia, Ukraine, Belarus, Moldova, Armenia, Georgia, Azerbaijan, Turkmenistan, Kazakstan, Uzbekistan, Kyrgyzstan, and Tajikistan, the Balts possessed states, civil societies, market economies, and rule of law, and, thanks to their Soviet-era status as laboratories for various social and economic experiments, they managed to retain some of these institutional features into the 1980s. As a result, the Baltic states deserve to be compared with the east-central European states. The definitive work on the Baltic states is Romuald J. Misiunas and Rein Taagepera, *The Baltic States: Years of Dependence, 1940–1980* (Berkeley: University of California Press, 1983).

4. John Mueller, "Democracy, Capitalism, and the End of Transition," in Michael Mandelbaum, ed., *Postcommunism: Four Perspectives* (New York: Council on Foreign Relations, 1996), pp. 102–167. Anders Aslund also writes that "if two people meet to exchange anything, a market exists" ("The Russian Road to the Market," *Current History,* vol. 94, no. 594 [October 1995], p. 314).

5. For an elaboration of this argument, see Alexander J. Motyl, *Dilemmas of Independence: Ukraine after Totalitarianism* (New York: Council on Foreign Relations, 1993), pp. 51–75.

6. I examine these issues at greater length in "Reform, Transition, or Revolution? The Limits to Change in the Postcommunist States," *Contention,* vol. 4, no. 1 (Fall 1994), pp. 141–160.

7. Stephen Holmes, "Cultural Legacies or State Collapse? Probing the Postcommunist Dilemma," in Michael Mandelbaum, ed. *Postcommunism: Four Perspectives* (New York: Council on Foreign Relations, 1996), pp. 22–76.

8. See Alexander J. Motyl, "The Conceptual President: Leonid Kravchuk and the Politics of Surrealism," in Timothy J. Colton and Robert C. Tucker, eds., *Patterns in Post-Soviet Leadership* (Boulder, CO: Westview, 1995), pp. 103–121.

9. Revolution as rapid, fundamental, and comprehensive change is only one possible definition. For a discussion of others, see Christoph M. Kotowski, "Revolution," in Giovanni Sartori, ed., *Social Science Concepts* (Beverly Hills: Sage, 1984), pp. 404–451, and Alexander J. Motyl, "Concepts and Skocpol: Ambiguity and Vagueness in the Study of Revolution," *Journal of Theoretical Politics,* vol. 4, no. 1 (January 1992), pp. 93–112.

10. In essence, the argument for pursuing radical economic reforms at the same time as democracy, civil society, and rule of law is an argument for rapid, fundamental, and comprehensive change—i.e., revolution. It hardly matters that contemporary proponents of revolution do not call themselves revolutionaries. For examples of revolutionary thinking, see Jeffrey Sachs, *Poland's Jump to the Market Economy* (Cambridge: MIT Press, 1994); David Kennett and Marc Lieberman, eds., *The Road to Capitalism* (Forth Worth: The Dryden Press, 1992); and Anders Aslund, ed., *Economic Transformation in Russia* (New York: St. Martin's, 1994).

11. Karl Popper, *The Poverty of Historicism* (New York: Harper and Row, 1964); *The Open Society and Its Enemies* (London: Routledge and Kegan Paul, 1945), vol. 2. Also arguing variants of this position are Kazimierz Z. Poznanski, ed., *The Evolutionary Transition to Capitalism* (Boulder, CO: Westview, 1995); Peter Murrell, "Conservative Political Philosophy and the Strategy of Economic Transition," *East European Politics and Societies,* vol. 6 (Winter 1992), pp. 3–16; and Stephen E. Hanson, "The Utopia of Market Society in the Post-Soviet Context," in Stephen E. Hanson and Wilfried Spohn, eds., *Can Europe Work?* (Seattle: University of Washington Press, 1995), pp. 206–230. See also Beverly Crawford, ed., *Markets, States, and Democracy* (Boulder, CO: Westview, 1995).

12. See Dominique Arel and Andrew Wilson, "Ukraine under Kuchma: Back to 'Eurasia'?" *RFE/RL Research Report,* vol. 3, no. 32 (19 August 1994).

13. Oleh Havrylyshyn, "Economic Reform in Ukraine," unpublished manuscript, June 1995.

14. Yaroslav Hrytsak, "Shifting Identities in Western and Eastern Ukraine," *The East and Central Europe Program Bulletin,* vol. 5, no. 3 (February 1995), pp. 3, 5. See also Robert S. Kravchuk and Victor Chudowsky, "The Political Geography of Ukraine's 1994 Presidential and Parliamentary Elections," unpublished manuscript, April 1996, and Volodymyr Zviglyanich, "Ukrainian Reforms: A Sociological Analysis," *The Ukrainian Weekly,* 14 July 1996.

15. Hrytsak, "Shifting Identities," p. 7.

16. See Ole Diehl, *Kiew und Moskau* (Bonn: Europa Union Verlag, 1994), and Olga Alexandrova,"Russland und sein 'nahes Ausland,' " in *Zwischen Krise und Konsolidierung* (Munich: Carl Hanser Verlag, 1995), pp. 323–335.

17. See Motyl, "The Conceptual President," pp. 112–113.

18. This section draws on Alexander J. Motyl, "Structural Constraints and Starting

Points: The Logic of Systemic Change in Ukraine and Russia," *Comparative Politics,* vol. 29, no. 4 (July 1997), pp. 433–447.

19. See Marta Kolomayets, "New Constitution Changes Political landscape," *The Ukrainian Weekly,* 7 July 1996, and *Ukraina: Khronika podii,* 28 June 1996.

20. Dmitrii Vydrin, "Ukrainskaia politicheskaia elita," *Kievskie vedomosti,* 3 September 1994.

21. Sherman W. Garnett, *Keystone in the Arch: Ukraine and the New Political Geography of Central and Eastern Europe* (Washington, DC: Carnegie Endowment for International Peace, 1997), pp. 10–14.

22. Olexandr Dergachov and Volodymyr Polokhalo, "The Metamorphoses of Postcommunist Power," *Politychna Dumka,* no. 1 (1996), p. 120.

23. See Volodymyr Polokhalo, "Vid Ukrainy komunistychno-totalitarnoi do Ukrainy neototalitarnoi?" *Politychna Dumka,* no. 2 (1994), p. 19.

24. *Ukraine: Current Events,* 17 July 1996.

25. See the chapter by Mykola Riabchouk, "Civil Society and National Identity in Ukraine," in this volume.

26. Interview in Kyiv, June 1996.

27. Peter Reddaway makes a similar point in "Russia on the Brink?" *The New York Review of Books,* 28 January 1993, and "Desperation Time for Yeltsin's Clique," *The New York Times,* 13 January 1995.

28. John Edwin Mroz and Oleksandr Pavliuk, "Ukraine: Europe's Linchpin," *Foreign Affairs,* vol. 75, no. 4 (May-June 1996), pp. 52–62, and Alexander J. Motyl, "Russia, Ukraine, and the West: What Are America's Interests?" *American Foreign Policy Interests,* vol. 18, no. 1 (February 1996), pp. 14–20.

29. Taras Kuzio, *Ukrainian Security Policy* (Washington, DC: Praeger and Center for Strategic and International Studies, 1995), pp. 52–63, and Garnett, *Keystone in the Arch,* pp. 67–83.

30. For a variety of sober, and sobering, analyses, see Peter Reddaway, "Russia Heads for Trouble," *The New York Times,* 2 July 1996; Amy Knight, *Spies without Cloaks: The KGB's Successors* (Princeton: Princeton University Press, 1996); Leslie Dienes, "Corporate Russia: Privatisation and Prospects in the Oil and Gas Sector," *The Donald W. Treadgold Papers,* no. 5 (March 1996); Lynn D. Nelson and Irina Y. Kuzes, *Radical Reform in Yeltsin's Russia* (Armonk: M.E. Sharpe, 1995); Sergei Kovalev, "On the New Russia: An Interview with Jeri Laber," *The New York Review of Books,* vol. 43, no. 7 (18 April 1996); Viktor Jerofejew, "In Russland keine Wahl," *Die Zeit,* 14 June 1996; David Remnick, "Hammer, Sickle, and Book," *The New York Review of Books,* vol. 43, no. 9 (23 May 1996); and Christian Schmidt-Hauer, "Die zwei: Duett oder Duell?" *Die Zeit,* 5 July 1996.

2

The Post-Soviet Transition in Ukraine: Prospects for Stability

Roman Solchanyk

It is difficult to overestimate the importance of the role that Ukraine plays in the context of regional stability and security, both in the so-called post-Soviet space and in Central and Eastern Europe. Given the country's size, population, and, perhaps most important, its strategic geographic position between East and West, Ukraine has quite rightly been characterized as a linchpin of European security.[1] As the contours of a new post–Cold War security structure begin to take shape with the eastward enlargement of NATO, Ukraine's pivotal position between a Europe that is in the process of being redefined and a Russia that remains uncertain about its identity and future will very likely assume even greater significance. Continued Western engagement in Ukraine, the modalities of NATO enlargement, particularly with respect to Russia, and the attitudes and policies of Moscow will be important components in determining Ukraine's place and role in the new European security order.[2] Ultimately, however, the deciding factor rests with the prospects for stability in Ukraine itself—that is, on the success or failure of the nation- and state-building agenda. The outcome of this work in progress is far from certain. Ukraine, as one perceptive observer has noted, does not fit easily into the new security arrangements implied by either Russia or NATO, " yet its fate is crucial to the shape, costs, and consequences of both."[3]

Ukraine in the Old Soviet Neighborhood

Five years after the collapse of the Soviet Union, developments in most of the newly independent successor states have served only to underscore

17

Ukraine's role as a force for regional stability. The three Transcaucasian states of Armenia, Georgia, and Azerbaijan have all experienced serious and intermittently violent domestic political crises. The most recent flare-up occurred in Armenia—previously described as an oasis of civility and democracy compared to its neighbors—whose presidential elections in September 1996 were accompanied by opposition protests of vote-rigging, mob violence, and armed troops and tanks in the streets of the capital. All three states are embroiled in ethnically fueled territorial conflicts that had already erupted during the late Soviet period. Georgia's territorial integrity is threatened by the breakaway regions of Abkhazia and South Ossetia, and Armenia and Azerbaijan remain locked in their dispute over Nagorno-Karabakh. In the meantime, Russia has been an active player in the region, particularly in the Georgian-Abkhaz conflict, manipulating one side or the other in pursuit of its economic and strategic interests. With military bases in Armenia and Georgia, Moscow has emerged as the main arbiter in the conflict-prone Transcaucasus.[4]

With the exception of Tajikistan, which has served as the battleground for the armed forces of rival regional, clan, ethnic, and religious groups since 1992, the remaining four Central Asian states (Kazakhstan, Uzbekistan, Turkmenistan, and Kyrgyzia) have managed their transition to independent statehood without civil war and ethnic conflict. But the price for maintaining stability in Central Asia appears to be a tendency toward the institutionalization of authoritarian, one-man rule throughout the region, particularly in Turkmenistan and Uzbekistan. Central Asia was one of the first to experience outbreaks of ethnic violence unleashed by perestroika that involved disgruntled national minorities on the 'wrong' side of artificially created borders, a problem that has not disappeared with the passing of time. Kazakhstan has a special problem with its Russian minority, which constitutes 37 percent of the total population (ethnic Kazakhs number 42 percent) and is heavily concentrated in the northern border regions with Russia that many Russians view as their own. There are significant Uzbek minorities in Tajikistan, Kyrgyzia, and Turkmenistan. With little or no experience of modern statehood and after having independence unwillingly thrust up on them, the newly independent states of Central Asia are now growing more assertive in their relations with Russia and seeking to define their geopolitical identities in a region increasingly subject to competing influences from key neighboring states such as Iran, Turkey, Pakistan, and China.

The prospects for Ukraine's immediate neighbors—Belarus, Moldova, and Russia—are no less problematic. In Belarus, power is concentrated in the hands of an erratic leader with anti-Western inclinations and scant regard for the principles and practices of democratic government. Alyaksandr

Lukashenka, who was elected the country's first president in 1994, had already achieved a certain degree of notoriety by casting the sole dissenting vote in parliament against the Belovezh agreements that sealed the fate of the Soviet Union and created the Commonwealth of Independent States (CIS) at the end of 1991. The Belarusian president is on record praising the leadership qualities of Hitler and threatening to redeploy nuclear weapons on Belarusian territory in response to NATO enlargement. Confronted, like all of the former Soviet republics, with the formidable task of political and economic reform, Lukashenka has opted instead for one-man rule, political repression of the opposition, and a vaguely defined 'union' with Russia. Characterizing the situation in Belarus in the fall of 1996, a senior foreign diplomat in Minsk warned: "A country in Europe that doesn't want to be part of Europe is a destabilizing force. That's what we have here under the current leader."[5] In the aftermath of the controversial November 1996 referendum that greatly expanded Lukashenka's powers and the subsequent dismissal of the legitimately elected parliament, the Council of Europe suspended Belarus's guest status in that body.

In Moldova, the problem of the breakaway Transdniester Republic, which has plagued the central authorities in Chisinau since before the country gained independence, remains unresolved. A local referendum at the end of 1995 revealed that more than 80 percent favored an independent Transdniester state and almost 90 percent wished to join the CIS.[6] Russia tacitly supports the region's separatist drive and, despite the 1994 agreement with Moldova on the phased withdrawal of the former Fourteenth Russian Army from the Transdniester, Moscow is determined to maintain a military presence in Moldova in the form of peacekeeping forces. In November 1996, the State Duma, the lower house of Russia's parliament, adopted a resolution reaffirming that the Transdniester constituted a "zone of special strategic interests of the Russian Federation" and proposed that Russian forces be permanently stationed in the region.[7]

Finally, there is the recurring question "Whither Russia?" After the abortive coup in Moscow in August 1991, which precipitated the collapse of the Soviet Union, Russia has experienced an armed revolt by opposition parliamentarians against the president led by, among others, the vice president, which was suppressed by the shelling of the parliament building in October 1993; parliamentary elections in December of that year that witnessed the stunning victory of Vladimir Zhirinovsky's extremist Liberal Democratic Party of Russia; the December 1994 invasion of Chechnya by Russian forces, a conflict that has cost the lives of an estimated eighty thousand Russian citizens and the political outcome of which remains unclear; and the electoral victory of the communist-nationalist coalition in the parliamentary elections of December 1995. The new State Duma wasted little time in unveiling its vision of Russia's future—and that of its neighbors—by adopting resolutions in March 1996 denouncing and retracting Russia's role in the dissolution of the Soviet Union and the creation of the CIS. In effect, Russia's lawmakers restored the USSR on the territory of the Russian Federation. Finally, although President Boris Yeltsin was able to defeat his communist challenger in the 1996 presidential elections, his uncertain state of health has already set the stage for speculation about what might be expected from a post-Yeltsin Russia.

Viewed against this background, Ukraine's post-Soviet transition—particularly during the administration of President Leonid Kuchma—is widely seen as a relative success story.[8] In the spring and summer of 1994, Ukrainian voters went to the polls and chose a new parliament and president; the transfer of power occurred peacefully and in a democratic fashion. Despite fears of a widening regional split between the 'pro-Russian' eastern and the 'pro-Ukrainian' western parts of the country, which were accentuated by the voting patterns in 1994, Ukraine does not show signs of being in imminent danger of fragmenting along overlapping regional and ethnic/ linguistic lines.[9] Indeed, one can reasonably argue that Kuchma's victory at the polls, which was made possible by the overwhelming support of 'pro-Russian' voters in the eastern oblasts, has served to legitimize Ukrainian independence and statehood in precisely that part of the country that, by all accounts, is least committed to such ideals. Even in Crimea, which remains Ukraine's most serious regional problem, the separatist movement has subsided considerably after Kyiv's crackdown in the spring of 1995 and the removal of the peninsula's separatist president and parliamentary speaker. The current Crimean leadership, although faced with a troublesome opposition in the local parliament, appears committed to resolving existing differences with the central government within the framework of Ukraine's new constitution, which was finally adopted in June 1996. Relations with Russia remain difficult, even after Kyiv and Moscow finalized the long-awaited bilateral treaty on friendship and cooperation in May 1997. There were serious disagreements on a number of important issues, particularly regarding the division of the Black Sea Fleet and the status of Sevastopol, which surfaced once again at the end of 1996 when Russian legislators renewed de facto claims to Ukrainian territory. The major problem in Russian-Ukrainian relations, however, is much more fundamental and enduring: Russia has yet to fully come to terms with the existence of an independent Ukrainian state. Most Russian elites are inclined to view Ukrainian independence as a temporary phenomenon, while public sentiment in Russia overwhelmingly favors the unification of the two countries. In a poll conducted in the fall of

1996, 76 percent of respondents agreed that Russia and Ukraine should reunite.[10] In spite of such difficulties, Moscow and Kyiv have succeeded in managing their relations without open confrontation. Finally, Ukraine's standing in the eyes of the West, particularly the United States, has improved markedly, largely as a result of Kyiv's decision to abandon its nuclear arsenal. Overall, from a country that several years ago was thought by many to be near total economic collapse and on the verge of ethnic turmoil and possible disintegration, Ukraine has moved steadily forward in its post-Soviet transition.[11]

While recognizing the considerable progress that has been made thus far, one cannot lose sight of the fact that political and economic reform is still in its early stages and has yet to be fully consolidated and institutionalized. Both Western analysts and domestic critics have argued convincingly that the most serious and immediate challenges that Kyiv faces are internal rather than external. The economy arguably ranks highest on the list of Ukraine's primary domestic concerns. Some observations on the political impact of market-oriented reforms are, therefore, in order. The economic difficulties that Ukraine continues to experience in the course of its post-Soviet transition have been felt most directly and forcefully by ordinary citizens in the form of widespread socioeconomic dislocation and serious strains on the social fabric. This, in turn, has inevitable political ramifications—on the policies of the president and the government; on the legislative agenda in parliament; on regional problems; and on relations with other countries, notably Russia. In this connection, it is useful to recall that in December 1991 over 90 percent of Ukraine's voters opted for independence. The expectation that independent statehood would facilitate their economic and social well-being was a major factor for many voters, perhaps even the majority. Such expectations have long since vanished—along with the initial level of political support. According to a nationwide survey conducted at the end of 1995, people's standard of living was seen by 72 percent of respondents as Ukraine's most important problem. Almost 85 percent were dissatisfied to one degree or another with the overall situation in the country. The political side of this story is that 31 percent favored the unification of Ukraine and Russia in a single state. In a similar poll conducted at the end of 1996, 67 percent felt that "things are going in the wrong direction," and few believed that economic conditions would improve during the following year. As many as 58 percent agreed that Russia and Ukraine should reunite.[12]

Beyond the economy, the prospects for stability in Ukraine will be conditioned by such important components of the state- and nation-building agendas as forging a national political consensus that accommodates the executive and legislative branches, managing the deep-seated and overlapping regional and ethnic/linguistic cleavages in the country, and normalizing relations with Russia.

The Politics of Transition

Leonid Kuchma was elected president in the summer of 1994 largely as a result of widespread popular discontent—particularly in Ukraine's predominantly Russian-speaking eastern and southern regions—with the catastrophic economic situation in the country and the strained relations with Russia that prevailed during the administration of Ukraine's first president, Leonid Kravchuk. For many voters, these two issues were closely linked; economic problems were often seen as a direct result of Kyiv's overly independent stance vis-à-vis Moscow and the breakdown of previously established economic ties. Accordingly, Kuchma's electoral campaign focused primarily on the need for economic reform and normalization of relations with Russia.[13]

The new Ukrainian leader's first major initiative came in the fall of 1994, when he proposed a 'socially oriented' program of economic reform, which was closely linked to the establishment of a strong executive. The implementation of that program was impeded from the very start by two major stumbling blocks. First, it was not until June 1996 that Ukraine succeeded in replacing its Soviet-era constitution, which had been altered on a piecemeal basis by innumerable amendments over the past five years, with a new fundamental law that clearly delineated the division of power between the executive and legislative branches of government. During the first two years of his administration, Kuchma and parliament were engaged in a drawn-out struggle over the basic tenets of the constitution, thereby overshadowing the reform process. Second, the parliamentary elections in 1994 seated a sizable contingent of left-wing deputies opposed to the bulk of Kuchma's market-oriented reforms. The coalition of communists, socialists, and agrarians accounted for slightly more than 40 percent of the parliamentary mandates. These two factors were closely interrelated. The clear delineation of power between the president and parliament would have served to facilitate implementation of the reform program, particularly if, as Kuchma had urged, the powers of the presidency were to be expanded and broadened. The bloc of leftist parties obviously had no interest in promoting this process, and certainly not along the lines envisioned by the president. Indeed, the program of the Communist Party of Ukraine, which still has the single largest contingent of deputies in parliament, goes so far as to call for the abolition of the institution of the presidency altogether.[14] Moreover,

Kuchma's vision of a powerful executive faced opposition to one degree or another from a broad spectrum of parliamentarians, including some reformers, whose natural instinct was to defend their corporate interests. The result was gridlock and a struggle for power between the two branches of government, a debilitating but by no means atypical phenomenon in most of the newly independent states.

The confrontation between the two branches of government was prompted by Kuchma's proposed draft law on state power and local government, submitted to parliament in December 1994, which delegated far-reaching powers to the presidency. The first phase of this conflict lasted six months and was resolved only after lengthy negotiations and the threat of a nationwide nonbinding referendum on confidence in the president and parliament. In May–June 1995, a compromise was reached and parliament passed a modified version of the so-called power law (May 18) and shortly thereafter agreed to a constitutional accord (June 8) that cleared the way for the power law to be implemented as an interim 'small constitution' until the adoption of a new constitution within a year's time.[15] The stage was now set for the final battle over the constitution itself.

Two points bear emphasizing with regard to the constitutional accord. First, it was agreed to by parliament not because the majority of lawmakers were won over by the president, but because it was clearly in their interest to avoid a referendum. Opinion surveys have consistently shown parliament ranking very low in popularity among voters, while Kuchma has, until recently, enjoyed unusually high approval ratings. A nationwide poll in December 1994, for example, found that 64 percent of respondents disapproved of parliament's work; conversely, more than 58 percent approved of Kuchma's handling of state affairs (almost 22 percent disapproved, and 20 percent were uncertain). In the fall of 1995, Kuchma's popularity was more than double that of the parliamentary speaker, Oleksandr Moroz.[16] Under these circumstances, a referendum might have led to new parliamentary elections, a possibility that the lawmakers wanted to preclude at all costs. Second, the constitutional accord was a stopgap measure, not a solution. It simply served to postpone the struggle among opposing political forces over a new constitution.

The second phase of the constitutional marathon began immediately after the constitutional accord was signed and focused on the actual text of the proposed fundamental law that had been drafted by a working group of the Constitutional Commission. In the process, the draft underwent numerous revisions by specially formed working groups, but it continued to be opposed by the left-wing parties in parliament. It was only in early June 1996 that parliament finally managed to approve a version of the draft in its first

Table 2.1

Parliamentary Blocs and Factions (April 1996)

Left (33.9 percent)	141
Communists	88
Socialists	28
Peasants' Party	25
Center (38.2 percent)	159
Unity	28
Center	28
Independents	26
Interregional Deputies Group	26
Social-Market Choice	26
Agrarians for Reform	25
National Democrats (21.4 percent)	89
Reforms	31
Rukh	29
Statehood	29

Source: Presidium of the Supreme Soviet of Ukraine, *Spysok deputats'kykh hrup i fraktsii u Verkovnii Radi Ukraiiny. Za stanom na 05 kvitnya 1996 roky.*

reading that had been agreed upon by a provisional committee of lawmakers representing the various factions and groups in parliament. Final approval came on the morning of 28 June 1996, after an all-night session by a vote of 315–36 with 12 abstentions and, once again, under a presidential threat of a popular referendum.[17] With the exception of one unaffiliated deputy, all of the negative votes were cast by communists (29) and socialists (6).[18]

Kuchma's problems with the current parliament have not been limited to disagreement over how power should be distributed between the branches of government. No less important is the fact that the president has not been successful in finding a stable and reliable majority of supporters in parliament. As Table 2.1 illustrates, in the spring of 1996 a coalition of opposition left-wing parties accounted for approximately one third of the parliamentary seats; a slightly greater proportion of deputies was distributed within an amorphous center that largely represented regional, economic, and nomenklatura interests; committed democrats and reformers held less than a quarter of the mandates.

It may be useful to examine the constellation of political forces in parliament in greater detail and note the recent shifts and realignments, particularly in the center of the political spectrum.

Left Coalition

The Communist Party of Ukraine, registered in October 1993 after having been banned following the abortive putsch in 1991, was the most successful political party in the 1994 parliamentary elections. It is also the most steadfast in its opposition to Kuchma and, indeed, to the existing political system in Ukraine. Symptomatically, the majority of communist parliamentary deputies refused to take the oath of allegiance, as required by the new constitution. The communists consider themselves to be the ideological heirs of the Communist Party of the Soviet Union. Their program is wholly restorationist. It seeks to put an end to what is described as the 'capitalization of society' by restoring the power of soviets, state regulation of economic and social processes, socialization of the means of production, and a revamped union of socialist states. Ukraine's communists have been in the forefront of an ongoing campaign advocating close political, economic, and security ties to Russia and full integration within the CIS. Overall, the communist parliamentary faction is quite stable, although there is a dividing line between its orthodox members and adherents of 'national communism.' This was demonstrated once again during the vote on the constitution, when twenty members of the faction cast their votes in support of the fundamental law and another ten abstained. In October 1995, more than twenty hardline communist deputies attempted to form a separate parliamentary group called Union, but ultimately failed to gain the sufficient number of members for official registration.

The socialists are moderate in their opposition. They favor a political system based on soviets, with the executive branch of government constituted, subordinated, and responsible to parliament; a state-regulated but mixed economy that places priority on state and collective forms of ownership and excludes private ownership of land except for personal plots; social guarantees for the population; and independent statehood with close ties to Russia as well as integration within the CIS.[19] The moderation of the socialist deputies is explained in part by the fact that their leader was elected speaker of parliament and, by virtue of his office, is obliged to seek compromise. It was primarily because of opposition to Moroz that a hardline group emerged within the Socialist Party of Ukraine at the end of 1995 and soon thereafter formed its own Progressive Socialist Party of Ukraine, which weakened somewhat the party's representation in parliament.

The agrarians, composed largely of chairmen of local rural councils and collective and state farm heads, are primarily a special-interest group and have been described as a rural version of the socialists. The agrarians, however, have not been able to sustain organizational unity and, increas-

Table 2.2

Parliamentary Blocs and Factions (February 1997)

Left (35.9 percent)	149
Communists	86
Socialists	25
Agrarians of Ukraine	38
Center (41.2 percent)	171
Constitutional Center	56
Unity	37
Interregional Deputies Group	28
Social-Market Choice	25
Independents	25
National Democrats (13.5 percent)	56
Reforms	29
Rukh	27

Source: Presidium of the Supreme Soviet of Ukraine, *Spysok deputats'kykh hrup i fraktsii u Verkhovnii Radi Ukraiiny. Za stanom na 01 lyutoho 1997 roku.*

ingly, a reform-oriented part of the group has sought to establish its own political identity and move toward the center of the political spectrum. Previously the agrarians were the second largest parliamentary group, but almost half of them walked out in the fall of 1995 to form the centrist Agrarians for Reform, leaving the remainder of the group to reorganize themselves as the parliamentary faction of the conservative Peasants Party of Ukraine. In September 1996, however, with both groups facing dissolution because of dwindling numbers, another reorganization resulted in the establishment of a single pro-reform parliamentary group that reverted to the original name, Agrarians of Ukraine, numbering thirty-eight members (see Table 2.2). There were not enough remaining anti-reform peasant party members to create a faction of their own, and so they joined the Socialists.

In principle, the differentiation of the left could have a positive effect with regard to prospects for reform, although in practice it has had little concrete impact thus far. The left, together with conservatives from the center, is still in a position to obstruct reforms, although it is not strong enough to dictate its own agenda. There are clear differences among the three left-wing parties that formed the coalition throughout most of 1996, which is reflected in the fact that each had its separate faction. Economic and social issues form the basis for cooperation within the left coalition, while issues of state work against a united front. The communists clearly stand out in the degree of their opposition across the board, while the socialists and agrarians have demonstrated their willingness to be flexible.

Amorphous Center

Overall, the six groups identified as centrist in Table 2.1 may be character-ized as political moderates, but their interests have proven to be so varied as to preclude a common political platform. The defining characteristics of the political center have been its largely amorphous nature and the absence of unifying and overarching political or economic convictions. Not surpris-ingly, the centrist groups tend to be organized not along party or political lines, but rather as regional or interest group lobbies. The Social-Market Choice group, which was formed in early 1996, represents an interesting combination of regional and party interests to the extent that it is under the patronage of the Liberal Party of Ukraine, which is based primarily in the Donets'k region in eastern Ukraine and is supported by influential local business interests. Social-Market Choice favors a 'socially oriented econ-omy of a market type' and has declared its commitment to 'strengthening the sovereignty of Ukraine.' Its first leader was Volodymyr Shcherban', head of the Liberal Party and, until his removal by Kuchma in July 1996, governor of the Donets'k region. Not long after, another prominent politi-cian who ran afoul of the president, former Prime Minister Yevhen Marchuk, joined the group and subsequently took over its leadership. Given Marchuk's undisguised presidential ambitions and the fierce competition among regional interests in Donets'k and Dnipropetrovs'k for power and influence in the country, observers have focused on Social-Market Choice as a platform for opposition to the president.

One of the largest groups in the center is Unity, which is made up almost exclusively of deputies from Kuchma's power base in Dnipropetrovs'k and represents the interests of local power structures and their allies from among the 'nomenklatura capitalists.' The group called Center, which was disbanded in the fall of 1996, initially brought together incumbent and former central government officials. The Interregional Deputies Group, which traces its origins to the electoral bloc cochaired by Kuchma (Interre-gional Bloc of Reforms), and the Independents are the most diverse in composition and in their political and economic views.

Taken together, the center accounts for a sizable proportion of parlia-mentary votes, but it remains largely fractured and unstable in the pursuit of diffuse, narrow, and often competing interests. Many centrist deputies either support or oppose reform legislation depending upon concrete issues and how these fit into their agendas. In many ways, the center holds the key to the transformation of the current parliament into an agent of reform, but only if it evolves into a genuine political center along European lines. The trend is progressively moving in this direction, and its continued progress depends on the further political structuralization of Ukrainian society, which has proven to be an inordinately slow process.

National Democrats

The national democrats have been consistent advocates of political and economic reform but reluctant supporters of Kuchma. With their main constituencies in the western and central regions and in Kyiv, the national democrats are firm supporters of market-oriented reform, represent principled anticommunism, and are strongly committed to independent statehood. The differences between the groups Statehood, which was also disbanded in the fall of 1996, and Rukh, which is led by the prominent former political prisoner Vyacheslav Chornovil, are based primarily on personalities. The Reforms group is one of the most variegated in its regional composition and gives precedence to the requirements of political and economic reform over 'nationalist' concerns. Reforms members Viktor Pynzenyk, deputy prime minister for economic reforms in the current government, and Volodymyr Lanovyi, a former deputy prime minister, are the two most prominent free-market economists in Ukraine.

Perhaps the most significant recent development on the political scene—and not only insofar as shifting allegiances and realignments in parliament are concerned—is the formation in September 1996 of the Constitutional Center parliamentary group, which ranks second only to the communists in numbers (see Table 2.2). Drawing strongly on the Center and Statehood deputies and thereby resulting in those groups' dissolution, the Constitutional Center is the product of a long-awaited rapprochement of reform-minded liberals and national democrats that was facilitated by the agonizing negotiations that ultimately led to the adoption of the constitution. Its leader is Mykhailo Syrota, who played a key role in guiding the draft of the new constitution through parliament as head of a special parliamentary conciliatory committee. The driving force behind the new group is the People's Democratic Party, formed in February 1996 largely on the basis of two centrist political parties (the Labor Congress of Ukraine and the Party of Democratic Rebirth) and the political association New Ukraine. The Constitutional Center sees itself as the nucleus around which the 'situational majority' that adopted the constitution could eventually be transformed into a stable parliamentary majority backing Kuchma's reform initiatives. The group includes such prominent political figures as former President Leonid Kravchuk and former parliamentary speaker Ivan Plyushch, Oleksandr Yemets', Ihor Yukhnovs'kyi, and Volodymyr Yavorivs'kyi. The fact that Kuchma chose to appoint Yevhen Kushnyar'ov—the head of New Ukraine and one of the leaders of the People's Democratic Party—as head of his administration prompted commentators to characterize the new group as representatives of an emerging 'party of power' that could serve as the foundation for Kuchma's reelection bid in 1999.

The realignments and shifts within the Ukrainian parliament during the past two years have witnessed the increasing strength of the center and, more important, the coalescence of a liberal-democratic nucleus determined to promote the reform process, but it has not dramatically changed the distribution of forces within the lawmaking body.

None of the parliamentary blocs has the votes to push through its agenda, but each is capable of blocking its opponents. A clear example of this is the failure of the left-wing forces to bring the question of Ukraine's membership in the CIS Interparliamentary Assembly to a vote. Thus far, this situation has not prevented Kuchma from winning parliamentary approval for such major national initiatives and issues as the economic reform program; ratification of the Nuclear Nonproliferation Treaty; Crimean separatism; the constitutional accord; and the new constitution. An important factor in Kuchma's success has been the degree of popular support that he has enjoyed. But the level of that support declined significantly in 1996. Whereas at the beginning of the year Kuchma had a net positive rating (52 percent to 43 percent), by the fall only 37 percent expressed confidence in the president, as opposed to 56 percent who did not.[20] While he continues to remain Ukraine's most favored politician, Kuchma's drop in popularity is a clear indication that voters are growing increasingly disenchanted with the absence of tangible short-term economic improvement in their daily lives. Moreover, the economic outlook for the country is not encouraging, a factor that will certainly makes itself felt during the next parliamentary and presidential elections, scheduled for March 1998 and October 1999, respectively.[21]

In spite of the social and economic difficulties associated with the post-Soviet transition, Kuchma has proved himself to be a skillful promoter of the state- and nation-building project, drawing both east and west to the national center. Although his election was secured by the predominantly Russian-speaking east largely in protest against the 'nationalist' incumbent, Kuchma now enjoys more popularity in the Ukrainian-speaking west than in the eastern regions. At the same time, he continues to staff the government and his own administration with associates from his eastern bailiwick of Dnipropetrovs'k. A case in point was the appointment of Pavlo Lazarenko, formerly governor of the Dnipropetrovs'k region, to succeed Marchuk as prime minister in May 1996. Critics have pointed to the growing and disproportionate number of national politicians coming from Kuchma's hometown—204 overall and 55 in high-level positions, according to one source—and raised the specter of the dangers of clan-dominated politics in Ukraine that are strangely reminiscent of the Dnipropetrovs'k group during the Brezhnev era.[22] Conversely, one could argue that linking local political and economic elites from the east to the center of power in Kyiv serves to 'nationalize' precisely those elites who have traditionally been weakest in their commitment to the national idea.

Regional Dimensions of Stability

Ukraine's regional and ethnic/linguistic fault lines constitute perhaps the most serious obstacle for the state- and nation-building agenda. The regional divide, primarily between the eastern and western regions, is a legacy of the country's historical development, and its effects on a wide range of domestic issues and foreign policy choices will continue to be felt for quite some time. However, the notion that the east is uniformly and solidly opposed to Ukrainian independence is flawed, and concerns about the disintegration of the state along regional lines are largely misplaced. There is a fair amount of diversity among the eastern regions, with a slight majority of easterners identifying themselves either with Ukraine or with their own region; identification with Russia is, in fact, minimal. Most important perhaps is that attitudes toward independent statehood are motivated primarily by socioeconomic factors rather than ethnic or linguistic considerations, which holds out the prospect that they are subject to moderation under more auspicious economic circumstances.

Ukraine's urban and industrial east has a high concentration of the country's 11.3 million ethnic Russians and is predominantly Russian-speaking; it displays a weak commitment to Ukrainian statehood and favors close ties to Russia and the CIS; and it is generally more supportive of the social and economic features of 'communism.' The West is Ukrainian-speaking; strongly committed to independence; suspicious of Russia and wary of the CIS; and more favorably disposed to Western models of political and economic development.

The most troubling feature of Ukraine's regional divide is the tenuous nature of the east's commitment to independent statehood. A poll conducted in May-June 1994 in eight eastern oblasts and in Crimea revealed that only 24 percent of respondents would vote for independence, while 47 percent would vote against.[23] Anti-independence sentiment was highest in the Donets'k and Luhans'k oblasts (63 percent), followed by the Crimean Autonomous Republic (55 percent), the southern oblasts of Mykolaiv, Odesa, and Kherson (36 percent), Dnipropetrovs'k and Zaporizhzhia (36 percent), and Kharkiv (30 percent). The proportion of opponents and supporters of independence were evenly split in Dnipropetrovs'k and Zaporizhzhia, and Kharkiv registered slightly more supporters (34 percent) than opponents. On the whole, the data show that the support for independence is minimal, although there are significant differences among the region's eastern and southern oblasts. Particularly interesting, however, is the question of how the east perceives its own identity. When asked "With which population do you identify?" most respondents opted for the seemingly contradictory choice of Ukrainian (34 percent), followed by the Soviet Union (27 percent) and their own region (23 percent). The smallest proportion identified itself with Russian (3 percent) and the CIS (7 percent).[24] It would appear, therefore, that the generally weak support for independent statehood in eastern Ukraine does not preclude a sense of Ukrainian identity and by no means signifies a preference for Russian identity. Thus, it might be suggested that the disaffection with independence in eastern Ukraine is motivated primarily by social and economic factors rather than ethnic and linguistic considerations. This is supported by the fact that the second largest group (27 percent) identifies with the former Soviet Union, which many associate with economic and social stability. Further, with the exception of the Crimeans themselves, a surprisingly high proportion of easterners, ranging from 45 percent to 67 percent, felt that Crimea should remain a part of Ukraine. Overall, it seems that the east represents a classic case of a deformed national identity in transition.[25] If this is indeed the case, the relative success or failure of the reform process will play a determining role in the shaping of state and national identity in eastern Ukraine. In this connection, it is worth remembering that the east has demonstrated once before that it is prepared to support an independent Ukrainian state if that state is able to accommodate its economic and social expectations.

The status of Crimea remains Ukraine's most sensitive and potentially destabilizing regional problem. The nature of the Crimean question is defined by a specific combination of factors that differentiate it from the eastern region and impinge directly on Ukraine's domestic stability and on its relations with Russia. First, the population of Crimea has from the very start consistently displayed the greatest degree of opposition to what might be termed 'political Ukrainianism.' The 1994 survey, for example, revealed that only 6 percent of respondents supported Ukrainian independence, while 55 percent were opposed. Conversely, Crimeans registered the highest level of identification with Russia (14 percent), although their primary allegiances were to the peninsula itself (40 percent) and to the former Soviet Union (37 percent).[26] The fact that Crimea is the only administrative subdivision of Ukraine with an ethnic Russian majority (67 percent, according to the 1989 census) is certainly an important factor in the Crimeans' level of antipathy to Ukraine and their relatively greater inclination toward Russia. But conventional wisdom notwithstanding, the ethnic composition of the peninsula is not the deciding factor.[27] Most important is the prevailing view among both Crimean political elites and the population at large that the peninsula was never an integral part of Ukraine. Crimea's argument with Kyiv, therefore, is primarily about history and jurisdiction rather than ethnicity, language, or the economy. When asked "To whom should Crimea belong?" Crimeans opt for Russia (55 percent) and independence (20 percent), and only 5 percent feel that the peninsula should remain part of Ukraine. For Kyiv, the problem is exacerbated by the fact that Russian elites and most Russians feel exactly the same. A nationwide poll conducted in Russia in mid-December 1996—shortly after the Council of the Federation, the upper house of Russia's parliament, in effect claimed the city of Sevastopol—revealed that 70 percent of respondents agreed that the city should belong to Russia.[28] Moreover, Moscow has strategic interests in Crimea, which are personified by the presence of the Black Sea Fleet in the peninsula's ports. The Crimean question, therefore, poses both a domestic and an international problem for the Ukrainian authorities, thereby increasing its potential to act as a destabilizing force.

Finally, the return of the Crimean Tatars is rapidly emerging as an ethnic as well a political issue of growing proportions. The ethnic dimension centers on the strained relations and incidents of violent clashes between the local Russian population and administration and the Crimean Tatars, who maintain that they are being discriminated against and harassed by the Crimean authorities. At the same time, the political support that Kyiv has grown accustomed to receiving from the Crimean Tatars in its struggle with the separatist movement is waning, and relations are becoming increasingly strained because of the lack of adequate financial support from the center to facilitate the social and economic integration of the returning Crimean Tatar population. The Crimean Tatar political spectrum has now been broadened to include the nationalist Adalet (Justice) party, which has taken a hard line toward the central authorities and is reported to have ties with a radical right Ukrainian party.[29] The Crimean Tatar question adds another dimension to the problem of stability in Crimea, one with clear and potentially explosive ethnic overtones.

In the course of 1995, Kyiv managed to deflate Crimea's separatist drive by a combination of decisive action, including the abolition of the local presidency, and a willingness to compromise on negotiable issues. Essentially, this policy succeeded in depriving the peninsula of its pro-Russian leadership, which was already losing support among the local population because of its political and economic incompetence. Russia, on the other hand, hampered and discredited by its violent crackdown in Chechnya, lacked the political will to exert pressure on the Ukrainian leadership. And lastly, ordinary Crimeans seem to have come to the growing realization that independence or reunification with Russia is a phantom, and that social and economic problems must take precedence over political confrontation.[30] Nonetheless, the Crimean problem will remain a sensitive issue for Ukraine. The long-term solution to separatist tendencies lies in economic improvement and a modus vivendi between Kyiv and Simferopol'. A key question, however, which is largely beyond the control of Ukraine's leaders, is how Moscow will play the Crimean card. The last two Russian parliaments were quick to demonstrate their support for Crimean separatists, and the current State Duma and Council of the Federation have demonstrated that they are prepared to follow suit. Parliamentary resolutions and declarations alone have little practical significance, but a post-Yeltsin Russia under communist-nationalist leadership is much more likely to exploit the Crimean question as a pressure point in its relations with Ukraine.

The main problem that regionalism poses for Ukraine is not the danger of secession and fragmentation, but the challenge of shaping a modern, post-Soviet identity that is grounded in a civic ethos. Cultural and linguistic characteristics combined with economic hardship have resulted in disenchantment with the notion of political independence in the eastern region. Much of the population there is perhaps best described as a political nation in the making, and the most important factor that will influence the direction that this process eventually takes is a steady recovery of the economy. An increasing number of prominent representatives of the local political and economic elites already have a stake in Ukraine: Kuchma is perhaps the best example.

Ukrainian-Russian Relations

The Ukrainian-Russian relationship, which remains fundamentally unstable and has been punctuated by periodic crises since both countries gained their independence in 1991, is a key determinant of Ukraine's stability and security. In October and December 1996, both houses of the Russian parliament adopted several resolutions and statements that called into question the status of Sevastopol, the Black Sea Fleet, and, indeed, Crimea as a whole.[31] Similar steps had been taken in 1992, when the Russian Supreme Soviet decreed that Moscow's transfer of Crimea to Ukraine in 1954 was "without the force of law," and again in 1993, when it declared the "Russian federal status of Sevastopol." In the meantime, the Ukrainian-Russian treaty on friendship and cooperation, although initialed in February 1995, has yet to be signed by the leaders of the two countries. Moscow's point of departure is that the treaty can be concluded only after the problem of the Black Sea Fleet and the related question of Sevastopol are resolved. By the end of 1996, Ukrainian-Russian relations were at one of their lowest points since the collapse of the Soviet Union, when, quite unexpectedly, it became clear that Ukraine had actually seceded from 'Russia.'

What is standing in the way of normalizing Ukrainian-Russian relations? Clearly, the status of Sevastopol, the disposition of the Black Sea Fleet, and the Crimean question were major stumbling blocks. Most would agree with Russian Foreign Minister Yevgenii Primakov that it is psychologically difficult for Russians to relate to the idea of Sevastopol being part of Ukraine.[32] Ukrainian and Russian negotiators have also found it difficult to agree on the question of dual citizenship, settlement of the former Soviet Union's foreign assets and debts, the role and function of the CIS, and a host of other lesser questions. But in order to fully understand the essence of the Ukrainian-Russian imbroglio, it would be useful to go beyond such issue-specific problems and focus on the underlying assumptions that inform Russia's attitude and, consequently, its policies toward Ukraine.

Most Russians, it seems, particularly among the political and cultural elites, have found it inordinately difficult to fully acquiesce to the notion that Ukraine is actually an independent state and no longer a part of Russia. This is a complex and multifaceted problem that is deeply rooted in the historical relationship between Ukraine and Russia, which has been shaped over several centuries. In the briefest of terms, the prevailing view in Moscow is that Ukraine, with the possible exception of its western regions, is historically an integral part of Russia—not only in the territorial sense, but culturally, linguistically, and spiritually as well.[33] From this standpoint, it follows that Ukrainian independence is an unfortunate result of circumstance, some sort of terrible mistake, a temporary phenomenon, and that in due time everything will return to 'normal.' This is more or less in line with the thinking of General Aleksandr Lebed, a front-runner to succeed Yeltsin as president. Asked what he thought about the disintegration of the Soviet Union, Lebed said:

> Whereas something can still be said about the Baltic states, Russians, Ukrainians, and Belarusians are people from one root, with essentially a single language—we understand each other without a translator. We are the heirs to one faith, one military glory. They took one people and tore it up in an artificial fashion. . . . But it doesn't matter, I think that by the end of this century we will arrive at a new state formation, founded on a confederative basis.[34]

Referring specifically to Ukraine and Russia, Lebed explained that "what happened was the completely artificial division of two parts of one people." Such views are by no means confined to the 'patriotic bloc' of communists and nationalists, but are widespread among Russia's democrats and reformers as well. Thus, Mikhail Yur'ev, the thirty-nine-year-old deputy speaker of the State Duma and a member of Grigorii Yavlinsky's reformist Yabloko group, is convinced that Ukrainians (and Belarusians) are a fiction:

> Ukraine and Belarus are not separate nations at all, they are Slavs, Russians [russkie] in the broad sense of the term. I think, for example, that the Ukrainian language is a hundred times more poetic than the contemporary Russian language, but nonetheless it is a dialect of Russian, just like, say, the Moscow accent or the Siberian dialect. . . . The question should not be posed in terms of integration or consolidation, but rather in terms of returning these lands to the Russian Federation on conditions analogous to those of, say, Tataria. This should be the cornerstone of our foreign policy.[35]

Significantly, the documents laying claim to Sevastopol that were adopted by the Council of the Federation in December 1996 were prepared and introduced by Moscow's mayor, Yurii Luzhkov, who enjoys a solid reputation as an energetic proponent of democratic and market-oriented reforms, and were approved by an overwhelming majority of 110 to 14, with 7 abstentions.[36] Luzhkov is also considered to be a leading presidential contender.

It is interesting to note that while the status of Sevastopol may well have been the major impediment to finalizing the Ukrainian-Russian treaty, during the course of past negotiations the most difficult stumbling block was the more fundamental and much broader problem of Russia's unwillingness to explicitly recognize the inviolability of the existing borders between the two countries and to expressly renounce existing or future territorial claims. Russian negotiators are said to have argued that such commitments would effectively preclude the treaty's ratification by the Russian parliament and were therefore not prepared to go beyond the wording in the Helsinki agreements of 1975.[37] This issue was reportedly resolved when the treaty was initialed. According to the Russian Ministry of Foreign Affairs, "in several articles of the document it is clearly and unequivocally stipulated that the sides recognize the territorial integrity of the states that are a party to the treaty."[38] Nonetheless, the treaty remained unsigned until May 1997.

The question of where Russia begins and ends, especially in relation to Ukraine, and the related problem of Moscow's ambitions in the post-Soviet space are not likely to be resolved in the short to medium term and will continue to plague Ukrainian-Russian relations in the foreseeable future. It is difficult to see how, even with the best intentions of the leaders of both countries, normalization of relations can proceed when influential politicians such as Konstantin Zatulin, the former head of the State Duma's Committee on CIS Affairs and Ties with Compatriots, expresses his skepticism about the need to recognize "the historically nonexistent borders of a historically nonexistent state [Ukraine]."[39] His successor in that post, Georgii Tikhonov, when asked recently what his committee sees as its main tasks, responded: "To gather together the Great Mother Rus' and, to that end, prepare the necessary legal groundwork. We will be speeding up this work. We have big plans."[40] Finally, one wonders what exactly Primakov had in mind when he argued that the Helsinki agreements regarding state borders do not apply to the new states that emerged on the territories of the former Soviet Union, Czechoslovakia, and Yugoslavia.[41]

Another characteristic aspect of the problem of prevailing attitudes and convictions in the context of Ukrainian-Russian relations is that, in spite of the conventional stereotypes concerning the long historic ties between Ukraine and Russia and the similarities in language, culture, and religion, the degree of Russian familiarity with and knowledge about Ukraine appears to be surprisingly low. The problem is a long-standing one. In July 1922, Lenin issued a directive to Stalin that contained a rather revealing insight: "Kharkov [Ukraine's then capital] should be ransacked—*we don't know it,* it is a 'foreign country' for us."[42] Unlike neighboring Poland, Russia apparently does not have a single institution of higher learning or academic institute that offers specialization in Ukrainian studies.[43] The result has been the continued persistence of superficial perceptions and entrenched prejudices about things Ukrainian. A content analysis of the Russian press after the collapse of the Soviet Union conducted by a Moscow historian that focused on the portrayal of Ukraine and Ukrainians revealed that directly after the December 1991 referendum on Ukraine's independence Russian newspapers, regardless of political orientation, proved incapable of providing their readers with a serious analysis of what was admittedly a very surprising and important development. In the ensuing years, Ukraine's independence continued to be described as largely the work of Ukraine's 'nationalist' or 'sovereign communist' elites, suggesting that the man in the street really had no role in these events. The result, according to the author, is a deformed picture that allows proponents of the "restoration of the [Russian] state" to argue that Ukrainian political elites are essentially the only obstacle preventing the simple folk from realizing their heartfelt desire to reunite with Russia. The study concludes that, for the most part, "Russian public opinion and the mass media evade serious discussion of the problems that are posed for Russian identity in connection with the formation of an independent Ukraine. A significant spectrum of public opinion continues to view the separation of Ukraine as something artificial and temporary."[44] Under the circumstances, it should not come as a great surprise that on the eve of the formation of the Russian-Belarusian 'union' in the spring of 1996, Yeltsin apparently entertained the notion that his Ukrainian counterpart "wants to join, but something's hindering him."[45]

The underlying abnormality of the Ukrainian-Russian relationship, when transferred to the realm of practical politics and the negotiating table, often results in a situation where the two sides talk past each other. Dmitrii Ryurikov, Yeltsin's foreign policy adviser, provides an instructive example. While recognizing that Ukrainian-Russian relations are burdened by a 'psychological layer,' at the same time he is genuinely puzzled and irritated by the fact that Kyiv refuses to build its state and conduct relations with Moscow on the basis of a 'special relationship'—that is, as a subordinate 'younger brother.' Instead, he complains, Ukrainian leaders and diplomats insist on proceeding from their own laws and internationally recognized legal norms.[46]

In spite of the difficulties during the past five years, Kyiv and Moscow have made important strides in normalizing their relations. Most important, both sides have worked to prevent any kind of open confrontation and conflict. There is a high level of diplomatic engagement, with delegations from Kyiv and Moscow continually shuttling between the two capitals. In 1995, Russia opened consulate generals in Odesa and L'viv and would like to do the same in Kharkiv, Donets'k, and Crimea. It was not that long ago that Moscow's first ambassador in Kyiv, Leonid Smolyakov, reportedly was urging his East European colleagues to scale down their diplomatic presence in the Ukrainian capital, suggesting that Ukraine would not be around much longer. And finally, much depends on the next generation of Ukrainian and Russian leaders and their determination and ability to transform the Ukrainian-Russian relationship from an agent of instability in Ukraine and a burden on democratization in Russia to a stabilizing force in both countries.

The normalization of relations between Ukraine and Russia, besides impinging directly on Ukraine's stability and security, is a key component of another, perhaps much more complex problem with considerably broader security implications—namely, the 'normalization' of Russia. How Ukraine and Russia interact will be a determining factor in defining Russia's role in the CIS, in Europe generally, and, indeed, in the global arena. Moscow's policy makers have chosen to pursue policies aimed at establishing Russian hegemony in the post-Soviet space and 'great power' status on the world stage. For all intents and purposes, neither of these objectives are realistic unless Ukraine remains entirely within the sphere of Russia's influence. At the end of 1991, in a rare moment of complete agreement, Gorbachev and Yeltsin recognized that the Soviet Union could not be preserved without Ukraine. Similarly, today Russia cannot realize its ambitions without the 'special relationship' that it would like to secure with Ukraine. Ukraine's leaders are faced with formidable challenges: they must work toward restructuring relations with Russia on a normal, cooperative, and mutually beneficial basis while at the same time pursuing integration into European political, economic, and security structures and sustaining and consolidating the political and economic reforms required to bolster Ukraine's security and stability.

Notes

1. Warren Christopher, "U.S. Policy toward the Newly Independent States: A Pragmatic Strategy Grounded in America's Fundamental Interests," *Problems of Post-Communism,* vol. 42, no. 3 (May–June 1995), p. 4.

2. For a detailed discussion of the external determinants of Ukraine's security, see F. Stephen Larrabee, "Ukraine's Balancing Act," *Survival,* vol. 38, no. 2 (Summer 1996), pp. 143–165, and John E. Tedstrom, "From Limited Enlargement to Meaningful Engagement: A Security Strategy for Ukraine," paper delivered at the The Center for Strategic and International Studies, Washington, DC, October 1996.

3. See Sherman W. Garnett, *Keystone in the Arch: Ukraine in the Emerging Security Environment of Central and Eastern Europe* (Washington, DC: Carnegie Endowment for International Peace, 1997), p. 7.

4. Russia's policies in the Near Abroad (the former USSR) are the subject of a lengthy and growing body of literature. See, among others, Fiona Hill and Pamela Jewett, *"Back in the USSR": Russia's Intervention in the Internal Affairs of the Former Soviet Republics and the Implications for United States Policy Toward Russia* (Cambridge, MA: Harvard University, John F. Kennedy School of Government, 1994); John W.R. Lepingwell, "The Russian Military and Security Policy in the 'Near Abroad,' " *Survival,* vol. 36, no. 3 (Autumn 1994), pp. 70–92; Mark Almond, *Russia's Outer Rim: Integration or Disintegration?* European Security Study no. 22 (London: Institute for European Defence and Strategic Studies, 1995); and Jeremy R. Azrael and Emil A. Payin, eds., *U.S. and Russian Policymaking with Respect to the Use of Force* (Santa Monica, CA: RAND Corporation, 1996). See also Stephen Sestanovich's controversial article "Geotherapy: Russia's Neurosis and Ours," *The National Interest,* no. 45 (Fall 1996), pp. 3–13, on the related question of what motivates Russian foreign policy.

5. Quoted in the *Los Angeles Times,* 15 September 1996.

6. *Infotag,* 27 December 1995. See also the *Washington Post,* 10 May 1996.

7. For the text, see *Sobranie zakonodatel'stva Rossiiskoi Federatsii,* no. 48 (November 25, 1996), p. 10552.

8. While upbeat commentary on Ukraine has recently been the norm in the West, praise has also come from some unexpected quarters. Thus, Dmitrii Furman, comparing developments in Ukraine and Russia, suggests that the 'younger brother' has reached a higher level of political maturity than the 'older brother.' See his "Ukraina i my. Natsional'noe samosoznanie i politicheskoe razvitie," *Svobodnaia mysl',* no. 1, 1995, pp. 69–83.

9. The east-west paradigm used here, although convenient, grossly oversimplifies Ukraine's rather more complex regional differences.

10. U.S. Information Agency, "Majorities in Russia and Ukraine Are Almost Equally Discontented," *Opinion Analysis,* M-240–96, December 23, 1996, p. 3.

11. According to the *Washington Post,* 25 January 1994, this was the scenario outlined by the U.S. intelligence community at the end of 1993. For a fuller exposition of this view, see Eugene B. Rumer, "Eurasia Letter: Will Ukraine Return to Russia?" *Foreign Policy,* no. 96 (Fall 1994), pp. 129–144.

12. *Hromads'ka dumka Ukrainy: Osin' 95–ho,* pp. 2 and 11 (unpublished report, Kiev International Institute of Sociology and the Sociology Department of the National University Kiev Mohyla Academy, October 1995), and U.S. Information Agency, "Majorities in Russia and Ukraine," p. 3.

13. See Taras Kuzio, "Kravchuk to Kuchma: The Ukrainian Presidential Elections of 1994," *Journal of Communist Studies and Transition Politics,* vol. 12, no. 2 (June 1996), pp. 117–144.

14. For the text of the program, see *Kommunist,* no. 19 (May 1995), pp. 3–10.

15. For the text of the constitutional accord, see *Holos Ukrainy,* 10 June 1995.

16. International Foundation for Electoral Systems, *IFES Poll of the Ukrainian Electorate,* February 6, 1995, and *Hromads'ka dumka Ukrainy,* p. 7.

17. For the text of the constitution, see *Holos Ukrainy,* 13 July 1996.

18. The names and party affiliations of deputies who voted against the constitution are published in *Nezavisimost',* 3 July 1996. For a complete register of the vote by name and faction or group affiliation, see *Holos Ukrainy,* 20 July 1996.

19. The economic program of the socialist faction is outlined in *Tovarysh,* no. 20 (May 1995).

20. U.S. Information Agency, "Kuchma Retains Trust of Half the Ukrainian Public," *Opinion Analysis,* M-78–96, April 10, 1996, pp. 1–2, and "Majorities in Russia and Ukraine," pp. 1–2.

21. According to *Interfax,* 25 February 1997, Ukraine's GDP decreased by 10 percent in 1996, with continued declines in industrial and agricultural output, increased unemployment, and year-end inflation of almost 40 percent. The average monthly wage was approximately $84.

22. See, for example, *The New York Times,* 18 October 1996; *The Washington Post,* 27 October 1996; and *The Wall Street Journal,* 28 January 1997.

23. Viktor Nebozhenko and Iryna Bekeshkina, "Politychnyi portret Ukrainy (Skhid, pivden')," *Politychnyi portret Ukrainy,* no. 9, 1994, p. 44. See also the survey results reported by Dominique Arel and Valeri Khmelko, "The Russian Factor and Territorial Polarization in Ukraine," in the special issue of the *Harriman Review* (entitled "Peoples, Nations, Identities: The Russian-Ukrainian Encounter"), vol. 9, nos. 1–2 (Spring 1996), pp. 81–91.

24. Nebozhenko and Bekeshkina, "Politychnyi portret Ukrainy (Skhid, pivden')," p. 45.

25. See Yaroslav Hrytsak, "Shifting Identities in Western and Eastern Ukraine," the *East and Central Europe Bulletin* (New School for Social Research), vol. 5/3, no. 18 (February 1995), pp. 1, 3, 5, and 7.

26. Nebozhenko and Bekeshkina, "Politychnyi portret Ukrainy (Skhid, pivden')," pp. 44–45.

27. The proportion of Russians in Crimea is now certainly lower than in 1989 because of the in-migration of the exiled Crimean Tatars. Most estimates place the current Crimean Tatar population at more than 250,000. Anatolii Franchuk, Crimea's former prime minister, has given the figure of 360,000. See *Molod' Ukraiiny,* 1 June 1995, and *Uryadovyi kuryer,* 31 October 1995.

28. *Izvestia,* 28 December 1996.

29. *Visti z Ukrainy,* 7–13 September 1995, and *Narodna armiia,* 19 March 1996.

30. For background, see Roman Solchanyk, "Crimea: Between Ukraine and Russia," in Maria Drohobycky, ed., *Crimea: Dynamics, Challenges and Prospects* (Lanham, MD: Rowman and Littlefield Publishers, 1995), pp. 3–13.

31. All three issues were raised, with the emphasis on Sevastopol, in the State Duma's appeal to the Ukrainian parliament of 24 October 1996. For the text, see *Sobranie zakonodatel'stva Rossiiskoi Federatsii,* no. 45 (Nov. 4, 1996), pp. 10050–10052.

32. *Kievskie vedomosti,* 24 January 1997. Moscow's current ambassador in Kyiv, Yurii Dubinin, expressed similar views in an interview in *Kievskie vedomosti,* 21 September 1996.

33. For a detailed discussion, see R. Solchanyk, "Russia, Ukraine, and the Imperial Legacy," *Post-Soviet Affairs,* vol. 9, no. 4 (October–December 1993), pp. 337–365.

34. *Kievskie vedomosti,* 28 August 1995.

35. *Nezavisimaia gazeta,* 30 March 1996.

36. *Nezavisimaia gazeta,* 6 December 1996.

37. Interview with Ihor Kharchenko, head of the Political Analysis and Planning Administration, Ukraine's Ministry of Foreign Affairs, Kyiv, 4 October 1994. The problem of recognizing borders was also a major issue during the negotiations of the 1990 treaty between Russia and Ukraine. See also S. Garnett, *Keystone in the Arch,* p. 25.

38. *Diplomaticheskii vestnik,* no. 3, 1995, p. 66.

39. *Nezavisimaia gazeta,* 24 March 1995.

40. *Delovyi mir,* 6 February 1997.

41. E. Primakov, "Mezhdunarodnoe otnosheniia nakanune XXI veka: Problemy, perspektivy," *Mezhdunarodnaia zhizn',* 1996, no. 10 (1996), p. 9.

42. Eugene D. Genovese, "Natural Born Killer," the *New Republic,* October 1996, p. 50, quoting from Richard Pipes, ed., *The Unknown Lenin: From the Secret Archive* (New Haven: Yale University Press, 1996) (emphasis in original).

43. *Segodnia,* 19 August 1994.

44. A.I. Miller, "Obraz Ukrainy i ukraintsev v rossiiskoi presse posle raspada SSSR," *Politicheskie issledovaniia,* no. 2, 1996, p. 135. President Nursultan Nazarbaev of Kazakstan recently singled out the negative image of the newly independent states purveyed in the Russian mass media as a complicating factor in relations with Russia. See his interview in *Nezavisimaia gazeta,* 17 January 1997.

45. Quoted in the *Financial Times,* 27 March 1996.

46. See his interview in *Kievskie vedomosti,* 28 April 1995.

3

State and Institution Building in Ukraine

Marc Nordberg

Writing thirty years ago, Gerald Caiden complied a list of administrative problems facing states made newly independent by decolonialization.[1] This list, which includes problems such as a lack of experienced administrators, the need for systemic reform, transition pains, an increase in corruption, and the need for international aid, is also applicable to post-Soviet Ukraine. Further depicting modern Ukraine, Caiden explained how these new states attempted to cram hundreds of years of Western development and experience into less than a decade of reform, and how "in this, most were doomed to failure. They attempted too much too quickly and fell victim to their own maladministration."[2] As the difficulties of reform became clear in these states, many lost the will to continue reform, with disastrous consequences.

Perhaps ominously for Ukraine, many of these states had administrators and elites educated in the colonial center prior to, and in anticipation of, independence. Ukraine received no such aid from the Soviet Union. But Ukraine does have the benefit of hindsight; it can see the problems that were faced by other newly independent states and perhaps learn from them. This makes Ukraine a useful case to study for two reasons. First, it is interesting as a comparative study in relation to the paths followed by the majority of postcolonial states in state and institution building. Secondly, Ukraine's current value to the West makes the country's ability to successfully reform itself immediately relevant as a policy issue.

Many scholarly articles have addressed the macroeconomic and political reforms of Ukraine, yet most of these assume that if political will to reform on the national level exists, then such reform will progress. Very little attention has been paid in a systematic manner to what factors influence this national will, or what impediments may appear at both the national and the local levels. Many works have also detailed Ukraine's efforts at nation building. But state building, a necessary corollary of nation building, has been largely neglected. Public administration, institutions, and economic reform are core aspects of state building.

This chapter seeks to examine the progress made since 1991 by Ukraine in state and institution building. The chapter divides the issue into institutional, civic culture, macro policy and planning, change, and transformational factors. By necessity, economic and political reform will be referred to only in passing (see the chapters by Paul Hare and John Tedstrom) This chapter will show the problems that Ukraine has faced in state and institution building, but concludes that Ukraine's economic collapse has bottomed out and that the next few years will show progress and growth.

Institutions

Ferrel Heady points out several characteristics that are generally agreed to be present in developed polities.[3] Ukraine today possesses many of these, notably a highly differentiated governmental organization where allocation of roles is by merit rather than by ascription, a highly diverse and specialized bureaucracy, and the existence of a politically mobilized population. These are either traits that the communist system encouraged or those that precipitated political change in the country (i.e., mobilization).

In some categories Ukraine receives mixed reviews such as a rational and secular decision-making process, high correlation between political power and legitimacy, and effective political control over the bureaucracy. These characteristics are all in flux with the transition from centralized control. After a period of upheaval, these are beginning to improve in Ukraine, especially since the election of Leonid Kuchma and the new parliament.

In two areas Ukraine is failing: professionalization of civil servants and a clear role for the bureaucracy in the political process, areas that overlap significantly. This failure is due to basic structural changes in the system. Serious problems exist with Ukraine's civil servants. The civil service remains underpaid and undertrained, and it lacks a clear vision of its role in management. Corruption is a widely cited example of the failings of the bureaucracy, but lingering adherence to communism by some and lack of knowledge about how to proceed with reforms are just as damaging. One example of the latter is that by the end of 1993 the Ministry of the Economy had submitted eight economic stabilization plans, each of which failed for lack of details on implementation.[4]

The civic culture in Ukraine, as with other aspects of the country, is misdeveloped. Ukraine inherited a diverse and professional (according to communist demands) bureaucracy, which was firmly under political control. On the other hand, it was largely subsumed within the Communist Party, discouraged real political mobilization, was too tightly tied into the economy, and was overly centralized. This has changed somewhat in the past five years. The number of ministries has dropped from 57 in 1989 to 27 today (with plans to take this number down to between 16 and 18), and many of the tasks that were handled by the central government have devolved onto local administration. These are not necessarily planned changes; the greater role of local government is as much a function of Kyiv's lack of funds and inability to collect taxes as it is of organized reform.

In addition to the above problems, Ukraine's civil service is too small to run an independent state and lacks many of the needed skills. In the centralized Soviet Union, many important decisions on local administration were made in Moscow, where the experts were located. At the time, Ukrainian authorities controlled just 5 percent of Ukrainian GDP. With the collapse of the union, Russia inherited the lion's share of administrative structures. Kyiv had to build many state bodies from scratch, such as the Ministries of Defense, Finance, and Foreign Affairs. (Because of its Soviet-era UN representation, prior to 1991 Ukraine did have a Ministry of Foreign Affairs. However, this was a vassal of Moscow, with no experience in taking care of the needs of an independent state. Further, it had but twenty employees, far too few for modern Ukraine.)

Ukraine's postindependence central ministries inherited about thirteen thousand administrators, a small number for a state of fifty-two million people (in contrast, Britain has around half a million).[5] Most of these civil servants lack the necessary training for running an independent, free-market state. The previous experience they do have is of a state that blurred the dividing line between politics and administration, casting doubt on many of these people's ability to impartially implement policy. Furthermore, Western governments are now experiencing growth in both the level and the range of activities for which they are responsible.[6] Facing many of the same demands for government services, Ukraine is decreasing the size of its administrative structures, beginning to lay off 20 percent of government employees in order to cut the budget and pay some wage arrears.[7]

Until very recently Ukraine was operating under a modified version of the 1978 Soviet constitution. That communist constitution was in no way appropriate for a free-market system (i.e., it proscribed the right to own property).[8] Without a new constitution, the dividing line between politicians and bureaucracy was unclear. Furthermore, the distribution of powers, both among the politicians in Kyiv and between the center and peripheries, was ambiguous. This hampered the ability of the government to handle its myriad of problems, sparked conflict between the oblasts and central government, and was a key factor in the institutional power struggles.

In June 1996 Ukraine adopted a new constitution.[9] The constitution of Ukraine creates three ostensibly equal branches: executive, legislative, and judicial (Article 6).[10] Of these, the executive is created as slightly more equal than the others. The president appoints judges for their first term—except to the Constitutional Court, where he only appoints 6 of 18 (Articles 128 and 148); appoints the prime minister (with consent of parliament), who in turn chooses the Cabinet of Ministers (the highest organ of executive power) with the president (Articles 106.9 and 106.10); and can unilaterally revoke decisions of the Cabinet of Ministers (Article 106.16). The president can also dismiss ministers, create or dissolve ministries (Articles 106.10 and 106.15), and call national referenda (106.6), and he is granted three years in which to issue decrees on economic reform (Transitional Provision 4). Parliament, among the usual powers of legislation, has the right to impeach (Article 111) and can override the president's economic decrees.

The executive has a great deal of power at the local level. Article 118 states: "Executive power in oblasts, districts, and the cities of Kyiv and Sevastopol is exercised by local state administrations. The composition of local state administrations is formed by the heads of the local state administration. Heads of local state administrations are appointed to office and dismissed from office by the president of Ukraine upon submission by the Cabinet of Ministers." The president controls who is in the Cabinet of Ministers, and can dismiss heads of local state administrations, so he has effective command over local administration. This creates a prefectoral system of administration, which, as Edward Page points out, is not rare in Europe.[11]

Local elected councils also exist (Article 141), but the division of power between them and the central executive is unclear. Article 118 claims that the local state administrations are accountable to both local councils and executive authority. A council may express no confidence in the head of the local state administration, whereupon the president must only decide whether or not to replace that individual. Article 119 gives the local state administration power over implementation of acts of executive power, "legality and public order," the local budget, and "the realization of other powers vested by the state and also delegated by the respective councils."

In other matters the constitution is nothing if not detailed. It has 161 specific articles, many of them with subarticles. There are 48 articles simply on rights, freedoms, and responsibilities. These include such items as the right to work (Article 43), and the right to vacations (Article 45), housing (Article 47), and marriage (Article 51). This raises a serious problem. Governments may enforce negative rights—those that restrict government interference—but they cannot realistically protect positive rights, such as those just listed. This inability to enforce the basic law of the land decreases the government's legitimacy.[12]

Many see the new constitution as a panacea for Ukraine's problems. While it may resolve some issues, much yet needs to be done. The ratification of the constitution, besides clarifying the division of powers in the government, has increased the apparent stability of the state, thereby increasing foreign investment opportunities.[13] But this is just the basic law of the state, regardless of how detailed. Much legal work needs to be done, including the implementation of property and bankruptcy laws; the reduction and rationalization of existing economic regulations and the alignment laws at the state, regional, and local levels. Less tangible changes also have to be made, such as increasing people's trust in banks in order to increase savings.

An important debate in independent Ukraine is the division of power between center and periphery. Whether to be a federal or unitary state is at the heart of this. After 1991, Ukraine remained a unitary state. Communists believed this would enhance state control and nationalists thought it would promote nation building, while Kyiv bureaucrats used it to maintain the status quo of administrative systems. Reformers thought a strong central government was necessary to enact change, and others believed that a unitary system would remove centrifugal threats from regionalism—especially over a perceived east-west divide.[14]

As time progressed, several factors came to light that challenged these assumptions. The east-west polarities have been shown to be exaggerated; power is instead nested in several key regional cities (L'viv, Donet'sk, Kharkiv, Dnipropetrov'sk, and Odesa), and a unitary state has done little to prevent regionalism from growing. The unitary state has also done more to hurt economic reform than to assist it. A federal structure would allow greater experimentation with local reform than a unitary state does. Increased regional administration allows greater focus on local problems, which local administrators now try to pass on to Kyiv. Because of the weakness of the center, some regions, such as Donet'sk, have been speeding reform regardless.

Likewise, with more powers falling upon local administrators, federalism would allow separate tax structures reflecting the specific demands of the regions and limiting unfunded mandates from Kyiv. Most importantly, the eastern oblasts have grown tired of economically supporting western Ukraine. In 1994, four eastern oblasts each paid in to Kyiv about one trillion *karbovantsi,* while four western oblasts each received the same amount. This is a trend that has continued since 1991.[15] Such redistribution has been blamed on the unitary system, and many believe that federalism would level the economic field and thus promote reforms. While Kuchma supports greater economic autonomy for the regions, he is against federalism. Article 2 of the constitution states that Ukraine is a unitary state, so the best that the federalists can hope for is a move toward some form of decentralized unity.

Another factor in the state unity debate has been Crimea. It is a region of Ukraine that until 1954 was part of Russia and contains a majority Russian population, many of them military. In December 1991, 54 percent of Crimea voted for the independence of Ukraine, compared to 91 percent nationwide. Since independence it has been the only autonomous region in Ukraine, with its own constitution and greater local economic control. Crimea adopted an independent constitution in 1992 that gave it the right to secede from Ukraine.

Ukraine's constitution devotes six articles to clarifying the autonomous status of Crimea. Although its constitution must be approved by the Verkhovna Rada in Kyiv, Crimea is allowed its own prime minister and parliament along with greater regulatory and budgetary freedoms. This settled the issue until late 1996, when the Russian parliament again claimed the autonomous republic of Crimea and particularly the city of Sevastopol as Russian. Fueled by the visit of Moscow's mayor, Yuri Luzhkov, in January 1997 the Crimean parliament again began to challenge Kyiv's rule, showing that this situation remains far from concluded.

Political parties are important for the modern state. Samuel Huntington and Robert Dahl have both shown how essential parties are for political mobilization and economic development.[16] Heady also believes this, and presents four models of state systems based upon their party typology.[17] Ukraine was until relatively recently a communist totalitarian system. Of the other types, Ukraine is almost by default a polyarchal competitive system, that is, a Western-style democracy, however embryonic. There is no dominant party in the country (although some say a 'party of power' has arisen formed from the ranks of the nomenklatura and Kuchma's Dnipropetrov'sk power base—see below) and free elections do take place. On the other hand, there are no firmly established parties and the system of freely contested elections is still quite new. Social mobility exists for some, while many are trapped in poverty. The main problem is the large number of parties with representation, ensuring that any effective government will be a coalition, with the inherent weaknesses that entails.

Institutional reform is under way in Ukraine, but it must be done in an organized manner so as to garner trust in the consistency and long-term stability of the system. Such predictability is now lacking and is limiting international interest in investment. Despite its faults, the constitution does greatly curtail the earlier struggle over executive and legislative powers. While differences remain between the two, now more attention is being shifted to legal reform. This is necessary for clarifying the responsibilities of local administrators and for encouraging reform in general, but much remains to be done in changing the attitudes of civil servants with regards to reform.

Civic Cultures

As with all bureaucratized states, Ukraine has to deal with the influence of civic cultures among its public servants as it transforms. Again, as with most states, this is not a unitary culture but does display some generalized traits. Many of these are legacies of Soviet rule and of centralized communist ideology. One aspect of this culture that has had significant impact on reform is the fact that many public servants do not adhere to the principles of a free market. Some of them, especially in the east and south of Ukraine, value the social safety provided by communism and hinder privatization or work to prevent other disruptions caused by the market (the coal mining industry of the Donbas is a particularly striking example). Victoria Egorova, researching reform in the coal industry, stated, "The new market economy, an economy completely foreign to the psyches of the Ukrainian peoples, represents an extraordinary psychological burden on the general public, forcing them to adapt to new ideas, concepts, institutional structures and at the same time accepting total destruction of values established within the previous regime."[18] Even Kuchma exhibits these tendencies, as when he proclaimed, "We will find a way out of the crisis ourselves. The IMF finds unemployment a necessary condition for market reform. But I am going to eradicate this shameful phenomenon."[19]

Due partially to lack of will, partially to lack of knowledge, and partially to conflict with parliament, Kravchuk's tenure as president was accompanied by indecision and economic crisis. There was little communication between ministries, cabinet meetings were rare, and standard bureaucratic practice was to avoid responsibility. Compounding this was the fact that Ukraine's first postindependence parliament had been elected in March 1990, as a Soviet body. Ukraine's democratic bloc controlled just 25 percent of the 450 seats, with the remainder controlled by communists and the left. The majority of communist and agrarian parliamentarians supported independence, but many had misgivings about free-market economics. This combination of a hesitantly proreform president and an antireform parliament ensured that those few economic reforms Kravchuk undertook were largely ineffective.

Events changed matters in 1994. New parliamentary elections brought a much larger proportion of proreform deputies to power. The power of the right remained almost unchanged, but many businessmen from eastern and central Ukraine were elected. The left continues to be a powerful group, but they are generally now more proreform. The Agrarian Party split, with a significant portion forming the Agrarians for Reform party. Despite, or perhaps because of, only 55 members of the old parliament being reelected, the new parliament has so far proven more willing to make decisions and has exhibited a greater degree of professionalism. Also in 1994, Ukraine held presidential elections. Leonid Kuchma won with 52.2 percent of the vote. He is much more committed to economic reform, having launched an ambitious reform program in October 1994 and having attracted several billion dollars in foreign economic assistance.

Another aspect of civil culture that must be faced deals with the division of power between the politicians and the civil servants. As is borne out in greater detail in Heady's work, bureaucratic overinvolvement in the political process is generally undesirable.[20] Civil servants should be responsible for implementing policy, not altering it. The Soviet Union had a strong bureaucracy held in check by, and overlapping with, a dominant political party. When the former Soviet Union collapsed, the bureaucracy remained but the controlling party disappeared. In Ukraine this bureaucracy affects politics in two major ways. First, its members are winning elected positions in the government. President Kuchma is a prime example of this, as he formerly headed Pivdenmash, a massive factory in Dnipropetrov'sk, eastern Ukraine, that used to produce nuclear missiles. After taking power, Kuchma seems to have brought a lot of his local power base with him to Kyiv. By mid-1996 over 160 of these people were in the president's administration.[21] The 'Dnipropetrov'sk Mafia,' as they are sometimes called, also hold influential positions in parliament with their own political representation—25 of the 28 members of the Unity faction hail from there, as does the prime minister.[22] This is an ominous centralization of power given that it has been estimated that only about two hundred people actually govern Ukraine, but perhaps understandable given that the city earns nearly half of Ukraine's hard currency through its metallurgy industry (much as Prime Minister Viktor Chernomyrdin's clan have ridden Gazprom profits to power in Russia).[23]

Civil servants often play a role in counteracting political decisions. This happened in June 1993 when Ukraine issued 14.2 trillion *karbovantsi* (about $710 million at that time) worth of credits at a time when Kyiv was trying to control inflation, much of this from the Ministry of Agriculture.[24] This helped to fuel the hyperinflation that Ukraine experienced in that year. Local officials have also had a negative effect on privatization. A large number of enterprises have been 'spontaneously privatized' by their management or local officials. Prime Minister Lazarenko supposedly used this method with metallurgical and energy firms to become the wealthiest man in Ukraine—again like Chernomyrdin in Russia. This was more profitable in the short term than actually producing anything. However, since Kuchma has become president there has been a greater attempt to control civil servants.

Macro Policy and Planning

The economy is of essential concern to a reforming state, as a strong economy facilitates reform.[25] Conversely, a weak economy, as in Ukraine, can hinder reform. Macroeconomic all-inclusive planning in Ukraine has been discredited after the failure of the Soviet system. Yet economic planning of some sort is a necessity for a modern state. Therefore, Ukraine is in the process of creating a looser system for macroeconomic management. This differs from planning in that it attempts to control only some of the broader aspects of the economy, such as inflation, the velocity of currency, and taxes. Through tinkering with these and other macroeconomic tools, the government can hope to influence the economy as a whole, but not to the level seen under communism.

In theory this is a good idea. It is the system used by the major Western countries and the one that the World Bank and IMF are encouraging former Eastern bloc states to adopt. However, theory is a long way from reality. Removing price controls illustrates the problem. As Naomi Caiden points out, the freeing of prices is of primary importance in this sort of management.[26] Without it, international trade (necessary today for economic development) becomes distorted and more difficult. But the freeing of prices can cause major disruptions, possibly leading to economic or political collapse. Even with Ukraine's attempt to carefully manage the lifting of price controls, the process generated inflation of nearly 5,000 percent in 1993.

Little real economic reform was managed until 1994. That October Kuchma introduced a radical reform plan that entailed many of the changes pushed by the IMF and Western experts. This package sought to free prices and cut state subsidies, reduce government spending and the budget deficit, reduce inflation, and promote privatization in order to westernize Ukraine's economy. These reforms succeeded in many of their goals, amongst which was attracting IMF and World Bank funds. But they also sparked protests at home. Many socialist-oriented politicians saw market reforms being introduced at the expense of social stability. Among some parts of the population there was the widespread belief that free-market reforms and social stability policies are not contradictory. Kuchma himself believes this, as the earlier quote on unemployment demonstrates. In 1995 he put before parliament an economic plan that incorporated aspects of both free-market economics and socially regulated stabilization policies.[27]

Such attitudes have resulted in a compromise 'Ukrainian Model' of economic development that calls for less stringent austerity measures than those advocated by the IMF, allows state supervision in much of the economy (including regulation of pricing), creates a mixed economy with state-owned and state-controlled (51 percent ownership) enterprises, and exempts 6,100 'strategic' firms from privatization—including such diverse enterprises as missile complexes and bread shops.[28] Article 95 of the constitution supports this, saying: "The budgetary system of Ukraine is built on the principles of a just and impartial distribution of social wealth among citizens and territorial communities." While this challenges the experts at the IMF and World Bank, it may be a necessity given Ukraine's inherited political culture. Western reforms that push unwanted Western social mores would be doomed to eventual failure.

Budgeting has been another problem in Ukraine. Economic decline, tax evasion, and high inflation cause problems with predicting correct income and expenditures. This, along with last-minute social subsidies, led to a 1993 budget deficit of 20 percent, yet parliament optimistically submitted a balanced budget for 1994.[29] More recent budgets have shown lower deficits, with the budget for 1996 achieving its target of a 6.2 percent deficit.[30] Industrial and agricultural subsidies drain government coffers, yet quickly eliminating them would vastly increase unemployment and therefore would be highly destabilizing. Social subsidies in the 1997 budget make up 12.7 percent of predicted GDP.[31]

Ukraine's falling GDP means that more people are relying on the government social safety net and less tax revenue is being collected. Desperate for revenue, the government created a progressive tax structure, with the top category imposing a 90 percent rate, and created a high VAT that assessed taxes on a firm's income, not profit. This high tax rate and the overly complicated manner in which it was assessed resulted in decreased foreign investment, were responsible for the failure of existing businesses, hurt privatization, and caused widespread tax evasion (tax avoidance costs $1.7 billion annually, with some two thirds of enterprises avoiding some or all of their taxes).[32]

New tax laws after January 1995 have improved the situation, but problems remain. Because of excessive optimism surrounding reform, the 1997 budget assumes an unrealistic 50 percent increase in tax revenue. Of government revenue, 35 percent is to be raised by treasury bills, but because of high returns it is feared that this program is starting to resemble a pyramid scheme.[33] In an effort to create a more attractive environment for business, taxation legislation was loosened in January 1997. While this move may promote investment, the chairman of Ukraine's National Bank has predicted it will lead to a 70 percent drop in tax revenue.[34] These revenue problems may add to future debt, and they show the relative inexperience of Ukraine's reformers, who often worsen one problem in the course of solving another.

Less revenue means less funds available for government expenditures, many of which are necessary for reform and improvement of infrastructure—which in turn are necessary to attract foreign investment. To improve this, the constitution outlines the division of responsibility for the budget between parliament and the Cabinet of Ministers. This will hopefully prevent future extrabudgetary credit emissions, and it creates the institutional basis for needed legal reform.

Ukraine's shadow economy is the largest in Europe, accounting for some 60 percent of GDP.[35] This means that a large portion of taxable activity is occurring outside the grasp of tax collectors. This estimate for the shadow economy does not include Ukraine's vast traditional economy, which also remains outside the purview of government. Economic activity will remain hidden as long as Ukraine's taxes remain high and regulation is large-scale and complicated. As things currently are, these factors have essentially legitimized the bribing of officials, many of whom have not received wages for months. It has also resulted in massive capital flight from Ukraine, with some $12 billion to $15 billion stashed abroad.[36] Until this changes, bureaucrats have an entrenched interest in inhibiting reform. Paradoxically, deregulation may in the short term increase the size of the shadow economy unless enforcement measures are improved. Laws to rectify this situation were submitted to parliament with a reform package in October 1996.

Foreign trade is another important area for the future of Ukraine's economy. The trade regime that Ukraine inherited from the Soviet Union had many problems. It focused almost entirely on interrepublic exchanges, with very little trade to non-COMECON states. The end of centralization meant that there was no mechanism in place for payment, and the banking structure remains underdeveloped. Ukraine is further hurt since the goods it may have a comparative advantage to produce (agriculture, metallurgy, textiles, chemicals) are the same goods that are on the European Union's sensitive products list for restricted import to Europe.

Ukraine has finally succeeded in currency reform. In 1992 an interim currency, the *karbovanets,* or coupon, was issued. This was to rectify a liquidity crisis caused by rising prices and the lack of printing presses (Russia claimed these presses for the ruble). Massive inflation quickly drove down the value of the *karbovanets.* Despite many false promises, Ukraine put off introducing the permanent currency until inflation settled down. In 1996 inflation dropped to 80 percent annually and was predicted to fall to 30 percent in 1998.[37] Therefore, in September 1996 the *hryvnia* was introduced. Despite many macroeconomic problems, Ukraine seems to be adjusting, with economic growth predicted for 1997 and 1998.

Change and Transformation

Ukraine is facing changes in state building and public administration different from those in the West. Superficially they are similar, with privatization, a decreasing role of the state, and the devolution of power to localities. But Ukraine's transformation dwarfs in scope any changes being made in the West. Furthermore, reform is being hindered by the government's lack of an overall program. According to Egorova, "The transformation policy has been initiated without a well-defined strategy and a real conception of how to work within the managerial, organizational, economic, social, and cultural constraints existing in Ukrainian society."[38] Instead, reform seems to be on an ad hoc basis.

Data on local politics for Ukraine are limited and focus almost exclusively on the regional divisions (west versus east and south, Crimea versus Kyiv) of the country. Ukraine is divided into 24 oblasts, 2 regional cities (Kyiv and Sevastopol), and the Crimean autonomous republic. This is further subdivided into 481 districts, 436 towns, and 9,211 rural councils. Local government employs 38,500 people plus another 57,300 in the rural councils.[39] This is a very low figure, even when compared to the central government, which in 1993 had just 12,400 employees.[40] In addition, these people lacked experience in administration, since the Communist Party exercised many of these functions during the Soviet era. This is reflected in a 1991 poll of local administrators, a vast majority of whom thought their chief role was to provide leisure and entertainment for the people.[41] As the local councils were elected in March 1990, the Soviet legacy also carried through in these personnel until the first postindependence election in 1994.

Since independence, power has been transferred from Kyiv to the localities. In 1992 the Law on Local Self-Government was amended to remove central control and to give localities the right "to arrive by collective means at decisions relating to all questions of local development."[42] Further powers and responsibilities have devolved onto local government, since Kyiv lacks the resources to handle them. Theoretically local councils had the right to create their own budgets, but in practice they were heavily dependent on subsidies from Kyiv and on what local needs had to be filled that the center could not cope with. Several laws were passed in the hope of clarifying this situation but served only to confuse it.

Local administration was the victim of a power struggle between parliament and the president over control. The constitution now places this firmly in the hands of the presidency. Nonetheless, some power remains in the regions. Locally elected councils can make decisions not proscribed by state law and retain certain budgetary powers. Article 142 allows state intervention in local budgeting, but also demands reimbursement by the state for expenditures of local administration forced by state action. In addition, Article 143 provides for the executive to devolve further powers and funds onto local administrators as needed.

Conclusions

Ukraine clearly has many major hurdles to conquer before it successfully moves away from being a quasi state. Ukraine must somehow find the means to diversify its energy supply, privatize thousands of large and unprofitable enterprises, decrease government subsidies, and train professional and pro-reform civil servants. But this is not to say that Ukraine faces an insurmountable task. The policy blunders of the early years have been partially alleviated by a new president and parliament who are more pro-reform. They will continue to make mistakes, but now have financial and technical assistance from the West, which is eager to see Ukraine reform because of its fifty-two million potential consumers and as a geostrategic buffer to Russia. The new constitution clarifies institutional roles; while political conflict certainly still exists, it is now focused on policy more than on power struggles.

Ukraine's civil servants have now had five years in which to gain experience running a state, and many Western organizations have moved in to help with further transformation. Crimea remains a problem, but as Ukraine further cements its independence and builds successful state institutions Russian claims to this area will carry less weight. A powerful sign that things are improving is that foreign direct investment doubled in 1996 from the previous year. If risk-averse foreign firms are starting to invest, then Ukraine may be on the right track. Nevertheless, the completion of state and institution building at the central and local levels will remain more of a medium-term objective than a short-term one.

Notes

1. Gerald E. Caiden, *Administrative Reform* (London: Penguin, 1970), pp. 99–100.
2. Ibid., p. 102.
3. Ferrel Heady, *Public Administration: A Comparative Perspective* (New York: Marcel Dekker, 1996), p. 203.
4. Economist Intelligence Unit (EIU), *Country Report: Ukraine, Belarus, Moldova,* 1st quarter 1994 (London, EIU, 1994), p. 18.
5. See Judy Hague, Aidan Rose, and Marko Bojcun, "Rebuilding Ukraine's Hollow State: Developing a Democratic Public Service in Ukraine," *Public Administration and Development,* vol. 15, no. 4 (October 1995), pp. 417–433.
6. See B. Guy Peters, *The Politics of Bureaucracy* (New York: Longman, 1995).
7. "Government Shake-up Continues in Ukraine," *OMRI Daily Report,* 17 June 1996.
8. *Constitution (Fundamental Law) of the Union of Soviet Socialist Republics* (Moscow: Novosti Press Agency Publishing House, 1985).
9. For greater detail on this process, see Chapter 7, by Kataryna Wolczuk in Part C, "Politics and Civil Society."
10. "Konstytutsiia Ukrainy," *Uriadovyi Kurier,* 13 July 1996.
11. Edward C. Page, *Localism and Centralism in Europe: The Political and Legal Bases of Local Self-Government* (Oxford: Oxford University Press, 1991), pp. 28–29.
12. Bohdan A. Futey, "Comments on the Constitution of Ukraine," *East European Constitutional Review,* vol. 5, nos. 2–3 (Spring/Summer 1996), pp. 29–34.
13. Janusz Bugajski, *American-Ukrainian Advisory Committee Report* (Washington, DC: Center for Strategic and International Studies, 1996), p. 5.
14. Volodymyr Zolotaryov, "A Federative System of Government as a Means of Resolving the Present Crisis in Ukraine," *Demos,* vol. 1, no. 7 (28 November 1994).
15. Andriy Dmytrenko, "A View on 'Unitarism' through Holes in the Budget," *Demos,* vol. 1, no. 7 (28 November 1994).
16. See Samuel P. Huntington, *Political Order in Changing Societies* (New Haven, CT: Yale University Press, 1968), and Robert A. Dahl, *Polyarchy: Participation and Opposition* (New Haven, CT: Yale University Press, 1971).
17. Heady, *Public Administration.*
18. Victoria B. Egorova, *The Process of Management Change in Ukraine with Reference to the Coal Industry, Conflict Studies Research Center* (Sandhurst, UK: Royal Military Academy, E87, April 1996), p. 1.
19. "Leonid Kuchma: 'Narod Ukraiiny hidnyi krashchoi doli . . . ,' " *Holos Ukrainy,* 6 July 1994.
20. Heady, *Public Administration.*
21. Sherman W. Garnett, *Ukraine: Europe's New Frontier, Conflict Studies Research Center* (Sandhurst, E88, July 1996), p. 4.
22. Victor Chudowsky, Taras Kuzio, and Oliver Vorndran, "Factions in the Ukrainian Parliament: From Regionalization to Consolidation," unpublished paper presented to the workshop "State Building in Ukraine," University of Birmingham, 3 March 1997.
23. Garnett, "Ukraine: Europe's New Frontier, " p. 3.
24. "How to Wreck an Economy," *The Economist,* 7 May 1994.
25. For greater detail, see two chapters on Ukraine's economy in this book: Chapter 10 by Paul Hare, Mohammed Ishaq, and Saul Estrin; and Chapter 11 by John Tedstrom.
26. Naomi J. Caiden, "Unanswered Questions: Planning and Budgeting in Poor Countries Revisited," in A.I. Farazmand (ed.), *Handbook of Comparative and Developmental Public Administration* (New York: Marcel Dekker, 1991), p. 427.

27. "Obrashchenie prezidenta Ukrainy Leonida Kuchmy k Verkhovnomu Sovetu Ukrainy 4 Aprelia 1995 goda," *Holos Ukrainy,* 6 April 1995.

28. Volodymyr Zviglyanich, "Ethnic Economics: Is a 'Ukrainian Economic Model' Possible?" *Ukraine Business Review,* vol. 4, nos. 1–2 (December 1995–January 1996), pp.1–4.

29. EIU, *Country Report: Ukraine, Belarus, Moldova,* 1st quarter 1994 (London: EIU, 1994), p. 19.

30. EIU, *Country Report: Ukraine, Belarus, Moldova,* 4th quarter 1996 (London: EIU, 1996), pp. 18–19.

31. *Ukrainian Economic Trends* October 1996."

32. EIU, *Country Report: Ukraine, Belarus, Moldova,* 4th quarter 1996, p. 19, and Taras Kuzio, "Crime Still Ukraine's Greatest Enemy: Organized Crime and Corruption in Ukraine," *Jane's Intelligence Review,* vol. 9, no. 1 (January 1997), pp. 10–13.

33. Natalia Gurushina, "The Trouble with T-Bills," *Transition,* vol. 2, no. 23 (15 November 1996).

34. "Yushchenko Warns of Tax Collection Crisis," *The Rukh Insider,* vol. 3, no. 1 (17 January 1997).

35. Kuzio, "Crime Still Ukraine's Greatest Enemy."

36. Bugajski, *American-Ukrainian Advisory Committee Report,* p. 5.

37. EIU, *Country Report: Ukraine, Belarus, Moldova,* 4th quarter 1996, p. 9.

38. Egorova, "The Process of Management Change," p. 2.

39. Adrian Campbell, "Regional and Local Government in Ukraine," in Andrew Coulson, ed., *Local Government in Eastern Europe: Establishing Democracy at the Grassroots* (Aldershot: Edward Elgar Publishing, 1995), p. 116.

40. These figures obviously do not include the military and most likely do not include police and educators. Therefore too deep a reliance on these numbers should be avoided.

41. See Oleksandr Boukhalov and Sergei Ivannikov, "Ukrainian Local Politics after Independence," *American Academy of Political and Social Science Annals,* vol. 140 (July 1995), pp. 126–136.

42. As quoted in Campbell, "Regional and Local Government," pp. 125–126.

National Identity and Regionalism

Introduction

Judy Batt

The breakup of the Soviet Union led to the formation of a set of new states all proclaiming the 'right to national self-determination' as their basic raison d'être. However, as the following chapters demonstrate, in the case of Ukraine this interpretation of the state-formation process is extremely misleading, and, if pursued to its logical conclusion by the new political elites in charge of the process of state building, is likely to have counterproductive if not catastrophic results. Ukraine is not and cannot be a 'nation-state,' not only because it contains a sizable minority of Russians with deep historical roots on the territory, but also because Ukrainians themselves are far from constituting a coherent and unified nation. The most obvious sign of this is the fact that a large (although, as the chapters in Part B also show, indeterminate) proportion of Ukrainians use Russian rather than Ukrainian as their first language. The linguistic divide is overlain by divergent political values and economic interests. There are three major linguistic groups in Ukraine: Ukrainian-speaking Ukrainians, Russian-speaking Ukrainians, and Russians. But it is also important to note that a majority of Ukrainians and some Russians are bilingual, so the borders between these three groups are fluid and changeable.

What are the political implications of this from the point of view of Ukrainian state building? From the point of view of Ukrainian nationalists, this is seen as a great obstacle to political integration, and they advocate deliberate state policies, especially in language use and education, to bring about a homogenized, uniform Ukrainian nation and marginalize the Russian community. But, as Chapter 4, by Valeri Khmelko and Andrew Wilson shows, this policy served to further polarize the country between east and west, alienating Russian-speaking Ukrainians as well as Russians—who together form a majority of the population. The dangers of this are clear not only for the internal stability of the state, but also for its external relations with Russia.

But some scholars would argue that the issue of language as a marker of national identity has been overplayed, especially in light of the extent of bilingualism, as noted above.

Mykola Riabchuk argues in Chapter 5 that the incoherence of Ukrainian national identity, or rather the existence of two different Ukrainian national identities, has been a positive factor in Ukrainian state building: it exerts a moderating influence, constraining the potential for ethnonationalist mobilization and promoting an alternative 'civic' model of state building, based on tolerance and mutual respect. But he also notes the weakness of the 'civil society' that is supposed to be the basis of this 'civic' Ukrainian identity. Ukrainian society remains heavily marked by the legacy of 'socialist corporatism' and dependence on the state; insofar as it shows any capacity for self-organization, this tends to take a defensive form, evading the state rather than engaging with it and calling it to account.

Chapter 6, by Louise Jackson focuses on the identities of the Russian-speakers in Zaporizhzhia and their reactions to Kyiv's national and language policies. This microlevel study reveals the complexity of the situation, and Jackson rightly warns against the dangers of over generalization. Many Western scholars extrapolate the inherited complexities found in the Donbas to the entire region of eastern and southern Ukraine.

In particular, Jackson notes the fluidity and multilayered nature of national identities in both regions. What Jackson's paper also shows, however, is the difficulty this poses for would-be state builders. It seems that major conflict over the language issue was avoided in this *oblast* mainly because the central government's policy was ignored. The depressing conclusion is that political stability is conditional on *lack* of effective state penetration of the regions. But if the state is unable to secure implementation of its education policies, it is also unlikely to muster the capacity to implement a coherent economic transformation strategy, which would in turn threaten the cohesion and stability of Ukraine.

But Ukraine is not only divided by national identities; these both coincide with and are further subdivided by distinctive historical and economic regional differences. The extent of regional diversity would appear to argue for a decentralized, if not explicitly federal, state structure as the most promising framework for noncoercive political integration. But federalism is by now a 'dirty word' in Ukraine, as in most other post-Soviet states. The institutionalization of national and regional diversity in the Soviet federation did not promote integration, but rather provided the launchpad for nationalist separatism—as the current Ukrainian elite is all too well aware, having itself secured power by exploiting this opportunity. Moreover, regional elites can—and do—act as a block on the center's policies for reform whenever these challenge the socioeconomic interests of their region. When socioeconomic interests coincide with a distinct national identity on a given territory, the ingredients are there for a major threat to the integrity of the state. The case of Crimea, however, gives cause for hope that the center can, under certain conditions, reach a negotiated compromise in the form of an 'asymmetric' federation (following, for example, the post-Franco Spanish pattern). The question is whether the experience of managing this crisis will provide food for thought for Ukraine's state-building elite and check the instinctive tendency, characteristic of former communists, to reassert central control whenever challenged from the regions.

4

Regionalism and Ethnic and Linguistic Cleavages in Ukraine

Valeri Khmelko and Andrew Wilson

The independent Ukrainian state came into being as a result of the collapse of the former Soviet Union. In the aftermath of the failed coup attempt in Moscow in August 1991, the legislature of the then Ukrainian Soviet Socialist Republic (the *Verkhovna Rada* or Supreme Council) passed the Act of Independence of Ukraine on 24 August and voted to submit the act to a national referendum on 1 December 1991.

Referendum and Presidential Election

In December 1991 the population of Ukraine amounted to some 52 million and the electorate to approximately 39 million. Of these, 84 percent participated in the referendum and in Ukraine's first-ever presidential election, held on the same day; 90 percent of these voted to support the declaration of independence (76 percent of the total electorate).[1] In competition with five other candidates (three nationalists and two centrists), Leonid Kravchuk, who until August 1991 had been head of the Ideology Department of the Communist Party of Ukraine and a member of the party Politburo, was elected president with 62 percent of the vote (52 percent of the total electorate). His opponents received 34 percent of the vote (29 percent of the electorate), with the lion's share (23 percent) going to his main nationalist rival, Viacheslav Chornovil (the remaining 4 percent of votes were wasted, spoiled, or cast against all candidates).

However, despite Kravchuk's decisive overall victory, he was unable to win a majority in all regions of Ukraine. In the west he lost ground to the three nationalist candidates, winning only 30 percent of the vote compared to their total of 68 percent. In southern and eastern Ukraine, on the other hand, some of Kravchuk's support was siphoned off by Volodymyr Hryn'ov, then second deputy chairman of parliament, who championed the cause of Ukraine's Russian-speaking population. However, at this stage Russophone discontent was muted and Kravchuk's overall score of 69 percent in the south and east was relatively high. Kravchuk's highest level of support was in central Ukraine, Kyiv city excepted, where he faced no strong challenge from either flank and won 70 percent of the vote (see Map 4.1).

Before the presidential election, the Kyiv International Institute of Sociology conducted a nationally representative survey in collaboration with the Research Institute of Radio Free Europe/Radio Liberty, which demonstrated that at the time the center of political gravity in Ukraine still lay firmly toward the center-left. (A total of 2,056 respondents age eighteen and over were interviewed in all Ukrainian oblasts and in the Crimean autonomous republic.) According to the survey data, only 13 percent of the adult population expressed what could be classified as nonauthoritarian political attitudes, while 32 percent were strongly authoritarian.[2] Only 33 percent accepted to some degree that Ukraine must move to a capitalist path of development (22 percent were in full agreement), while 43 percent were in some degree opposed (32 percent were completely opposed). Although he later gained a reputation for nationalism, it should therefore be remembered that in 1991 Kravchuk actually campaigned from the center-left. His victory was due mainly to support from electors who held negative or mixed attitudes toward private enterprise, had positive or mixed attitudes toward the socialist system, and displayed authoritarian political attitudes. Among supporters of Kravchuk, 72 percent had authoritarian attitudes, 75 percent had socialist sympathies, and 85 percent expressed negative attitudes toward private enterprise. Only 11 percent of the last group planned to support any of the five opposition candidates. Kravchuk had the support of only 30 percent of those who expressed positive attitudes toward private enterprise, compared to 43 percent for the opposition candidates. This helps to explain the strength of the reaction against Kravchuk's subsequent move to the right.

As stated above, there were also considerable regional variations in support for Kravchuk, but without any marked polarization in any definite geographical direction. However, the variation of the vote for independence between the same regions was quite different (see Map 4.2). In west Ukraine 90 percent or more of the regional electorate voted for independence; in central Ukraine the vote was from 75 percent to 90 percent; in south and east Ukraine it was from 50 percent to 75 percent, and in Crimea it was less then 50 percent (taking differential turnout into account). Sup-

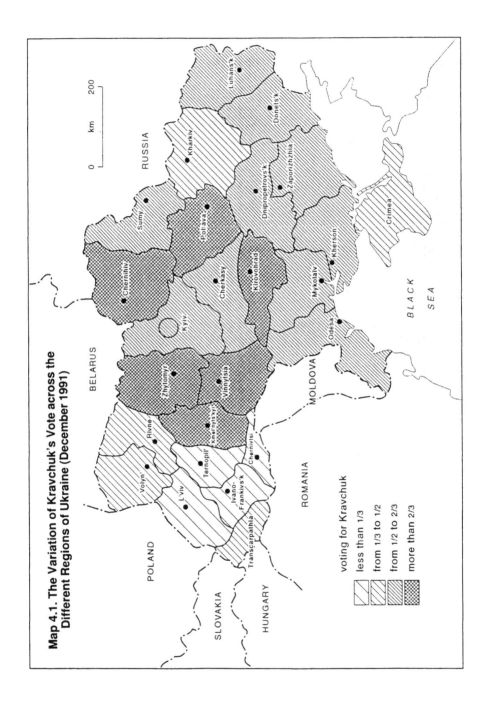

Map 4.1. The Variation of Kravchuk's Vote across the Different Regions of Ukraine (December 1991)

voting for Kravchuk

less than 1/3

from 1/3 to 1/2

from 1/2 to 2/3

more than 2/3

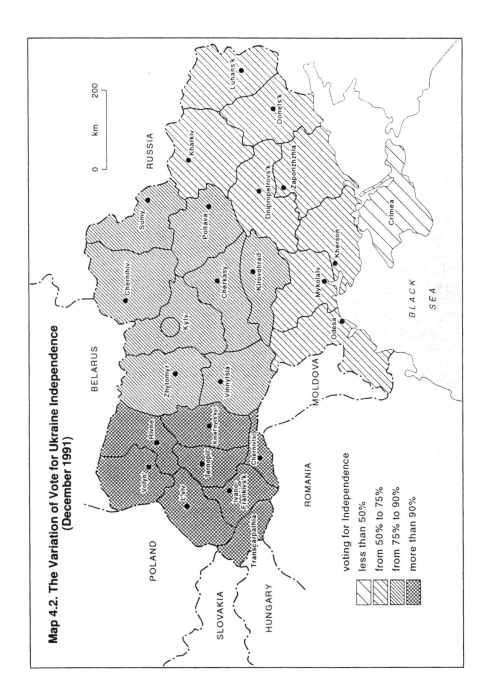

Map 4.2. The Variation of Vote for Ukraine Independence (December 1991)

voting for Independence

- less than 50%
- from 50% to 75%
- from 75% to 90%
- more than 90%

Table 4.1

Parliamentary Seats Won in 1994 by Representatives of the Main Left- and Right-Wing Parties, by Region

Regions	Number of mandates* (N)	Percentage of mandates received					
		Left (L)	Right (R)	Balance (R-L)	Left (L)	Right (R)	Balance (R-L)
Western	95	40	3	37	59	4	55
Central	135	11	19	−8	17	22	−5
Southern	120	—	28	−28	1	32	−31
Eastern	100	—	51	−51	—	55	−55
Total	450	11	25	−14	17	29	−12

*According to official data on party membership as assessed by experts.

port for independence therefore fell the further one traveled from the west of Ukraine toward the east and south, but at the time the degree of polarization was not considerable and failed to attract sufficient attention either from politicians or researchers.

Parliamentary Elections (1994)

By the time of the two-round parliamentary elections in March and April 1994, however, the situation had changed markedly, and this change became even more apparent during the presidential election that took place the following June and July.

The parliamentary elections demonstrated sharply contrasting patterns of regional support for the parties of the left and right.[3] Historical, geographical, and political divisions between the four main regions of modern Ukraine, namely the west, center, south, and east (see Map 4.3), became much more apparent.[4] Table 4.1 shows how the number of seats won by representatives of the various political parties after the two rounds of voting was significantly polarized along the east-west axis. (The main parties of the left were the Communist Party, the Socialist Party, and the Peasant Party; the main parties of the right were the Ukrainian National Assembly, the Congress of Ukrainian Nationalists, the Ukrainian Conservative Republican Party, the Ukrainian Republican Party, and Rukh; centrist political parties are relatively weak in Ukraine.)

The first four columns in Table 4.1 show figures derived from official

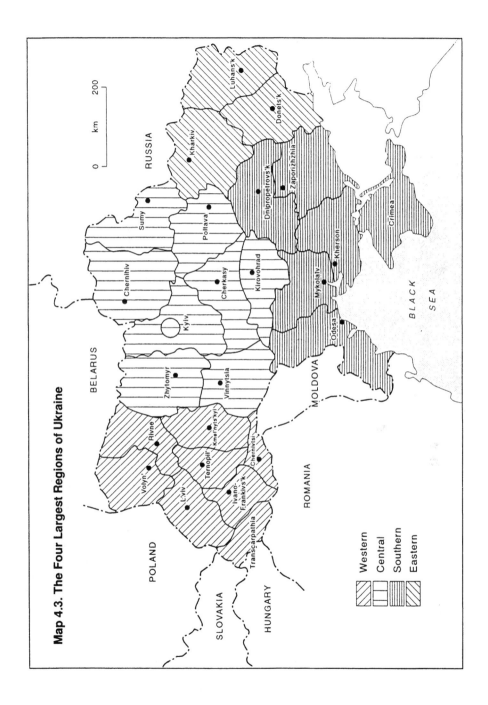

Map 4.3. The Four Largest Regions of Ukraine

Western
Central
Southern
Eastern

data about party membership in parliament, but because this data is far from complete it is supplemented by more comprehensive data supplied by the Kyiv Center of Political Studies and Conflictology and, for the western region, data published in the newspaper *Post-postup.*[5] However, the two sets of figures demonstrate the same trend in the distribution of seats between left and right across the different regions, namely the overwhelming dominance of the right in the western region, a relative balance between right and left in central Ukraine, a clear advantage for the left in the south, and its absolute dominance in the east.

Regional Polarization

In order to investigate the factors behind this regional polarization we will use the data of a second selective, nationally representative survey conducted in the run-up to the elections by the Kyiv International Institute of Sociology in collaboration with the Department of Sociology at the National University of the Kyiv-Mohyla Academy. A total of 1,737 respondents age 18 and above, living in 183 villages, towns, and cities from all 24 administrative regions and Crimea, were interviewed for the survey from mid-December 1993 to late January 1994. The respondents were a representative sample of the Ukrainian population, with a margin of error of 2.4 percent at the 0.05 level of significance.[6]

The survey was designed to probe respondents' voting intentions, as well as their judgments on a wide range of socioeconomic and political issues. A high degree of consistency between the survey data and the election results was demonstrated by the value of the correlation coefficient (0.98) between the balances of preferences for right-wing and left-wing parties in the four regions computed from the survey data and those demonstrated by the election results. Therefore, we are able to use this data to analyze the correlation of voters' party preferences with the political and socioeconomic attitudes revealed by the same survey. Factor analysis was used to classify respondents' attitudes toward twenty major political and economic issues into six general sets, which were responsible for more than half of all the variations in the evaluative judgments analyzed (see Table 4.2).[7] Table 4.2 illustrates the contents of each of these six factors by means of clustered demonstration variables.

Taking into account the signs and values of the coefficients shown in Table 4.2, it can be seen that the first factor (F1) differentiates respondents according to their attitudes toward private property and private enterprise. On the other hand, the other loads of this factor demonstrate that for the majority of Ukrainian voters these attitudes are weakly correlated with

Table 4.2

Factor Loadings of Respondents' Evaluative Judgments on Selected Social, Economic, and Political Issues

Subject of judgments	Factor Loadings					
	F1	F2	F3	F4	F5	F6
Attitude toward:						
Private ownership:						
of land	.68	−.03	−.10	−.00	.05	−.16
of small enterprises	.75	−.07	−.10	.13	.10	.02
of large enterprises	.69	−.08	.04	.06	.07	.10
Private business	.60	−.03	−.19	.35	.07	.02
Importance of private property for ordinary people	.69	−.05	−.02	.14	.02	.01
Allowing bankruptcy of inefficient state-owned enterprises	.28	−.15	−.06	.55	−.04	.12
Free prices	.25	−.09	.07	.62	−.01	.15
Personal responsibility for one's well-being	.02	−.03	−.05	.71	.10	−.13
Right to publish newspapers of any political orientation	.13	.04	−.05	.10	.80	.02
Right to free discussion even of the issues increasing tension in society	.10	−.05	−.06	−.03	.82	−.02
Liberty of assocation in political parties competing in elections	−.09	.01	.59	−.29	−.06	−.00
Liberty to criticize the government	−.00	.05	.67	−.11	−.26	.01
Equal justice for everbody	−.09	−.03	.69	.10	.04	−.03
Protection of the rights of minorities	−.08	−.06	.71	.11	.06	−.08
Ukraine's membership in the CIS	.00	.76	−.08	−.04	.01	−.02
Ukraine's membership in the CIS economic alliance	−.03	.74	.00	−.11	.01	.01
Establishing closer links with Russia	−.16	.70	.13	−.16	.02	.14
Official status of the Russian language in Ukraine	−.07	.71	−.06	.04	−.05	.08
Nuclear disarmament of Ukraine	.05	.07	−.04	−.08	.06	.75
Selling to Russia a significant share of the Black Sea Fleet warships	.06	−.08	.06	−.16	.07	.73
Dispersion of factors	3.52	2.18	1.61	1.35	1.18	1.00

attitudes toward such natural consequences of the development of private property and private business as the freeing of prices and the bankruptcy of inefficient enterprises. Moreover, there is no correlation with willingness to assume the major responsibility for one's own well-being instead of shifting this duty onto the state.[8] In other words, support for market principles is not always consistent. Many Ukrainians accept the market in principle but balk at its consequences. Attitudes toward personal responsibility for one's well-being and toward market-controlled prices and employment form the other (properly social) aspect of respondents' socioeconomic orientations, or the fourth factor (F4), which can be identified as attitudes toward the conditions of life under a market economy.

The second factor (F2) differentiates respondents according to their attitudes toward the membership of Ukraine in the Commonwealth of Independent States (CIS) and its would-be economic union, to establishing closer economic links with Russia, and toward granting the Russian language official status, either as the second official language in those regions of Ukraine where this is desired by the majority of the population or as the second state language in Ukraine as a whole.

The third and fifth factors (F3, F5) characterize attitudes toward the two principal political institutions of democracy, namely political liberty and legal equality. The third factor represents attitudes toward the problems of equal justice for all and protection of the rights of minorities, free criticism of the government, and free association into political parties with a right to free competition in elections. The fifth factor shows attitudes toward freedom of speech and freedom of the press.

Finally, the sixth factor (F6) differentiates respondents according to their attitudes toward two key aspects of Ukrainian disarmament, namely Ukraine's nuclear disarmament and the possible sale to Russia of a significant proportion of the ships due to Ukraine from the Black Sea Fleet.

We then used the technique of discriminant analysis to evaluate how respondents' socioeconomic and political values were correlated with their attitudes toward political parties of the left, right, and center. First of all, our analysis shows that the differentiation between supporters of *left-wing* and *centrist* parties was associated most of all with different attitudes toward private property and private business. This factor was responsible for about 38 percent of the total influence of the six factors shown. Another factor having a comparable effect (26 percent) was different attitudes toward freedom of speech and the press. Next in importance (20 percent of the same total influence) were attitudes toward the CIS, Russia, and the use of Russian as an official language. Finally, least significant were attitudes toward the conditions of life under a market economy (about 16 percent of the

Table 4.3

Indices of Voter Orientations in the Four Ukrainian Regions

	Average values for the regions				
	West	Center	South	East	Correlation
Attitudes toward:					
Private property	0.35	0.12	0.07	0.01	−0.11
The CIS, Russia, and the Russian language	−1.41	−0.12	0.29	0.49	0.55
Personal responsibility for one's well-being, free prices, possible bankruptcy of enterprises	0.23	0.24	0.18	0.15	−0.04
Freedom of speech and mass media	0.09	0.12	0.01	−0.07	−0.06

same influence). Attitudes toward the principal legal institutions of democracy, except for freedom of speech and the press (F3) and Ukrainian disarmament (F6), had no statistically significant influence on whether voters gravitated toward left-wing or centrist parties.

As regards the differentiation between supporters of *centrist* and *right-wing* parties, the crucial issues were attitudes about the membership of Ukraine in the CIS and its economic union, closer links with Russia, and the use of Russian as an official language. These orientations accounted for as much as 95 percent of the total influence of the six factors. All other orientations had little, if any, significance.

Moreover, the same factor—that is, attitudes on national political questions—was also critical in dividing voters into supporters of *left-wing* and *right-wing* parties (73 percent of the total effect of the six factors). Other influences, including socioeconomic issues and questions of political liberty, were much less significant.

Domestic Cleavages

The next important question is which particular sets of attitudinal differences have contributed most to the political polarization between east and west Ukraine. To find the answer to this question we compared indices of voter orientations across the four Ukrainian regions (see Table 4.3).

As can be seen from the above table, attitudes toward private property were indeed less favorable in the east than in the west (the difference between the average values of the respective indices was 0.34). Willingness to live under the conditions of a market economy was also slightly lower (0.08), as was commitment to the principles of freedom of speech and the press (0.16). However, the most significant difference between the regions was revealed by voters' opinions on questions of national policy. Attitudes toward the CIS and its proposed economic union, and toward Russia and the status of the Russian language in Ukraine, were extremely negative in west Ukraine but significantly positive in the east (the difference between the indices was a very high 1.90). Overall, therefore, we can conclude that the regional political polarization in Ukraine that became apparent during the 1994 parliamentary elections was correlated mainly with national political orientations rather than socioeconomic ones.[9]

Language Preferences

A second and even more marked manifestation of political polarization between east and west Ukraine came in the second round of the 1994 presidential election between the incumbent president, Leonid Kravchuk, and his Russian-speaking former prime minister, Leonid Kuchma.[10] Kuchma failed to win a majority in any of the twelve oblasts west of a line running through Chernihiv, Poltava, and Kirovohrad, while Kravchuk could not carry a single oblast to the east and south of that line (see Map 4.4). By mid-1994, therefore, it was clear that the most important manifestation of political differentiation in Ukraine was a sharp and growing regional polarization. Proper analysis of the roots of this phenomenon is not just a matter of academic interest; it is also of utmost importance to the future territorial integrity and independence of Ukraine. If the true sources of east-west polarization amongst the peoples of Ukraine are not uncovered, then actions designed to alleviate an already dangerous situation may simply aggravate it instead.

The following three conclusions can be drawn from our 1993–1994 survey findings. First, there was a high degree of correlation (0.63) between the regional distribution of votes for Kravchuk and Kuchma and the distribution of Ukrainian-speakers and Russian-speakers in Ukraine (see Map 4.5). Second, there was an even higher correlation (0.93) between the regional breakdown of votes for Kuchma (or Kravchuk) and the regional breakdown of supporters (and opponents) of the idea of uniting Ukraine and Russia in a single state. Third, attitudes toward national independence in the two parts of Ukraine diverged markedly after 1991. In the December 1991 referendum the vote against independence was a mere 2 percent in the westernmost oblasts of L'viv, Ternopil', Ivano-Frankivs'k (the historical region of Galicia), Rivne, and Volyn' (Volhynia), while at the opposite end of Ukraine it was 19 percent in Donets'k and Luhans'k (the Donbas) and the Crimea. The difference was therefore only 17 percent (our 1991 survey measured a similar gap of 19 percent), whereas our 1994 survey revealed that the west-east gap in terms of attitudes toward independence between the same regions had soared to 53 percent.

Sources of Division in Ukraine's Polity

The most common explanation of the growing gap between east and west is that the serious fall in the standard of living in Ukraine (and Russia's comparatively better economic performance) in the two and a half years of Kravchuk's presidency left those with an underdeveloped national consciousness disillusioned with the idea of Ukrainian independence they had supported back in December 1991. Their hopes for material improvement became linked to the idea of restoring the USSR or some other form of state union with Russia, and such sentiments were fanned by nostalgists and imperial restorationists both in Ukraine and abroad.

A second hypothesis admits that the waning commitment to the idea of Ukrainian independence in recent years is partly due to popular dissatisfaction with falling relative living standards, but attributes primary importance to cultural rather than material factors. In the years since independence the prospects for the future development of the cultures of Ukrainian-speaking and Russian-speaking Ukrainian citizens have diverged markedly. Ukrainian-speaking Ukrainians have found new opportunities for the free development and wider use of their language and culture, while Russian-speaking Ukrainians have come to fear that the possibilities for using their language and preserving their culture will sooner or later be restricted.

Analysis of our survey data across the Ukrainian regions shows that, contrary to the predictions of the first hypothesis, support for the idea of uniting Ukraine and Russia in some form of single state had no statistically significant correlation with the level of left-wing or so-called welfare-dependent attitudes in the same regions, and was only slightly correlated with judgments concerning how standards of living had changed since independence (the relevant coefficient of determination was 0.07). On the other hand, such support was much more closely (by a factor of more than eight) related to attitudes in the same regions toward the status of the Russian language in Ukraine (the coefficient of determination was as high as 0.61).

Further analysis shows that this correlation was not accidental. Differing attitudes in different regions of Ukraine toward the status of the Russian

72

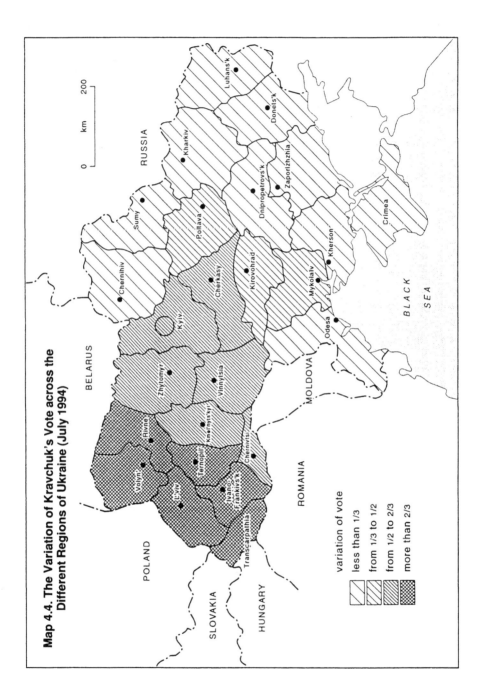

Map 4.4. The Variation of Kravchuk's Vote across the Different Regions of Ukraine (July 1994)

variation of vote

less than 1/3

from 1/3 to 1/2

from 1/2 to 2/3

more than 2/3

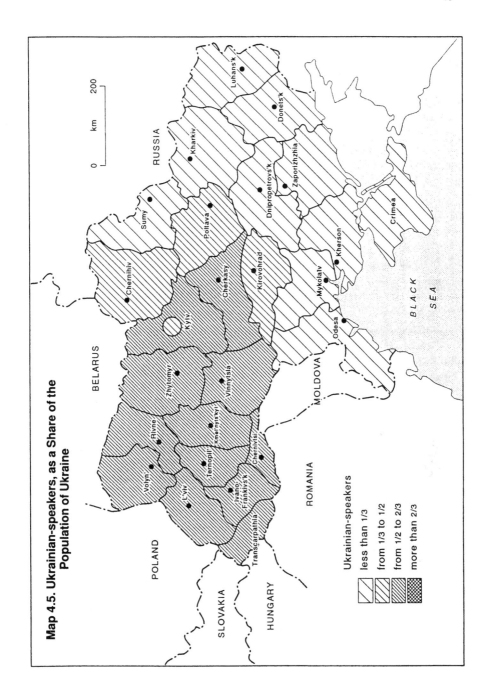

Map 4.5. Ukrainian-speakers, as a Share of the Population of Ukraine

Ukrainian-speakers

less than 1/3

from 1/3 to 1/2

from 1/2 to 2/3

more than 2/3

language in Ukraine and toward relations with Russia reflected the geographical distribution of social and cultural differences in Ukraine, and above all differences in the ethnic and linguistic composition of its regions. Not surprisingly, the percentage of people wishing Ukraine to have closer links with Russia, or wanting the Russian language to receive official status, was closely linked to the percentage of Russian-speaking Ukrainians and ethnic Russians in a particular region.

However, our studies also reveal that Ukraine has a more complex socioethnic structure than indicated by official population censuses dating from the Soviet period. This was due to the fact that censuses conducted by the Soviet authorities did not allow for multiethnic (or biethnic) self-identification by respondents. Only monoethnic identification was registered, multiethnic possibilities were excluded.

Moreover, the censuses never recorded the language the respondent actually spoke or preferred to speak. Only the language named by the respondent as 'native' was recorded (*ridna mova* in Ukrainian, *rodnoi iazyk* in Russian), irrespective of the actual language used in everyday life. 'Native' language, however, was often taken to mean the language spoken by respondents' parents, or even by their mothers alone.

According to the 1989 census, the population of Ukraine was 73 percent ethnic Ukrainian and 22 percent ethnic Russian, with 64 percent claiming Ukrainian as their 'native tongue' and 33 percent claiming Russian. However, our studies show that the phenomenon of biethnicity (i.e., self-identification of a person as belonging in some respect to two ethnic groups rather than óne) is quite common in contemporary Ukraine. According to our data, about 57 percent of the adult population identify themselves as Ukrainians only, and about 11 percent as Russians only, whereas 25 to 26 percent identify themselves as somehow both Ukrainian and Russian. Moreover, Ukraine's socioethnic structure is further complicated by ethnolinguistic heterogeneity. Even among those identifying themselves as Ukrainian only, about 36 to 37 percent are Russian-speaking Ukrainians who use Russian when they can choose their language of communication.

Amongst the population as a whole, according to data gathered by the Kyiv International Institute of Sociology, less than half (44.1 percent) of all adults in Ukraine use Ukrainian for day-to-day communication, while more than half (56.1 percent) typically use Russian for this purpose.[11] Moreover, it is reasonable to suppose that the phenomenon of bilingualism is also quite common in Ukraine. When asked about the language (Ukrainian or Russian) more convenient for them to use with the interviewer (it should be emphasized that this question is always formulated in both languages), 17 to 18 percent of respondents replied that it is equally convenient for them to speak either of these languages. (However, only 5 to 6 percent give this reply in Ukrainian, with 12 to 13 percent replying in Russian.)

As a first approximation, therefore (leaving aside the phenomena of biethnicity and bilingualism for the moment), we can say that, in terms of socioethnic structure, more than 94 percent of the adult population of Ukraine belong to one of three large ethnolinguistic groups. The largest group (about 40 percent of the population) comprises Ukrainian-speaking ethnic Ukrainians; the second largest group (about 33 to 34 percent) consists of Russian-speaking ethnic Ukrainians; and the third group (20 to 21 percent), Russian-speaking ethnic Russians. A fourth group (by size), Ukrainian-speaking ethnic Russians, only accounts for some 1 to 2 percent of the population (the remainder of the population belong to Ukraine's various ethnic minorities).

Furthermore, the regional distribution of these ethnolinguistic groups is extremely uneven. For example, in western Ukraine (if we consider the compact group of the eight western-most oblasts) more than 90 percent of the population are Ukrainian-speaking Ukrainians. Only 2 to 3 percent are Russian-speaking Ukrainians, and about 3 percent are Russian-speaking Russians. At the opposite extreme, in Crimea Russian-speaking Russians constitute about 62 percent of the population, Russian-speaking Ukrainians slightly over 20 percent, and Ukrainian-speaking Ukrainians a mere 4 to 5 percent.[12]

We therefore argue that the second of the two hypotheses outlined above is in better agreement with the facts and is better able to explain the divergence between east and west Ukraine in the 1994 presidential election. According to this hypothesis, the crucial factor in explaining regional polarization was cultural rather than material. Confirmation of this hypothesis sheds new light on our data concerning the linguistic and ethnic profile of the voters who supported Kravchuk in the two presidential elections of 1991 and 1994.

According to our data, ethnolinguistic divisions were more marked in the 1994 election than in 1991. In 1994, 70 percent of those who usually speak Ukrainian supported Kravchuk, while 72 percent of those who usually speak Russian opted for Kuchma. Among Kravchuk supporters, 71 percent were Ukrainian-speaking and 29 percent Russian-speaking, while Kuchma supporters were divided between Ukrainian-speakers (23 percent) and Russian-speakers (77 percent). Ethnically, the majority of the voters who voted against Kravchuk were not Russians but Ukrainians (62 percent). Only among Ukrainian-speaking Ukrainians did Kravchuk win a majority. Among Russian-speaking Ukrainians, his supporters numbered only 31 percent, with 60 percent intending to vote for Kuchma. Generally, Russian-

Table 4.4

Support for Leonid Kravchuk as a Candidate for President among the Main Linguistic and Ethno-Linguistic Groups in Ukraine in 1991 and 1994

| | Attitudes to Kravchuk's candidacy (%) | | | |
| | November 1991 | | July 1994 | |
Electors	Pro	Con	Pro	Con
Ukrainian-speakers	44	51	71	23
Russian-speakers	56	49	29	77
Total	100	100	100	100
Ukrainian-speaking Ukrainians	41	50	68	22
Russian-speaking Ukrainians	35	28	20	40
Russian-speaking Russians	19	19	7	32
Others	5	3	5	6
Total	100	100	100	100

speaking Ukrainians contributed to Kravchuk's defeat in the election more than any other linguistic or ethnic group.[13]

On the other hand, during the previous presidential election in 1991 there was as yet no significant linguistic and ethnic polarization between supporters and opponents of Kravchuk. In 1991 Kravchuk drew his support almost proportionally from all linguistic and ethnic groups amongst the Ukrainian electorate (see Table 4.4).

Once the representation of the main linguistic and ethnic groups in the different regions of Ukraine is taken into account (see Table 4.5), it is striking that in 1991 Kravchuk was supported almost equally by all linguistic and ethnic groups, but by 1994 had been transformed into a candidate who polarized the nation, attracting Ukrainian-speakers and alienating Russian-speakers to an almost equal degree.

Conclusion

Clearly, the policies of the first president alienated the majority of Russian-speaking citizens of Ukraine, and this effect was particularly strong amongst Russian-speaking Ukrainians (see Table 4.4).[14] The data cited above are insufficient to give a full explanation of this phenomenon, but the general trend is evident. During Kravchuk's period in office the state-controlled mass media demonstrated an increasingly negative attitude toward the public use of the Russian language in Ukraine.[15] Moreover, newspaper space and airtime were given to nationalist politicians who denied the very

Table 4.5

Linguistic and Ethnolinguistic Groups in Right-Bank Ukraine and Left-Bank Ukraine (in percent)

	Right-Bank	Left-Bank	Ukraine (Total)
Ukrainian-speakers	78	16	44
Russian-speakers	22	84	56
Total	100	100	100
Ukrainian-speaking Ukrainians	73	16	40
Russian-speaking Ukrainians	14	48	33
Russian-speaking Russians	7	30	21
Others	6	6	6
Total	100	100	100

Note: Because the balance between Russian-speakers and Ukrainian-speakers changes dramatically roughly along the line of the River Dnipro, a simplified twofold division ("West" or "Right-Bank" Ukraine against "East" or "Left-Bank" Ukraine) is used here instead of the previous division between western, central, eastern, and southern Ukraine. This alternative division once again reflects historical divides. The Right Bank includes western Ukraine and all the central *oblasts* west of the line from Kyiv down to Cherkasy and Kirovohrad. The Left Bank includes those east-central *oblasts* that fell under Russian influence in 1654 rather than 1793–95, all of eastern and southern Ukraine, and Crimea.

existence of a Russian-language Ukrainian culture. More precisely, nationalist politicians do not deny the use of the Russian *language* amongst ethnic Ukrainians, but they do not accept that there is a specific *culture* of Russian-speaking Ukrainians in the same sense that there is an indigenous Ukrainian-language culture.[16] Although Ukraine is formally a model civic state, committed to equal rights for all its ethnic and linguistic groups, different political messages are given out by the political discourse of Ukrainian nationalists. Like ethnonationalists the world over, they base their conceptual framework on the unique rights of 'indigenous' culture, and dismiss Russian-language culture in Ukraine as the result of the forcible acculturation policies of the tsarist and Soviet regimes. Moreover, they have tended to assume that the resultant unnatural bifurcation of ethnic Ukrainian society would automatically wither away after independence.[17] However, the carriers of this Russian-language Ukrainian culture see it as the result of voluntary interchange and mutual affection rather than forcible 'Russification.'[18] The implied threat to their very identity was therefore, we have argued, the main factor behind their alienation from the language policy directed by Kravchuk.

Given the parlous state of the Ukrainian language and Ukrainian-language culture in 1991, the deep concern of Ukrainian-speaking Ukrainians for their preservation and popularization is natural enough—as are their attempts to encourage all citizens of Ukraine, irrespective of their ethnic origin, to learn the Ukrainian language and to study Ukrainian-language and Ukrainian culture, for example by creating Ukrainian-language schools, colleges, and libraries to attract young people; by promoting Ukrainian television, radio, and film; and by Ukrainian-language publishing of the best Ukrainian and foreign books. However, there was also a perception of actual or potential future discrimination *against* Russian-language culture.[19] As well as stigmatizing that culture as 'artificial,' Ukrainian nationalist politicians have also argued against granting legal status to the continued de facto right of Russian-speaking Ukrainian citizens in the south and cast, to communicate in Russian with local authorities, and to send their children to Russian-language secondary schools and institutions of higher education on the territory of Ukraine, arguing that only Ukrainian-speaking Ukrainians deserve official status for their language.

About half of all Ukrainian citizens are currently Russian-speaking, including more than a third of all ethnic Ukrainians. Russian-speaking Ukrainians are potentially a swing group whose identity depends on a mixture of ethnic and linguistic factors. However, the 1994 presidential election demonstrated the potential dangers if nationalist doctrines of indigenous rights produce overly hasty 'nationalizing' policies that collide with the realities produced by the historical bifurcation of Ukrainian culture. The result can only be to widen the differences between mainly Ukrainian-speaking west Ukraine and the mainly Russian-speaking east and south, and play into the hands of imperially minded politicians in Russia who are already seeking to protect and, if possible, 'reunite' all Russian-speaking people, including Russian-speaking Ukrainians living in Ukraine.

Notes

1. On the 1991 elections, see also Valeri Khmelko, "Referendum: khto buv 'za' i khto 'proty,' " *Politolohichni chytannia,* no. 1, 1992, pp. 40–52, and Peter J. Potichnyj, "The Referendum and Presidential Elections in Ukraine," *Canadian Slavonic Papers,* vol. 33, no. 2 (June 1991), pp. 123–138.

2. Respondents were asked about the need for the retention of censorship and whether they agreed with the statement that Stalin "was a great leader" *(vozhd').* Positive answers were taken as indications of 'authoritarian' attitudes.

3. On the 1994 parliamentary elections, see V. Khmelko, "Politicheskie orientatsii izbiratelei i itogi vyborov v Verkhovnyi Sovet (mart-aprel' 1994 goda)," *Ukraina segodnia,* 1994, no. 5, pp. 55–63; Dominique Arel and Andrew Wilson, "The Ukrainian Parliamentary Elections," *RFE/RL Research Report,* vol. 3, no. 26 (1 July 1994), and Marko Bojcun, "The Ukrainian Parliamentary Elections of March–April 1994," *Europe-Asia Studies,* vol. 47, no. 2 (March-April 1995), pp. 229–249.

4. 'Western Ukraine' refers to the eight most westerly oblasts of Ukraine; L'viv, Ternopil', and Ivano-Frankivs'k (Galicia), Rivne and Volyn' (Volhynia), Chernivtsi (Bukovyna), Transcarpathia, and Khmel'nyts'kyi (Khmel'nyts'kyi is included because of the imprecise association between tsarist and Soviet, or post-Soviet, borders). Western Ukraine as a whole was only incorporated into the USSR between 1939 and 1945; only Volhynia (between 1795 and 1917) and parts of Khmel'nyts'kyi had previously been parts of the Russian empire. 'Central Ukraine' refers to the city of Kyiv and the following eight oblasts: Zhytomyr, Vinnytsia, Kyiv, Cherkasy, Kirovohrad, Chernihiv, Sumy and Poltava. The last three oblasts, all of which are east of the Dnipro River, mainly came under Russian control in 1654; those to the west of the Dnipro were incorporated between 1793 and 1795. 'Southeastern Ukraine' includes the remaining oblasts, namely Kharkiv, Donets'k, and Luhans'k (that is, eastern Ukraine, with Donets'k and Luhans'k together forming the Donbas region); and Dnipropetrovs'k, Zaporizhzhia, Odesa, Mykolaïv, Kherson, and Crimea (southern Ukraine). Although Ukrainian Cossacks based in Zaporizhzhia settled many parts of the southeast from the sixteenth century onward, the high number of Russian-speakers throughout the region is the result of multiethnic settlement after Russian conquest in the second half of the eighteenth century, and the consequent displacement of the Crimean Tatars and Ottoman Turks.

5. "Verkhovna Rada. Spektral'nyi analiz. Prohnozovanyi sklad parlaments'kykh fraktsii," *Post-postup,* 15–21 April 1994.

6. The technique used was stratified cluster sampling.

7. The factor scores were obtained from principal component analysis with rotation by the varimax method.

8. V. Khmelko, "U svidomosti ukraïntsiv perevazhaie syndrom utrymans'koï psykholohiï," *Demos,* no. 5, 1995, pp. 23–24.

9. See also Vicki L. Hesli, "Public Support for the Devolution of Power in Ukraine: Regional Patterns," *Europe-Asia Studies,* vol. 47, no. 1 (January–February 1995), pp. 91–121.

10. On the 1994 presidential elections, see D. Arel and A. Wilson, "Ukraine under Kuchma: Back to 'Eurasia'?," *RFE/RL Research Report,* vol. 3, no. 32 (19 August 1994), and A. Wilson, "Ukraine: Two Presidents, but No Settled Powers," in Ray Taras, ed., *The Post-Communist Presidents* (Cambridge: Cambridge University Press, 1997).

11. The parameters of the ethnolinguistic composition of the population were calculated from the data collected in thirteen nationally representative surveys conducted by the Kyiv International Institute of Sociology from December 1991 to December 1994 (the last seven were in collaboration with the Department of Sociology at the National University of the Kyiv-Mohyla Academy). The total number of respondents was 18,586.

12. See also V. Khmelko, "Dva berehy—dva sposoby zhyttia," *Demos,* no. 1, 1995, pp. 17–20.

13. See also V. Khmelko, "Tretii rik nezalezhnosti: Shcho vyiavyly druhi prezydents'ki vybory," *Ukraina segodnia,* no. 6, 1994, pp. 22–30.

14. See also D. Arel, "Ukraine: The Temptation of the Nationalizing State," in Vladimir Tismaneanu, ed., *Political Culture and Civil Society in Russia and the New States of Eurasia, The International Politics of Eurasia,* vol. 7 (Armonk, New York: M. E. Sharpe, 1995), pp. 157–188, and D. Arel and V. Khmelko, "The Russian Factor and Territorial Polarization in Ukraine," *The Harriman Institute Review,* vol. 9, nos. 1–2 (March 1996), pp. 81–91.

15. See, for example, Kravchuk's statement that it was "painful and offensive when a Ukrainian does not wish to speak his native language, and in official declarations registers himself and his children amongst the legion of the Russified," in Leonid

Kravchuk and Serhii Kychyhin, *Leonid Kravchuk: Ostanni dni imperiï . . . Pershi roky nadiï* (Kyiv: Dovira, 1994), p. 118.

16. See, for example, Yevhen Repet'ko, "Narid i natsiia," *Holos natsiï,* no. 24, 1993, and Mar'iana Chorna, "Solom''ianyi bychok znaishov sobi hospodaria," *Post-postup,* 14–20 July 1994.

17. See A. Wilson, *Ukrainian Nationalism in the 1990s: A Minority Faith* (Cambridge: Cambridge University Press, 1997). For a typical example of nationalist argument, see Vasyl' Lyzanchuk, *Navichno kaidany kuvaly: Fakty, dokumenty, komentari pro rusyfikatsiiu v Ukraïni* (L'viv: Institute of Ethnology, Academy of Sciences of Ukraine, 1995).

18. See, for example, Volodymyr Hryn'ov, *Nova Ukraïna: Yakoiu ya ïï bachu* (Kyiv: Abrys, 1995), pp. 60–64.

19. As Rogers Brubaker has pointed out, the important factor in alienating ethnic or linguistic minorities is that state policies "are *perceived* as nationalizing by representatives of the national minority." See his "National Minorities, Nationalizing States, and External National Homelands in the New Europe," *Daedalus,* vol. 124, no. 2 (Spring 1995), p. 114 (emphasis in original).

5

Civil Society and Nation Building in Ukraine

Mykola Riabchouk

The fall of communism in Eastern Europe and in the Soviet Union has not yet resulted in the full-fledged democracy that was supposed to replace totalitarianism as soon as free democratic elections were held, independent mass media permitted, and all other Western-style liberties guaranteed. The formal democracy that has been established in postcommunist (and, especially, post-Soviet) countries 'from above' proved to be merely that and not a substantial feature of political life and social behavior in these countries; it seemed to be a necessary but not sufficient condition for democracy as developing (and functioning) 'from below.' Eventually the notion arises that "liberty is not about freedom from government, but about the capacity for self-government, which alone makes the practice of freedom possible."[1]

As more skeptical scholars have put it, "Much of what is considered to be a successful 'transition to democracy' in the world is no such thing. One finds almost as many democratic facades in the period after the Cold War as one found national facades in the aftermath of decolonization."[2] And the optimists are also reserved: "It is too early to stop watching the progress of Eastern Europe, too early to assume that everything there will simply turn out for the best. This is a region whose future is still far from assured."[3]

In order to understand why democracy 'from above' (as well as the free market and many other Western inventions and impositions) does not work properly in most postcommunist countries, and why democracy 'from below' is being established so tardily, some preconditions for the emergence and functioning of democracy should be considered. The notion of 'civil society' seems to give us the necessary clue to the East European puzzle: "It is more useful than 'democracy' only, because it refers to social conditions that must be fulfilled for a democracy to prevail, that is, for people to be able to act independently of, or in opposition to, the state authority in a sustained way."[4]

Most scholars define civil society as "the sphere of social life where people as private citizens interact with each other, creating their own organizations not controlled by the state."[5] However significant all the aspects of civil society are for the establishment of democracy, the most important is "people's capacity to act jointly and in a sustained and regulated way to influence the government." In the West it was precisely the gradual institutionalization of this challenge to the state (first liberal-bourgeois, then social-democratic) that came to be known as 'civil society.'[6]

Its emergence (or reemergence) in postcommunist countries, therefore, is of the utmost importance and urgency. As the numerous theoretical elaborations and, even more graphically, Western practical experience show, civil society implies the denial of ideological monopoly, the acceptance of compromise on fundamental issues, and the abandonment of messianism, chauvinism, and national exclusiveness in their various forms. However, there is another available basis for political mobilization that can easily dispense with civil society. Nationalism, based on cultural identification, on the role of culture as the marker of collective boundaries, on a direct linkage between the leader(s) and the followers, and frequently on political exclusiveness, does not require painstaking institution building, but can be activated quickly, not least in conditions of increasing economic misery and an alleged (or real) threat to national sovereignty.[7]

Nationalism is too broad and fickle a phenomenon to be defined here briefly and definitely. And even less possible is its ultimate evaluation as a 'positive' or 'negative' factor of social life. In fact, it is ambivalent and, what is more important, unavoidable—that is, inherent to human beings, since it has roots in some biological instincts such as xenophobia (fear of things alien and unusual) and in an existential fear of nonexistence (which forces human beings to extend the narrow limits of their corporeal lives through the imagined belonging to a wider, eternal, 'spiritual' community). My basic assumption, thus, is that nationalism cannot be avoided or eliminated completely, but it can and must, as any instinct, be controlled, 'humanized,' and properly channeled.[8]

For all practical purposes, I have confined the broad phenomenon of nationalism to one very particular manifestation: the emancipation of the Ukrainian nation from the political bonds of empire and from the cultural pressure of dominant Russian discourse. This restriction may enable me to find and to emphasize a functional connection between the very nebulous phenomenon of nationalism and the quite concrete processes of state and nation building. And, on the other hand, it may provide my research with a good 'common denominator' for two seemingly incompatible phenomena: democracy and nationalism. In Ukrainian terms, these phenomena interact as two different (but compatible) processes of emancipation: that of civil society from the totalitarian state, and that of the Ukrainian nation from the Soviet Russian empire.

The Ukrainian case, therefore, is considered as both postcommunist and postcolonial, as both typical and unique. Its typicalness means that many political processes in Ukraine are similar to those taking place in Russia and other Eastern European countries, while some developments resemble those of the developing world. Its uniqueness is reflected in an unusual combination of different processes and phenomena, caused by Ukraine's regional, ethnic, and historical peculiarities. The Ukrainian case, however, is not only of purely academic interest. Ukraine's geopolitical situation makes the country a "linchpin of the new post–Cold War Europe" (in Strobe Talbott's words) and forces Western policy-makers to adopt different attitudes about this "unwanted stepchild of Soviet perestroika."[9]

Eastern rather than western Ukraine is the major concern of this research, not only because it is four times bigger and probably more important, but also because the processes in the east are much more complicated and interesting than in western Ukraine, which in general follows the well-researched patterns of development of neighboring East European countries.[10] It means not that western Ukraine is to be completely ignored, only that western Ukrainian developments are considered to the extent that they have an impact on the entire nation.

Unfortunately, most opinion surveys consider Ukrainians in Ukraine as a single entity, paying little if any attention to their linguistic preferences and language-based identities. But Russophone Ukrainians constitute a large, separate group, which substantially differs in its values, attitudes, and orientations both from Russians in Ukraine and from Ukrainophone Ukrainians. It is this very group that largely determines Ukraine's 'uniqueness' and decisively complicates both the process of national emancipation and, as I try to show, the development of civil society. At the same time, this 'middle' group with a mixed identity moderates potential interethnic conflicts in Ukraine and prevents two other groups, Russophone Russians and Ukrainophone Ukrainians, from directly clashing. Since no ethnic group in Ukraine is strong enough to gain the upper hand, all of them are doomed to mutual toleration and the search for compromise.[11]

My major point, therefore, is that Ukraine has the possibility to develop modern civil society and stable democracy despite the heavy burden of the Soviet totalitarian legacy and delayed and misguided market reforms. The weakness of Ukrainian nationalism makes ethnic mobilization impossible and impels political elites toward state and nation building on a civic basis rather than an ethnic one. An atmosphere of tolerance is being established, and in turn this facilitates a slow—but peaceful—development of Ukrainian society within the framework of civility and legality. The measures that can be applied in order to promote this development are considered in the final part of this chapter.

Civil Society

The concept of civil society is not a major concern of this chapter, since the theory of it has been extensively elaborated by Western scholars. Thus, the concept is employed just as a working term for this case study. Here and throughout, the term is defined as a "set of diverse non-governmental institutions, which is strong enough to counterbalance the state, and, whilst not preventing the state from fulfilling its role of keeper of the peace and arbitrator between major interests, can nevertheless prevent the state from dominating and atomizing the rest of society."[12]

In general, the numerous studies of civil society in the former USSR and Russia can be applied to the Ukrainian case—with some substantial amendments and corrections, which, by and large, are the main concern of this chapter. As everywhere in the former USSR (with the slight exception of Ukrainian Galicia and the Baltic states), civil society in Ukraine can be characterized as weak, underdeveloped, and heavily burdened with a postcommunist legacy. Neither political nor economic liberalization has created, so far, the sufficient conditions for the emergence of full-fledged civil society.

The so-called nomenklatura privatization has not separated the economy from the state and has contributed little if anything to the emergence of a middle class—a broad stratum of private owners, the 'bourgeoisie'—which is the social base of civil society (*bürgerliche Gesellschaft*). The caricatural 'privatization' leads rather to a 'corrupt economy,' comparable to the economies of the Latin American countries, where exchange is based on social-political power instead of on economic relations.[13] Since property remains a form of organization dependent, above all, on holding office, privatization in the former Soviet bloc is, in effect, "piratizations, in which nomenklatura connections matter as much as ever."[14] As the Russian experience shows most graphically, it leans heavily on the shadow economy or the 'mafia,' consolidated in the last years of the Soviet period in a symbolic relationship with state structures.[15]

In social terms, Ukrainian society is also far from being modern in

Western terms, despite large-scale urbanization and industrialization carried out first in the 1930s and again in the 1950s. As some scholars aptly point out, this forced modernization in the Soviet Union led to a specific kind of separation between political discourse and everyday life, a remarkable autonomy of the society vis-à-vis the sphere of politics. "The impressive figures of growth of the industrial and urban population, reflecting the political determination of the party-state, were not matched by corresponding changes in social relations. Rather, the figures covered an increasing gap between the administrative efforts from above and the reaction of a restive society that adapted itself to changes only insofar as it was necessary." In fact, it meant the ruralization of cities rather than the urbanization of the country.[16]

In this perspective, a high level of industrialization and urbanization did not imply modern social relations. While in statistical terms the social structure in Ukraine resembled that commonly found in the West, at the level of social relations it still represents the traditional, Soviet-style 'network of distribution'—that is, family relations, 'functional friendship,' et cetera—so characteristic of the socialist economies. The reintroduction of market mechanisms (in their peculiar, highly corrupted, and limited form) reinforced the orientation of the existing networks instead of eliminating them.[17] As a result, a Ukrainian scholar concludes, "we have to face and deal with a new 'bourgeoisie,' whose negative traits pose a serious threat to the successful transition to capitalism and the market economy."[18]

Thus, the increasing autonomy of the social sphere does not lead to a sustained popular effort to enter the polity; the 'social networks of distribution,' which used to function in symbiosis with official structures or exploit them, now restrain the capacity of the population to organize and act collectively, not develop it. The individual and group-based survival strategies stifle active mobilization and organization rather than promote them (at least among the majority, which is not highly educated).[19] In fact, the "corporatist-participatory political culture of the late Soviet period" (in Molchanov's words) remained untouched.[20]

As for political liberalization, its impact on the emergence of civil society in Ukraine proved to be also ambivalent if not ambiguous. The postcommunist or, more precisely, cryptocommunist elites that replaced the pro-Moscow nomenklatura in Kyiv in 1990–1991 did not dismantle the former political structures. A number of old arrangements still exist—and not only in the economic sphere, where they are the most visible. To a large degree, Ukrainian independence meant just a "rearrangement within the confines of the old polity."[21] The nomenklatura ostensibly adopted the democrats' slogans of independence, democracy, market reforms, and Western orientation. But the cryptocommunist policy, pursued under this guise, not only resulted in further economic stagnation but also deeply alienated the population from these misused slogans and from the political sphere in general; nihilism ('defensive mobilization,' in Charles Tilly's understanding)[22] came to be the prevailing political attitude in Ukrainian society.

On the other hand, the Ukrainian democrats who came into existence between 1990 and 1992 tended to be easily co-opted to the existing power structures. Since the democratic movement emerged not so much as an organized challenger to the empire and to the party-state but rather as the result of their dissolution, it was able to fill the vacuum rapidly, adapting itself to the political struggle in the upper echelons of the state and society and being ready to leave the organizational efforts to a secondary plane. Thus, the political parties (or 'protoparties') still resemble informal organizations, and their leaders are usually 'generals without armies.' There are dozens of them, and they are in a perpetual process of emergence, division, and disintegration.[23] Their mode of organization recalls, in effect, that of the Ukrainian intelligentsia in the late nineteenth century—the clubs *(hromady)*. As a matter of fact, the anticommunist opposition shares equal responsibility with the postcommunist nomenklatura for the moods of frustration and alienation that has engulfed Ukrainian society. What they claimed was their patriotic duty—to participate in state building and to defend a vulnerable Ukrainian independence from various threats—proved to be an unconditional collaboration with the nomenklatura and resulted in further discreditation of the misused democratic slogans.[24]

And finally, the democratic potential of the labor collectives proved to be dubious as well. As most analysts agree, socialist industrialization transformed social relations in the USSR much less than it appeared at first sight to have done. "Discontent was not directed against the paternalistic control as such but against its excesses. Workers were not conscious of a common interest even in terms of the labor collective . . . and they tended to see conflicts in a local framework only."[25]

Even though there were some democratic demands in the declarations of the independent workers' movements, an alliance between them and the intellectuals' democratic movement was difficult to establish, thanks to the psychological alienation of the worker milieu from the intelligentsia in general, and from any Ukrainian cause in particular. As the postindependence developments in Ukraine have revealed, the workers' movement in the southeast (the most industrialized and, at the same time, the most Russified region) is much more under communist than democratic influence, and very often is skillfully manipulated by the local postcommunist (cryptocommunist) nomenklatura for its regional and clannish purposes. Still, the workers' social behavior follows a preclass or nonclass pattern and can hardly create the basis for civil society.

All these sad observations are firmly confirmed by opinion surveys carried out in Ukraine. For example, 83 percent of respondents are not members of any public or political organization;[26] just 10 percent are interested in politics, while 63 percent are interested only to some extent and 27 percent are not interested at all.[27] On the eve of the 1994 parliamentary elections, only 13 percent of respondents were familiar with the policy statements of Ukrainian political parties and movements;[28] only 19 percent believed that there were political leaders who could govern the country in the future; and only 14 percent felt that there were political parties and movements in Ukraine that deserved to achieve power.[29] Despite the common dissatisfaction with the deteriorating standard of living (80 percent) and the common belief that Ukraine, by and large, is ruled by the same people as in the past, only 16 percent of the respondents thought that their personal participation in the elections was important,[30] and only 12 percent were ready to participate in strikes (more radical forms of protest attracted even smaller numbers of people).[31]

The measure of alienation and atomization of Ukrainian society was most graphically revealed by Evhen Holovakha in his survey of Ukraine's population conducted in 1994. When asked about their attitude toward political parties oriented toward either return to socialism or a push in the direction of capitalism, only 22.2 percent of the respondents supported the proponents of capitalism, and even fewer (only 12.7 percent) supported the proponents of socialism. But 20.1 percent declared that they supported none of them, and 23.8 percent surprised everybody by answering that they supported both sides in order to avoid conflict. (The rest of the respondents found the question difficult to answer.)[32]

In fact, what is revealed here is an absolute fear of conflict, which not only prevents any violence in the country but also hampers dramatically any attempt to overcome the socioeconomic crisis—since any attempt of this sort would unavoidably include a very serious clash between outdated totalitarian administrative structures and civil society. In order to gain mass support for (or at least to head off resistance to) its cryptocommunist policy, the ruling nomenklatura deliberately fosters this fear among the population, who, frightened by the possibility of social chaos due to the radicalization of social changes and semimythical 'Ukrainization,' hold the same political line as the ruling structures. But while declaring their support for democracy, market reforms, and the rule of the law, they do nothing for the actual achievement of these political goals. Due to its self-imposed role of a guarantor of 'bad peace,' the nomenklatura successfully maintains the ancien régime, that is, holds power and property in its hands, and even more successfully degrades the economy and discredits national independence.[33]

In many aspects, Ukrainian (and any postcommunist) society resembles that of a developing country.[34] However, industrialization, the character of urbanization, and the population's relatively high level of education make the Ukrainian case rather different. And Ukraine's both geographic and 'spiritual' (semireal, semimythical—'imagined') belonging to Europe makes the prospects for civil society and democracy in Ukraine even more inviting. Even the multiethnicity of the Ukrainian state, which contributes greatly to the country's sense of fear and makes Ukrainian society very rigid, conservative, and manipulable by the nomenklatura, can prove advantageous—because it eliminates completely the possibility (and temptation) of political mobilization under the slogans of ethnic nationalism.[35]

This belief in belonging to Europe is another substantial difference between Ukraine and Russia. Since no ethnic group is strong enough to dominate the political scene, and since fear of conflict is still predominant, both Russophones and Ukrainophones in Ukraine are doomed to coexistence if not mutual tolerance; thus, civil society in Ukraine may emerge in the process and, to a certain degree, as a result of these mutual negotiations and compromises. Of course, for these purposes, the appropriate strategies should be applied—and I will formulate some of them later, at the end of this chapter.

National Emancipation

The widespread and rather misleading idea about the ethnic composition of Ukrainian society is based on the results of the last 1989 Soviet census, which found 11.4 million ethnic Russians in Ukraine (22.1 percent of the total population), 37.5 million ethnic Ukrainians (72.7 percent of the population), and 2.7 million other minorities (5.2 percent of the population). These figures, however, do not reflect the real alignment of forces between the two major ethnic groups. Any empirical observation easily shows that the Russian (that is, 'minority') language and culture predominate, if not dominate totally, in most Ukrainian cities, where the majority of population lives and where the major cultural and political developments are occurring. No minority, however numerous and powerful as it used to be, could ever change an urban milieu so substantially without the support of assimilated members of the indigenous majority.

The same 1989 census revealed that 4.6 million ethnic Ukrainians in Ukraine (9 percent of the population) listed Russian as their native tongue, along with approximately 1 million other minorities (2 percent of the population). In total, therefore, some 17 million individuals (33 percent of the population) said that Russian was their 'native tongue' in 1989.[36] But even this figure hardly explains the nearly total dominance of Russian language and culture in Ukraine's urban centers. Only recently have some scholars questioned the census formula 'native tongue' *(ridna mova)* as methodologically incorrect.[37] In their view, this formula can be interpreted to mean either the language that one speaks best at the present time or the language one first learned as a child. Due to the process of Russification, these two languages are not necessarily identical. Therefore, scholars have now applied the formula of the 'language of convenience' or the 'language of everyday preference.'

The surveys based on this formula disclosed a shocking fact: Ukrainophone Ukrainians make up a minority of the population (approximately 40 percent), while ethnic Russians account for 20 to 21 percent and Russophone Ukrainians a massive 33 to 34 percent.[38] Of course, these figures can also be questioned because, in the Ukrainian circumstances, the formula 'language of preference' is as dubious as that of 'native tongue'. Since the Ukrainian language has traditionally been of a low status (as a shameful proof of village backwardness or of semicriminal Ukrainian 'bourgeois nationalism'), many respondents probably feel that it is more respectable and prestigious to use higher-status Russian for public discourse.[39] In any case, we may conclude that the number of Ukrainophone Ukrainians varies somewhere between 63 percent ('native tongue' data) and 40 percent ('language of preference' data).[40] For our purposes, the precise figure is not so important: Even if this figure is closer to 60 percent than to 40 percent, we must remember that approximately half of these Ukrainophone Ukrainians live in rural areas, that is, the places where civil society emerges last, and which usually play a minor role in the processes of national and political emancipation. The major implication of these alignments is that in any case, in urban areas, Ukrainophone Ukrainians are a minority that can hardly dream about any dominance but may try, at best, to defend their rights vis-à-vis the dominant and traditionally privileged Russophones.[41]

Yet, despite their de facto minority status, Ukrainophone Ukrainians prove to be much more active and visible on the political and cultural scene than their more numerous and better-established Russophone counterparts. There are a few reasons for this, which should be explained in order to understand better why civil society in Ukraine emerged largely as a 'Ukrainian' ('Ukrainophone') phenomenon. First of all, as an oppressed and humiliated minority, Ukrainians have had more reasons to protest; the dissident movement in Ukraine consisted mostly of Ukrainians, with some Jews and Crimean Tatars and almost no Russians.[42] During perestroika, Ukrainians raised both democratic and national demands; the political emancipation of civil society from the totalitarian state coincided for them with the national emancipation of Ukrainian society from the empire.[43]

Russians, meanwhile, found themselves in a more difficult situation. Most of them supported the political emancipation of Soviet society from the party-state, but only a few favored the national emancipation of Russian colonies from the center. They disliked the center as oppressive and undemocratic, but they tolerated and even supported it because it was Russian, that is, their own, and many considered it a protector of their real or imagined privileges in the Near Abroad. In the Baltic republics, this kind of schizophrenia led the Russians to create antinational and antidemocratic 'interfronts' (Internationalist fronts created by the Communist Party to block moves to independence); in Ukraine it just made Russophones passive and neutral (or, rather, ambivalent) toward the republic's political life. Despite its primarily urban location, favorable for civic development, the Russophone population has not significantly contributed to the emergence of civil society in Ukraine. Having no democratic leaders nor parties of their own, these people have little choice but to opt for the communists as a 'known evil' over the unknown (hence suspicious) Ukrainian democrats—who are perceived mostly as 'nationalists.'

This segment of the population was 'lost,' to some extent, by the national democrats, who resorted to a fatal collaboration with the former communist nomenklatura. However, the same part of the population was 'won' by the nomenklatura, which managed to identify as a mass awareness the notion of 'democracy' with something purely 'Ukrainian,' hence 'nationalistic' or merely 'Galician,' that is, western Ukrainian. The fear of conflict, as mentioned above, makes these people very susceptible to various myths invented and disseminated by the nomenklatura. The scarecrow of Ukrainian nationalism makes them more 'procommunist' and 'pro-Russian' than they really are. According to the Democratic Initiatives survey, Ukrainian voters, if they were living in Russia, would have supported mostly Yegor Gaidar's Russia's Choice party (11.2 percent), Grigori Yavlinsky's Yabloko (4.8 percent) and so forth, while only 3.8 percent would have supported Gennadiy Ziuganov's Communists and only 2.7 percent Vladimir Zhirinovsky's Liberals.[44]

As a result, civil society in today's Ukraine mainly embraces ethnic, Ukrainophone Ukrainians while the Russophones—that is, civic Ukrainians—are apparently underrepresented in all of its structures (except the Communist Party of Ukraine, which, however, is neither civic nor Ukrainian but rather imperial and totalitarian). The nucleus of the unformed civil society practically coincides with that of an unformed political nation.[45] The purposeful attempts of Ukrainian democrats to enlarge civil society so as to encompass the nationally indifferent segment of the population (mostly the urban Russophones, but also the rural Ukrainophones) has proved to have little success so far, because of three reasons.

1. Both consciously and subconsciously the Russophones have a strong bias against the Ukrainophones, who may allegedly challenge their real (or, rather, symbolic privileges), and whose very existence is psychologically uncomfortable.

2. Anti-Ukrainophone biases and stereotypes among the urban Russophones (as well as among the rural Ukrainophones who have a 'local' rather than national identity) had been actively promoted by the Soviets, and still are successfully fostered by the postcommunist nomenklatura as a part of its strategy for survival ('divide and rule') and for intimidating society with potential conflicts (self-imposed role of the guarantor of a 'bad' peace).

3. Some mistakes and incoherent steps of the Ukrainian democrats facilitated their opponents with additional means to discredit both 'Ukrainianness' and 'democracy.'

Yet the main reason civil society in Ukraine emerges so slowly and painfully is the same as elsewhere in postcommunist countries: the ambiguous character of economic reforms and distorted social relations. In many terms, it faces the same problems as in Russia, where little if any tradition of civil society has ever existed. One difference, however, is very substantial. While in Russia political mobilization can be (and actually is being) achieved by means of nationalism, in Ukraine this easier (but very dangerous) path is impossible.[46] Ethnic nationalism in Ukraine can mobilize only a minority of the population and in no way can challenge the dominant Russophone majority backed by Russians. The only way left, however difficult and complicated it might be, is civic consolidation. Paradoxically, national emancipation in Ukraine may succeed only to the extent to which civic integration will be achieved.

Conclusion

Economic reforms should be the major priority for the Ukrainian democrats because only a free-market economy can provide the social base for civil society, and because economic problems are indeed of bread-and-butter importance for the entire population. This is the primary field where the

Ukrainian democrats may find a common language with the Russophone liberals and some more progressive clans of the nomenklatura, and to make their slogans appealing to the masses.

Under the peculiar circumstances of an external threat and internal vulnerability of the newly emerged Ukrainian state, the Ukrainian democrats perhaps cannot afford any large-scale confrontation with the ruling nomenklatura and would probably cooperate with it, in some form and to some extent. But the form and conditions of this cooperation should be clearly defined, and the principal differences between nomenklaturian and democratic policies should be loudly articulated. They must learn from their recent experience how easily their moral advantages were wasted by collaboration with the nomenklatura, incompetence, and corruptibility. They also should take a more resolute stand against extreme nationalistic groups, which are marginal but vociferous and rather successful in compromising the Ukrainian movement in general.

The fear of social conflicts that paralyzes Ukrainian society and results in people's passivity and alienation cannot and, as long as the society is immature, should not be completely rejected on the grounds that a 'bad peace' is better, so far, than a 'good war'. Conflict of interests is a basic feature of any dynamic, competing society, and does not necessary lead to violence or other excesses. Civil society is precisely a means to mediate and to moderate those conflicts. This idea should be articulated in the public consciousness by all possible means—education, the mass media, and political activity.

The divisive ethnic-linguistic question in Ukraine cannot be ignored completely, but it should not, in any case, dominate the Ukrainian political agenda.[47] From the very beginning the Ukrainian state was defined as a juridical and territorial—rather than an ethnic—identity, and both the Ukrainophones and the Russophones have been recognized as its citizens. A civic—rather than an ethnic or a linguistic—definition of citizenship is broadly recognized in Ukraine, and no serious political force questions it.

Equal political rights, however, do not necessarily guarantee cultural-linguistic equality for all of its citizens. The legacy of colonialism still makes Ukrainophone Ukrainians second-class citizens: The low social status of their language, as well as of villages where they mostly live or originate from, contributes greatly to their social inferiority vis-à-vis the dominant Russophones. Certainly no minority would agree with this status, and especially not a minority that feels it lives on its own historical territory and has no other place to cherish its language and culture. Thus, some very careful and well-thought-out measures should be implemented in order to put an end to the 'linguistic apartheid' in the cities of eastern Ukraine, to hamper

Russification, and to ensure a real (not just formal, as now) opportunity for the Ukrainophones to use their language in all possible spheres of public life.

Of course, this subtle and delicate problem cannot be resolved by merely administrative measures. Centuries-old Ukrainophobia (or, more precisely, Ukrainophonophobia), still promoted by the local nomenklatura, makes any affirmative action in the cities of eastern Ukraine extremely suspicious and often hostile in the eyes of the predominantly Russophone population. (Arel, who was then at the Harriman Institute and who interviewed some politicians in Donets'k in 1993, confirmed that "several of them expressed hostility to the presence of the one and only Ukrainian-language school in Donets'k," a city of 1.1 million inhabitants).[48] Unfortunately, this Ukrainophonophobia is a prevalent attitude not only among some politicians and not only in Donets'k. Apparently all these state-run affirmative actions should be preceded and supported by a well-considered explanatory campaign, with the agreement and help of the most prominent Russophones (politicians, professionals, cultural figures), whose favorable attitude is absolutely necessary.

The sphere of education should be a prime concern of the democrats, since the future citizens of a democratic country are formed by this sphere. As some sociological research has shown, there is wide agreement in Ukrainian society that study of the Ukrainian language (as a second if not the first language) in schools should be mandatory; the research has also shown rather favorable attitudes toward Ukrainian as the language of instruction. Many Russophones who oppose any Ukrainianization of their own lives, prove to be much more tolerant and flexible with regard to the Ukrainianization of their children's lives.[49] But, of course, however important the language of instruction might seem to be, much more important should be its content and quality.

The independent mass media is another special concern for Ukrainians. Hardly any civil society can exist without an influential free press, and hardly any nation can be consolidated without an national information network. In Ukraine, however, national television is still inferior to Russian public television, and national newspapers are still less popular than Russian-based and, ironically, local publications. The only Ukrainian newspaper that has a daily circulation of half a million is the parliamentary *Holos Ukrainy,* but it still reaches only 7.8 percent of Ukrainian citizens.[50] And again, the language of the national media should be of secondary importance, while the major concern should be their content, quality, and competitiveness with those from Russia.

Western political, economic, and/or technical support is absolutely necessary for all these strategies to be implemented. Ukraine deserves much attention not only as a potential buffer, and counterbalance of an unpredictable Russia, but also as an exemplary state where political mobilization can be achieved by civic solidarity rather than by ethnic nationalism and where the emergence of civil society precedes—rather than follows—national emancipation.

Notes

1. Andrew Sullivan, "Democracy's Discontent," *The New York Times Book Review,* 19 May 1996.

2. Ken Jowitt, "Our Republic of Fear," *The Times Literary Supplement,* 10 February 1995.

3. Anne Applebaum, "Nice Guys Finish Last," *The Freedom Review,* vol. 27, no. 1 (January–February 1996), p. 30. Six years ago, amidst the general euphoria in the West over the seeming collapse of communism, the restraints had been shown rather implicitly; the general tone was that "events in Eastern Europe seem too pat, maybe even too good, to be true." See Ellen Frankel Paul, "Introduction," in E.F. Paul, ed., *Totalitarianism at the Crossroads* (New Brunswick and London: Transaction Books, 1990), p. 4.

4. Risto Alapuro, "Civil Society in Russia?" in Jyrki Iivonen, ed., *The Future of the Nation State in Europe* (Aldershot and Brookfield: Edward Elgar, 1993), p. 194.

5. Vladimir Shlapentokh, *Private and Public Life of the Soviet People: Changing Values in Post-Stalin Russia* (New York: Oxford University Press, 1989), p. 190.

6. Alapuro, "Civil Society in Russia?" p. 198.

7. Alapuro, pp. 213–214. This tendency was noticed by Ernest Gellner as early as 1990: "In the painful revival of civil society, it quickly became obvious that ethnic associations can be revived far more quickly and effectively than any others. The new political parties tend to be relatively small clubs of intellectuals, whereas it is the 'national fronts' which rapidly acquire real and persisting grass roots." See E. Gellner, "Nationalism and Politics in Eastern Europe," *New Left Review,* no. 189 (September–October 1991), p. 133.

8. I have covered this problem in greater detail in "Xenophobia," *News from Ukraine,* nos. 36–37 (1992). See also my article "Vid 'Malorosii' do 'Indoevropy,' " *Politolohichni Chytannia,* no. 2, 1994, pp. 120–122.

9. As quoted by Taras Kuzio in "Ukraine: The Linchpin of Eastern Stability," the *Wall Street Journal,* 11 May 1995.

10. See Mykola Ryabchuk, "Two Ukraines?" *East European Reporter,* vol. 5, no. 4 (July–August 1992).

11. Fear of any conflict, as I will show later in this chapter, is another 'moderating' factor that makes Ukrainian transition evolutionary and nonviolent. Apocalyptic forecasts of Ukraine's future in the Western periodicals have been replaced lately by surprise and attempts to examine the reasons for Ukraine's unexpected stability. See, for example, George Zarycky, "A Resilient People," *The Freedom Review,* vol. 26, no. 6 (November–December 1995); Elizabeth Pond, "Poland Is Not Yugoslavia. Neither Is Ukraine," *The Harriman Review,* vol. 8, no. 2 (July 1995), pp. 1–4; and T. Kuzio, *Ukraine: Back from the Brink,* European Security Study no. 23 (London: Institute for European Defense and Strategic Studies, 1995).

12. E. Gellner, "The Importance of Being Modular," in John A. Hall, ed., *Civil Society: Theory, History, Comparison* (Cambridge: Polity Press, 1995), p. 32.

13. "Yegor Gaidar once said that Russia faced the choice between aspiring to be like

America, or being forced to become like Africa. But Latin America is an option, too: huge gaps between the rich and poor, political violence, massive slums, perennially unstable fiscal and monetary policies" (Applebaum, "Nice Guys Finish Last," p. 27).

14. J.A. Hall, "In Search of Civil Society," in John A. Hall, ed., *Civil Society: Theory, History, Comparison* (Cambridge: Polity Press, 1995), p. 19.

15. Alapuro, "Civil Society in Russia?" p. 200.

16. Ibid., p. 201.

17. Ibid., p. 202.

18. Yuri Pakhomov, "The Postcommunist 'Bourgeoisie' as a Threat to a Civilized Market," *Politychna Dumka,* no. 1, 1995, p. 154. He goes on to say: "First and foremost this is the orgy of criminality which horrifies the world. Second, it is a lack of a constructive basis. And the issue here is not only the absence of desirable conditions and stimuli for a capital inflow to the production sphere and that the upstart 'bourgeois' makes his fortune solely from middle-man activities, commerce, financial speculation, racketeering, and comprador servility to foreign capital. What also matters is that the *nouveau riches* have made their huge fortunes in practically no time from scratch, by plundering the people and redistributing the national wealth and property to their own (and the foreign partners') advantage. Third, it is the unprecedented gap between the upstart *nouveau riches* and the rest of the people. An eight-fold gap in incomes between the richest and poorest 10 percent is considered a danger for society. And in Ukraine this index is already three times higher."

19. Alapuro, "Civil Society in Russia?" p. 202.

20. See Mykhailo A. Molchanov, "Political Culture in Transitions from Authoritarian Rule: The Post-Soviet Case," *The Harriman Review,* vol. 9, nos. 1–2 (Spring 1996), pp. 43–56.

21. Alapuro, "Civil Society in Russia?" p. 199.

22. Charles Tilly, *From Mobilization to Revolution* (Reading: Addison-Wesley, 1978), p. 73.

23. Alapuro, "Civil Society in Russia?" pp. 205–206.

24. For more details, see my articles "Democracy and the So-Called 'Party of Power' in Ukraine," *Politychna Dumka,* no. 3, 1994, pp. 154–60, and "Deshcho pro 'partiyu vlady' ta kryzu democratychnoho rukhu," *Suchasnist,* no. 12 (December 1994), pp. 50–60.

25. Alapuro, "Civil Society in Russia?" p. 208.

26. "The Results of Four Polls Conducted During the 1994 Election Campaign in Ukraine," *A Political Portrait of Ukraine: Bulletin* (Kyiv: Democratic Initiatives Research and Educational Center, 1994), p. 50.

27. Ibid., p. 41.

28. Ibid., p. 2.

29. Ibid., p. 42.

30. Ibid., p. 27.

31. Evhen Golovakha and Natalya Panina, "Public Opinion in the Regions of Ukraine: The Results of a National Poll," *A Political Portrait of Ukraine* (1995), p. 14. The same poll revealed that 32 percent of the respondents did not believe in any means of protest as effective and acceptable enough to take part in it, while 30 percent were not able to answer. Moreover, only 12 percent of respondents believed they would be able to do something if local authorities were to make a decision that infringed upon their interests; only 5.6 percent thought they would be able to resist a similar decision of the Ukrainian government (ibid., p. 13).

32. *A Political Portrait of Ukraine* (1994), p. 41.

33. For a detailed analysis of this phenomenon, see E. Golovakha, "Osoblyvosti

politychnoi svidomosti: ambivalentnist suspilstva ta osobystosti," *Politolohichni chytannia,* no. 1, 1992, pp. 24–39.

34. As far back as 1989, John Gray predicted that after perestroika we should expect "not the reconstitution of civil society, but Ottomanization—the process of decline, corruption, and the waxing of the institutions of the parallel economy that characterized the era of stagnation in the Soviet Union, but in a context of worsening economic conditions for the entire bloc." His major assumption was that "important elements of civil society must remain intact if the transition to a full civil society is to be achieved." Since Soviet totalitarianism had been profoundly hostile to Western civil societies, it was to be succeeded "only by authoritarianism or chaos—or, most likely, a mixture of the two." This gloomy view was supported also by the firm belief that "the task of reforming a Communist economy confronts problems that are in most cases insoluble," and that few states of the Soviet bloc could fulfill "the first condition of a stable post-totalitarianism, which is a stable market economy." See John Gray, "Totalitarianism, Reform, and Civil Society," in E.F. Paul, ed., *Totalitarianism at the Crossroads* (New Brunswick and London: Transaction Books, 1990), pp. 134–135.

35. When asked, "What impact would it have on your decision to vote for a candidate if he advocates the idea of Ukrainian nationalism?" only 13 percent of the respondents defined the impact as positive, while 67 percent felt a negative attitude toward such a candidate (*A Political Portrait of Ukraine* [1994], p. 3). In political terms it meant that 19 to 20 percent of the respondents would vote for nationalist-democratic candidates (i.e., moderate nationalists), and only 1 to 4 percent supported radical nationalists (ibid., pp. 31, 34). The 1994 parliamentary elections confirmed the results of this poll quite closely. As sociologists summarized it, "In Ukraine the main problem is not one of nationalism but of mutual imposition of the fields of economic, social, cultural, and political heterogenity" (Svitlana Oksamytna and Serhiy Makeev, "Sociological Aspects of the Political Geography of Ukraine," *A Political Portrait of Ukraine* [1995], p. 6).

36. This figure nearly coincides with the result of a recent opinion poll in which 34.9 percent of the respondents claimed Russian as their native language. It coincides also with the number of respondents who claim to speak only Russian in their families (32.7 percent). Yet, the number of Ukrainophones is rather unclear: while 62.6 percent of the respondents claim their native language to be Ukrainian, only 37 percent use it in their families; another 29.6 percent claim to speak both languages, "depending on circumstances."

37. See, for example, Valeri Khmelko and Dominique Arel, "The Russian Factor and Territorial Polarization in Ukraine," *The Harriman Review,* vol. 9, nos. 1–2 (Spring 1996), pp. 81–91.

38. Ibid., p. 7. The figure, by the way, coincides proximately with the number of the respondents who claim to speak both Ukrainian and Russian, "depending on circumstances" (29.6 percent; see note 36). In practice, however, it means that they speak mostly Russian because "circumstances" in heavily Russified urban centers are neither supportive of nor friendly toward Ukrainian-speakers. As Western scholars and politicians have recognized long since, formal equality does not mean de facto equality: "The rights of language, education, and culture are really group rights, requiring social institutions for their implementation and realization" (Oscar I. Janowsky, *Nationalities and National Minorities* [New York: Macmillan, 1945], p. 132).

39. Khmelko and Arel ("The Russian Factor") express, in fact, the same reservation: "The convenience that some people felt in using Russian for the interviews was of a social nature" (for example, a respondent felt that it was more suitable to use Russian to discuss public matters).

40. This figure coincides with the number of votes (45.5 percent) received by Kravchuk during the 1994 presidential elections. His rival, Kuchma, won 51.1 percent—

a figure that probably coincides with the number of Russophones in Ukraine. What makes this rough extrapolation possible is the fact that, during the election campaign, Kuchma represented himself as a 'protector' of the Russophones, and his major slogans were "Integration with Russia" and "Russian as the second state language in Ukraine." Meanwhile, Kravchuk represented himself as a firm defender of Ukrainian sovereignty and strove to transform elections in one more, de facto, referendum on independence. (See Kuzio, *Back from the Brink.*)

41. "The Russians have been such privileged immigrants, that any nationally-minded government in Kyiv is bound to try to redress the balance by restoring state support for Ukrainian language, culture and education, thus provoking easily manipulable fears of Ukrainianization, whether justified or not." All these measures, so far, "offered little practical threat to Russian linguistic dominance" (T. Kuzio, *Ukraine: The Unfinished Revolution,* European Security Study no. 16 [London: Institute for European Defense and Strategic Studies, 1992], p. 9).

42. "By nationality, 77.2 percent of dissidents were Ukrainian, 0.5 percent were Russians, 9.9 percent belonged to other nationalities (mostly Jews and Crimean Tatars) and the nationality of 12.4 percent of our total sample of 942 was impossible to determine. Bearing in mind that almost 20 percent of the total population in the republic was Russian, and their representation in the urban population was higher, Russians were clearly under-represented among dissidents" (Bohdan Krawchenko, *Social Change and National Consciousness in Twentieth-Century Ukraine* [New York: St. Martin's Press, 1985], p. 251).

43. For a more detailed elaboration of this problem, see my article "Civil Society and National Emancipation: The Ukrainian Case," in Zbigniew Rau, ed., *The Reemergence of Civil Society in Eastern Europe and the Soviet Union* (Boulder, San Francisco, Oxford: Westview Press, 1991), pp. 95–112.

44. *A Political Portrait of Ukraine* (1994), p. 6. The nationwide opinion poll held in Ukraine on the eve of the presidential elections in Russia appeared no less revealing. Again, nearly half of Ukrainian respondents could not imagine themselves taking part in these Russian elections or did not want to answer. But of the rest, 12 percent would have voted for Yeltsin, 8 percent for Yavlinsky, 7 percent for Fedorov, 6 percent for Lebed, and 5 percent for Gorbachev. Ziuganov has the support of 11 percent of Ukrainian citizens, while Zhirinovsky would run the worst, with only 4 percent support (*Vysokyi Zamok,* 23 May 1996).

45. According to opinion polls, only 34 percent of respondents identify themselves primarily with the Ukrainian population as a whole, while 37 percent identify with the region or city where they live. Still, 17 percent consider themselves Soviet, while 6 percent identify themselves primarily with the population of 'Europe' or the whole world (*A Political Portrait of Ukraine* [1994], p. 19).

46. "The main difference between post-Soviet Ukraine and Russia is that the alliance of communists and nationalists in Ukraine is impossible. . . . Both the history and geography separate them" (Dmitrii Furman, "Ukraina i my," *Svobodnaia mysl',* 1995, no. 1, p. 79). This Russian scholar believes that the election of Kuchma as president in 1994 meant not only a peaceful transition of power from one political elite to another, but also the entering of the Russified south eastern regions into Ukrainian political life, and the eventual identification of the millions of Russophones with the Ukrainian state as their own, not just of the Kyiv literati and L'viv nationalists. He asserts that "moreover the very character of the political blocs that competed during the presidential elections, may create a firm basis for the stable political life. To certain degree, these blocs resemble those of the classical two-party system in America—with the permanent regional bases (Donets'k will be always in opposition to L'viv, and the struggle will be over the 'middle,' ambivalent regions)" (p. 82).

47. This view is shared by most scholars. See, for example, the analysis by Roman Szporluk, "Reflections on Ukraine after 1994: The Dilemmas of Nationhood," *The Harriman Review,* vol. 7, nos. 7–9 (March–May, 1994), pp. 1–10.

48. Personal communication, November 1993.

49. According to Ian Bremmer's survey in L'viv, Kyiv, and Simferopol, 96 percent of the surveyed Russians in Lviv and 91 percent in Kyiv agreed that their children must be fluent in Ukrainian, and even in Simferopol, where Ukrainian had never been taught, 55 percent of the surveyed Russians wanted their children to be fluent in Ukrainian. Also, 54 percent of the surveyed Russians in L'viv and 65 percent in Kyiv would prefer that their children study in Ukrainian schools (i.e., be instructed in Ukrainian). See I. Bremmer, "The Politics of Ethnicity: Russians in the New Ukraine," *Europe-Asia Studies,* vol. 46, no. 2 (April 1994), p. 277.

50. *A Political Portrait of Ukraine* [1994], p. 52.

6

Identity, Language, and Transformation in Eastern Ukraine: A Case Study of Zaporizhzhia

Louise Jackson

This study surveys the current political situation in Zaporizhzhia, a region located in east Ukraine.[1] It is suggested that although the area has a high proportion of Russian speakers, especially in urban areas (see Table 6.1), a strongly 'pro-Russian' political orientation has not evolved in the region, and there has been little resistance to proposed increases in Ukrainian-language education. It is proposed that this is because political/national orientation and cultural identity are not solely determined by language. Although a significant proportion of the population in Zaporizhzhia is Russian-speaking, it might be more helpful to view the region as having a mixed 'Soviet' identity, which includes Russian and Ukrainian elements.[2] That there is a low level of mass political activity in the area, and that the political and economic elites have diverse and fractured interests, are also important factors. In addition, the slow manner in which changes in education have been implemented has been of crucial significance.

This study suggests that national and cultural identity are much more multilayered and dynamic than is often assumed in studies of regional differences in Ukraine. It is argued that language alone does not define a person's identity; rather, in the post-Soviet context identities are much more ambiguous, have many layers, and are constantly being reconstructed. The paper also questions the assumption that Ukraine is neatly divided into east and west along lines of cultural and political allegiances and seeks to understand differences in Ukraine in terms of less static and absolute conceptualizations.

Table 6.1

Zaporizhzhia Oblast: Nationality and Language

Nationality	Population (000)	%	Native Language of Nationality Groups		
			Ukrainian (%)	Russian (%)	Other (%)
Ukrainian	1,308.0	63.1	77.0	23.0	
Russian	664.1	32.0	1.7	98.3	
Bulgarian	34.6	1.7	2.4	49.4	48.0

Source: 1989 Soviet Census

Notes: Total population 2,074,000; urban population 897,500; natural increase −2.8%; as a part of Ukraine population 4.5%, territory 4.1%.

There have been many studies of change in Ukraine on the macro scale, including opinion polls and general surveys, and they have provided us with valuable information about general trends and patterns. However, there is also a need to conduct intensive research on the micro scale. Intensive small-scale research complements the larger-scale studies by shedding light on some of the subtleties within wider processes, and testing the theoretical assumptions upon which they are based.[3]

Regional Cleavages in Ukraine

Recently, attention has been focused upon regional differences in Ukraine.[4] This was especially the case in the wake of the 1994 presidential and parliamentary elections. There was even speculation as to whether Ukraine would survive as a unitary state or split along regional lines.[5] Ukraine does display great regional diversity; however, the significance of such differences and how they should be interpreted is open to debate.

The main differences in Ukraine are ethnic, linguistic, and socioeconomic. Ukraine has a population of 52 million, with an ethnic makeup (according to the 1989 Soviet census) of 73 percent Ukrainian, 22 percent Russian, and 5 percent other.[6] However, these ethnic groups are territorially concentrated, with most Russians in the east and south. For example, in Donets'k 43.6 percent of the population is Russian, in Luhans'k the figure is 44.8 percent, in Zaporizhzhia 32 percent, and in Dnipropetrovs'k 24.3 percent.[7] The 1989 census recorded that 30 percent of the population in Ukraine regarded Russian as its native tongue; this means that around 12 percent of the population who classified themselves as ethnically Ukrainian see Russian as their native tongue. In the east and south this is as high as 25 percent.[8] The actual level of Russian-language use is much higher, and Ukrainian is rarely heard in the major cities. East and south Ukraine are also more urbanized, with oblasts such as Donets'k and Luhans'k having over 80 percent of the population living in urban areas, whereas provinces such as L'viv display levels of around 45 percent.

The differing regional histories and socioeconomic characteristics translate into different political interests. This was most clearly expressed in the presidential elections of June–July 1994. As two authors wrote, "The results show a country deeply split along geographical, historical and linguistic lines."[9] Kravchuk, who stressed that protection of Ukrainian independence was more important than economic issues, won 87.4 percent of the vote in western Ukraine in the final round, and only between 9 and 37 percent in the eastern oblasts (except Mykolaiv). Kuchma put forward a platform of greater attention to the economy, closer integration with the CIS and Russia, and official status for the Russian language. He achieved overwhelming support in the eastern and southern regions of the country, winning 75.6 percent of the vote in the east and 72.5 percent in the south. The voting patterns were taken to indicate that there were strong divisions among Ukrainians about how to define themselves and their identity vis-à-vis Russia and the Russian language.

While undoubtedly there are important differences between the regions of Ukraine, it is a matter of debate as to how they will affect the future of the Ukrainian state and what their wider implications are for the development of Ukrainian society and the Ukrainian nation, both civic and ethnic. It is also a matter of contention as to which factors are the most important, how different factors interact and are interpreted, and how the different regions will develop in the future.

This study suggests that while east-west differences exist, there is also a need to examine subtler differences and processes of change on a smaller scale. 'East' Ukraine is highly varied, and attention tends to focus on the Donbas region. This chapter seeks to suggest that an examination of change in less politically active centers can also shed light on some of the transformations taking place in Ukraine. Indeed, the predictions that Ukraine would split into two have turned out not to be accurate, and it is precisely the existence of less politically charged areas in eastern and central Ukraine that has been a crucial stabilizing factor.[10] This study focuses on change in the Zaporizhzhia region, and seeks to understand processes occurring on the micro scale. By examining regional change at such a level we can begin to conceptualize the nature of wider political and cultural change in Ukraine.

Theoretical Aspects of National Identity

National identity is "the identity of a territorially organized community or . . . a polity."[11] In addition, the term 'national identity' is also used at the individual level to describe the feelings of loyalty and attachment that people have toward the nation and the state.[12]

Recent theories of cultural and national identity have suggested that although identities may appear fixed and permanent, they are continuously being constructed. Writers such as Bhabha have conceptualized the nation as a process of 'cultural narration.' Conceiving of the nation in this way draws attention to the ways in which the nation is continually being reproduced. In addition, rather than viewing the nation as something unproblematic, such theories stress its ambiguity. Although it may appear that the process of the construction of the nation clearly draws boundaries between insiders and outsiders, in reality this is blurred and is continually changing: "The other is never outside or beyond us: it emerges most forcefully within cultural discourse, when we think we speak most intimately and indigenously 'between ourselves.' "[13] Bhabha also stresses that there are always alternative constituencies who give new meanings and different directions to the processes of historical change. Although the narrative of the nation may seem to be about similarity and drawing boundaries, in reality these borders are shifting and national culture is always hybrid, as when it talks about 'us'; it automatically invokes those who are not 'us.' Hence, the idea of the nation is a dynamic process and one that is always being given new meanings and interpretations.

Hall has also drawn attention to the produced nature of national and cultural identities. This does not mean to imply that they do not have real effects and histories, but that: "Cultural identity . . . is not something which already exists, transcending place, time, history and culture. Cultural identities . . . have histories . . . but they undergo constant transformation."[14] Thus, Hall also moves away from the idea that identities are fixed, with a definite beginning and straight, defined trajectories. He stresses that similarity and difference, continuity and rupture can coexist and are a part of each other.

Although postmodernist accounts have been criticized for their highly theoretical and abstract nature, they can offer useful insights that can aid our understanding of the processes occurring in the former USSR. While we need to be aware of the problems with such conceptualizations, attention to the dynamic nature of national identity, and the coexistence permanence and change, can help us to approach questions of identity and regional difference in Ukraine in a new and useful way. It allows us to explore the attempted nation-building process and reactions to it, not in terms of fixed groups who react in predetermined ways, but in terms of evolving processes, responses, and identities.

Zaporizhzhia: A Case Study

The geographical location and historical development of Zaporizhzhia are crucial influences on present-day processes. Until the eighteenth century the area was relatively uninhabited, as the original Slavic inhabitants had been driven out due to constant Tartar attacks. In the fifteenth and sixteenth centuries Cossacks set up fortresses in the area, particularly on the island of Khortitsa. A town grew up at the site of present-day Zaporizhzhia at the end of the 1770s, linked to the establishment here of a fortress called Alexandrovsk. After the defeat of the Crimean khanate in 1783, the fortress lost its military importance and became a trading post. The town's name was changed to Zaporizhzhia in 1921.

The main growth of the town came with the construction of the Dniprohes dam from 1927. The dam was ordered by Soviet leader Vladimir Lenin in 1921 in order to supply power to the nearby regions. With the construction of the dam a whole industrial complex was built in Zaporizhzhia, which included aluminum enterprises as well as steel, coke-by-product, ferroalloy, and refractory materials plants. A transformer complex was constructed in 1949, as were high-voltage equipment plants and cable plants. Car and aircraft engine production was also established in the city. Zaporizhzhia was devastated by the Second World War and had to be rebuilt, which led to the influx of around 50,000 workers from throughout the USSR. The population increased by three times after 1940, reaching 900,000 in 1989. Zaporizhzhia was an important Soviet city, accounting for half of all the USSR's stainless and ball-bearing steel, a third of the cold rolled sheets, and half of all transformers. It was the most important producer of the Zaporozhets car, titanium, aluminum, and ferroalloys.

The city of Zaporizhzhia therefore is basically a Soviet creation. The area's historical development has two important implications: the ethnic mixture of the population, and the highly industrial character of the city. The first factor is reflected in Zaporizhzhia's present-day ethnic composition, as the settlement here of people from throughout the Soviet Union means that it has a high concentration of national minorities, as is shown in Table 6.1 (page 100).

It has been suggested that it is helpful to view the region as having a mixed identity, which contains Russian and Ukrainian elements.[15] This has important implications for the political and cultural development of the region. The geographical location of the region is also significant. Unlike regions such as the Donbas, Zaporizhzhia is not on the border of Ukraine.[16] In addition, the region's Cossack heritage means that its the rest of status as part of Ukraine is relatively unquestionable. The debate is more about what *kind* of a Ukraine it should be a part of. This question involves what kind of state Ukraine will evolve into in terms of its relationship with other countries, what kind of economy and political system it will create, and the official status accorded to its various languages and regions.

Political Activity in Zaporizhzhia

Zaporizhzhia is characterized by a low level of mass political activity. Political parties, which are the main potential vehicle for public participation in political activity, are extremely small and still not fully formed.[17] The main political power in the region is still in the hands of the former nomenklatura and industrial elite. However, these groups are also fractured and still evolving; they have not formally structured themselves or aligned themselves with any political party. There are fifteen active political parties in Zaporizhzhia,[18]

Active Parties in Zaporizhzhia Oblast
Left-Wing:
  1. Communist Party of Ukraine (CPU)
  2. Socialist Party of Ukraine (SPU)
  3. Peasant Party of Ukraine
  4. Party of Slavic Unity

Center/Liberal:
  5. Party of Labor
  6. Labor Congress of Ukraine (TKU)[19]
  7. Liberal Party of Ukraine (LPU)
  8. The All-Ukrainian Party of the Center for Civic Agreement
  9. Party for the Democratic Revival of Ukraine (PDVU)
  10. Interregional Bloc for Reform

Center-Right:
  11. Rukh (NRU)
  12. Ukrainian Conservative Republican Party (UKRP)
  13. Democratic Party of Ukraine (DPU)
  14. Ukrainian Republican Party (URP)
  15. Congress of Ukrainian Nationalists (KUN)

The largest party at the oblast level in Zaporizhzhia is the Communist Party, with more than 4,000 members. The second largest is the Peasant Party, 2,000 members, followed by the Party of Labour, which has 1,800 members. Of the rest of the parties, the largest is the Socialist Party, with around 600 members. The Liberal Party, Rukh, and the other democratic parties are much smaller and consist of around 20 to 30 members each. All fifteen of the party leaders interviewed except those of the communists, the socialists, and the Party of Slavic Unity claimed that they supported Ukrainian independence in some form. There is no visible, effective pro-Russian lobby in Zaporizhzhia. The Party of Slavic Unity and the Rus' cultural society, which aim to protect Russian culture and promote unity of all the Slavic states, are extremely weak. The Communists are the only strong group expressing support for a union of Ukraine with Russia. However, the Communist Party leader in Zaporizhzhia confided that they would probably not want to enter into a union with Russia unless it was a communist state.[20] Many parties have no clearly defined social base, as they have not adequately outlined their programs and objectives. Therefore, it is difficult for the electorate to understand the differences between them, particularly between the programs of highly similar groups such as the CPU and SPU, and between the centrist parties.

There seems to be two contradictory processes of party development taking place in the region.[21] First, there is a growing tendency for parties to unite and cooperate. For example, the Liberals and Labor Congress work closely together. In addition, the Communist Party, the Socialist Party, and the Party of Labor joined together to form a coalition in the 1994 local and parliamentary elections. However, at the same time there is also a tendency for parties to divide. Thus, although the number of parties has risen, this does not signify that ever-growing numbers of people are joining political parties. Rather, there seems to be a fragmenting of the same group of people into different parties. This process can especially be seen amongst the national democrats in Zaporizhzhia. The URP was initially quite a large organization, but its membership has dwindled as former members have gone on to form other parties, such as UKRP and KUN. Hence, the increase on the number of political parties in Zaporizhzhia should not be taken to signify an increase in popular political activity in the area. Even the Cossacks in Zaporizhzhia were divided between one group loyal to the Ukrainian Orthodox Church—Moscow Patriarchate and the other to the Ukrainian Orthodox Church—Kyiv Patriarchate.

Although the CPU has the largest support, in reality it could be argued that no party has a significant power base. The CPU relies on the older population and memories of the past, rather than having built up a new membership and image, which is why it has a higher membership than other parties.[22] The centrist parties, such as the All-Ukrainian Party for the Center of Civic Agreement, recognized that they had a small power base and a small potential electorate. They based their activity on influencing decision making through personal contacts, rather than seeking mass popular support.[23] The national democrats also have a very low level of support, as they tend to be seen as nationalists rather than as democrats.[24] Soviet propaganda portrayed Ukrainian nationalists as the 'enemies of the people' and 'fascist collaborators.' Such images are extremely difficult to eradicate, and nationalist democratic activists are still subject to verbal abuse in public, although this has declined in recent years.[25] In addition, the national democrats have experienced some degree of conflict and disagreement amongst themselves, so it is difficult for them to present a united front. The low level of mass political activity in regions such as Zaporizhzhia does guarantee stability for the region, but, at the same time, it also means that there is little pressure for change.

The real power in the region still belongs to the former nomenklatura and industrial elite. Although these groups are typically former communists, this does not mean that they follow a procommunist orientation. Their attitude seems to be rather more ambivalent. Hence the celebration of official state holidays and the display of blue and yellow flags coexist, perhaps rather uneasily, with old communist street names and statues. There has been no formal structuralization of the political elite, and the majority of the members of the local legislative and executive bodies are not affiliated with particular parties.

Zaporizhzhia is a highly industrial town, and the industrial elite plays a major role in the political and economic life of the region.[26] In order to appreciate its influence it is important to note that the industrial plants are not just places of work; they also typically provide accommodation and leisure facilities, organize vacations, and offer educational support (although such support has declined recently). Hence, the potential influence that the directors have over their workers is immense. The industrial elite is not simply 'pro-Moscow,' as might be assumed. They do not act as a unified group; rather, their interests are fragmented and depend on the economic orientation of the particular plant.

Where a factory has established a strong export market beyond the CIS (and many companies, such as Zaporizhstal, ZTZ, and Dniprospetsstali, have been highly successful in this), then the directorship is not simply pro-Russian in its political orientation. For such firms the collapse of the USSR has not been an economic blow, and indeed they have increased contacts both in Russia and the rest of the world.[27] However, other plants, particularly those of a military-industrial nature, that formerly relied on Soviet markets, such as Motor Sich and the aluminum plants, have suffered from the collapse of traditional markets and supply routes.[28] Their political interests are correspondingly different from those of the other industries mentioned.

Education Policy

The 1989 Soviet Ukrainian language law granted the Ukrainian language the status of the state's language. It seems likely that at the time this was intended only as a symbolic gesture by the communist elite. The law makes it clear that although the language of the state is to be Ukrainian, beyond this language use is the choice of the individual. There was a distinct lack of progress in the implementation of the law, except in western Ukraine. However, after independence there was a change: Official papers began to be published only in Ukrainian, and in Kyiv the language of government and administration has largely switched to Ukrainian.

The 1989 language law stipulated that Ukrainian must be taught as a second language in all schools and that higher educational institutions were to switch to Ukrainian over a ten-year period. In the autumn of 1992 the Ministry of Education directed that all local education departments should ensure that the proportion of first-graders studying in Ukrainian should correspond with the national composition of the population in each region. In theory school changeover was to correspond to the wishes of the parents. However, the directive seems to assume that parents' wishes will correspond with their ethnicity. Thus, the right to be educated in Russian is guaranteed only for ethnic Russians and not for Russophone Ukrainians. Russophone Ukrainians are therefore not seen as a legitimate linguistic minority, with the right to determine the language of education of their children. Arel has argued that such policies display 'nationalizing tendencies.'[29] Indeed, the stress on Ukrainian-language teaching does seem to indicate that there is an attempt to create some kind of a Ukrainian-speaking 'nation' in Ukraine, beginning with schoolchildren.

But the implementation of the policy was left entirely to bureaucrats. This meant that the number of schoolchildren studying in Ukrainian barely increased in the east and south. Enrollment increased by 5 percent from 1988 to 1993, to 28.1 percent, though there were regional differences—in Dnipropetrovs'k and Mykolaiv it went up by 12 percent, but no increases were registered in the Donbas and the Crimea.[30] One should also take into

Table 6.2

Percentage of Schoolchildren Studying in Ukrainian

	1991–1992	1992–1993	1993–1994	1994–1995
Ukraine	49.3	51.4	54.3	56.5
Kyiv (city)	30.9	41.7	54.7	63.5
Zaporizhzhia	22.7	24.9	27.5	29.7
Donets'k	3.3	3.9	4.9	5.4

Source: Informatsiynyi Biuleten' of the Ukrainian Ministry for National Minorities, Religions and Cults, no. 3 (September 1995), pp. 33–41.

account the financial means allotted to the implementation of such policies. In an interview, Ivan Dziuba, the former minister for culture, stated that although the need to support Ukrainian culture was frequently expressed by other ministers he felt that, in reality he had lacked the funds to fully implement these policies.[31]

The Impact of Education Policies in Zaporizhzhia

In Zaporizhzhia there has been some development of Ukrainian schools, but the process has been very gradual.[32] The information given by the Zaporizhzhia City Department of Education states: "In the city conditions are being created for the provision of the constitutional right of citizens to educate their children in their native language; the network of educational institutions is being brought into conformity with the needs/ demands of the population."[33]

At the beginning of the 1995–1996 educational year in Zaporizhzhia City, there were 33 Ukrainian-language educational institutions (out of a total of 129) and in 29 there were classes with Ukrainian as the language of instruction.[34] A network of Ukrainian-language preschool establishments has been founded. In the 1994–1995 educational year, 22 Ukrainian-language preschool establishments, out of a total of 132, were functioning; besides this, Ukrainian-language groups were created in 63 preschool establishments in the city. Parent preferences about language are taken into consideration by questionnaire surveys, plus parents are represented on the schools' governing bodies.[35] The proportion of pupils studying in Ukrainian has slowly increased in Zaporizhzhia oblast, as can be seen in Table 6.2.

At first sight these figures seem to indicate that change *is* taking place in Zaporizhzhia, although slowly. While some policies arguably may have 'nationalizing' tendencies when they are issued in Kyiv, by the time they actually reach schools in Zaporizhzhia they have become radically diluted. Therefore, we need to examine both documentation in Kyiv and how these policies are being implemented in the localities and in individual schools in order to understand processes of change in education.

In reality, the way that change is taking place in the language of education is highly complex. In an interview, the headmaster of a Ukrainian school stated that there are more children who want to enter this school than there are places.[36] The fact that this is a school that offers English at all levels is likely to be important as a consideration for parents. The fact that higher educational institutions and exams are now increasingly in Ukrainian also means that parents realize that knowledge of the Ukrainian language is important.

The increase in the teaching of Ukrainian language and culture should not be seen as the simple imposition of culture from outside. In an interview with the local educational methodology center it emerged that local teachers are involved in the development of the Ukrainian culture classes, which take on a local character—for example, concentrating on the legends and myths of the Cossacks.[37] It was thought that west Ukraine had its own traditions, different from those in the east. In addition, the schools are helped by local Ukrainian museums, which existed in Soviet times.

It should not be assumed that Russian-speaking parents will automatically be against Ukrainian-language teaching. A survey conducted by the Educational Methodology Center in Zaporizhzhia found that when asked about choice of language for children to study in school, around 50 percent said they would choose both Ukrainian and Russian.[38] It therefore seems that parents see Ukrainian and Russian as having equal significance in their children's education. The survey reported that 80 percent of those questioned did not insist that their children study only in Russian; rather, they wanted both languages, or just Ukrainian.[39] In an interview with seventeen-year-old Russian-speaking students, the students stated that they would like their children to be educated in two languages—Russian and Ukrainian.[40] The students were also not against studying the Ukrainian language themselves. The Ukrainian-language class was in fact popular, as it concentrated on business language, which was felt to be useful. Therefore, the attitude toward language seemed to be very pragmatic.

In interviews with the heads of school and students it became clear that language is not the major issue in Zaporizhzhia. When speaking about the main issues and problems of education, the groups' main concerns seemed to be the quality of teaching and the economic provision for education. In the Russian school, for example, there was felt a need to specialize more and become a gymnasium, with the question of language taking second place to this. In the Ukrainian school, although lessons were in Ukrainian, the informal language of the school was still Russian, and there was no perceived contradiction in this.

The local culture in Zaporizhzhia is not purely 'Russian,' or 'Ukrainian.' We can see this cultural mix in the languages used. In the cities, people speak Russian mixed with Ukrainian words and ideas *(surzhyk)*. Similarly, in the villages Ukrainian is mixed with Russian. It is likely that such mixed and bicultural identities will persist. However, it is possible that identification with some civic form of Ukrainian identity could increase. In addition, it needs to be recognized that in the past people chose to adopt Russian because it offered them the best chances for advancement and was seen as the language of modernization and access to the outside world. It is possible that in this area such pragmatic attitudes could lead people to adopt the Ukrainian language if this is perceived as necessary to gain the most prestigious jobs and access to the outside world.

Conclusions

This study found that there was a lack of organized pro-Russian-language political activity in Zaporizhzhia, even in the face of proposed increases in Ukrainian-language teaching. It has been proposed that this is due to the lack of development of political parties and mass popular political activity, the divided interests of the elite, the mixed cultural character of the city, and the slow way that reforms have been implemented.

One of the main factors seems to be that no real political or cultural pressure was being placed on Russian-speakers. There seemed to be little perception of a threat to the Russian language, as it was the only language heard in the large cities. Even in schools where Ukrainian has become the major language of instruction, Russian is still the dominant language outside the classroom; hence a mixture of languages is used. It is possible that identification with a civic form of Ukrainian identity could increase in the area, and that the use of the Ukrainian language might increase over time. However, it does need to be stressed that at the time of the study there was no strong pressure being placed on people in Zaporizhzhia, as changes in areas such as education were occurring very slowly, allowing people to gradually adapt to change. Were people suddenly faced with extreme pressure, then it is possible that language issues might suddenly take on a crucial significance.

Appendix A6.1

Employment Structure, Zaporizhzhia Oblast (in thousands)

Industry	303.7
Agriculture (of this, state farms)	58.1 (46.1)
Transport	47.4
Building	56.1
Trade	34.7
Catering	12.0
Housing	12.6
Communal economy	21.6
Health	51.9
Education	71.0
Culture	9.1
Art	1.8
Total	757.4

Appendix A6.2

Employment Structure in Industry (town, 1993)

Electrical energy	258
Metallurgy	
Heavy	36,473
Light	14,042
Machine building	109,156
Chemicals	3,695
Timber	1,197
Building materials	6,137
Light industry	3,854
Food	6,177
Microbiology	594
Printing	338
Total	181,894

Source: Zaporozh'skia Oblast' v Tsifrakh (Zaporizhzhia: Ministerstvo Statistiki Ukraini, Zaporozh'skoe Oblastnoe Upravlenie Statistiki, 1994).

Notes

The research for this chapter was conducted with support from an Economic and Social Research Council Research Studentship Award (R00429334168), which the author acknowledges with thanks.

1. At the crudest level Ukraine can be seen as divided into two halves roughly along the line of the Dnipro River. This division can also be seen reflected in the results of the second round of the 1994 presidential elections. There is much debate as to how accu-

rate such divisions are, and even within small regional areas relatively major differences can be observed.

2. This study will concentrate mainly on the city area of Zaporizhzhia. It is appreciated that there are crucial differences between the urban and rural areas of the oblast.

3. See Hilary Pilkington, *Russia's Youth and Its Culture* (London: Routledge, 1994).

4. For example, see Dominique Arel and Andrew Wilson, "The Ukrainian Parliamentary Elections," *RFE/RL Research Report,* vol. 3, no. 26 (1 July 1994); D. Arel and A. Wilson, "Ukraine under Kuchma: Back to Eurasia?" *RFE/RL Research Report,* vol. 3, no. 32 (19 August 1994); D. Arel, "Ukraine: The Temptation of the Nationalizing State," in Vladimir Tismaneau, ed., *Political Culture and Civil Society in Russia and the New States of Eurasia, The International Politics of Eurasia,* Volume 7 (Armonk, NY: M.E. Sharpe, 1995) pp. 157–188; and Sven Holdar, "Torn between East and West: The Regional Factor in Ukrainian Politics," *Post Soviet Geography,* vol. 36, no. 2 (February 1995), pp. 112–132.

5. For example, see "Ukraine—The Birth and Possible Death of a Country," *The Economist,* 7 May 1994.

6. Roman Solchanyk, "The Politics of State Building: Center-Periphery Relations in Post-Soviet Ukraine," *Europe-Asia Studies,* vol. 46, no. 1 (January–February 1994), pp. 47–68.

7. One should approach this census data with caution, however, as Alexander Motyl has suggested. It is likely that the number of Russians recorded in the census is higher than the real proportion of the population which sees itself as Russian, due to the frequent association of Russianness with Soviet identity in the USSR. Also, Ukraine had a high proportion of mixed marriages, and this factor of mixed parentage is obscured by the data. See Alexander J. Motyl, *Dilemmas of Independence: Ukraine after Totalitarianism* (New York: Council on Foreign Relations, 1993).

8. Taras Kuzio and Andrew Wilson, *Ukraine: Perestroika to Independence* (London: Macmillan; New York: St. Martin's Press; Edmonton: Canadian Institute for Canadian Studies, 1994).

9. Arel and Wilson, "Ukraine under Kuchma: Back to Eurasia?"

10. Interview with Mykola Riabchouk, Kyiv, September 1996.

11. Bhikhu Parekh, "The Concept of National Identity," *New Community,* vol. 21, no. 2 (April 1995), p. 225.

12. For a fuller analysis, see Homi Bhabha, *Nation and Narration* (London: Routledge, 1990); B. Parekh, "The Concept of National Identity," *New Community,* vol. 21, no. 2 (April 1995), pp. 255–268; and Anthony D. Smith, *National Identity* (London: Penguin, 1991).

13. Bhabha, *Nation and Narration,* p. 4.

14. Stuart Hall, "Cultural Identity and Diaspora," in Jonathan Rutherford, ed., *Identity, Community, Culture and Difference* (London: Lawrence and Wishart, 1990), p. 225.

15. Interview with a local deputy to the Supreme Soviet, Zaporizhzhia, 21 August 1995.

16. See A. Wilson, "The Donbas between Ukraine and Russia: The Use of History in Political Disputes," *Journal of Contemporary History,* vol. 30, no. 2 (April 1995), pp. 265–289.

17. See Karen Dawisha and Bruce Parrot, *Russia and the New States of Eurasia: The Politics of Upheaval* (Cambridge: Cambridge University Press, 1994).

18. Interview with a consultant for political parties and movements from Zaporizhzhia Oblast Council, Zaporizhzhia, August 1995. The definition of 'active' parties was reached on the basis of information supplied by Zaporizhzhia Oblast authorities.

All fifteen leaders of the active political parties were interviewed in 1995; in addition, where possible, the author also attended any meetings and demonstrations held during her period of fieldwork in the city.

19. The Labor Congress of Ukraine united with the Party for Democratic Revival and New Ukraine in February 1996 to form the People's Democratic Party.

20. Interview conducted by the author in Zaporizhzhia, 26 August 1995.

21. Interview with a consultant for political parties and movements from Zaporizhzhia Oblast Council, Zaporizhzhia, August 1995.

22. Interview with a journalist in the politics department at *Zaporiz'ka Pravda,* Zaporizhzhia, August 1995.

23. Interview with leader of the Party for the Center of Civic Agreement, Zaporizhzhia, August 1995.

24. Interview with Mykola Riabchouk, Kyiv, September 1995.

25. Interview with the president of the local Prosvita organization, Zaporizhzhia, September 1995.

26. See appendices.

27. Interview with a representative from *Zaporizhstal,* Zaporizhzhia, August 1995.

28. Mar'yana Chorna, "Tykha Hryznya v Zaporiz'kykh Plavnyakh," *Demos,* no. 8, 1995, pp. 14–21.

29. Arel, "The Temptation of the Nationalizing State."

30. Ibid.

31. Interview conducted by the author, Kyiv, October 1995.

32. In order to explore changes that might be occurring in the educational sphere, the head of the education department in the city and staff at the local Educational Methodology Center (which is responsible for studying parental attitudes and recommending how policy should be implemented) were interviewed. Local schools, Russian and Ukrainian, were visited, and interviews were conducted with the heads, teachers, and some pupils. In addition, the study was also interested in life beyond the classroom, and in the corridors and staff rooms, and a considerable amount of time was spent in a local school participating in daily life.

33. *Informatsiya,* Zaporizhzhia Department of Education document, 6 June 1995.

34. *Dovidka,* Zaporizhzhia Department of Education document, 14 August 1995.

35. Interview at the Educational Methodological Center in Zaporizhzhia, 7 September 1995.

36. The interview was conducted by the author at a Ukrainian school in Zaporizhzhia in September 1995; school number withheld to respect confidentiality.

37. Interview at the Educational Methodological Center in Zaporizhzhia, 7 September 1995.

38. This survey was conducted by the Scientific Methodological Center's Informational Sociological Laboratory in the Zaporizhzhia City Education Department. The number of respondents was 119, at kindergartens numbers 219 and 164. In the same survey, 67 percent of respondents chose to describe themselves as Ukrainian; 30 percent discribed themselves as Russian, and 3 percent were other. However, 93 percent had been born in Ukraine and only 7 percent in other former Soviet republics.

39. General support for Ukrainian-language teaching for children amongst Russian speakers was also found in Bremmer's 1994 questionnaire study of Ukraine. See Ian Bremmer, "The Politics of Ethnicity: Russians in the New Ukraine," *Europe-Asia Studies,* vol. 46, no. 2 (March 1994), pp. 261–283.

40. This was an interview conducted by the researcher with twelve students at a higher education college in Zaporizhzhia. The interview took place in an informal classroom environment on 18 September 1995.

Politics and Civil Society

Introduction

Marko Bojcun

The concept of civil society, drawn essentially from the historical experience of Western democracies, has several interpretations that are useful for the analysis of Ukrainian society and its engagement with the state. 'Civil society' refers to a space of autonomous citizens' activity that has arisen (again) in Ukraine only in the past decade. It refers to society's self-organization and its progressive liberation from the state as the mediator of all social relations. More pertinent with respect to democratic politics is the idea of civil society as a process of aggregation and articulation of societal interests by citizens' groups with the specific aim of influencing public policy, both in the time between elections to public office and during election campaigns. The development of Ukrainian civil society in this last sense is in a relatively infant state, yet it already contains some attributes of Western civil societies, such as a democratic constitution, political parties, and competitive elections.

But can one readily apply the concept to contemporary Ukraine? In the Western experience a strong civil society presupposes a developed state and an integrated national community, and few would contend that Ukraine has either.

Ukraine inherited an incomplete state structure five years ago, an administrative arm of the complete Soviet state that was woefully inadequate for its independent statehood. Moreover, the subjective unification of Ukraine's citizens into a common national identity remains an unfinished historical process. The regional, ethnic, religious, and other subnational and prenational identities have yet to be 'digested' and transcended by modern Ukrainian nationhood.

Therefore, we apply these concepts of civil society, state, and national identity with some caution, knowing they denote interrelated phenomena in the West that have matured after two centuries of capitalist economic development, the consolidation of bourgeois states, and the achievement of democratic rights by their subjects. Ukraine's historical experience has been different from that of Western Europe. And we cannot readily assume that its future evolution will or even can replicate the Western pattern.

Kataryna Wolczuk's contribution (Chapter 7) chronicles the preparation of Ukraine's new constitution over the past six years. It provides an insight into the political process at its pinnacle—that is, within central state institutions—during a period of concerted systemic transition. For here we have not only 'the rules of the game' analyzed, but also (and primarily) the contest between the key players over what the rules of their own game will be. The key players—the president and the Verkhovna Rada (the parliament)—have been concerned with more than adopting a blueprint of an effective system of checks and balances of power, defining representative government, proclaiming judicial supremacy, and so on. They have simultaneously been fighting each other for power and for enduring institutional preeminence within the state. What makes this constitutional process even more complex is that the key players do not all agree that Ukraine should have an independent state.

Sarah Birch's contribution (Chapter 8) examines the 1994 parliamentary elections on the basis of regional variations in the structure of competition. Her analysis reveals the disjointed nature and incompleteness of the country's new multiparty system. She shows that the major parties in the 1994 elections were regionally concentrated and so competed directly against each another in only half of the constituencies. On that basis she argues that they could not yet serve an integrative role at a pan-national level.

Birch seeks to relate voting behavior in the 1994 elections to voters' geographic location, ethnicity, age, and education. Like other chapters in this book, hers grapples with the much-disputed significance of ethnicity in the Ukrainian political process. Birch offers other insights about electoral participation and party competition that defy conventional expectations of democratic politics.

How can we understand the political process evolving in Ukraine, in particular the engagement of the citizenry with the state? The chapters in this section attempt to analyze these questions with the tools of Western political science and in the hope that the Ukrainian political system will approach the ideals of Western democracies. However, a strong civil society is but one possibility for the future. There is evidence of an emergent civil society and democratic process, but it must be weighed against strong evidence of an entrenched patron-client system operating in the relational space between the individual citizen and the state. In other words, the public allocation of scarce resources has been somewhat overshadowed by private allocation involving state officials suborned by powerful new business interests.

Furthermore, the still-grave economic situation and its attendant social tensions affecting the overwhelming majority of people prevent us from ruling out altogether an authoritarian-populist solution to the looming crisis. Should it come to pass, all autonomous civic activity would be suppressed and replaced by a direct, mobilized relationship between individual citizens and the leader of the state.

In their various guises, all three kinds of 'workable' political systems—liberal democratic, clientelist, and authoritarian-populist—cohabit in Ukraine's political arena today. It is too soon to say which of them will become the dominant historical tendency.

7

The Politics of Constitution Making in Ukraine

Kataryna Wolczuk

Constitutions serve as an organizing principle in the modern state. They set up the parameters of political relationships by delineating the boundaries of authority between institutional actors, citizens, and the state. Constitutions define means of peaceful, structured conflict resolution and provide conditions for accountability, under which those decision makers that have not been elected by universal suffrage should be accountable to those that have been—an indispensable attribute of representative democracy. It is facilitated by the implementation of the principles of the 'separation of powers' and 'checks and balances,' which, although an ambiguous set of concepts, are recognized as inherently linked to representative democracy.[1]

Constitution-making dragged on in Ukraine for nearly six years, and by 1996 Ukraine remained the only Soviet successor state without a new post-Soviet constitution.[2] The process was marked by long periods of deadlock and overall fitful progress until 1995. However, along with apathetic constitution making, the simultaneous revision of the Soviet-era constitution was taking place in order to adjust it to the needs of an independent state. This revision was an outcome of the juxtaposition of the interests of institutions, elites, personalities, and—to a much lesser extent—the political parties and groupings. Furthermore, the amendments made to the old constitution had a direct bearing on the drafting of the new constitution, which closely mirrored the shifting political landscape. The constitution was finally adopted in June 1996, and, like all previous drafts, was an outgrowth of the temporary configuration of forces at that time.

As a result, in Ukraine, as indeed in all postcommunist states, constitution making has been highly politicized in that political actors negotiated the rules while 'playing the game,' which Elster neatly alluded to as "rebuilding the boat in the open sea."[3] Ukraine illustrated the perils of such an approach extremely well. The presidency was the main driving force behind constitution making in its final stages, and the constitution mirrored the 'presidentialization' of Ukraine's polity and reflected President Leonid Kuchma's quest for power.

Furthermore, in post-Soviet republics, constitution making constituted an integral part of the state-building process, something that set it apart from most Central–Eastern European states, where the transformation is concerned more with socioeconomic and political reform. Apart from having an organizing function (establishing the basis for the institutional delineation of authority), a constitution also performs legitimizing and integrating functions in a new state. However, in Ukraine the heterogeneity of the society was projected onto politics through the lack of fundamental agreement on government according to a common set of rules. Conflicting views on the essential principles of the political system meant that the creation of consensus between political actors proved anything but a straightforward task. The troubled constitution-making process exposed the fragile foundation of Ukrainian statehood.

Before I continue with an empirical analysis of constitution making in Ukraine, some theoretical issues need addressing. Whether one holds that the reform of the constitutional framework is an end in itself (a procedural definition of democracy) or the means to achieve socioeconomic democracy, the study of it is the point of explanatory departure for the understanding of the transformation of the state and its relations with society. Analysis of the change of institutional frameworks utilizes the descriptive-inductive method—known as 'contemporary history'—which is about contextual explanation and understanding, not the formulation of laws.[4] Thus, the focus will be not on abstract formal rules and arrangements but rather on the motives for, interests involved in, and circumstances surrounding their formation. It needs also to be pointed out that no theory on constitution making has been developed in general. Comparative studies of the subject are basically nonexistent and the case study approach dominates, as the nature of the constitutional process, which is embedded in the particular history, social divisions, culture, and political circumstances of each country, renders any generalizations extremely difficult. Nevertheless, the case study of constitution making in Ukraine as one of the Soviet successor states provides illuminating insights into the wider dialectics of democratization and state building in the first postindependence years.

Preindependence Developments

Following Russia's steps toward sovereignty and the departure of the Ukrainian communist leader Volodymyr Ivashko to Moscow, on 16 July 1990 the Ukrainian Supreme Council (*Verkhovna Rada*) announced its Declaration of Sovereignty. It was to serve as a basis for the new Ukrainian constitution.* The radicalism of the declaration was surprising given that the democratic opposition—the Narodna Rada (People's Council)—had only 25 percent of the seats. For example, the declaration stated that only following the adoption of the new Ukrainian constitution could the new federal treaty proposed by Mikhail Gorbachev be signed by Ukraine. In practice, however, the constitution-making process formally started in October 1990, when the Supreme Rada resolved to form a Constitutional Commission. The body prepared the 'Concepts of the New Constitution,' which, after fierce debates in parliament, were officially endorsed in June 1991. Most debate centered on the form the government was to take, with Leonid Kravchuk—then the chairman of the Supreme Rada and a prominent candidate for the presidency—favoring an executive presidency and a bicameral parliament; he was backed by a parliamentary majority on the former suggestion but defeated on the latter.[5]

In 1991, however, still before independence, the drafting of the constitution took on an anti-Gorbachev and anticenter character and thereby symbolized the emancipation of national elites rather than expressing the principal concerns of the legislators. But soon the rate of political change exceeded the predictions of even the most farsighted spectators: the aborted coup in Moscow (19–21 August 1991), the proclamation of Ukrainian independence (24 August 1991), the abolition of the Communist Party (30 August 1991), the referendum on Ukrainian independence (1 December 1991) and the Belovezhskaia Pushcha Agreement establishing the Commonwealth of Independent States (8 December 1991). The pace of the breakup of the USSR took Ukrainian elites—including the national democrats of Rukh—by surprise.

Apathetic Constitution Making: 1992–1994

Despite all these changes, the Ukrainian ruling elites did not relinquish power, and instead switched their allegiance from the Communist Party to national liberation. In other words, the communist elites underwent an ideo-

---

*In this chapter the term 'Supreme Council' (Verkhovna Rada) will be used interchangeably with the term 'parliament' or 'legislature.'

logical 'transition to nationalism' prompted by the proreform and anti-communist movement taking place in fact not in Ukraine but in Russia. The Ukrainian 'route to independence' offers clear evidence of what Holmes refers to as the "cultural and structural residue of the communist period," which dictated the (desperately slow) pace of reform.[6] No power base for radical change existed in the country—the Ukrainian SRR just drifted into independence.

While feelings about the communist regime and Soviet influence were made explicit in the Central–Eastern European countries, there was only a limited condemnation of Soviet domination in Ukraine. In the former, constitutions were often drafted as human-rights logbooks, focused on circumventing state prerogatives and protecting citizens against the state. The need for a circumscribed yet well-defined and efficient framework of state was only gradually recognized.[7] Such dilemmas of 'antipolitical' politicians in central-eastern Europe were of little interest to Ukrainian constitution drafters. Of more significance to them were the fundamentals of statehood, that is, the symbolic attributes of the state and, in particular, the form of government.

As in other postcommunist states, however, Ukraine was preoccupied with issues of legality, such as respect for the provisions of the communist constitution, which subsequently became the framework guiding political action. As Elster points out, communist-era constitutions—paradoxically—were given 'life after death.'[8] The Soviet system fell apart, but the fundamental laws it produced—nominal and decorative constitutions serving as a facade for popular sovereignty—became the frameworks for the building of new regimes. On 17 September 1991 the 1978 Ukrainian Soviet Socialist Republic's constitution became the constitution of Ukraine following only minor amendments by the Supreme Rada. Thus, independent Ukraine inherited the institutional infrastructure of the Soviet era, with the institution of the presidency added in July 1991. According to the constitution, the Supreme Rada was the highest state authority, with broad oversight powers, a presidium and chairman performing some higher executive functions, and a prime minister as head of government, naming ministers and other top officials. The Cabinet was the highest executive body, subordinated to the president and accountable to the Supreme Rada. At the local level, the radas (soviets) were representative organs, which in accordance with the principle of Soviet centralism were subordinated to the rada at a higher level.

After the referendum on independence in December 1991, in which over 90 percent voted for independence and over 60 percent elected Leonid Kravchuk as president, it soon became clear that urgent changes to the machinery of government were necessary, not only in terms of running a modern state but also in terms of turning formal independence into a reality; the existing constitution was incapable of either. The resulting power vacuum allowed the president to gradually extend his powers, and following the amendment of the constitution in February 1992, the president was named both the head of state and the chief executive; in addition, he was granted the right to issue decrees having the force of law, to appoint some ministers and top officials, and to form administrative and consultative bodies. Furthermore, in March 1992, in the Law on the President's Representatives, the president was also granted the right to create a centralized vertical structure of presidential prefects equipped with extensive authority in the regions, that is, the right to annul the decisions of the local radas.

In the months following the referendum, the issue of the new constitution was put on the back burner; although important, it was seen as something of a luxury under the circumstances. The first draft prepared by the Constitutional Commission was published for consideration and discussion only in June 1992. It dealt with the president's broader prerogatives as head of state and of the executive branch. Although it proposed a compromise between a presidential and parliamentary systems (with two possible versions: one a unicameral legislature and the other a bicameral legislature), it clearly reflected the wide-ranging prerogatives granted to the president in early 1992.[9]

However, by that time the power of the president was beginning to ebb away. In November 1992 parliament granted Prime Minister Kuchma additional prerogatives to intensify economic reform and simultaneously suspended the corresponding presidential powers. President Kravchuk, by agreeing to the limitation of his powers, in effect disengaged himself from the direct leadership of the executive branch and focused his attention on the mainly representative, international functions. Kravchuk's foreign visits were used as part of his nation-building policies to project Ukraine onto the international arena.

Quite apart from that, the undercurrent of a simmering intraelite conflict within the former first echelon of communists elites, by then competing for the top state posts, were increasingly evident. One of its most prominent members—the chairman of the Supreme Rada, Ivan Plyushch—had vested interests in preserving the Soviet-era structure of the radas, the powers of which were challenged by presidential representatives. Plyushch engineered a coalition to dismantle the presidential executive structure in the localities and reendow the radas with their previous power; he claimed that being in principle highly democratic, the "system of radas had to be given a chance."[10] The intention was to use them as a vehicle for his candidacy for the presidency. As part of this strategy, Kravchuk's representatives were first marginalized by parliament's measures and subsequently abolished after the June 1994 local elections.

The new constitutional draft prepared in 1993, after nationwide discussion, reflected both the elites' reduced trust in Kravchuk's leadership skills and the presidential ambitions of Plyushch. It foresaw a form of government based on the 'principle of a division of powers' combined with the 'principle of unity'; it also endorsed the superiority of the bicameral legislature *(vse-narodna rada)* over the executive branch and a more limited—symbolic and representative—role for the president as the head of state.[11] Up till this point, 'pure' constitution making lagged behind real-life developments, which basically dictated the content of each subsequent draft.

Nevertheless, the amended 1993 draft was never tabled in parliament. In the summer of 1993 a massive miners' strike broke out in the Donbas, orchestrated by regional elites. The main demand was for referenda on confidence in parliament and the president. To defuse the tension, early presidential and parliamentary elections were opted for in the hope of averting a crisis of government. Under such circumstances, the Constitutional Commission liquidated itself in the autumn of 1993, and work was halted until the elections in 1994.

In Ukraine, the window of opportunity provided by the state of confusion would have facilitated the early ratification of a new constitution in 1992. The euphoria of international recognition and the pressure to attain international standards (e.g., through having a constitution—a tangible attribute of a new state) was accompanied by relative indifference to and ignorance of the importance of such a document. Instead of focusing their effort on that goal immediately after the referendum on independence, the political forces united behind the populist slogans of national liberation (with the leftist forces still keeping a low profile). Attention was directed at symbolic manifestations of nationhood rather than the erection of an institutional infrastructure.

By autumn 1992, however, the opportunity to create a consensus was gone as rifts began to emerge not only between Ukraine's left and right wings (proreform, pro-Western versus antireform, antinational, pro-Russian), but also on a more personal level between the president and the chairman of parliament. The amorphous mass of deputies underwent some ideological crystallization (and polarization) as the left consolidated their position, capitalizing on the catastrophic economic performance of the young state. By the spring of 1993 the left commanded enough votes to block amendments to the existing constitution, which required a two-thirds vote of parliament. The idea of a constitutional assembly—a purpose-made body with exclusive responsibility for constitution drafting—enjoyed little support. The Ukrainian legislators' reluctance to relinquish control over constitution making is characteristic of all postcommunist states, none of which opted for a constitutional assembly.

At the same time, the 1978 Soviet constitution was not sufficient for the needs of an independent state, which was evidenced by the fact that between 1991 and 1995 it was amended over 220 times. Effectively, it grew into a register of shifts in the political balance, eventually coming to lack any clarity and consistency. The principle of the 'unity of soviet power' (this could be called Soviet parliamentarism—a very different animal from Western parliamentarism) was interwoven with elements of the 'separation of powers.' This meant that there were three branches of combined legislative-executive power, with overlapping competencies, and each of them could legislate on any issue almost freely: ministers through 'normative acts,' the president through *ukazy* (decrees), and the Supreme Rada through *postanovy* (resolutions) and *zakony* (laws) ranging from writing off the debts of the coal industry to raising minimum social security payments and setting up children's Christmas holidays. And the fundamental issues remained unaddressed: How is the structure of local government to be determined? To whom is the state administration to be subordinated: parliament, president, or government? What are the relations between the president and the cabinet? Who represents the executive branch before parliament? What is the mechanism of accountability of policy makers? The fact that governments (or at least prime ministers) changed on several occasions did not mean that there was a sanctioned procedure at work. Without dealing with such issues, the whole machinery of the state was driven by an incomprehensible array of political machinations rather than being the result of the application of any recognized rules and procedures. Inevitably this had detrimental repercussions for the economy. Holmes argues that some false starts and trial and error in constitution drafting are desirable, as they provide the opportunity to master the rules, thereby preventing hastily made 'quick-fix' solutions.[12] Looking at the situation of Ukraine at the end of 1993, however, the extremely slow progress made lends credence to Alexis de Tocqueville's belief that in certain circumstances having any constitution is better than drafting a perfect constitution.[13]

Politics of the Constitutional Process: 1994–1995

After the 1994 elections the constitution-making process got under way again. However, the hope that elections would result in decisive leadership capable of turning the country around and end the period of drift proved futile.[14] The national democrats especially badly miscalculated in their hopes for a majority in parliament. More than anything else, the historic polarization of the country came to the fore and regional, linguistic, and cultural cleavages were clearly reflected in the composition of the new parliament. Soon after conflict between the president and the leftist forces (both elected in southern and eastern Ukraine) surfaced in the winter of 1994–1995, something occurred that reduced the likelihood of consensus over the new constitution even more than that in the previous parliament. In order to implement economic reforms, President Kuchma demanded more executive power. In this way he challenged the leftist agenda, which advocated the reincarnation of the Soviet-era system of radas and either the strict recentralization of the economy (favored by Communists) or an ambiguous antimarket direction (pushed by the Socialists), while blaming the 'reforms' (and the resulting economic disaster) on the national democrats and liberals. Aside from its abhorrence of the nationalistic Kravchuk, the left was less than enamored with the institution of the presidency itself, as it did not fit easily with their ideas on *narodovladya* ('popular rule' or 'peoples power').

Nevertheless, the communist grip on the legislature weakened. Centrist deputies—mainly deputies from left-bank constituencies with no or limited ideological affiliation—initially grouped around the leftist bloc, attracted by its sheer size; they also had little in common with the 'nationalistic' right wing. After noting the decisive, pragmatic, and de-ideologized style of Kuchma's presidency, they switched their loyalty and became supportive of the president. In the legislature pro- and antireform blocs gradually emerged, although the balance of power depended on the issue under consideration. The left, with just over one third of the seats, could not easily block ordinary legislation, which required a simple majority, yet could still control the constitutional process. It boiled down to a question of mathematics: The changes to the existing constitution required at least two thirds of the total number of the mandates (450), yet as approximately 50 seats were vacant at the end of 1994 (due to the high turnout and 'winning threshold' in the electoral law), in practice the constitutional majority was close to three fourths of the actual number of members (301 out of 450).

The newly elected president, exasperated with the 1978 constitution, which had clearly outlived its usefulness, was unwilling to work in such an amorphous legal environment. One month after the election Kuchma asserted his authority by issuing two decrees: The first one stated that the president, as the head of the executive branch, directed the activities of the cabinet of ministers, while the second *ukaz* subordinated directly elected heads of radas at oblast and rayon levels to the president and made them personally responsible for the execution of state powers. The *ukazy* indi-

Table 7.1

Breakdown of the Ukrainian Parliament in December 1994

Left	
Communist Party of Ukraine	84
Socialist Party of Ukraine	25
Agrarians of Ukraine	36
Center	
Interegional Block of Reform	25
Unity (Yednist)	25
Center	36
Right	
Rukh	27
Reform	29
Statehood	27
Nonaffiliated	89
Total	403 of 450

Source: Verkhovna Rada Ukrainy: Paradyhmy i Paradoksy (Kyiv: Ukrainska Perspectyva, 1995)

cated that the 1978 constitution had ceased to perform an organizing function and was no longer even nominally respected.

A new Constitutional Commission was formed in October 1994. However, rather than being a parliamentary commission, as was its predecessor, it was a state commission consisting of 'subjects with the right of legislative initiative.' President Kuchma and the new chairman of the Supreme Rada, Oleksandr Moroz, cochaired the 40–member body, consisting of 15 representatives of the Supreme Rada (proportionally representing the parliamentary factions), 15 representatives of the president, 1 representative of the Supreme Rada of Crimea, and 7 members from the judicial branch (the Supreme, Arbitrary, and Constitutional Courts and the Procuracy).[15] The Commission was an all-inclusive forum for political actors (both institutions and partisan groupings), and the contradictory objectives of its members soon came to the fore. As expected, progress on the draft was sluggish (as was the case with the work of the previous Constitutional Commission), so much so that the president decided to take action by proposing a temporary solution to the constitutional crisis, while simultaneously extending his powers: in December 1994 the draft Law on Power, the aim of which was to provide a stopgap constitution until the new one was ready, was tabled in parliament.

A number of considerations underlay this decision. First, its aim was to challenge the July 1994 law On Local Radas of People's Deputies (sponsored by the left wing in parliament), the purpose of which was to revive the system of radas. With the Supreme Rada as the highest state organ, the president would be deprived of any means of controlling the executive structure and thereby would be limited to ceremonial functions. Second, constitutional changes favorable to the presidency would be disguised as an 'ordinary' law. This, of course, would also enable the president to neatly circumvent the two-thirds requirement. Third, it would provide a precedent suggesting that the future constitution ought not to be very different from the Law on Power and thereby provide for a strong executive presidency. At this stage the Constitutional Commission had not yet decided on the form of government and the president's role.[16]

After the first reading in the Supreme Rada, in which the draft was approved for further consideration with the support of the six center and center-right factions, a special conciliatory commission was created to deal with the areas of dispute.[17] The quandary of the center and center-right factions was either to back the strengthening of the proreform president or to guard parliamentary prerogatives. At that point they opted to support the president for the sake of reform of the Soviet-type state structure (especially at the local level, at which reactionary pro-Soviet and antireform forces had become entrenched in eastern Ukraine). However, they still favored a power-sharing system based on a balance between the legislature and a strong, yet accountable, executive branch. Hence, Kuchma's draft was effectively amended and the presidential prerogatives were watered down following some horse trading—for example, articles on the dissolution of parliament and impeachment of the president were dropped.[18]

After a six-month delay, in May 1995, an amended law mustered only a simple majority in its second reading (224 in favor, 93 against, 14 abstentions). And yet, in order for the bill to become operational, the suspension of a number of articles of the 1978 constitution (which required a qualified majority) was necessary. Therefore, the last word on the matter belonged to the leftist faction, which flexed its muscle and voted against the constitutional revision on 30 May 1995. Kuchma decided on a gamble and decreed a referendum on the populace's confidence in both the president and parliament, conscious of his popularity rating in contrast to that of the legislature.[19] Eventually, behind-the-scenes negotiations with the center and center-right wing parliamentarians ended in an extraordinary constitutional agreement *(konstytutsiynyi dohovir)* between parliament and the president on the principles of temporary organization and functioning of state powers and local self-government in Ukraine until the new constitution was ratified. It stipulated a suspension of certain sections of the 1978 constitution and the adoption of the Law on Power for twelve months until the new

Table 7.2

Breakdown of the Ukrainian Parliament in May 1996

Left	
Communist Party of Ukraine	87
Socialist Party of Ukraine	28
Agrarians of Ukraine	25
Center	
Interegional Block of Reform	26
Independents	26
Unity (Yednist)	28
Agrarians for Reforms	25
Center	28
Social Market Choice	26
Right	
Rukh	29
Reform	31
Statehood	29
Nonaffiliated	27
Total	415 of 450

Source: Holos Ukrainy, 31 May 1996.

constitution was sanctioned in a nationwide referendum. The dohovir's trademark was a shift toward a semipresidential system in Ukraine and the abolishment of the soviets at the rayon and oblast levels. Thus, the Communists and some Agrarians and Socialists repudiated its constitutionality, as it was voted in with only a simple majority (240 in favor).

Although the dohovir mitigated the confrontation, it was only a momentary ceasefire in the unfolding conflict over power rather than its resolution. Indeed, the law failed to live up to Kuchma's expectations, being a sketchy piece of legislation with some contradictory provisions, such as those concerning the local administration (Articles 46 and 53). Its lifespan was thus finite, so much so that one of its authors commented that "by October [1995] the konstytutsiynyi dohovir had outlived itself and to rely on it any longer was mistaken."[20]

However, the implications of the dohovir were far-reaching. According to the president's plans, it was to become the basis for the new constitution. These plans contradicted the agenda of Moroz, the chairman of the Supreme Rada. Although he adopted a more 'independent' position, vacillating between communist and social-democratic lines, and signed the dohovir, he nevertheless remained the spokesman of the leftist factions. Moroz stressed the temporary and unbinding nature of the dohovir, totally separate from and in no way contiguous with the new constitution. However, while the one-year deadline mobilized the parliament and the president to some extent, no agreement on the general principles of the new constitution was forthcoming. Instead, the commission took the 1993 draft as its point of departure and started working in sections of the separate chapters. The results were so poor (owing to the lack of overall coherence) that in the summer of 1995 an ad hoc working group of 10 specialists (4 presidential representatives, 4 parliamentary representatives, and 2 representatives of the legal system) was delegated the task and started working under a shroud of secrecy. As a result, events started to acquire momentum. Being more inclined to support the strong presidency, the working group prepared a draft which closely resembled the dohovir. It was then passed to the Constitutional Commission in November 1995, where after some amendments it was ratified by a majority (though not the communists, who voted against it) and handed over as an official draft to parliament in March 1996.[21]

The March 1996 draft constitution, as the president put it, was intended "to end Soviet rule in Ukraine once and forever."[22] It provided for a bicameral legislature *(natsyonalni zbory)* with legislative and budget functions. The upper chamber—the Senate, was more representative of the regions and was given extensive nominative authority, mostly to approve presidential candidates for top state posts.[23] Most important, the draft envisaged a strong executive presidency, which had the right to:

- appoint and dismiss from (most) judicial, military, and state posts (though in some cases only with the approval of the Senate);
- appoint the prime minister and cabinet on approval of the House of Deputies, though he/she may dismiss the prime minister and other ministers unilaterally;
- issue decrees with the power of laws;
- initiate legislation;
- veto parliamentary bills, a decision that could be overruled only by a qualified majority of two thirds of the House of Deputies;
- personally endorse the vertical state administration (by nominating heads of oblast and rayon state administrations);
- dissolve the legislature (if the House of Deputies rejected the program of government twice within sixty days).

Furthermore,

- the legislature could not veto presidential legislative acts (and only the ruling of the Constitutional Court—nominated by the Senate and president—could suspend them); parliament could remove the president only through a complex procedure of impeachment;

- the Cabinet of Ministers, proposed by the prime minister, would have to be approved by the president and would exist for the duration of the president's term in office; it would not have the right of legislative initiative.

When analyzing the text of the draft, one observer sarcastically commented that the system of "checks and balances" in the draft constitution was actually a "system of checks" for parliament and a "system of power" for the president.[24] To this end, Kuchma's upper hand in constitution making was to lead to a "free hand" in the managing of the executive branch through the concentration of legislative and nominative powers under his control. However, the 'ideological' issues—seemingly of little concern to the president—were utilized so as to attract the support of the national democrats. Thus, when examining the role of national symbols (i.e., flag, emblems, and the anthem), initially it was decided that they be determined by ordinary law; yet according to the March 1996 draft the 'nationalistic' symbols (yellow and blue flag, trident, and the anthem "Ukraine Has Not Yet Perished") were to be sanctioned by the constitution.

Toward the New Constitution: Compromise Without Consent

Both the specific provisions and the general spirit of autocratic rule in the draft sparked wide-ranging criticism, not confined to leftist forces, as the programs of most Ukrainian parties were affected. In December 1995 Vyacheslav Chornovil, the leader of rukh, criticized its provisions as "anti-national, anti–organized (political) party and anti-parliamentary," although the March 1996 draft was viewed somewhat more positively.[25] Yet other voices pointed out that it religiously copied the 1993 Russian constitution. Effectively, there was limited enthusiasm for the March 1996 draft across the center-right part of the political spectrum, although there was some relief that at least there was now something to work on.

Nevertheless, the communists were by far the most vocal in their criticism. Amongst other things they objected to:

- the abolition of the structure of radas with the Supreme Rada as the highest authority;
- the bicameral legislature;
- the dominance of the president over the legislature with prerogatives more extensive than in the dohovir;

- inadequate protection of state and collective property, in contrast to that of private property;
- the introduction of capitalist social relations;
- insufficient social guarantees to preserve 'socialist achievements';
- nationalistic state symbols;
- the elevation of the Ukrainian nation (in the form of a national state) and Ukrainian as the sole state language.[26]

By the beginning of 1996 the Communist Party had launched a campaign by collecting three million signatures in support of a referendum on the principles of the new constitution (subsequently ruled illegal by the Minister of Justice). In addition, the communist faction tabled its own draft, the Constitution of the Ukrainian Soviet Socialist Republic (signed by 125 members of parliament), a week after the draft of the Constitutional Commission was passed to parliament.[27] The communist leadership questioned the authority of the Constitutional Commission to draft the constitution because—as they argued—its working group consisted only of propresidential specialists and the communist representatives did not approve the final draft. In the context of the upcoming Russian presidential elections in June 1996, the intention of the left (with the agrarians and some socialists siding with the CPU) was to block the adoption of a new constitution in the hope that if the Russian communists were to come to power it would bolster the communist quest for power in Ukraine.[28]

The desperation of the communists—as it was interpreted—to shape the destiny of Ukraine by returning to the past served only to consolidate the fragmented center and center-right of the political spectrum, which tended to look to the president for support. While Kuchma was above all concerned with a division of power favorable to the presidency, the national democrats' main objective, apart from weakening the antireform leftist bloc, were 'national' issues, such as the state language and symbols, and the 'correct' definition of the population as the 'Ukrainian people' rather than a denationalized 'people of Ukraine.' As regards the political regime, it was made clear that under the circumstances it was more than a matter of ensuring institutional advantages, that is, a presidential or parliamentary system; for them the overarching goal was the protection of the sovereignty of Ukraine. Serhiy Holovatyi, the Minister of Justice, commented on the content of the draft, "These are only details. Because, today, what concerns me the most is the problem of survival. And that very much depends on whether or not Ukraine will have its own constitution before the elections in Russia."[29] The quick ratification of the constitution finally became an uttermost priority.

However, progress was hindered by the lack of an accepted procedure. According to the 1978 constitution, any changes to the fundamental law existed only within the competencies of the Supreme Rada and required a qualified majority. The dohovir, in turn, stated that the text of the draft constitution agreed between the president and parliament would be subject to a referendum. As the meaning of the phrase 'agreed text' was unclear, it was interpreted as having to be first passed in parliament. Soberly recognizing that mustering a two-thirds majority would be nothing short of a miracle, the national democrats began to argue that a straight simple majority in parliament would be sufficient for the president to subject the draft to a referendum. Thus, the president, through the powerful Council of Regions (an advisory body consisting of oblast governors), began to work towards 'raising public awareness on the constitutional question' in the localities.[30] Overall, a corollary of the prevailing legal confusion was that it provided ample opportunity to conduct all sorts of blocking maneuvers.[31]

Still, for many mainly center-left but also some centrist and right-wing deputies, the March 1996 draft necessitated further improvements, especially the chapters on human rights, judiciary, and local government. Overall, the bicameral legislature evoked the most zealous resistance. The national democrats, except for the Ukrainian Republican Party and its Statehood faction, viewed the Senate as a step toward the federalization of Ukraine, and claimed that in a unitary state there was no need for such regional representation. To smooth out the rough edges of the draft, an informal conciliatory group emerged within parliament even before the draft became a subject of discussion in the plenary session on 18 April 1996. And, as the ideologically loaded debates did not bode well for the achievement of consensus, this body was transformed into a formal extraordinary parliamentary commission chaired by Mykhailo Syrota. It represented all center-right factions, with agrarians and socialists as 'observers,' although the communists refused to participate and continued to impede the ratification process.

The extraordinary commission produced an amended version—the so-called Syrota draft constitution at the end of May. Although various tactics were used by all sides to control or hinder the debates, on 4 June 1996 the draft finally underwent its first reading, in which it obtained a simple majority (258 in favor, 106 against, 19 abstentions, 9 did not vote).[32] National democrats were overwhelmed that at least an improved draft could be taken to 'the people' with 'parliamentary blessing.' The chance of a successful passage was perceived as minimal when a day later the Supreme Rada's vote to initiate procedures for dismissal of its chairman, Moroz, for his apparent politically motivated abuse of parliamentary procedures in favor of the leftist bloc failed to get even a simple majority. When two weeks later the debate on the constitution resumed for the second reading the Supreme Rada decided that its rules and procedures *(rekhlament)* would not be binding for debates on the draft any longer; effectively the ratification procedures became improvised and negotiated on the spot.[33] However, the urgent need for progress on the constitution and at least a facade of legality imposed a degree of discipline sufficient to ensure that the mundane debates on each article soon restarted. Their protracted nature resulted in a deep skepticism about the whole endeavor, as even the text of the preamble failed to get a qualified majority vote, and the growing (and indeed well-justified) conviction was that a simple majority in the first reading was the best result the Supreme Rada could deliver.

At that point, the president reemerged as the dominant force in the process of constitution making. Until then, the president had been officially left out of the process, as the parliamentary commission only 'consulted' him, although at the same time he and his administration embarked on intensive behind-the-scenes lobbying, negotiations, promises, and deals. The president's very evident reticence made sense as long as the internal divisions in parliament in effect protected his interests. But gradually he lost patience with the volatile parliament, which amended 'his' March draft. On 25 June 1996 the president announced that, with no prospect of the constitution being adopted by the Supreme Rada, a nationwide referendum would be held in September 1996. Most important, the referendum was to be held on the March draft, which was viewed by all parliamentarians, regardless of their ideological connotations, as inferior to the already approved Syrota draft. The decree invoked mixed feelings even with the national democrats, who themselves had began to urge the president to put the Syrota draft to the referendum.

Although media attention shifted away from the Supreme Rada and focused on the referendum, the decree acted as a catalyst in forging some sense—even if faint—of collective solidarity in parliament as the highest representative body with sole responsibility for the adoption of the constitution. The parliamentarians set to work in a desperate attempt to prove their worthiness and ability to produce results. This determination can at least partly be attributed to the institutional inferiority complex vis-à-vis the president and the other parts of government, which stemmed from the parliament's extremely low rating in public opinion polls. The constitutional debate itself only reinforced the conviction of parliament as little more than an inefficacious 'debating society' characterized by fruitless, emotionally charged polemics. The decision of parliament to carry on was perhaps also motivated by the fact that its fate was at stake, as preterm parliamentary elections after the referendum could not be ruled out. Nevertheless, emotionally arousing questions such as the status of the Russian language or the property regime remained unresolved, although the ad hoc rules created room for truce.

In an atmosphere bordering on hypertension and with deputies on the verge of exhaustion after the all-day and all-night session, on the morning of 28 June 1996 the Syrota draft was put to vote as a whole for its final reading; a qualified majority was reached with 315 in favor, 36 against, 12 abstentions, and 30 nonvoters. This result was met with astonishment by all sides. There is little doubt that the result was a product of a temporary relinquishing of their principal position by some deputies of the leftist bloc rather than the emergence of consensus following the conclusion of a rational and thoughtful debate on contested issues. The ratification of the constitution was immediately interpreted as a triumph of proreform centrists, national democrats, and President Kuchma (none of whom attempted to conceal their joy) and the defeat of the antinational, conservative communist faction. The former succeeded in ratifying the Ukrainian constitution before the decisive second round of the Russian presidential elections, at which stage Yeltsin's victory seemed far from certain.

The constitution provided for a semipresidential system. However, in comparison with the March 1996 draft, presidential power was somewhat circumvented by a switch to unicameralism. The nominative functions of the Senate (envisaged in the March draft) were placed with the Supreme Rada (symbolically, the Soviet-era title was kept). The president was not given the right to dissolve parliament, and his legislative power to issue decrees on economic issues was limited to a period of three years; yet the presidential veto on parliamentary laws, which required a two-thirds majority to be overridden, was continued. The legislature was given the right to vote the government out of office under certain circumstances, while the president could be dismissed only in a complex criminal-legal procedure of impeachment. The right to appoint the Constitutional Court (with the sole competency to interpret the constitution) was given to the president, parliament, and judiciary, each of which was to appoint six judges. The status quo of Crimea was confirmed, as evidenced by its title, Autonomous Republic of Crimea, although Ukraine was designated a unitary country. In addition, of crucial symbolic importance was the confirmation of the national symbols, albeit in a somewhat modified form. The Ukrainian language was sanctioned as the only state language, whereas "Russian and languages of national minorities are entitled to develop freely." Finally, the transitional provisions stipulated that the parliamentary and presidential elections were to be held in 1998 and 1999 respectively, hence affirming that the president and parliament would serve their full terms.

Conclusion

Regardless of the grandiose rhetoric on state building, the institutional delineation of power was not of primary concern in Ukraine during the period 1992–1994. Thus, it could be concluded that, ironically, the institutionalization of the new state slowed down after the referendum on independence and that the Ukrainian state started taking shape only after the 1994 elections. At the same time, shackled by constitutional paralysis since independence, the political process in Ukraine had taken the form of an ongoing crisis.

The slow progress in the constitution-making process can clearly be attributed to the lack of vested interests in the creation of a coherent institutional framework. No political force was both powerful and willing to push the issue forward. And yet unceasing changes to the constitution resulted in a situation in which "no firm distinction has been established between the tools of action and the framework of action."[34]

Nevertheless, by 1996 the somewhat surprising realignment of forces that took place once Kuchma was in power provided am environment more conducive to progress. Although due to its composition, parliament remained weak and fractured, the ideological crevasse running through it was briefly and almost miraculously bridged during the third and final vote on the draft constitution. The ideological cleavages in the Ukrainian polity were modified and finally overcome by the institutional and personal interests of constitution drafters. Undoubtedly, the president's determination to clarify power relations and to strengthen the presidency was a catalyst in pushing the whole process forward.

However, the accumulation of formal powers in the hands of the presidency does not necessarily imply efficient government, as the case of Yeltsin has illustrated. And yet, the semipresidential system that was adopted—due only to a temporary weakness of the leftist bloc, with whom an enduring compromise on this matter was unobtainable—fuels the feelings of defeat and ostracism. As a result, the communists' commitment to the new political rules of the game may be weakened, and this may lead to a prolonged rebellion against the new state. Leftist forces command the support of 30 percent of the electorate, predominantly in Russophone eastern Ukraine and Crimea. Although not homogeneous, the Communist Party of Ukraine remains the biggest and best-organized political party, with a disciplined faction voting virtually unanimously in parliament, all of which is in addition to the considerable power and influence the party still wields in localities.

The manner in which a constitution was adopted in Russia is an illustration of this danger: The dissolution and shelling of parliament, the 54 percent turnout in the referendum and the 58 percent vote in favor (that is, 31 percent of all eligible voters in favor) show that "too few Russian politicians view the constitution as a mutually beneficial pact" and thus have little stake in respecting it.[35] The parallels to Ukraine are thus evident. The long-term participation and consensus of the communist forces, however reactionary, conservative, and obstructive in the process of change, have to be secured if the new constitution is to fulfill its integrative function of binding the new polity by bridging the ideological gap and stimulating political cooperation. However, in contrast to Russia, the predicament in Ukraine is that some of the communists are not just the 'systemic' political opposition but a potential fifth column of Russia's neoimperialist forces, and thus a threat to the sovereignty of the young state.

When the new constitutional framework is adopted, its aim is to serve as a means of resolving underlying conflict. However, as Holmes noted, in the process of its formation "all parties must be assured that 'ultimate values'— the things they care about most—will not be dragged through the mud of contestation. When factions negotiate, they put their differences aside and build on common ground."[36] In other words, the process of constitution making is about conflict and compromise on the understanding that the 'boundaries of disagreement' are respected and not crossed. In Ukraine, however, this process of consensus building through bargaining and the gradual closing down of distance was not available, as it was not just the occasional point that was a source of altercation—ultimately it was the ideological and institutional blueprint of the Ukrainian state that was being contested. The nature of the issue being disputed reflected the fundamental disagreement on the very notion of Ukrainian statehood. The months of intense political struggle preceding the adoption of the constitution gave little hope that the new fundamental law would resolve the underlying conflict; at least the new constitution provides a framework for its structured mediation. In addition, although the constitution is far from perfect, the delineated institutional competencies and functions contribute to the capacity to combat the acute socioeconomic collapse Ukraine confronts.

Finally, Staniszkis has pointed out that "the lack of well-articulated interests in post-communist societies often gives the elites the illusion of a free hand."[37] In Ukraine, the ease with which the old party elites took advantage of the post-Soviet disarray resulted in a deep cynicism and distrust of the politics of self-interested turncoat politicians. This poses problems for the creation of democratic institutions in an alienated society, as the populace is left with the impression that the constitutional process has been hijacked by a coterie of government officials. The continuing facade of Soviet-style public participation and consultation (as, for example, in the case of the 1992 draft constitution) can no longer conceal the growing gap between the ruling elites and the society at large.

Therefore, the broader question emerges of how the process of constitution making and the provisions of the new constitution itself affect the prospects of the 'rule of law' in Ukraine. The constitution is only a point of departure and per se is not sufficient for a viable constitutional order. The latter is modified by cultural, social, and economic as well as political factors, the relative importance of which is a subject of debate. Therefore, it is the mutual dependencies and interactions of political institutions, culture, and socioeconomic background in non-Russian post-Soviet states that will determine the quality and degree of constitutionalism, and that have yet to be explored in further research.

Notes

Research for this chapter was carried out as part of the ESRC-financed project "The Political Economy of New States in Central and Eastern Europe and the Former Soviet Union" (research grant no. R000 23 5650).

1. See, for example, M.J.C. Vile, *Constitutionalism and the Separation of Powers* (Oxford: Clarendon Press, 1967).

2. This chapter is based on interviews with members of parliament, politicians, journalists, and scholars conducted in Kyiv in November 1995 and on an analysis of the Ukrainian central press, *The Ukrainian Weekly,* and official Ukrainian documents.

3. Jon Elster, "Constitution-making in Eastern Europe: Rebuilding the Boat in the Open Sea," *Public Administration,* vol. 71, no. 1/2 (Spring/Summer 1993), pp. 169–217.

4. R.A.W. Rhodes, "The Institutional Approach," in David Marsh and Gerry Stoker, eds., *Theory and Methods in Political Science* (London: Macmillan, 1995), pp. 43–44.

5. Roman Solchanyk, "Ukraine Considers a New Republican Constitution," *Report on the USSR,* vol. 3, no. 23 (7 June 1991).

6. Stephen Holmes, "Conceptions of Democracy in the Draft Constitutions of Post-Communist Countries," in Beverly Crawford, ed., *Market, States and Democracy* (Boulder, CO: Westview Press, 1995), p. 71.

7. Ibid, pp. 77–78.

8. Elster, "Constitution-making in Eastern Europe," p. 171.

9. The draft was published in *Holos Ukrainy,* 17 July 1992.

10. *Holos Ukrainy,* 18 March 1992.

11. *Holos Ukrainy,* 28 September 1993.

12. Holmes, "Conceptions of Democracy," p. 75.

13. Elster, "Constitution-making in Eastern Europe," p. 184.

14. The electoral law adopted in November 1993 was based on the system of plurality, favoring candidates nominated by workers' collectives and groups of voters over those nominated by political parties.

15. *Vidomosti Verkhovnoi Rady Ukrainy,* no. 40 (1994).

16. *East European Constitutional Review,* vol. 4, no. 2 (Spring 1995), p. 33.

17. The numbers were 176 in favor, 135 against, and 30 abstentions (see *Ukrains'ka Perspektyva,* no. 2, 1995).

18. In the original draft the president would have the right to adopt this move if parliament rejected the budget law submitted by the Cabinet of Ministers twice or rejected its program twice.

19. Parliament declared that decision unconstitutional on 1 June 1995 (with only nine votes against) and attempted to block it by refusing to authorize funding to carry it out.

20. Within four months after the signing of the *konstytutsiynyi dohovir* approximately ten deputies requested to remove their signatures from it (interview with Deputy of Supreme Rada Roman Bezsmertnyi in Kyiv, November 1995).

21. It was published in *Uryiadovyi Kuryer,* 21 March 1996.

22. Interview with Kuchma, Ukrainian TV, 24 November 1995.

23. The Senate was to be elected in direct elections. However, the main candidates in direct elections tended to be state administration officials, who, according to the draft, had to be nominated by the president. Thus, as the Senate would be likely to consist of individuals subordinated to the president, it would become a propresidential organ.

24. *Holos Ukrainy,* 3 February 1996.

25. *The Ukrainian Weekly,* 31 December 1995.

26. *Holos Ukrainy,* 26 December 1995.

27. *The Ukrainian Weekly,* 31 March 1996.

28. *The Rukh Insider,* vol. 2, no. 4 (25 March 1996).

29. *The Ukrainian Weekly,* 17 March 1996.

30. *The Ukrainian Weekly,* 5 May 1996.

31. When Moroz—the chairman of the parliament—suggested that a law on the procedure for the adoption of the constitution should be put to parliament, the head of presidential administration replied that the president would veto it. See *Demokratychna Ukraina,* 23 March 1996.

32. The most frequent method to obstruct sessions (known as 'constructive destruction'), used by both leftist and center-right blocs, was the refusal to register, so that a quorum could not be reached.

33. As the draft with comments (approximately a thousand pages) was distributed in parliament only on 18 June, the communists demanded two weeks to review it; the factions of the right accused them of delaying ratification, arguing that the 'bones of contention' were well known to all sides anyway.

34. Holmes, "Conceptions of Democracy," p. 73.

35. Eric Hoffmann, "Challenges to Viable Constitutionalism in Post-Soviet Russia," *The Harriman Review,* vol. 7, no. 4 (November 1994), pp. 46–47.

36. S. Holmes, "Gag Rules or the Politics of Omission," in Jon Elster and Rune Slagstad, eds., *Constitutionalism and Democracy* (Cambridge: Cambridge University Press, 1993), p. 37.

37. Jadwiga Staniszkis, "Main Paradoxes of the Democratic Change in Eastern Europe" in Kazimierz Poznanski, ed., *Constructing Capitalism: The Re-emergence of Civil Society and Liberal Economy* (Boulder, CO: Westview, 1992), p. 181.

8

Party System Formation and Voting Behavior in the Ukrainian Parliamentary Elections of 1994

Sarah Birch

As in many new democracies, electoral politics in Ukraine is characterized first and foremost by geographical heterogeneity. The rapid changes experienced by Ukrainian society in the first years of independence created a situation in which geography came, almost by default, to structure political organization at the mass level. This was undoubtedly made possible by the considerable variations across Ukrainian regions in sociodemographic composition and political history, but it was exacerbated by the dynamics of the transformation process and the institutional structures that were chosen to guide it. In the parliamentary elections of 1994, the distinction between west and east was most striking; nationalist deputies were overwhelmingly elected from the west, whereas the strong Communist contingent in the new parliament hailed primarily from the east. But closer examination reveals that there were notable differences in the voting patterns of other parts of the country as well. The parliament elected in 1994 was only loosely integrated and subject to periodic realignments, and I would argue that this outcome can be largely explained in terms of geographical disjunctions in political party formation and electoral mobilization.

The nature of electoral competition in Ukraine has been strongly determined by the peculiarities of local political organization ever since the first semicompetitive elections to the Soviet Congress of People's Deputies in 1989. In Ukraine's first truly competitive elections in 1990, the umbrella Democratic Bloc managed to field candidates in only about two-fifths of all constituencies.[1] The Bloc was itself a temporary coalition of organizations with different aims, and it was in 'opposition' to an extremely diverse collection of candidates, many of whom were virtually apolitical. For most constituencies, then, the 1994 elections were the first taste of organized party competition.

Yet this is not meant to imply that the structure of competition in 1994 approximated that of elections in Western countries. Commentators invariably remark upon the large *number* of parties active in Ukrainian politics; what they often neglect to mention is that these parties are for the most part regionally concentrated, such that in any given constituency the number represented is much smaller. In one sense this makes for a more 'manageable' structure of competition at the constituency level, but it also means that the party system as a whole is highly fragmented along regional lines.

For this reason the study of the national attributes of Ukrainian electoral behavior is rather problematic; local factors are so influential in determining the context in which that behavior occurs that the analyst faces severe difficulties of comparability. It is perhaps for this reason that the majority of quantitative work that has been done on recent Ukrainian elections has focused on the presidential election of 1994, rather than the parliamentary contests of the same year.[2] These studies have pointed to the importance of two sets of determinants of voting behavior: regional differences and ethnically linked variables such as language. The purpose of this chapter is to build on previous work by constructing a multivariate model of the social determinants of vote choice in the parliamentary elections of 1994, taking into account regional and constituency-level variations in the structure of competition.

It is important to emphasize the incomplete nature of the party system in Ukraine. A common characteristic of new party systems is that they are regionally divided; only gradually do they grow to become uniform structures with nationwide relevance.[3] It is thus not surprising that the Ukrainian party system should be fragmented at this stage. But the Ukrainian party system was also notable in the 1994 elections for the partial nature of its occupation of the terrain of competitive politics. The large number of independent candidates in the race can be accounted for primarily by two factors: the electoral law, which made it more difficult for parties to nominate candidates than for groups of voters or workers to do so, and the fact that the nascent parties had been allowed to incubate for four years in the closed realm of parliamentary politics, giving them little incentive to establish strong grassroots support bases.[4] In the first round of the elections, party candidates gained a majority of the votes in only 205 of 450 constituencies, and the composition of the party palatte varied widely from seat to seat.[5] Any analysis of voting behavior must therefore start by analyzing the peculiarities of the structure of competition that characterized the race in different types of seats.

The Structure of Competition

Four party 'camps' are commonly distinguished in Ukrainian politics: the Left, the Center, the National Democrats, and the Extreme Right. Though members of thirty-two parties contested the first round of the 1994 elections, there were considerable variations in the extent of regional penetration of the different parties. No party contested all constituencies; in fact, the party that came closest, the Communist Party of Ukraine, had members standing in only two thirds of the seats (294 of 450), and the party with the next highest level of penetration, Rukh, managed to field candidates in fewer than half (214). The first column of Table A8.1 in the Appendix (p. 151), gives the number of seats contested by each party. It can be seen from these figures that the majority of parties had extremely low penetration: the median was 22.3 and the average 44.7. If we classify the parties according to the number of candidates they stood, we can distinguish three groups of parties: 'major' parties, defined as those that stood candidates in at least 20 percent of all constituencies (90), 'significant' parties, defined as those which stood candidates in at least 10 percent of constituencies (45), and all the rest.[6] According to these definitions, Ukraine had four 'major' parties in 1994: The Communist Party (KPU), the Socialist Party (SPU), Rukh (NRU), and the Ukrainian Republican Party (URP), as well as five 'significant' parties: the Liberal Party (LPU), the Democratic Party (DemPU), the Party of Democratic Revival (PDVU), the Peasant Party (SelPU), and the Congress of Ukrainian Nationalists (KUN). These nine parties are spread across the political spectrum, but it is clear from Table A8.1 that party support is most concentrated on the Left and least concentrated in the Center.[7]

The regional distribution of party candidates is presented in Table A8.2 in the Appendix (pp. 152–3). These figures show that differences in the party systems of different parts of the country were the result of overlapping distributions of activity on the part of a core group of political organizations. The Communist Party and Rukh are the only parties that qualify as 'major' in all regions, though candidates from these parties stood together in fewer than a third of the seats nationally and in no more than two fifths of the seats in any one region. While these two can be termed national parties, they do not as yet form the basis for a national party system. There is a good deal of overlap in the areas of activity of the other large parties as well: of those classified as 'major' or 'significant' at the national level, all are also so classified in more than one of the five regions, and all the 'major' national parties are 'major' in at least three of these regions. Regional variation in the structure of competition is therefore due primarily to variation in the local prominence of different parties.

If we aggregate up to the level of the ideological party camp, it is possible to view the regional aspect of the structure of competition more clearly. Table A8.3 in the Appendix (p. 154), presents the distribution of seats contested by the different party groups. The Right and the Left clearly have the highest degree of overall penetration, yet they have inverse patterns of geographical distribution. The Left fielded candidates in at least four fifths of all constituencies, with the exception of the west, where it failed even to reach the 50 percent mark. The distribution of Rightist candidates exhibits a more gradual reduction as one moves across the country, from virtually universal coverage in the west to just over half the constituencies in the east. Centrist candidates stood in a solid majority of eastern and southern seats, whereas their presence in the rest of the country was patchier.

These patterns have important consequences for electoral politics in Ukraine. Although the Ukrainian party spectrum is composed of distinct Left, Center, and Right blocs of parties, a minority of voters had a choice from among these three options, while an equal percentage could choose only from among the candidates of one camp. Furthermore, only a bare majority could make the basic choice between left and right. In many cases the most significant axis of competition was between parties from the same camp. It could be said that Ukraine has not one but three party systems. Each macroregion has what might be described as a two-and-a-half-party-camp configuration. In the west the National Democratic parties constitute the dominant group; they vie in the majority of cases with the Extreme Right, with the Left playing a minor role. In the east the Left is the dominant camp, and its main competitor is the Center. In this case the Right is in a subordinate position. It is in the central and southern regions of the country that we find structures of competition most similar to those found in Western countries; here the main axis of competition is between the Left and the Right, with Centrists squeezed in the middle. Yet it is the East and the West that are generally considered to be the most politicized regions, and it is from these regions that the majority of party candidates were elected.

If we compare the geographical penetration of parties with their rates of success, we find that those that fielded candidates in the greatest number of constituencies were also, by and large, those whose electoral support was strongest, both overall and within those constituencies. The correlation between number of seats contested by a party and the total vote share of that party is 0.75; that between the number of seats contested and average vote share per seat contested is 0.68. There are, however, some striking anomalies. The Peasant and the Communist Parties were by far the most 'efficient' at turning candidates into deputies: the ratio of total vote share to number of seats contested was 0.05 for the Peasant Party and 0.04 for the Communists, whereas no other party managed to achieve more than half that level. The Liberal Party, on the other hand, stood seventy-six candidates nationwide, putting it fifth in rank order after the URP, yet it persuaded on average only 4 percent of registered voters in these seats to vote for it. This translated into a mere 0.5 percent in the country as a whole (0.6 percent of those who voted). The regional distribution of support for the seven parties that gained over 1 percent of the national vote can be seen in Table A8.4 in the Appendix (p. 155), along with that for the main party camps. The following sections will consider the ways in which the geography of party organization interacted with the demographics of electoral participation and party support.

The Social Determinants of Electoral Behavior: Hypotheses

Past experience leads to two contradictory hypotheses regarding electoral participation in Ukraine. On the one hand, high rates of turnout are in most countries associated with high levels of education and high socioeconomic status.[8] This can be interpreted as a propensity for those who are more 'cognitively mobilized' to be more politically mobilized as well. But affluence is only one path to political mobilization; the second principal route is institutional affiliation. Membership in political parties and secondary organizations has been found to affect the likelihood with which a person will go to the polls.[9] In most developed countries the residents of rural areas are also more disposed to exercise their franchise.[10] Comparative analysis would thus lead us to speculate that the groups with the highest turnout rates would be rural residents, those with high status, and those most involved in civil society. Given that independent civil society began to develop first in western Ukraine in the late 1980s, and given that many western Ukrainians had previous experience of involvement in party politics during the period of Polish rule between the wars, we should not find it surprising that this region of the country should consistently have exhibited the highest turnout levels since competitive elections were introduced during the final years of perestroika.

But it may be that, for reasons having to do with the Soviet experience, late- and post-Soviet voters will not conform to turnout patterns observed elsewhere. Commenting on the 1989 elections, a group of Soviet geographers remarked that, in Western democracies, "the proportion of the electorate which takes part in elections is the traditional indicator of the level of social activity [of the citizenry]. Here the reverse is true. The more active the population of a region, the lower the degree of participation of electors in elections and the higher the level of absenteeism."[11] Likewise, the Soviet Interview Project found that nonvoting in the USSR was associated with levels of political interest similar to those of voters in Western countries.[12] Not only did voters represent an older-than-average section of the voting-age population, but they also tended to be less educated and more working-class.[13]

The advent of truly competitive elections could have radically altered the determinants of electoral participation in Ukraine, and Ukrainian participation patterns may have come to resemble those observed in Western countries. Yet it could also be that vestiges of Soviet-era habits will linger for some time. A final hypothesis is that the cleavage structure underlying turnout patterns may come to resemble that underlying attitudes toward the new regime, in which case those sections of the electorate hostile to Ukrainian statehood would be reluctant to participate in the new state's political processes.

As far as electoral choice is concerned, the above discussion points to the importance of regional and constituency-level variations in the electoral menu Ukrainian voters faced when they went to the polls in March of 1994. The outcome of the vote in each constituency can thus be expected to be a function of a combination of contextual factors and the political dispositions of the electorate. What factors, in addition to political context, can we expect to be important in influencing vote choice?

Many who analyze post-Soviet politics assume that voters in countries such as Ukraine are motivated in their choice of candidate by individual material interest. There are, however, a number of reasons to doubt the plausibility of this assumption. First, many voters' interests are too various, too ill-defined, and subject to too much uncertainty to be determinate—from either a subjective or an objective point of view. Second, even those voters who are able to determine with a fair degree of confidence where their interests lie are likely to find difficulty in making a connection between those interests and a political party, given the number of parties in the political arena, the vagueness of many of their platforms, and the weakness of information—economizing devices such as party identification or standing voting decisions that are commonly used by voters in established democracies. Finally, there is evidence that Ukrainian voters have little confidence in the efficacy of the representative process as a vehicle for aggregating interests. The perceived and actual lack of parliamentary accountability, combined with the frequent inability of parliament to pursue even those aims upon which it can agree, have discredited the institution in the eyes of the electorate, which is thus not likely to view the voting situation as one in which it is worthwhile or even appropriate to vote on the basis of personal interest. Rather than voting instrumentally, Ukrainian voters are more likely to vote according to group loyalties and perceptions of the common good. Their behavior is, in other words, more likely—for perfectly rational reasons—to approximate the sociopsychological models developed in relation to Western electorates of the 1940s and 1950s than to resemble the rational-choice models of more recent times. It is thus necessary to determine the underlying social divisions that will characterize this behavior.

In the absence of the conditions necessary to facilitate instrumental voting, much of the Ukrainian electorate can be expected to vote according to perceptions of group interest. But because problems associated with party formation have hampered the development of a true party system, candidate-voter relations are characterized by diversity. This diversity is in part a function of idiosyncratic factors associated with local politics; some politicians and party organizations are more successful than others in building clienteles and mobilizing voters through the use of selective incentives. The differential success of these efforts is also in large measure determined by the interaction between regional and sociodemographic cleavages. The relevance of ethnicity to many of the political debates in Ukraine points to ethnic and ethnolinguistic characteristics as strong determinants of vote choice. We might also expect stratification cleavages such as socioeconomic level to be significant. Finally, the importance of factors such as age and urban residence in influencing vote choice in Ukraine in the past suggests that they also played a role in the 1994 elections.[14]

Methodology

The method chosen to test the above hypotheses is statistical analysis of aggregate-level electoral results in conjunction with constituency-level demographic data.[15] Though individual-level survey data would in many respects have provided a more appropriate means of conducting such a test, there are a number of benefits to using aggregate data that make them well suited to the task at hand. First, aggregate data have the advantage of relative completeness, in that they include information on the entire population, in contrast to a small sample, which excludes those unwilling to be interviewed. Second, electoral data represent highly accurate reflections of actual electoral behavior, whereas survey data yield at best respondents' accounts of whether and how they voted. This is especially true as regards respondents' reports of their participation in elections, and, in the Ukrainian case, the reported vote choice of those sectors of the electorate that supported certain alternatives.[16] Third, in order to test the above hypotheses, it is important to determine the factors that differentiate voters and the ways in which these factors interact. Given that some of the factors hypothesized to be significant pertain to relatively small segments of the population—ethnic minorities and nonvoters—it is necessary to employ a method that will enable analysis of the behavior of small groups. This is notoriously difficult when using survey data, because members of such groups tend to compose minute portions of any representative sample. This problem is, of course, compounded when one attempts to analyze the interactions between variables. For the same reason, national samples are problematic when there is reason to believe there is regional variation in voting patterns. Finally, a common problem encountered when using survey data is the 'individualistic fallacy' of neglecting to account for the effects of contextual factors on individual behavior.[17]

A relevant instance of the 'individualistic fallacy' is the isolation of voting behavior from the immediate political environment in which it takes place. Definition of the relevant political environment will vary from country to country and from period to period, depending on the nature of the political system in question, the cleavage structure of the country, and the issues that are electorally salient. In the Ukrainian case, there is reason to believe that an examination of the effects of constituency-level 'political ecology' variables on electoral behavior is crucial to an understanding of electoral outcomes. While constituency-level factors are undoubtedly of some importance in any majoritarian system, they are especially significant in situations of rapid sociopolitical change and a high degree of heterogeneity across constituencies, as has been the case in Ukraine. Support for a given party depends not on the absolute popularity of that party, but on its popularity relative to the alternatives on offer. When the range of alternatives varies greatly from constituency to constituency, the structure of competition within each constituency becomes one of the most important aspects of the decision process.

The main disadvantage of using aggregate-level data pertains to the statistical difficulties that arise in attempting to infer individual-level behavior from models of causal effects at the aggregate level. But with adequate theorization of the model to be estimated and careful specification, the dangers of the so-called ecological fallacy can be minimized.

Analysis

Three types of regression models were constructed to test the hypotheses elaborated above: one for electoral participation, one each for the main camps in the Ukrainian party system, and one each for the four largest parties. These models will be examined in turn.

The role of different demographic characteristics in affecting turnout was modeled using variables representing the following characteristics of the population of each constituency: percentage with higher education, percentage retirement-age residents, and percentage of rural residents. As it was hypothesized that attitudes toward the Ukrainian state might be instrumental in influencing turnout, and statehood is an issue to which ethnicity is highly relevant, ethnic variables were also entered into the equation.[18] Finally, a set of dummy variables was constructed to represent each of Ukraine's five regions, with the Right Bank serving as a baseline against which the others are compared. Table A8.5 in the Appendix (p. 156), presents the resulting equation.

The magnitude and the direction of the coefficients in this equation suggest that older, rural people in Ukraine vote with greatest frequency, as do residents of the west; fewer non-Ukrainians and highly educated citizens appear to vote, and the same is evidently true for residents of the south. These findings support the above hypotheses about rural residence, region, and an antistatehood ethnic vote on the part of non-Ukrainian groups. They also, however, suggest that the Soviet-era habit of the highly educated of voting with less frequency is still dominant. In this respect, Ukrainian electoral behavior differs from that of Western democracies.

Similar models were constructed for the electoral support of the three main party camps. In this case each model included only those constituencies contested by parties of the camp in question, so as to take into account the distribution of candidates.[19] In addition to the demographic and regional variables included in the model for turnout, a set of dummy variables representing the presence in a constituency of candidates from the other blocs was entered to control for the differential effects of varying structures of competition. As it turned out, none of the variables achieved significance, but this in itself is instructive, for it suggests that the main axis of competition in most constituencies is that among parties of the same camp, rather than between camps (see also below). The models for the Left and Right votes yielded significant equations (see Table A8.6 in the Appendix, p. 157), but not that for the Center. Support for Centrist parties is evidently too various and too fragmented for a meaningful sociodemographic or geographical analysis of the electoral center in Ukrainian politics to be possible.[20]

The largest effect on the vote for candidates of leftist parties is exerted by the percentage of retirement-age voters in a constituency. The second main effect of demographic characteristics is more complex, in that it involves an interaction between ethnicity (defined here in terms of native language) and level of education. Though higher education is not significant on its own, it appears to diminish the tendency of Russophones to vote for parties of the left. In a hypothetical constituency in which no residents had higher education, each 1 percent increase in the number of Russophones would correspond to a 0.47 percent increase in the Left vote. But with increasing education levels, this trend decreases, and it is reversed at the level of 8.5 percent. In other words, less-educated Russophones would seem to be more likely to vote for the left, whereas highly educated members of this group exhibit the opposite tendency.

Region constitutes the second set of significant variables in the Left equation. It is noteworthy that the west is not distinguished from the Right Bank in this model; instead the main dividing line is that which separates the south and the east from the rest of the country.

The model for support of the Right is distinguished by the fact that only regional variables are significant, but they are so significant that the model as a whole explains considerably more of the variance in support than its Left counterpart. In the case of Right support, the main dividing line runs between the west and the rest of the country, with rightist candidates polling on average twenty points higher in western Ukraine. Thus, though there are clear dividing lines in support for the two camps, they fall at different places.

The lack of significant demographic variables in the Right model can perhaps be explained by the hegemony exerted by the Right over its western stronghold. Residents of this region who do not support the Right may simply not vote at all, or not support party candidates. As the main axis of structured competition in this region is that between right-wing parties, we should expect to see the vote for different parties of this camp distinguished in demographic terms. In this context, it will be instructive to consider support for different parties individually.

Unfortunately, the small number of seats contested by most of these parties limits analysis of subsections of the party spectrum to the four major parties: the KPU, the SPU, Rukh, and the URP. Unsurprisingly, the support bases of the largest parties within the Left camp—the Socialists and the Communists—contain features of the model for the Left vote overall. As can be seen from Table A8.7 in the Appendix (p. 158), higher education has a depressant effect on the vote for both parties, yet there is no evidence of an interaction between education and ethnicity in the models for the individual party votes. Ethnicity does not appear to be a significant determinant of the Communist vote, though Russophones evidently support the Socialist Party with greater frequency than their Ukrainophone counterparts. Interestingly, region proves in these equations to be a significant determinant of the Communist but not the Socialist vote.

Demographic variables were not found to be significant in the vote for the Right camp overall, and they are only weakly significant in the models for Rukh and the Ukrainian Republican Party. URP supporters would seem to be drawn disproportionately from the older population, while Rukh voters appear to be more highly educated than the average voter. Given that Rukh stood significant numbers of candidates in all parts of the country, it is not surprising that regional variables should be more important determinants in this model than they are in the model for URP support, where only the basic east-west divide is significant.

It is notable that the two largest parties in the country are those with the most distinctive support bases, and those whose support is best explained by sociodemographic factors. This might seem to bode well for the development of a structured party system in Ukraine, but the regional dimension of voting patterns has the effect of isolating the Communists from Rukh and preventing any true competition between them. This can be observed from examination of the effects of dummy variables entered into these equations for the presence of candidates from other 'major' and 'significant' parties. It will be recalled that this type of variable was not significant in the model for the party camps, but for all parties except the URP, the presence of other individual parties was linked to support levels. The Communist vote was most strongly affected by the presence of a Socialist candidate; the presence of a Liberal also appears to have had a depressant effect on the Communist vote. A similar pattern was evident in the model for Rukh support, where the presence of URP and KUN candidates was associated with a drop in support. This suggests that the Communists were engaged in both intracamp and intercamp competition, but that the range of their rivalry extended only as far as the Center. As conjectured above, Rukh faces competition mainly from within its own camp.

In this context, the effects of party dummies in the model for the Socialist vote are anomalous. The parties whose presence is most strongly associated with the Socialist vote include one in the Center, the LPU, and one on the right, Rukh. Curiously, the presence of a Liberal candidate coincides with an *increase* in Socialist support, which runs contrary to what we would expect on the basis of the hypothesized effects of party competition. It may well be that the significance of these variables points less to a competition effect than it does to the dominant political tendency in the different parties where the Socialists stood candidates. The Socialists had a relatively broad regional penetration in comparison with other parties (see Table A8.2 in the Appendix, pp. 152–3), and these coefficients most likely reflect the fact that the Socialists performed better in what were generally more Left-wing constituencies, which were also those in which Liberal candidates tended to stand. In other words, though regional variables were not found to be significant in this equation, the party dummy variables could be registering quasi-regional effects.

This analysis of the Socialist vote model might lead one to question the foregoing interpretation of the party variables in the other models; the causal relationship might be the reverse of that posited by the hypothesis of competition effects. In fact, it is likely that reciprocal causation is at work in this case. Parties stand candidates for seats that they believe, on the basis of their local knowledge, they have the best chances of winning. But their presence in the race further enhances these chances, and the most successful parties are able to draw votes from those near them on the political spectrum. Either way, it is clear from the patterns of interaction observed in these models that there is little direct competition between the Left and the Right, confirming the analysis of party camps offered above.

Conclusion

The results of this investigation can be summed up as follows: Region and ethnicity are both important determinants of voting behavior in Ukraine, but they clearly have distinctive effects, in that they operate on different segments of the electorate. Perhaps the most significant general finding of the analysis is the difficulty of making generalizations as to which factors are most important determinants of the vote, for different factors are characteristic of the support bases of different parties, and because the parties have characteristic regional distributions, the most important factors vary from region to region. What has been depicted here is a proto–party system: the structure of overlapping support bases implies that though the system is disjointed in electoral terms, it is not fractured. Nevertheless, such a situation is not conducive to further party system development, because there is little common ground—either social or geographical—for structured competition. The newly adopted semiproportional electoral system will go some way toward remedying this problem, and its implementation will undoubtedly represent a significant advance for the process of party system consolidation in Ukraine.

APPENDIX

Table A8.1

Competitive Characteristics of the Parties

	No. seats contested[1]	Average vote share in seats contested[2]		Total vote share[3]
Left				
Communist (KPU)	294	19.9%	(15.4)	9.7%
Socialist (SPU)	166	8.3	(10.0)	3.1
Peasant (SelPU)	55	20.2	(18.0)	2.7
National Salvation (PNVU)	1	0.8	—	0.0
Center				
Liberal (LPU)	76	3.8	(3.1)	0.1
Democratic Revival (PDVU)	47	8.7	(10.1)	0.8
Social Democratic (SDPU)	30	5.6	(9.4)	0.4
Green (PZU)	37	2.9	(4.6)	0.3
Labor (PPU)	25	8.2	(8.6)	0.4
Civic Congress (HKU)	23	6.1	(6.3)	0.3
Labor Congress (TKU)	16	7.8	(9.9)	0.3
Justice (UPS)	15	4.7	(4.1)	0.1
Liberal Democratic (LDPU)	9	1.8	(2.0)	0.0
Slavic Unity (PSE)	8	4.3	(3.3)	0.1
Solidarity and Social Justice (UPSSS)	6	3.7	(2.7)	0.0
Constitutional Democratic (KDP)	6	4.4	(2.4)	0.0
Economic Rebirth of Crimea (PEVK)	5	8.1	(3.7)	0.1
Beer Lovers (UPShP)	2	1.6	(0.6)	0.0
National Democratic				
Rukh (NRU)	214	10.5	(11.4)	5.2
Republican (URP)	126	8.3	(10.6)	2.5
Democratic (DemPU)	67	7.0	(7.8)	1.1
Christian Democratic (KhDPU)	31	4.7	(1.9)	0.4
Peasant Democratic (USDP)	8	2.1	(2.4)	0.0
Ukrainian Christ. Dem. (UKhDP)	6	1.4	(1.3)	0.0
Free Peasants (PVSU)	2	1.2	(0.7)	0.0
Extreme Right				
Congress of Ukr. Nat. (KUN)	55	8.8	(13.1)	1.3
Ukr. Conserv. Repub. (UKRP)	28	4.7	(11.6)	0.3
Ukr. National Assembly (UNA)	22	8.5	(14.1)	0.5
Social Nationalists (SNPU)	21	3.2	(2.2)	0.2
Org. of Ukr. Nat. (OUN)	11	1.9	(1.5)	0.1
State Independ. of Ukr. (DSU)	11	3.7	(4.4)	0.1
Ukr. Nat. Conserv. (UNKP)	6	2.0	(2.5)	0.0

Source: Compiled by the author from the Vybory-94 database, constructed by the Petro Mohyla Scientific Society of Kyiv.

Notes: [1]A seat is considered to have been contested by a party if a member of that party stood as a candidate there.

[2]These figures are percentages of the registered electorate. Figures in parentheses are standard deviations

[3]Percent of the registered electorate.

Table A8.2

Regional Distribution of Candidates: "Major" and "Significant" Parties

Parties	Regions[1]					
	West	Right Bank	Left Bank	South	East	All Parties
Left						
KPU	21(26%)	67(63%)	31(76%)	90(75%)	85(85%)	294(65%)
SPU	14(17%)	56(52%)	23(56%)	36(30%)	37(37%)	166(37%)
SelPU	9(11%)	13(12%)	10(24%)	19(16%)	4(4%)	55(12%),
Center						
LPU	2(2%)	12(11%)	7(17%)	19(16%)	36(36%)	76(17%)
PDVU	2(2%)	9(8%)	4(10%)	14(12%)	18(18%)	47(10%)
Right						
NRU	57(70%)	62(58%)	21(51%)	45(38%)	29(29%)	214(48%)
URP	45(55%)	36(34%)	7(17%)	25(21%)	13(13%)	126(28%)
DemPU	22(27%)	20(19%)	3(7%)	6(5%)	16(16%)	67(15%)
KUN	25(31%)	22(21%)	1(2%)	3(3%)	4(4%)	55(12%)
KPU+NRU	14(17%)	40(37%)	16(39%)	39(33%)	27(27%)	136(30%)

(continued)

	West	Right Bank	Left Bank	South	East	Ukraine
"Major" parties	NRU URP KUN DemPU KPU	KPU NRU SPU URP KUN	KPU SPU NRU SelPU	KPU NRU SDP URP	KPU SPU LPU NRU	KPU NRU SPU URP
"Significant" parties	SPU SelPU LPU	DemPU SelPU PDVU	LPU URP URP	SelPU LPU SelPU	PDVU DemPU KUN	LPU DemPU PDVU
Total constituencies	82	107	41	120	100	450
Turnout	85.66%	76.87%	82.54%	68.80%	73.81%	76.19%
Average no. of candidates/seat	14.28	14.42	11.98	11.21	12.88	12.97
Average no. of party candidates/seat	4.17	3.97	3.15	2.96	3.52	3.56

Source: Compiled by the author from the Vybory-94 database, constructed by the Petro Mohyla Scientific Society of Kyiv.

Notes:[1] The historic regions are defined as follows: West = L'viv, Ternopil', Ivano-Frankivs'k, Volyn', Rivne, Transcarpathia, and Chernivtsi; Right Bank = Vinnytsya, Khmel'nyts'kyi, Kyiv oblast, Kyiv City, Zhytomyr, Kirovohrad, Cherkasy; Left Bank = Poltava, Sumy, Chernihiv, South = Odesa, Mykolaiv, Kherson, Crimea, Zaporizhzhia, Dnipropetrovs'k; East = Donets'k, Luhans'k, Kharkiv.

[2] In each column the first number is an absolute figure and the second is the ratio of this to the total number of candidates in the region in question.

Table A8.3

Regional Distribution of Candidates: Party Camps

Party camps	Regions					
	West	Right Bank	Left Bank	South	East	All
Left	38(46%)	87(81%)	39(95%)	105(88%)	91(91%)	360(80%)
Center	15(18%)	46(43%)	10(24%)	57(48%)	63(63%)	191(42%)
Right	78(95%)	96(90%)	27(66%)	72(60%)	51(51%)	324(72%)
Left + Right	35(43%)	78(73%)	25(61%)	65(54%)	49(49%)	252(56%)
Left + Center	9(11%)	40(37%)	10(24%)	50(42%)	61(61%)	170(38%)
Right + Center	15(18%)	43(40%)	8(20%)	37(31%)	33(33%)	136(30%)
Left + Right + Center	9(11%)	37(35%)	8(20%)	34(28%)	33(33%)	121(27%)
Left only	3(4%)	6(6%)	12(29%)	24(20%)	14(14%)	59(13%)
Center only	0(0%)	0(0%)	0(0%)	4(3%)	2(2%)	6(1%)
Right only	37(45%)	12(11%)	2(5%)	4(3%)	2(2%)	57(13%)
Total constituencies	82	107	41	120	100	450

Source: Compiled by the author from the Vybory-94 database, constructed by the Petro Mohyla Scientific Society of Kyiv.

[1]In each column the first number is an absolute figure and the second is the ratio of this to the total number of candidates in the region in question.

Table A8.4

Regional Distribution of Vote Share among "Major" and "Significant" Parties (in percent)

Parties	West	Right Bank	Left Bank	South	East	All Parties
Left						
KPU	1.45	6.87	11.32	9.41	19.38	12.72
SPU	0.64	3.23	4.31	1.62	2.95	3.09
SelPU	0.97	2.26	4.91	3.04	0.54	2.74
National Democratic						
NRU	9.44	4.99	3.06	2.06	0.72	5.15
URP	6.65	2.74	1.13	1.19	0.36	2.52
DemPU	1.80	1.07	0.31	0.24	0.65	1.08
Extreme Right						
KUN	3.93	0.75	0.13	0.03	0.11	1.25
Party Camps						
Left	3.07	12.35	20.55	14.07	22.86	18.55
Center	1.09	2.16	1.81	2.93	4.13	3.37
National Democratic	17.96	8.55	4.34	3.16	1.68	9.16
Extreme Right	7.93	1.09	0.40	0.21	0.15	2.44
All party candidates	30.05	24.15	27.1	20.37	28.82	33.45

Source: Compiled by the author from the Vybory-94 database, constructed by the Petro Mohyla Scientific Society of Kyiv.

Table A8.5

OLS Regression for Turnout

Variable	B	Standard error
Retirement age	0.49[c]	(0.29)
Higher education	−0.70[c]	(0.11)
Urban residence	−0.08[c]	(0.03)
Ethnic Russian	−0.11[b]	(0.06)
Other ethnic[1]	−0.14[b]	(0.07)
Regional dummy variables:		
West	5.10[c]	(1.22)
Left Bank	−0.02	(1.13)
South	−2.80[b]	(1.41)
East	1.53	(1.55)
Constant	81.47	(3.36)
N	192	
Adjusted R^2	0.74	

Notes:

Coefficients are unstandardised.

[a]The category "other ethnic" is composed of members of ethnic groups other than Ukrainian and Russian.

[b]$p < 0.05$

[c]$p < 0.01$

Table A8.6

OLS Regression for Party Camps

Variable	Left B	Left Standard Error	Right B	Right Standard Error
Retirement age	0.91[b]	(0.33)		
Higher education	0.69	(0.83)		
Native language Russian	0.47[c]	(0.02)		
Interaction between native language Russian and education	−0.04[b]	(0.02)		
Regional dummy variables:				
West	−10.57	(6.93)	19.86[c]	(2.38)
Left Bank	3.78	(3.69)	−2.82	(2.91)
South	6.65a	(3.70)	−5.18[a]	(2.81)
East	8.87a	(4.97)	−5.96[b]	(2.73)
Constant	−9.57	(12.43)	10.50	(1.50)
N	118		164	
Adjusted R^2	0.24		0.41	

Notes: Coefficients are unstandardized.

[a]$p < 0.1$

[b]$p < 0.05$

[c]$p < 0.01$

Table A8.7

OLS Regression for Major Parties

Variable	KPU	SPU	NRU	URP
Retirement age				0.68^c
Higher education	-0.59^b	-1.19^c	0.29^a	
Native language Russian		0.21^b		
Party dummy variables				
SPU	-8.81^c			
LPU	-7.72^b	10.93^c		
NRU		-4.84^a		
URP			-5.30^c	
KUN			-5.61^b	
Regional dummy variables:				
West	-14.43^c		10.14^c	6.36^c
Left Bank	3.43		-1.55	
South	1.66		-4.31	
East	14.94^c		-5.99^b	
Constant	23.16	$b14.43^b$	7.60^b	-11.24^b
N	134	49^b	99^b	58^b
Adjusted R^2	0.33	0.22^b	0.24^b	0.16^b

Notes: Coefficients are unstandardized.
[a] $p < 0.1$
[b] $p < 0.05$
[c] $p < 0.01$

Notes

1. Peter J. Potichnyi, "Elections in the Ukraine, 1990," in Zvi Gitelman, ed., *The Politics of Nationality and the Erosion of the USSR* (London: Macmillan, 1992), pp. 176–195.

2. See, for example, Valeryi Khmel'ko, "Politicheskie orientatsii izbiratelei i itogi vyborov v Verkhovnyi Sovet (mart-aprel' 1994 goda)," *Ukraina segodnya,* no. 5 (May 1994), pp. 55–63, and Valeryi Khmel'ko and Dominique Arel, "The Russian Factor and Territorial Polarization in Ukraine," *The Harriman Review,* vol. 9, nos. 1–2 (Spring 1996), pp. 81–91.

3. This is not to deny that the vestiges of regionalism remain in many developed party systems, from the nationalist parties of Belgium, Quebec, and the Celtic fringe in Britain, to the Christian Social Union in Bavaria.

4. Oleksa Haran', " 'Bahatopartiynist' na Ukrainy: formuvannya, problemy, perspectyvy" in O. Haran', ed., *Ukraina bahatopartiyna: prohramni dokumenty novykh partiy* (Kyiv: Pam"yatky Ukrainy, 1991), pp. 5–32; Volodymyr Lytvyn, "Pro suchasni ukrains'ki partii, ikhnykh prykhil'nykiv ta lideri," *Politolohichni chytannya* no. 1, 1992, pp. 62–101;

Artur Bilous, *Politychni ob"yednannya Ukrainy* (Kyiv: Ukraina, 1993); Andrew Wilson and Artur Bilous, "Political Parties in Ukraine," *Europe-Asia Studies,* vol. 45, no. 4 (1993), pp. 693–703; and Taras Kuzio and Andrew Wilson, *Ukraine: Perestroika to Independence* (London and New York: Macmillan and St. Martin's Press, 1994).

5. For reasons of comparability and comprehensiveness, this analysis will concentrate on the first round of elections only (held on 27 March 1994).

6. Strictly speaking, most of the candidates included in this analysis were not actually nominated by their parties (primarily due to the organizational hurdles this would have involved and the ease with which candidates could be nominated by other means), but all candidates who were party members will be considered, for the purpose of the present analysis, to have represented their party in the elections. Though this might in some instances involve a distortion of the truth, it is most likely a reasonable assumption for the majority of cases.

7. The reasons for this can no doubt be traced to the organizational infrastructure inherited by the left from the Soviet-era Communist Party, as well as the organizational experience gained by certain right-wing parties over the course of the perestroika period (primarily Rukh and the URP).

8. Sidney Verba and Norman H. Nie, *Participation in America: Political Democracy and Social Equality* (London and New York: Harper and Row, 1972), and Sidney Verba, Norman H. Nie, and Jae-on Kim, *Participation and Political Equality: A Seven-Nation Comparison* (Cambridge: Cambridge University Press, 1978).

9. Angus Campbell, Philip Converse, W. Miller, and Donald Stokes, *The American Voter* (New York: Wiley, 1960), pp. 99–100; Verba, Nie, and Kim, *Participation and Political Equality;* Bingham Powell Jr., "Voting Turnout in Thirty Democracies: Partisan, Legal, and Socio-Economic Influences," in Richard Rose, ed., *Electoral Participation: A Comparative Analysis* (Beverly Hills and London: Sage, 1980), pp. 5–34; and Ivor Crewe, "Electoral Participation," in David Butler and Austin Ranney, eds., *Democracy at the Polls: A Comparative Study of Competitive National Elections* (Washington and London: American Enterprise Institute, 1981), pp. 216–263.

10. Verba, Nie, and Kim, *Participation and Political Equality.*

11. A.V. Berezkin, V.A. Kolosov, M.E. Pavlovskaya, N.V. Petrov, and L.V. Smirnyagin, "The Geography of the 1989 Elections of People's Deputies of the USSR (Preliminary Results)," *Soviet Geography,* vol. 30, no. 8 (October 1989), p. 618; cf. A.V. Berezkin, V.A. Kolosov, M.E. Pavlovskaya, N.V. Petrov, and L.V. Smirnyagin, *Vesna 1989: Geografiia i anatomiia parlamentskikh vyborov* (Moscow: Progress, 1990), p. 107.

12. Rasma Karklins, "Soviet Elections Revisited: Voter Abstention in Non-competitive Voting," *American Political Science Review,* vol. 80, no. 2 (1986), pp. 449–469; cf. Georg Brunner, "Elections in the Soviet Union," in Robert K. Furtak, ed., *Elections in Socialist States* (London: Harvester Wheatsheaf, 1990), p. 39, and Theodore H. Friedgut, *Political Participation in the USSR* (Princeton, NJ: Princeton University Press, 1979), p. 113.

13. Karklins, "Soviet Elections Revisited," pp. 455–457.

14. For an analysis of the role of these variables in elections between 1989 and 1991 in western Ukraine, see Sarah Birch, "Electoral Behavior in Western Ukraine in National Elections and Referendums, 1989–91," *Europe-Asia Studies,* vol. 47, no. 7 (November 1995), pp. 1145–1176.

15. This includes data from the 1989 census gathered from oblast statistical administrations. The data were fitted to constituency boundaries where possible, but in many cases constituency boundaries crossed the lines of the *rayony,* which are the main unit of aggregation of the demographic data. All in all, it was possible to fit 225 of 450

constituencies, though gaps in the census data mean that some of the analyses that follow are based on a smaller sample size. The numbers of constituencies included in each analysis are given in the tables.

16. Turnout is chronically underestimated in survey research (William L. Miller, "Measures of Electoral Change Using Aggregate Data," *Journal of the Royal Statistical Society,* vol. 135, no. 1 [1972], pp. 122–142), obliging many researchers in this area to resort to ecological analyses. In Ukraine there has also been a well-evidenced tendency among survey respondents to underreport support for the Socialist and Communist Parties. See *Politychni portret Ukrainy,* no. 8 (May 1994), and Jaroslaw Martyniuk, "The Demographics of Party Support in Ukraine," *RFE/RL Research Report,* vol. 2, no. 48 (3 December 1993), p. 39.

17. Erwin K. Scheuch, "Cross-national Comparison Using Aggregate Data: Some Substantive and Methodological Problems," in Richard L. Merritt and Stein Rokkan, eds., *Comparing Nations: The Use of Quantitative Data in Cross-national Research* (New Haven and London: Yale University Press), pp. 131–168; "Social Context and Individual Behavior," in Mattei Dogan and Stein Rokkan, eds., *Quantitative Ecological Analysis in the Social Sciences* (Cambridge, MA: MIT Press, 1969), pp. 133–155.

18. A number of different variations on ethnicity were compared, including language fluency, native language, and declared ethnic group, but declared ethnic group was eventually chosen for this equation, as it was found to have the strongest effect.

19. Unfortunately, the numbers of seats contested by the national democratic parties and the extreme right were too small to allow for meaningful statistical analysis, so these camps were conflated into one right-wing bloc.

20. Though it is common in many countries for centrist parties to be a repository for an eclectic collection of disillusioned leftists and rightists (as well as those who do not fit well into the left-right spectrum), the regional divisions that characterize the Ukrainian situation make for an even greater dispersion of centrist support, which may in part account for the large number of parties that make up the center. Nearly half of the parties that contested the elections of 1994 fall into this category, though as a group these parties polled less than 4 percent of the total vote. It is thus not surprising that Centrist support should be most difficult to characterize.

Economics and Society

Introduction

Neil Malcolm

The history of Ukraine during the 1990s provides a good illustration of the impossibility of analyzing economic change in isolation from other political and social dimensions. International factors have been particularly important.

Ukraine's four transitions of democratization, marketization, state and nation building, discussed in Taras Kuzio's chapter, make the entire post-Soviet transformation process in Ukraine far more complicated and fraught with unpredictable consequences for Ukraine than for some of the country's Central and East-European neighbors. Economic reform has tended to be perceived as part of a wider Westernizing project embracing all spheres of society. From Kyiv, however, the European Union appears much more distant than it does from Prague or Budapest. Ties with Russia are much stronger. The Russian-Ukrainian political and cultural entanglements dealt with in other chapters are arguably less serious in their immediate impact than the legacy of Soviet-era economic links, still deeply entrenched in many sectors. In particular, there is a profound energy dependency on Russia. The fate of Ukrainian economic reform is inseparable from events in Moscow, something that complicates scenario writing for the Ukrainian economy.

The Ukrainian political leadership under Kravchuk cannot be said to have ignored the international dimension. Their mistake, if anything, was to rely too much on it. Foreign policy (asserting independence of Moscow and a pro-Western orientation) took precedence over internal reform. In the economic field, foreign trade liberalization measures, for example, ran far ahead of domestic liberalization, with the result that they remained empty gestures and in many cases came to be reversed.[1] The slow pace of internal change meant that the support for independence of powerful opponents of reform in the government camp could be maintained. As for the opposition, it fastened its hopes, in an equally unrealistic way, on support from Russia to salvage Soviet-era economic ties. Meanwhile, the economy itself stagnated.

As John Tedstrom notes in his chapter, this "period of denial" was terminated by the arrival of Leonid Kuchma as president in the summer of 1994. It was by now quite apparent that rather than looking abroad for solutions to its economic problems, Ukrainians had to take determined steps in the direction of economic renewal as a prerequisite for acquiring more leeway in international affairs. The government had to persuade the industrialized states and international financial organizations that it was serious about reform, and it had to begin implementing the kind of changes that would ultimately weaken Russia's powers of economic leverage.

Putting a serious program of economic reform into practice has not been easy, and assessments of its progress and prospects vary widely. Tedstrom emphasizes the successes that have been achieved since 1994 in the field of macroeconomic stabilization, with some nudging from the IMF. The budget has moved closer to balance, and inflation has dropped steeply, albeit from very high levels. Privatization has been slow to get under way, he acknowledges, but seems to have been gathering pace in 1996; liberalization has made progress in retail pricing and in the foreign exchange market, but many restrictions on exports remain in place.

Exploring the reasons for the disappointingly low level of foreign investment in Ukraine, Tedstrom identifies five key hindrances to an inflow of capital. Potential investors fear political instability and doubt Kyiv's commitment to reform. There is a shaky legal foundation for business, and the workings of the taxation system are obscure and weak; worse still, there is insufficient confidence in the inviolability of property rights. Nevertheless, he argues that if its leaders display sufficient boldness and good judgment, Ukraine can pursue the path trodden by Poland and the Czech Republic, halt the decline of the economy by 1997, and achieve positive growth in the course of 1998.

Paul Hare, Mohammed Ishaq, and Saul Estrin paint a less encouraging picture in Chapter 10. They focus on the reasons for the sluggish pace of change, which has led the World Bank to categorize Ukraine as a slow-reforming state. They home in on the "unpredictable, complex, and bureaucratized" policy-making system in Kyiv. The authors concur with Tedstrom that Ukraine is not unique in the sense claimed by its champions of an interventionist 'third way' in economic reform strategy. They nevertheless consider it important to identify specific characteristics of the Ukrainian situation that must be taken into account if the correct mix of policy instruments is to be found.

The first special feature that they point to has its origins in the Soviet period, when Ukraine became the location of many large industrial enterprises USSR subordinated to the ministries in Moscow. The leaders of the industrial sectors concerned, and friendly politicians in their regions, developed a powerful lobbying capacity. With the demise of the ruling Communist Party bureaucracy, these industrial lobbies appear to have increased their influence. They have had a great deal of success in demanding subsidies from Kyiv and resisting the implementation of privatization and bankruptcy measures. The second is that, in contrast to more rapidly reforming states, a large proportion of the old industrial planning apparatus, including some of the sectoral ministries, has been allowed to remain in place. At the same time, creation of a legal, regulatory, and fiscal framework for private business has been neglected.

The third is that many enterprises see their products (rightly) as uncompetitive in world markets, and view the traditional orientation toward Russia (possibly wrongly) as a more secure option. Fourth, there is what they describe as the "conceptual" problem—there is simply a shortage of people in senior positions who understand how a market economy might operate. Finally, the black markets and corruption generated by incomplete liberalization help to entrench public opposition to reform in general.

Hare, Ishaq, and Estrin trace the way in which these political and social factors have worked together to hamper and distort the government's privatization and antimonopoly programs. At the national level, they note the significant powers exercised by the conservative majority in parliament and the conservatives' success in bogging down the privatization process. They describe how regional authorities have preferred to deal with shortages not by relying on free pricing to balance supply and demand, but by prohibiting the 'export' of commodities from their domains. Similarly, local employment is protected by preventing the 'import' of competing goods and by distributing tax concessions and subsidies.

In the face of powerful social resistance to liberalization and the continuing lamentable condition of the Ukrainian economy, it is naturally tempting to consider the workability of the alternative 'industrial policy' that Kyiv appeared to be favoring in the second half of 1995. It seems clear, however, that many of the factors that hamper liberalization would make a more interventionist policy even more unworkable. As Andrew Wilson and Ihor Burakovsky have pointed out elsewhere, the experience of East Asia suggests that the most important element for the latter is "a relatively autonomous and managerially adept state, capable of identifying sectors with long-term comparative advantage . . . and favoring them with far-sighted protection policies . . . rather than a weak state succumbing to domestic political pressure to maintain open-ended subsidy to an excessively broad range of enterprises regardless of any assessment of their long-term trading potential."[2]

It seems likely, then, that the broad trajectory of any successful transition to market-based economic recovery in Ukraine will be similar to that followed by its Western neighbors. To bring it about, however, will require great ingenuity from political leaders in Kyiv, and imaginative support from outside.

Notes

1. See V. Budkin et al., "Ukraine and the European Union: the Liberalization of Cooperation," *Political Thought,* nos. 2–3, 1995, pp. 148–158.

2. See Chapter 5, "External Aspects," in I. Burakovsky and A. Wilson, *The Ukrainian Economy under Kuchma,* RIIA Post-Soviet Business Forum Paper (London: Royal Institute of International Affairs, 1996), pp. 32–37; Oleh Havrylyshyn, "Reviving Trade amongst the Newly Independent States," *Economic Policy,* no. 19 (supplement) (December 1994), pp. 172–187; and P. Nolan, *China's Rise, Russia's Fall: Politics, Economics and Planning in the Transition from Stalinism* (London: Macmillan, 1995), pp. 65–66.

— 9 —

Ukraine: A Four-Pronged Transition

Taras Kuzio

Ukraine faced a number of difficult choices in December 1991 when it became independent from the former USSR. Ukraine had to undertake four transitions after the disintegration of the former USSR.[1] These include:

1. Moving from a command administrative system to a social-market economy (a market economy with a social welfare safety net).
2. Shifting from a totalitarian political system to a democracy with a civil society (including providing guarantees for human rights and liberties, free elections, peaceful transfers of power, and civilian control of the security forces).
3. Making the transition from a subject of empire to an independent state.
4. Evolution from a country possessing an uneven national identity to one with a civic, unified nation and political culture.[2]

In this chapter I discuss transition in postcommunist and post-Soviet countries. Then I survey the four-pronged transition that Ukraine had to face, arising out of its inherited legacies of external domination and totalitarianism.

Common Problems

The first obstacle facing postcommunist states in transition is the fact that we are largely dealing with an unknown area. There are no ready-made theories that can be lifted off bookshelves, dusted down, and then applied to all postcommunist states to guide them in their transition processes. "The problem of creating a liberal, stable and prosperous society on the ruins of a totalitarian industrial ideocracy is absolutely new—no one knows what the answer is, or indeed whether there is one," Ernest Gellner wrote.[3] In the case of nuclear powers such as Russia and China, which have pretensions to be recognized as great powers, promoting political transformation "is like spinning a roulette wheel: many of the outcomes are undesirable."[4] Similarly, after World War II the newly created states carved out from the former colonial empires of the West were not provided with stock answers as to how to sequence their transitions to democracies, market economies, states, and nations.

There were no theories and policies available to aid transition in postcommunist and post-Soviet countries. Jiri S. Melich commented that few Western scholars "have been able to predict all the difficulties, setbacks and deviations down the road." On the contrary, Melich believes, "they were time and time again surprised by actual developments."[5] Paul Hare and Junior Davis pointed out that even the term 'transition' is confusing. It implies "that there was (or should have been) a definite starting point, that the destination is also clear and substantially agreed, and that the mixture of policy measures and institutional changes required to shift a given society from starting point to destination can also be identified, agreed and imposed. Unfortunately, none of these assumptions is generally correct, since even at the start the countries of the region exhibited substantial differences, and after 3–5 years of transition experience these differences have become greater rather than smaller."[6]

Transition is inevitably both an economic process and a political one, Hare and Davis argue. But is democracy an impediment to the introduction of capitalism? Roger D. Markwick believes that it is: "The record suggests, both in Latin America and spectacularly in China, that the sequencing of economic reforms prior to political reforms has the greatest chance of success. Simultaneous reforms falter in the face of opposition facilitated by liberal and democratic openings."[7]

Observers of post-Soviet transition usually ignore nation and state building while focusing exclusively upon political and economic reform. This is mistaken. As Mettle Skak has conclusively argued, post-Soviet transition in the non-Russian republics of the former USSR is an 'imperial transition.' It therefore has many similarities to that undertaken by the former colonies of the Western powers. Decolonization "adds the politics of nation and state building to the agenda of reform in the country undergoing transition from communism."[8] The two polar choices open to new states are both unpalatable. At one extreme, a new state may attempt to institutionalize political and economic reform at the cost of possible internal strife and disintegration (Russia could be a good example of this). At the other extreme, a newly independent state, such as Ukraine, "may choose to restrain social and economic change to a level that can be handled by the existing political structure."[9]

The newly independent states can also choose between two other poles—transforming themselves completely for the benefit of the postnationalist elites, which will lose them popular support and their popular base, or "constricting access to the political elite, with the possibility of political stagnation and turning the younger generation of elites against the regime."[10] In the former USSR, the first seems closer to the Russian experience, while the latter resembles what occurred in Ukraine, where the stability of 1992–93 was replaced by the stagnation of 1993–1994.

Centrist policies, which are often pursued by post-Soviet leaders trapped between radical nationalists and hard-line communists in the early stages of reforms, over time become increasingly untenable, as they are attacked by both sides.[11] In the short term, they may work as a strategy for muddling through because they provide a platform upon which to unite all shades of political opinion. "The appeal of this political constellation in a context of decolonization results from the skillful manipulation of nationalism by third-way protagonists," Skak argues.[12] This unity of purpose was precisely what Ukraine required during the early years of its independence.

In view of the lack of a 'grand plan' that the postcommunist elites could have adopted in the their transitions perhaps the only policy open to them was to muddle through. Alexander J. Motyl, himself critical of Western 'grand plans' for postcommunist transitions, argues: "For the most part, states lumber along; they muddle through from problem to problem, from mess to mess. The business of states is business as usual. And surprisingly or not, they do manage to survive, even with relatively low levels of policy effectiveness and decidedly low levels of policy innovation."[13]

Ukraine was not ready for independence in December 1991, either professionally or psychologically. It inherited a quasi state, no united nation, few experts, and no international strategy. As two leading former members of the Kuchma administration wrote: "Mistakes in such a situation practically were inevitable."[14] Ukraine's deputy foreign minister, Kostyantin Hryshchenko, described Ukraine's first years of independence as a "transition period from infancy to at least childhood, and during these three years [that is, the Kravchuk era] our country was independent. During the next two years we learned what a firm and considered position on most important issues implied."[15]

The majority of Western advisers, international financial institutions, and governments gave prescriptions to postcommunist states advocating rapid transitions to market economies and democracies. One could argue that this was done more often out of concern for their own perceived national interests than because of any concern for the interests of the countries to whom the advice was being given. But, as Alexis de Tocqueville pointed out long ago, it is very dangerous for a country with few democratic traditions to introduce radical reform and change.[16] Perhaps, therefore, a slow transition process that muddles through and takes into account both the experience of transition in other countries as well as local conditions may be the best solution. After all, slow transition was the norm in most West European and North American countries, leading to more sustainable transformations and democracies.[17]

The conditions for rapid and radical change are absent in the majority of post-Soviet states; anyway, this would require enormous resources. Radical and rapid change can usually occur only in authoritarian environments, and therefore the promotion of such change by Western governments and international financial institutions serves only to undermine the transition to democracy and nation building. The postcommunist states should therefore sequence their transformations; it would be folly to assume that all four transitions could be undertaken simultaneously. The only realistic transformation with the limited resources at their disposal is "reform, certainly, transition, perhaps, revolution, never."[18] The creation of a state structure, the assertion of control over existing structures that the newly independent states inherited from the former USSR, and the formation of elites to man these inherited and newly created state structures are the necessary prerequisites for the successful launch of economic transition, political transformation, and nation and state building.[19] President Kuchma could not have launched his reform program in the autumn of 1994 without the groundwork undertaken by his predecessor in at least some of these areas.

To varying degrees the postcommunist states inherited fragile and inexperienced governments, ethnic minorities, disputed borders, economic recessions, economies that were deeply integrated with the former metropolis, and little knowledge of market economies or the short-run costs of transition.[20] Whenever a colonial power retreats, it leaves an administrative void—weak institutions and weak quasi states. Both Russia and the countries of the former Soviet empire in Eastern Europe inherited government apparatuses. But the non-Russian republics of the former USSR "were virtually born as quasi states and share their institutional handicaps."[21] Other handicaps that the postcommunist states inherited included a cultivation of victimization and political helplessness, intolerance of opposing views, inability to negotiate and compromise, a deep distrust of the authorities, and political passivity.[22]

There are, therefore, many obstacles to the institutionalization of liberalism in politics and economics in the postcommunist states. Liberalism developed successfully in the West as a result of three factors that do not necessarily exist in postcommunist states. Western Europe inherited the remnants of the old honorable elites and developed a new individual work ethic. A reactive egalitarianism then attempted to correct these two factors.[23] But in the postcommunist states there is confusion as to how far to drop state control and ongoing debates over the proper role of the state. Ukraine inherited only the outlines of the bureaucratic structure necessary to run an independent state. Many institutions—such as a tax inspectorate—simply did not exist. While state control over the economy was deemed to be excessive, other aspects of the state structure required enlarging. Even the transition to a social-market economy is deemed to be something that should be state-regulated whereby the state continues to act in the role of a 'comforter.'[24] Only in August 1996, five years into Ukraine's independence, did President Kuchma announce that Ukraine's state building (but not nation building) had been completed. In other words, five years were required for Ukraine to establish the full range of institutions required for the normal functioning of a state at least at the central (but not local) level.

There are a number of key factors required to ensure a stable and successful transition process. There should be an open political process allowing each citizen to become involved with an established rule of law that sets out the 'rules of the games.' Politicians should be willing to compromise and settle for less than a maximalist agenda, and there should be a gradual erosion of the 'us' and 'them' division of society between the authorities and its citizens (a legacy from the communist era). If citizens continue to see themselves as subjects with duties, but without the right to be involved in the policy-making process, then democratization will be slow.[25]

Another obstacle to liberalism in postcommunist states is the continued weakness of the newly emerging state, which creates barriers to the emergence of civil society and its institutionalization. In the case of Ukraine, this is made doubly worse by the fact that the growth of civil society is also hampered by low national consciousness in its eastern and southern regions (see Chapter 5 by Mykola Riabchouk). It is no coincidence that in eastern and southern Ukraine civil society is weakest and the feelings of citizens widespread that they are unable to influence the authorities.

As the late scholar of nationalism Ernest Gellner has pointed out, nationalist ideology arises as an inevitable consequence of modernization and industrialization.[26] Nationalism is as much a driving force of China's rush to the market as is communism. In the Ukrainian case, the weakness of its national identity and national consciousness are added factors slowing the process of transition.

In addition, the inheritance of corrupt, clannish-nepotistic ties from the communist era within the nihilistic postcommunist elites (usually termed the 'party of power') makes it highly unlikely that North American–style capitalism will develop in Central and Eastern Europe. Instead, the transition in the postcommunist states looks increasingly likely to resemble the corporatist pattern of links between state and private enterprise found in Latin America.

Studies of democratization in Asia and Latin America have also shown the correlation between high income levels and democracy. Few countries with a living standard of less than $5,000 per capita per annum operate as democracies.[27] The growth of income levels also leads to a growth in support for democratization. But there is little evidence to show that countries that have become democracies experience more rapid growth.[28] Indeed, many Asian and Latin American countries introduced market economic reforms under authoritarian regimes. The growing prosperity of these countries, such as South Korea, led to the rise of a new middle class, which then agitated for political reform and democratization. Hence the temptation for some postcommunist states to follow the East Asian model of combining authoritarian political rule with the transition to a market economy. (This, of course, assumes that the ruling elites would have an interest in pursuing market reform, which is not something that we can automatically assume would exist in Ukraine or elsewhere in the former USSR.)

Transition in the postcommunist states is a medium- or even long-term process.[29] Although Western governments have traditionally focused upon personalities such as Mikhail Gorbachev or Boris Yeltsin, to "guarantee" the continuation of the transition process, this personalization is a fatal mistake. The transition process cannot be 'guaranteed' and is unlikely to be halted by any one leader.[30] The West's personalization of the reform process in Russia led it to back Yeltsin in the 1996 presidential elections as the "lesser of two evils," despite his responsibility for the shelling of his own parliament in October 1993 and the appalling human rights record in the Chechnya conflict between 1994 and 1996.

The West's personalization of the reform process is also linked to its short attention span. Western leaders have to 'prove' to skeptical domestic audiences that there have been notable successes in the transitions to democracies and market economies in the postcommunist states targeted for assistance. This message, though, is unpalatable both to Western leaders and to the domestic audiences of postcommunist states, who remain cynical when told to 'tighten their belts' for a better tomorrow (it too closely resembles similar exhortations in the communist era). Kravchuk was therefore outlining reality but, nevertheless, a reality Ukrainian citizens did not wish to hear when he said: "In another five years, believe me, we will still be far from accomplishing everything. And in ten years we won't [accomplish everything]."[31]

This theme was reiterated by Kravchuk during the 1994 Ukrainian presidential election campaign in answer to charges that he had neglected the economy during his tenure as president. Kravchuk told his impatient Ukrainian citizens that transition required at least ten to fifteen years, just as it took more than a few years to deal with the ravages of World War II.[32] Kravchuk added that this transition would be especially long and difficult in Ukraine: "We want our people to change in the space of three to four years—we want them to be fully fledged citizens, protectors of their rights, their land, their culture. They hardly know their own culture."[33]

Obstacles Facing the Former Soviet Union

The consolidation of democracies and market economies within the post-Soviet states must inevitably be a lengthy process marred by instability. The Soviet regime leveled and atomized the population into a state of both confusion and disillusionment. The post-Soviet states inherited problems of political subcultures, mass alienation, lack of the rule of law, ethnic nationalism, absence of civil society, distrust of political parties, and diffuse identities and interests as well as legacies of intolerance. They lacked institutions to implement transition with systems that were unconsolidated and volatile.[34]

Ethnic conflict breeds authoritarianism.[35] Democratization will be slower in those postcommunist countries where domestic disputes are not solved peacefully and different racial, religious, or ethnic groups are unable to live together in mutual trust.[36] It is no coincidence, therefore, that in post-Soviet states where domestic conflict has erupted, authoritarian political environments usually exist.

Russia and Ukraine became independent states with different legacies of external domination and totalitarianism. Ukraine inherited no state and few elites, as well as an unresolved national identity; the resulting need to undergo four transitions means that these will be slow and sequential. Ukraine's leaders and policy makers have to search for the correct model(s) of nation and state building. Ukraine's muddling through its transition processes inevitably also leads to the search for compromise and moderation, an attempt to balance different bureaucratic and regional groups and interests within an overall nation- and state-building agenda (something that Kravchuk proved particularly adept at undertaking).

Yet it is in post-Soviet states such as Ukraine, where there is a balance between different branches of authority, that democratic transitions are more likely to be successful. Ukraine's post-Soviet bureaucratic clans (that is, many 'parties of power') demand greater parliamentary control and checks and balances between the executive and legislative branches of government; this "encourages development toward a democratizing compromise among factions."[37] Where politicians are forced to seek compromise and consensus politics, as in Ukraine, democratic transition is more likely to progress, albeit slowly.[38] Political reform and democratization therefore are more advanced in Ukraine than in Russia.

Radical transition was adopted in Russia by victorious anticommunist elites who took over the country in January 1992 (something in sharp contrast to Ukraine's former national communists, who retained power and who saw reform as a threat to their interests). Russia, after all, has a historical tradition and political culture in which reform has been implemented by an authoritarian leader from the top down (for example, Peter the Great and Josef Stalin). In Russia, "reforms often meant radical breaks [and] demonstrate renunciation, indeed condemnation of the old and the inclination to go from one extreme to the other."[39] In Russia's post-Soviet transition, history has reasserted itself. Yeltsin's personalization of the state has continued the Petrine traditions of 'enlightened absolutism' with Westernization and the implantation of capitalism upon a passive population from above.[40]

But Russia's radical policies led merely to confrontation, collapse of the center ground of politics, a huge growth of the state's bureaucracy and security forces, and institutionalization of an autocracy. Despite lacking the resources to rebuild an empire, which would damage its political and economic transitions anyway, Russia is destined to continue along this path, which finds supporters among the bulk of the population and the majority of political parties.[41]

In contrast, Ukraine inherited a deformed national consciousness in which only about half of its population was confident of its own national identity. The remainder of the population lacked a clear-cut Ukrainian (or even Russian) identity. This factor inevitably ensured that Ukraine would adopt moderate citizenship and national minority policies that would be based on territorial and inclusive—not ethnic and exclusive—criteria. The inheritance of an incomplete national identity and political subcultures also ensured the victory of a former national communist (not nationalist) in the December 1991 presidential elections, a man who stood for moderate reform and nationality policies as well as compromise, centrist politics. In the words of one author:

Its leadership could not have successfully pursued either rapid, comprehensive and fundamental change or change that was premised on the existence of preconditions that did not exist. These were the limits of the possible. In turn, they could have pursued state building, nation building, and elite formation.[42]

Obstacles Faced by Ukraine

Transition would therefore not be smooth or uniform throughout the very different post-Soviet states. No Western policy makers should have insisted that post-Soviet transition in Ukraine and Russia be identical. Nevertheless, comparative studies of Ukraine and Russia argue that Ukraine, like Russia, could have launched "a rapid and consistent economic reform" at the end of 1991.[43]

This point of view is the result of two factors. First, there is lack of deep knowledge of the conditions that exist in Ukraine and the specificity of its four transitions. Second, for the first two years of Ukraine's existence as an independent state, the majority of Western governments and policy makers regarded it as illegitimate and somehow 'Russian.' As it was really 'Russian,' then policy prescriptions should be the same as those applied to Russia.

The economic costs of the transition process are initially offset by the political and psychological benefits of statehood and a vision of a better future. Indeed, these factors played a decisive role in the Ukrainian referendum in December 1991, in which independence obtained its decisive 90 percent endorsement. But, as I have already argued, the transition to a market economy and democracy is not a short-term phenomenon. Consequently, a population willing to tolerate the initial hardships of the transition period because of their support for independence is vital to sustaining the momentum of the transition process in the medium-long term.

New states therefore go through three phases:[44]

1. Agitation for independence is considered important per se, especially by nationalists.
2. After the state achieves independence, the economic difficulties associated with separation from the former empire lead to political instability.
3. This instability compounds the difficulties that already exist in the transition to a market economy and economic viability.

On the eve of the disintegration of the former USSR, most commentators argued that an independent Ukraine seemed to have tremendous prospects for economic success. Ukraine possessed fertile land, and a large industrial base, a large population (which was 72 percent ethnically Ukrainian); it was a large exporter of foodstuffs and a net exporter of technology, metallurgical products, and machine tools. But these optimistic prognoses failed to take into account both that 80 percent of Ukraine's trade was with the former USSR and that it would be hit very severely by the raising of prices for its imported energy to world levels after 1993.

As the costs of economic transformation became more acute over time, public optimism about the future rapidly shrank. In a speech to the Ukrainian parliament in early 1992, President Kravchuk warned, "People are losing faith and this is dangerous to our ability to return the situation to the better."[45] Whereas 70 percent of Ukrainians in the capital city of Kyiv were optimistic in December 1991, when Ukraine became an independent state, a year later this had dropped to an alarming 10 percent. The stabilization of the political and economic situation under President Leonid Kuchma since mid-1994 increased the numbers of those with an optimistic outlook to the more respectable, but still low, 30 percent of Kyiv's inhabitants.[46]

Due to the legacy of external domination and inheritance of an unevenly developed national consciousness, the costs of the economic and political transition became particularly dangerous for Ukraine. By the end of 1995, according to one opinion poll conducted by *Sotsis*-Gallup, public support for independence had collapsed by more than half, to 43 percent, since December 1991. The major factors causing this collapse in support were economic. The poll pointed to a remarkable symmetry between those areas of Ukraine where support for independence remained high, at between 70 and 85 percent (west, northwest, and the capital city, Kyiv), and areas where national consciousness is higher. In those areas where support for independence was as low as between 48 and 57 percent (the Crimea, east, and south), national identity and consciousness are still weak and in greater flux.[47]

The improvement in Ukraine's economic situation since 1994, coupled with greater domestic stability, has contributed to the reduction of support for union with Russia. But just as the proindependence vote in December 1991 was in part due to economic factors, a correlation between low support for independence, poor economic performance, and low standards of living in areas of Ukraine where there is low national consciousness will remain. Hence the close interconnection between reform and nation and state building.

Although the commentaries presented during 1993–1994 by outside observers, policy makers, and academics suggested a Ukraine ready to 'disintegrate,'[48] the reality is that states do not lose their independence "because of an unsuccessful economic development, but rather by military conquest or as a consequence of settlement of scores by the victors in major international conflicts."[49] Former colonies do not usually resubjugate themselves to their former hegemon, especially in the case of newly independent states such as Ukraine. Republican elites are largely supportive of the new status quo, which is not threatened by a populace that may feel discontented with the costs of economic transition but lack the means (through a functioning civil society and institutionalized rule of law) to effect change or influence their situation.

The danger therefore faced by the newly independent post-Soviet states is not to be reabsorbed by their former hegemon, Russia, but to be pressured into joining confederations, monetary unions, or other new unions such as the Belarusian-Russian Community of Sovereign Republics, formed on 2 April 1996, to ease the pain of the transition process. These unions do not help economic reform—they are more a means to avoid the painful transition to a market economy. It is therefore rather confusing why a Russia that *is* reforming should be propping up communist or neo-communist regimes in the Transdniester separatist region of Moldova, Belarus, and Tajikistan that *do not* want to reform.

In all of Ukraine's *oblasts,* according to the 1989 Soviet census, ethnic Ukrainians are in a majority, giving an overall Ukrainian majority of 72 percent of the republic's population. But these figures do not give the full picture. After the election of Kravchuk as Ukraine's first post-Soviet president, Mykhailo Horyn, then a leading member of the Ukrainian Republican Party, said, "We are in the paradoxical situation that we have a president but we do not have a nation. Our task is diligently to supervise the president in building an independent Ukraine." As argued earlier, a strong national identity, such as in the Visegrad countries, eases the transition to a market economy by creating a unity of purpose. By bringing reformers to power, it increases the level of discomfort that the population is willing to tolerate during the short-term hardships that inevitably accompany transition.

"In this sense, state, nation and identity were and are at the very center of these processes of change in eastern Europe," one author has pointed out. Transition in Latin America, and in southern and Central Europe, amounted to only democratization and a change in the regime. In contrast, in the former USSR the transition process is far larger, involving the creation of a new social order, the nature of the state, the forging of a national identity, and creation of the basis for a capitalist economy. Ethnicity and national identity play a central role in the transition process throughout the former USSR, defining each country's nation and state building, democratization, tradition of a market economy (or lack thereof, as the case may be), practices of citizenship, existence of elites, contested borders, and relations with the former metropolis. Taking these factors into account Ukraine represents a difficult case of transition, one that will probably inevitably be both slow and muddled.[50]

Political and economic transition in a society that is divided and is itself in transition toward a new nation and state will invariably be more complicated and slower than in societies that are ethnically homogeneous and smaller. Political and economic transformation in Ukraine will therefore be slower than in states such as Slovenia, the three Baltic republics, and those of the Visegrad group. At the same time, the process will be faster than that experienced by postcommunist states in the throes of ethnic conflict (for example, Croatia, Serbia, Moldova, the Transcaucasus, Tajikistan, and possibly even Russia). Ukraine therefore belongs to that group of countries lying in the middle between these two extremes of severely divided countries and those where identity is fluid.

Conclusions

The Ukrainian transition is inevitably both an evolutionary process and a nonlinear one, for two reasons. First, there was a general lack of ready-made policies that could be applied to all postcommunist states. Second, Ukraine inherited specific legacies that made it very different from Russia and many other postcommunist countries. In contrast to most postcommunist states, Ukraine has to undertake four transitions (nation building, state creation, democratization, and economic transformation). In other words, any Ukrainian leader needs to combine the qualities of Abraham Lincoln, Adam Smith, and Nelson Mandela. Kuchma, his national security adviser Volodymyr Horbulin told us, has to be simultaneously a social democrat (ensuring social welfare), a liberal democrat (backing reforms), and a national democrat (by being a nation-state builder, a *derzhavnyk*).

The election of Kravchuk in December 1991 as president prevented the eruption of the ethnic conflict that would probably have arisen (especially in the Crimea) if a nationalist had been elected. This absence of ethnic conflict allowed Ukraine to escape the temptation of authoritarianism. To rule a country with such multifaceted inherited legacies necessitates compromise politics and the search for consensus and the central ground. Although this ensured the continuation of centrism in Ukrainian politics, at the same time it slowed the transition process. In the short run this inevitably caused problems, as the search for compromise looked to many outside observers suspiciously like a loss of direction and a lack of clear-cut policies by the Ukrainian leadership. The alternative to consensus-seeking politics might have produced short-term gains, such as in Russia. But this would only have led at a later stage to the collapse of the center ground, the polarization of society, and domestic crisis. The choice may have been between the imposition of liberalism by 'Bolshevik methods,' as in Russia, or the slow, muddled, but peaceful transition adopted in Ukraine. 'Full steam ahead' may not have therefore been the best advice to give post-Soviet countries such as Ukraine. Finally, despite their different economic strategies, the actual economic records of Ukraine and Russia have not been radically different. In Ukraine and Russia annual average GDP change amounted to -14 and -12 percent, respectively, during the period 1990–1994.[51] The contribution of the private sector to each country's GDP was over 50 percent in both Russia *and* Ukraine by 1995–1996. Ukraine had therefore largely caught up with Russia's transition process while escaping its domestic conflict. By 1996–1997 two-thirds of Ukrainians were employed in the nonstate sector.

Ukraine muddled through 1992–1993 by initially taking control of inherited structures and building new ones as well as forging new ruling elites. Kuchma was able to continue nation- and state-building policies by prioritizing political and economic transition after mid-1994. This was only possible because the former parliament under President Kravchuk had previously laid the foundations for the Ukrainian state. Ironically, therefore, "seen in this light, Kravchuk's greatest achievement may be that he made Kuchma possible."[52]

Notes

The author is grateful for the extensive comments provided by Prof. Paul G. Hare, based at the Center for Economic Reform and Transformation, Department of Economics, Heriot-Watt University, Edinburgh, Scotland, on the first draft of this chapter.

1. These four transitions were outlined by Hennadiy Udovenko, Ukrainian foreign minister, in a speech to the Royal Institute of International Affairs on 13 December 1995, where the author was present. Udovenko added a fifth task, that of creating new foreign and defense policies. Volodymyr Cherniak, a well-known economist, leading member of Rukh, and candidate for mayor of Kyiv in local elections in June 1994, also outlined these mutually compatible aims, arguing that they should constitute Rukh's program, in a speech to the sixth Rukh congress. See *Chas,* 29 December 1995.

2. A survey of students on the eve of independence found that only 44.2 percent viewed national issues to be a priority, whereas 56.7 percent argued in favor of the prioritization of human values. Students from western Ukraine viewed the achievement of independence, defense of national interests, and national revival as goals they wanted to become involved in, whereas eastern and southern Ukrainian students emphasized good ethnic relations and the promotion of consensus politics. See N.I. Chernysh, Yu.V.

Vasilieva, O.L. Holianka, and B.Yu. Poliarush, *Natsional'na samosvidomist' students'koi molodi (Sotsiolohichnyi analiz),* (Edmonton, Toronto, and L'viv: Canadian Institute of Ukrainian Studies, 1993), pp. 43–44.

3. Ernest Gellner, "An Identity Crisis in the East," *The Independent,* 29 April 1996.

4. Edward Mansfield and Jack Snyder, "Democratization and War," *Foreign Affairs,* vol. 74, no. 3 (May–June 1995), p. 80.

5. J.S. Melich, "The Post–Communist Mind—How Real a Phenomenon?" paper presented at the conference "Socio-Psychological Legacies of the Communist Rule, Carleton University, Ottawa, no date.

6. See P.G. Hare and J. Davis, "Transition to the Market Economy: Introductory Overview," in P.G. Hare and J. Davis, ed., *Transitions to the Market Economy* (London: Routledge, 1997).

7. Roger D. Markwick, "A Discipline in Transition? From Sovietology to 'Transitology,' " *Journal of Communist Studies and Transition Politics,* vol. 12, no. 3 (September 1996), p. 266.

8. M. Skak, *From Empire to Anarchy: Postcommunist Foreign Policy and International Relations* (London: Hurst, 1996), p. 21.

9. William J. Foltz, "Building the Newest Nations: Short-Run Strategies and Long-Run Problems," in Karl W. Deutsch and William J. Foltz, eds., *Nation-Building* (London and New York: Atherton Press, 1963), pp. 128–129.

10. Ibid.

11. Russell Bova, "Political Dynamics of the Post-Communist Transition: A Comparative Perspective," in Frederic J. Fleron and Erik P. Hoffman, eds., *Post-Communist Studies and Post-Soviet Methodology and Empirical Theory in the Soviet Union* (Boulder, CO: Westview, 1993), pp. 247–249.

12. Skak, *From Empire to Anarchy,* p. 19.

13. Alexander J. Motyl, "Reassessing the Soviet Crisis: Big Problems, Muddling Through, Business as Usual," *Political Science Quarterly,* vol. 104, no. 2 (Summer 1989), p. 274.

14. Dmytro Vydrin and Dmytro Tabachnyk, *Ukraina na porozi XXI stoletiya. Politychni aspekt* (Kyiv: Lybid, 1995), p. 63.

15. *Zerkalo nedeli,* 23 August 1996.

16. M.I. Mykhailchenko and B.I. Koroliova, eds., *Kudy Yidemo?* (Kyiv: Ukrainian-Finnish Institute of Management and Business, 1993), p. 63.

17. Bova, "Political Dynamics of the Post-Communist Transition," p. 252.

18. A.J. Motyl, "Reform, Transition or Revolution? The Limits to Change in the Post-Communist States," *Contention,* vol. 9, no. 1 (1995), p. 18.

19. A.J. Motyl, "Imperial Collapse and Revolutionary Change: Austria-Hungary, Tsarist Russia and the Soviet Empire in Theoretical Perspective," in Jurgen Nautz and Richard Vahrenkamp, eds., *Die Wiener Jahrhundertwende: Einflusse, Umweet, Wirkungen,* Studien zu Politik und Verwaltung, Band 46 (Koln, Graz, Vienna: Bohlau Verlag, 1993), p. 831.

20. Gertrude E. Schroeder, "On the Economic Viability of New Nation-States," *Journal of International Affairs,* vol. 45, no. 2 (Winter 1992), p. 573.

21. Skak, *From Empire to Anarchy,* pp. 36, 69.

22. See Beverley Crawford and Arend Liphart, "Explaining Political and Economic Change in Post-Communist Eastern Europe: Old Legacies, New Institutions, Hegemonic Norms and International Pressures," *Comparative Political Studies,* vol. 28, no. 2 (July 1995), pp. 171–199.

23. Gellner, "An Identity Crisis in the East."

24. George Schopflin, "Obstacles to Liberalism in Post-Communist Polities," *East European Politics and Society,* vol. 5, no. 1 (Winter 1991), p. 191.

25. Carol Barner-Barry and Cynthia A. Hody, *The Politics of Change: The Transformation of the Former Soviet Union* (New York: St. Martin's Press, 1995), pp. 212–213, 225.

26. E. Gellner, "Nationalism and Modernization," in John Hutchinson and Anthony D. Smith, eds., *Nationalism* (Oxford and New York: Oxford University Press, 1994), pp. 55–62. See also Mansfield and Snyder, "Democratization and War," pp. 83–87, for examples of the historical linkage between the growth of nationalism and democratization.

27. Peter Rutland, "Has Democracy Failed in Russia?" *The National Interest,* Winter 1994–1995, p. 12.

28. Mick Moore, "Democracy and Development in Cross-National Perspective: A New Look at the Statistics," *Democratization,* vol. 2, no. 2 (Summer 1995), p. 3.

29. Thomas Caruthers talks about the "chimera of instantaneous democracy" and points to the usual correlation between high incomes and democracy. See his "Democracy without Illusions," *Foreign Affairs,* vol. 76, no. 1 (January–February 1997), pp. 85–99.

30. Bill Bradley, "Eurasia Letter: A Misguided Russia Policy," *Foreign Policy,* no. 101 (Winter 1995–1996), p. 85.

31. *Chas,* 22 August 1995.

32. See Reuters, 26 June 1994, and *The Independent,* 27 June 1994. At a press conference Kravchuk said, "But we should all understand that it is impossible to destroy the old links and structures and to establish new ones in just one year" (*Molodi Ukrainy,* 12 November 1992, and *Uriadovyi Kurier,* 13 November 1992).

33. *The Ukrainian Weekly,* 29 January 1995.

34. See Robert S. Kravchuk and Victor Chudowsky, "The Political Geography of Ukraine's 1994 Presidential and Parliamentary Elections," paper presented at the annual meeting of the New England Slavic Association, 19–20 April 1996.

35. See Donald L. Horowitz, "Democracy in Divided Societies," *Journal of Democracy,* vol. 4, no. 1 (October 1993), pp. 18–38.

36. Barner-Barry and Hody, *The Politics of Change,* pp. 212–213.

37. Philip G. Roeder, "Varieties of Post-Soviet Authoritarian Regimes," *Post-Soviet Affairs,* vol. 10, no. 1 (January–March 1994), p. 74.

38. Ibid, p. 98.

39. Gerhard Simon, "Political Culture in Russia," *Aussenpolitik,* no. 3, 1995, p. 246.

40. Markwick, "A Discipline in Transition?" p. 268.

41. See A.J. Motyl, "Russia, Ukraine and the West: What are America's Interests?" *American Foreign Policy Interests,* February 1996, pp. 14–20.

42. A.J. Motyl, "Structural Constraints and Starting Points: Postimperial States and Nations in Ukraine and Russia," paper presented at the conference "Post-Communism and Ethnic Mobilization," Cornell University, 21–23 April 1995, p. 5.

43. See Marek Dabrowski and Rafal Antczak, "Economic Transition in Russia, Ukraine and Belarus: A Comparative Perspective," in Bartlomiej Kaminski, ed., *Economic Transition in Russia and the New States of Eurasia,* vol. 8 of *The International Politics of Eurasia*, Vol. 8 (Armonk, NY: M.E. Sharpe, 1996), p. 76.

44. Schroeder, "On the Economic Viability of New Nation-States," pp. 551–552.

45. *Holos Ukrainy,* 30 January 1992.

46. *Chas,* 22 March 1996.

47. *Demokratychna Ukraina,* 28 December 1995.

48. A typical example of a lack of knowledge about the four transitions Ukraine

faced after December 1991 could be found even in the knowledgeable *Economist* (6–8 December 1991) which claimed that Ukraine had chosen the Romanian, not the Visegrad, transition route. As this chapter argues, the Visegrad route was not available to Ukraine, whereas postcommunist Romania, in contrast, inherited both a state and a nation.

49. Schroeder, "On the Economic Viability of New Nation-States," p. 572.

50. Valerie Bunce, "Should Transitologists be Grounded?" *Slavic Review,* vol. 54, no. 1 (Spring 1995), p. 126.

51. *Economist* Intelligence Unit, *Ukraine: Country Profile 1996–1997* (London: EIU, 1997), p. 20.

52. Alexander J. Motyl, "The Conceptual President: Leonid Kravchuk and the Politics of Surrealism," in Timothy J. Colter and Robert C. Tucker, eds., *Patterns in Post–Soviet Leadership* (Boulder, CO: Westview, 1995), p. 120.

10

Ukraine: The Legacies of Central Planning and the Transition to a Market Economy

Paul Hare, Mohammed Ishaq, and Saul Estrin

Ukraine gained its independence when the Soviet Union disintegrated at the end of 1991. Like all the other postcommunist states, it had accepted and had begun to implement the process of transition from a planned economic system to a market-based economy where the forces of demand and supply would largely determine the allocation of resources. However, it was doing so without the support of a clearly articulated postindependence constitution, Ukraine being the only post-Soviet country lacking a new constitution as late as June 1996. Moreover, the collapse of the Soviet Union itself imposed a series of severe shocks on Ukraine, both political (in that independence came far faster than Ukraine's elites had anticipated) and economic (loss of mainly Russian markets, energy supplies available only at world market prices, etc.).

It was generally accepted and acknowledged that comprehensive reforms in several areas of economic life would be required to achieve a successful transition, that the reform process would extend over several years, and that it would involve fundamental changes in the economy. The principal areas for reform were: macroeconomic stabilization; price liberalization; liberalization of foreign trade and domestic supply arrangements; privatization and enterprise restructuring; the creation of a stable financial, fiscal, and legal environment in order to attract the foreign private investment essential to modernize and restructure Ukrainian industry; and the creation of private financial institutions such as commercial banks, as well as a wide range of financial markets.[1] Unfortunately, while several Central and East European countries have made great progress with their reforms (e.g., Estonia, Poland, Czech Republic, and Hungary), demonstrating a strong political commitment to the goal of constructing a market-type economy, Ukraine has been one of the slowest to reform.[2] Indeed, a World Bank survey ranked Ukraine in the category of slow reformers. This is despite Ukraine's having been rated very highly in terms of its prospects for successful reforms at the start of its transition process.

In the five years or so since independence, Ukraine has experienced numerous economic problems, such as persistently high rates of inflation, rapidly falling output, a rapidly growing shadow economy, and a sharply rising debt burden with Russia and Turkmenistan in particular, related to energy imports that must now be purchased at world market prices. Several of these problems were exacerbated by the country's own policy errors and misjudgments.

Since 1991 industrial production has been falling consistently, although the drop of 13.5 percent in 1995 was considerably more than the previous year. Inflation rates have been extremely high, reaching a peak of over 10,000 percent in 1993 (according to EBRD estimates). Monetary indiscipline and huge and erratic fiscal deficits have been the main causes. Unemployment, although officially recorded as low, is significantly higher if one considers the existence of hidden unemployment, which is not recorded in official statistics. Official unemployment was only seven thousand at the end of 1991. By the end of 1995 this had risen to 126.9 thousand, or about 0.4 percent of the labor force. At the same time the number of job vacancies has been declining.

The problem of Ukraine's foreign debt repayments to Russia and Turkmenistan for energy imports remains a serious one, and spurs pessimism about Ukraine's prospects of reducing its budget deficit significantly in the near future. In the area of stabilization policy, progress since 1991 has been very erratic. Initially, both monetary and fiscal policy had been far too lax. As the country moved toward hyperinflation, monetary policy was tightened in 1993, but this was not matched by sufficient fiscal restraint. Recent progress has continued to be erratic, but inflation does appear to be coming under control. Since Leonid Kuchma's election as president in 1994, much progress has been made in limiting the public sector deficit, controlling monetary emissions, and beginning to sell government bonds. But policy making is still unpredictable, highly complex, highly bureaucratic, and confused, so the advances are reversible. Subsidies to firms have been cut, but there is still significant commercial bank lending to already indebted and possibly nonviable firms.

Nevertheless, Ukraine has made some headway in certain areas of reform and has learned some painful lessons. However, it has not yet achieved a sustained macroeconomic stabilization. Of equal concern—from the standpoint of constructing a market-type economy—has been the country's limited progress in key microeconomic areas such as privatization and competition policy, the latter being interpreted broadly to include a wide range of measures and policies affecting the functioning of markets. It appears that Ukraine is facing barriers left over from the old system of central planning, barriers that are mainly political and ideological in nature and which are threatening to impede its progress.

There are serious contradictions in the execution of Ukrainian economic policy. For instance, while Ukraine is committed in principle to large-scale privatization and has passed laws regulating monopolies, it is noticeable that there has not been a wholehearted effort to implement reform policies in these areas. As a result, there still exists a large number of monopolies able to charge high prices, stifling competition. It is even claimed by some, not entirely convincingly, that these monopolies are partly responsible for inflation.[3] Although the process of privatization officially started in 1992, little was done until 1994. After gathering pace between 1994 and 1995, the process still failed to reach targets set by the government in agreement with the International Monetary Fund.

So, how can we explain and understand these apparent contradictions between the slow and erratic implementation of Ukraine's transition policy and the often-stated intention to progress toward some form of market economy? In this chapter we proceed as follows. First, we outline some features of the evolving political situation that have a significant bearing on reform progress. We then discuss the conception of economic reform that appears to be widely held in Ukraine, an uneasy and far from consistent mixture of ideas drawn from the experience of central planning, naive views of the 'market,' and economic nationalism. The following section takes the two examples referred to above—privatization and competition policy—and explores them in greater depth in light of the framework developed earlier in the chapter. Finally, the closing section summarizes and concludes.

Domestic Politics

When Ukraine became an independent state at the end of 1991, it was not immediately apparent what this would mean for the country's politics, economic policy, and evolving economic situation, especially as the country remained in the Ruble zone until 1993. On the economic side, monetary control by the Russian central bank was undermined both by the Ukrainian

National Bank's lax control of credit supplies and by the introduction of a 'temporary' currency, the coupon (or *karbovanets*), which eventually replaced the ruble. Ukraine introduced a permanent new currency, the *hryvnia,* in September 1996. Many state-owned enterprises in Ukraine were highly dependent on Soviet markets, mostly in the Russian Federation, and others relied on raw material deliveries from elsewhere in the Soviet Union. Hence the disruption of trade flows that resulted from the breakup of the USSR, with a shift to world prices and hard-currency settlement, had very severe effects on Ukrainian production. Exacerbating this effect was Ukraine's dependence on imported energy, already referred to.

This is the economic background against which the relevant political actors had to elaborate and introduce reforms while also seeking to regain control over the basic directions of the economy. The situation was undeniably difficult. However, it was not helped by the initial inability of Ukraine's key political actors, especially under the country's first postcommunist leader, Leonid Kravchuk, to agree on a reform program. The problems were partly conceptual, concerning what moving to a market economy really involved, and partly political, in the more conventional sense associated with different interest groups promoting their own perceived interests.

Thus an important factor delaying reforms was the constant bickering between the different branches of the political system, which generated much conflict. This was most evident in clashes between parliament and the president. The problem was that the boundaries of authority between central and local government, and between parliament, government, and the presidency, were in many areas poorly defined from the outset. The resulting confusion enabled parliament to obstruct the process of privatization. For instance, in early 1995 parliament rejected the program of privatization put forward by the government; this rejection was seen by the latter as a serious step back. Earlier, in July 1994, the Ukrainian parliament had voted to halt all privatization. It claimed that this was necessary in order to decide which state property should be privatized and how this should be done. Parliament then proceeded to draw up a list of 6,100 'strategic enterprises' that it claimed could not be privatized at all. Many members of parliament and their advisers profoundly objected to the whole idea of privatization.[4] The political clash between the legislature and the executive branch prevented Ukraine from developing a clear and consistent economic program to transfer the economy to a free-market system.

In addition, of the opposing political factions within parliament, some are in favor of the process of reform, some are strongly opposed. As recently as January 1996, the European Commission claimed that "the economic reform process in Ukraine is characterized by an ongoing struggle between reformers and conservative forces." It went on: "The President and former Prime Minister Yevhen Marchuk continue to be confronted with a conservative majority in parliament that manages to delay or even cancel reform measures." If we look at the composition of parliament (the Supreme Rada) we can see that a diverse range of political factions is present.

First, there is the left-wing group made up of the Communist and Socialist Parties of Ukraine plus the Peasant Party. This group can be regarded as 'conservatives'—in terms of their approach to economic reforms—who call for a return to socialist methods in the economy. These conservatives can in many ways be seen as the most dangerous threat to economic reforms. Indeed, they want more active intervention by the state in the economy, and they are generally opposed to privatization. The second group, called the 'national statehood group,' are supporters of capitalist-type reforms for Ukraine, and they can be viewed as the best hope for implementing market-oriented reforms. There is also a third group, referred to as the 'political middle' (center), which has much the same position on economic issues as the left. Thus parliament represents diverse groups, and its overall political orientation and makeup change frequently. The left-wing parties have been able to mount strong opposition to Kuchma's reforms.

As mentioned earlier, the political orientation of the Ukrainian parliament is very volatile, and there are even some deputies who have broken parliamentary regulations by belonging to more than one faction or by not yet having registered as deputies. The figures show that the two factions, the left-wing and the center, which both favor a socialist-type economy, are the dominant groups in parliament. Together they form a formidable opposition to the president's reform program.

A rift opened up between President Kuchma and former Prime Minister Marchuk; the latter's disagreement with the president on various aspects of economic reform may have cost him his post in May 1996.[5] A complication here was that there did not exist until May 1996 any clear guidelines about the respective roles and responsibilities of the prime minister (and his government) in relation to the president. The power-sharing agreement that Kuchma and parliament agreed upon in June 1995 has done nothing to clarify matters. The agreement was seen as an attempt to bypass parliament's opposition to reform. In effect, this agreement increased the president's power and was viewed as a necessary step to strengthen the president's authority over the executive. Under this agreement parliament's ability to challenge the government would be limited by the requirement that no attempt to unseat the government could be made for a year after parliament endorsed its annual program. Despite this, parliament could still block economic legislation. In fact, Kuchma had virtually coerced the reluctant deputies into signing the agreement by threatening to hold a national confidence referendum in which the Ukrainian people would have been able to decide between himself and parliament.[6]

A related problem for Ukraine has been the presence of interest/lobby groups, in some cases very powerful ones. Many with left-wing tendencies have been successful in impeding the passage of particular reform or disrupting their execution.[7] One example of this can be seen in the case of the National Bank of Ukraine (NBU), which has proved to be vulnerable to lobbies seeking to protect particular firms and sectors. As a result, the National Bank has not been able to conduct an independent monetary policy, though it has gradually managed to convince the government that budgetary discipline is important and has secured legislation limiting the government's power to borrow from the NBU.[8] This situation has been further complicated by the fact that the National Bank is subordinated both to parliament and to the president's office and therefore has to satisfy two bodies with very different, and at times strongly opposed views about the correct policy.

Another illustration of the power of interest groups and lobbies to impede the full implementation of policy was the passage of a law providing for a list of enterprises that were to remain in state hands. Initially it was intended that this provision should be confined to a limited number of firms in infrastructure and public utilities, but many lobbies argued for other firms to be included on the grounds that this might give them continued access to state subsidies and other budgetary supports (including tax favors and preferential access to credit). This led to the situation, noted above, where over six thousand firms were placed on the list. This is scarcely the way to a market economy. Even when state enterprise funds have ordered an enterprise to be sold to private individuals, managers and local bureaucrats have sometimes been able to prevent the sale by placing an unrealistically high price on its assets. Politicians, sometimes under the influence of interest groups, are inclined to take a short-term view, and in doing so they are affected by their past positions.[9] Most political leaders are still former communists but describe themselves today as independent professionals.

Some five years after attaining independence, Ukraine has not yet achieved an effective stabilization of the economy, though inflation has been brought down from its 1993 peak of over 10,000 percent to under 200 percent in 1995.[10] There has been strong opposition to firmer stabilization measures from the powerful industrialists and bureaucrats who depend on the patronage of the state. The political influence of industrialists and groups representing their interests may even have increased since the collapse of communism, because their activities are no longer checked by the Communist Party apparatus.

Since all societies contain lobby groups actively promoting their own interests, one cannot really insist that this fact per se is a problem for Ukraine. What is a problem, however, is the inability of the existing political system to find a way of developing and implementing policies for the whole country, including in the area of economic reform, without being completely swamped and dominated by these interest groups. Thus as presently constituted, the Ukrainian polity seems to be unable to sustain its own policies while also mediating sectional interests in a constructive way.

Conceptions of Economic Reform

A significant obstacle to rapid reform progress in Ukraine has been the lack of understanding of the functioning of a market-type economy and of the serious consequences of not reforming. Many are understandably fearful of the social problems transition may entail. Indeed, since independence Ukraine has tried several economic plans. But many politicians have argued that no serious attempt was made because no politician would accept the risk of bringing about a decline in living standards. Moreover, a large proportion of those employed in key ministries are very pessimistic about the prospects for a successful transition, and many are still hostile to the idea of radical economic reform. Admittedly, the transition from a planned economy to a free-market system is a painful process that is likely to have negative effects in an initial period, with significant benefits coming through later as growth resumes. Along the way, many social groups will lose out for shorter or longer periods, and the resulting dislocations need to be managed with great political sensitivity. Not surprisingly, the whole enterprise is seen as politically very risky.[11] Nevertheless, the evidence from other transition economies is that the perceived 'costs' of transition are not reduced by slower reforms, and those countries that reformed fastest and with greatest commitment suffered smaller output declines and resumed growth sooner than the more cautious countries.

Amongst the population there are contradictory and inconsistent attitudes toward market reforms. For instance, a recent survey indicated that 75 percent of the population of Ukraine favored privatization, but about the same percentage opposed price liberalization because they believed it was largely responsible for the high rate of inflation. Similar contradictions can be found in specifically Ukrainian approaches to transition, such as an economic model that still places great emphasis on state intervention.

In late 1994 President Kuchma's government put forward an economic program that was characterized by cuts in state subsidies, the freeing of many prices, reductions in government spending, and the establishment of markets for state securities including bonds. This model essentially proposed to follow the line advocated by the IMF and World Bank. But in April 1995 there was a sudden shift in the government's position with Kuchma insisting that "rapid market transformation of the economy must address the social needs of the population and provide a strong safety net." In effect, he was outlining what can be seen as a unique Ukrainian economic model. This model would involve a gradual rather than radical program of reform, characterized by much greater state interference than transition demanded. There was clearly much wider support for his new approach, with most of the population in favor of the state guaranteeing them a job, retaining control over economic policy, and providing free health care and education. All this suggests that citizens have little comprehension either of the personal responsibility involved in a free-market system or of the need to work hard to improve their lives rather than rely on the state for support.

The main feature of this 'Ukrainian model,' as outlined by Volodymyr Zviglyanich, is state control over price formation, using a variety of economic levers. The state, that is, will regulate prices indirectly rather than setting prices by command. This involves greater state involvement in the economy, and this was justified by the leadership on the basis that it was fully consistent with the historical traditions of the Ukrainian people and their mentality; with a mixed economy led by the market, creating the conditions for all forms of ownership, state and private; and with the preservation of the monopoly status of certain huge state enterprises. The acceptance of this model may help to explain why progress in certain areas such as privatization, competition policy, and stabilization has been slow.

At the same time, it is important to try to understand in what respects Ukraine might be 'special,' since the conditions just outlined—perceived as barriers to economic reform—are not greatly different in any of the transition economies, except perhaps in degree. A few points can be mentioned, but it is not yet clear whether they are sufficient to explain the observed situation of Ukraine.

First, much of Ukraine's industry was strongly oriented toward Moscow, either for supplies (energy and raw materials) or markets (heavy industrial products, especially in engineering and the defense industry), with the result that a high proportion of Ukraine's production took place in all-USSR enterprises subordinated to Moscow ministries. Lobbies of managers and local or regional bureaucrats to protect these enterprises and further their development were already well established under central planning, and they were strong enough to promote their interests within the all-USSR planning framework (albeit subject also to Communist Party controls and limits). Once Ukraine gained independence, there was no effective local counter-weight to these lobbies, especially as the Communist Party also lost its guaranteed monopoly of power.

Second, the suddenness of independence and the inability to agree on reforms led Ukraine to make serious mistakes in the institutional sphere. It retained a surprising amount of the supposedly outmoded institutional appa-ratus of central planning (including some sector ministries), whereas most other transition economies dismantled or transformed such structures very rapidly; and it failed to create the legal, regulatory, and fiscal conditions that would have encouraged large-scale private business formation. The consequence of these last two points was that political elites (rightly) lacked confidence in the ability of the Ukrainian private sector to fill the gap that would be left by large-scale employment reductions (or even outright clo-sures) amongst the larger state-owned firms. Hence there was a strong inclination to resist or delay such adjustments, with the result that many politicians found themselves siding with the lobbies already referred to. In addition, since old administrative structures were still intact, the natural response to a variety of economic problems that could have been addressed using market-type methods was administrative. We shall see some exam-ples of this practice below.

Third, for a relatively large transition economy such as Ukraine's, deter-mining the country's future orientation in regard to foreign trade is espe-cially problematic. Many of the larger firms, especially those located in the predominantly Russian-speaking eastern part of Ukraine, probably favor renewing links with Russia and former partners there, and are likely to resist market-type reforms until it is clear whether this is a real option or not. Other firms might favor a stronger orientation toward the West, espe-cially toward the potentially large EU markets, but this is feasible only with a great deal of product development, enterprise restructuring and adapta-tion, and a strongly market-oriented trade policy. None of this is yet in place to a sufficient extent, and moving further would require a much stronger commitment to market reforms. Proceeding in this way, moreover, would not actually shut out the 'Russian option,' since that direction of trade would not be closed to a market-oriented Ukraine. However, many of Ukraine's elites seem to perceive this issue—wrongly—as an either/or choice.

Fourth, as Tedstrom observes, Ukraine simply has far too few people, especially in senior positions, who understand market economics and are able to use this understanding effectively in their day-to-day work of public administration and economic management. This alone perhaps makes unsurprising the persistence of practices that would be more at home under central planning.[12]

Last, the important role of the shadow economy and pervasive corruption in Ukraine must be mentioned here. The fact that there is not a well-functioning legal and institutional framework for the market has opened up numerous opportunities for black-market and semilegal economic activity.[13] The incentive to engage in such activity is provided, for many people, by the collapse in their real personal incomes since 1990 (a combination of lower real wages and delayed payments) and hence the need to find other sources of income. The opportunity to engage in this sort of activity is fostered by inefficient tax collection, unclear and frequently variable rules and regulations concerning private business, the slow pace of liberalization, and onerous formal licensing procedures. The latter, in turn, stimulates petty corruption by officials to supplement their own meager and insecure salaries. Unfortunately, even though the resulting marketlike activity may often be an efficient and desirable response, the prevalence of such activity helps to create a climate of public opinion hostile to the market and all its manifestations. Black markets and corruption are viewed as market phenomena par excellence. This situation makes it all the easier for those politicians opposed to serious reforms to justify their positions, and to blame 'the market' for many economic problems.

Despite all these points, we shall emphasize below that there is no unique and distinct 'Ukrainian way,' since the same economic laws that apply to other countries also apply to Ukraine. Of course, Ukraine's initial position and current problems are somewhat different from those of other countries in the region, but this only implies that different combinations of policy tools might be required to advance reforms while restoring economic stability. The political economy of reforms in Ukraine is also more complex and difficult than in some other countries, and this has already sharply constrained Ukraine's feasible policy set and delayed reforms.

Privatization and Competition Policy

Privatization

As in Russia and elsewhere, Ukraine's legislation on privatization establishes funds which formally hold or own state-owned enterprises pending their privatization.[14] Thus there is a State Property Fund of Ukraine, with regional branches, plus local committees to deal with communal and municipal property. There are three main approaches to privatization included in the legislation: privatization for cash, free distribution to all citizens (via vouchers), and free distribution to working collectives. There is also privatization via leases with a buyout option. The relevant laws concern privatization of state enterprises, small-scale privatization, agricultural production, municipal housing, and so on.

As Tedstrom observes, Ukraine's privatization plan was set up in a rather similar way to the Czech and Russian plans, the main emphasis being on vouchers issued to the general population. However, in its implementation the procedures turned out to be very complex and bureaucratic, with many transactions requiring eighteen months to pass though all stages. However, the main features of the process seem to be as follows. Until 1995 the 'working collective' (managers and workers) chose whether to privatize (though others could also seek privatization). The 'value' of the firm was apparently set externally, linked to an indexed book value of assets; this provision, naturally, made it harder for working collectives to amass sufficient funds to secure a controlling interest in 'their' firms. The collective needed to raise the funds via their own (and family) privatization vouchers. Most privatizations in this period (70 percent) were in fact leased buyouts, in which the future profits of the firms were mortgaged to pay for shares. Outsider involvement was highly unpopular in the working collectives.

There have been major efforts to accelerate the process since 1994 and the election of Kuchma, though the basic approach is unchanged. Firms are now coming to privatization in blocks of 20 or 30 rather than singly, with privatization plans negotiated between the working collective and the state property fund, which holds the state's shares postcommercialization but preprivatization (and any residual state share holding postprivatization). There can be one or more 'emissions' of shares for any given firm—this need not be decided in advance.

Each firm will have a privatization plan in which the working collective proposes to buy a proportion of shares via their own privatization certificates. These share holdings are of necessity somewhat egalitarian in nature, in terms of their distribution across the workforce. Members of the working collective can put up to 50 percent more in to buy shares in cash. The value of each privatization certificate is around U.S. $5 and the value of each firm is, as we have seen, set by its book value. The remaining shares to be issued can be sold via certificate auctions or, at least in principle, on the stock exchange. The certificate auctions permit the general public to buy (vouchers are issued under particular names, so people cannot trade them). However, individuals can also place their certificates in the hands of investment funds, and these are in practice the main players in certificate auctions.

Finally, the government is issuing 'compensation vouchers' partially to compensate individuals for savings lost during the hyperinflation. These can also be used at the certificate auctions after April 1996.

In summary, this is a highly complex and bureaucratic process that has so far proceeded rather slowly. Kaufman of the World Bank has argued that this was because it gave the bureaucrats more opportunities for rent seeking at every stage. The process is also heavily weighted toward 'egalitarianism' and toward outsider (general public) owners. The latter effect comes from the high valuation implied by cost-based valuations, at least relative to the value of privatization certificates available to the working collective itself. This probably explains the slow pace and the lack of interest in or outright opposition to privatization among many managers and workers, and hence further explains the delayed implementation of the program.

Returning to the issue of insider versus outsider owners, the authorities do give some benefits to insiders. Workers and managers appear to be able to buy shares at a discount, and managers may receive 5 percent of shares free. Moreover, in the certificate auctions, if there is excess demand for shares, the price (to the general public) rises but the price paid by members of the working collective stays fixed at the nominal value of the privatization vouchers ($5). If supply exceeds demand, however, the certificate price does not fall—rather, the unsold element returns to the state property funds, perhaps for a later emission.

This scheme may appear moderately generous to workers and managers, but one suspects that, except in the case of small labor-intensive firms, the combination of high book values and low certificate values means that insiders cannot get majority stakes. Moreover, there are cases where outsiders who have bought majority stakes in certificate auctions immediately sacked the existing management. The previous system of leased buyouts, now outlawed, was in principle more advantageous for insiders. However, this all took place in a period when reform itself was in question—subsidies remained large, the state was still pivotal in decision making, and the prospects of renationalization were very real. Hence the atmosphere was not particularly favorable for working collectives to choose privatization.

Overall, certificate take-up has been quite slow; nevertheless, 40 million had been taken up by the end of 1996 out of a population of 52 million. Small privatization, i.e., the privatization of small businesses such as shops, restaurants, and other service establishments, has proceeded far more slowly than planned, with about 22,000 firms from a potential population of 50,000 small state-owned firms having completed the process by the end of 1995. Moreover, even this result was the outcome of a sharp acceleration in 1995, presumably related to the new decrees issued by the government. But by the summer of 1996 small-scale privatization was completed. Of large privatizations, 5,815 firms out of a possible total of 20,000 had been privatized by the end of 1995, as against only 2,600 privatized by the end of 1994. However, these figures are somewhat misleading, as they include many firms in which only small proportions of the equity have actually been sold to new private owners.

At a roundtable discussion on privatization organized by the Control Committee on Privatization of the Supreme Rada held jointly with the Institute of Transition Society, many speakers stressed traditional communist views about ownership and displayed a lack of understanding of market processes, some even fearing a foreign takeover. The view that privatization was a plot by foreign capitalists (especially from Russia) to take over Ukrainian firms seemed to be quite widespread, and even those who did not oppose privatization in principle sometimes believed that it had been set up in its current form solely to benefit international capitalists, who were going take over Ukraine.

A low standard of living is often regarded as a justification for arguing that unemployment could not be tolerated and that reforms must be introduced gradually.[15] On the question of the restructuring and associated employment reductions that would result from privatization, it is argued that these are impossible in Ukraine, as there is "no understanding of unemployment and it cannot be accepted." This view is hardly surprising given that countries such as Ukraine lack any culture of unemployment or the institutional network to cope with it. Moreover, many workers are likely to suffer from occupational immobility, as many possess one specific skill and are unable to make the switch to jobs in other areas; this implies that the social costs of unemployment are likely to be higher in Ukraine than in other countries undergoing rapid structural change. Hence it proves easy to win support for policies that inhibit adjustment and delay privatization. However, as noted above, these arguments apply to all transition economies, and most have found ways of adjusting and then coping with the resultant social costs.

The conservative parliament has often moved to increase controls over the privatization process, a process that is viewed as complicated and alien to such an extent that grassroots participation can be difficult to generate. Thus under a 1993 decree of the parliament, control commissions have been set up at all levels to supervise the privatization process, though their tasks are different at different levels.

At the lower levels, there are three main reasons for problems in the privatization process: lack of legislation, contradictions between laws and presidential decrees, and serious violations of the law. So part of the commissions' task is to interpret otherwise unclear or ambiguous legal rules, such as to do with asset valuations (including how to adjust for inflation). Commissions have very wide powers, even including the power to fire leaders of regional branches of the state property funds. Commissions win about 80 percent of the cases they have to deal with. In cases of disagreement, the parties can resort to commercial arbitration or the courts. Once per session, commissions report to parliament.

The various Property Funds apparently function badly due to: contradictions between laws and decrees, and 'temptations' for those allocating property. The laws change too frequently and are badly framed. However, it seems that in this whole approach there is far too much emphasis on control, and not enough on just getting privatization accomplished.

The overall responsibility for effective implementation often falls to local authorities, who do not necessarily adhere to central policy and who make their own deals with local businessmen. There has so far been little success in attracting foreign direct investment. Foreign firms are reluctant to invest in Ukraine not only because of the legal problems associated with its complex and vague privatization and property rights, but because of macroinstability and the burdensome regulatory environment.

The main factor that discredits privatization in Ukraine is that privatized firms do not yet work better, presumably at least in part because the general economic environment is not very favorable.[16] Privatization is often about power and the distribution of property to those already close to power—the nomenklatura. While probably true (and also probably inevitable), it appears that one's views about this must depend on the objectives of privatization. If they are to get firms into private hands, and preferably in the hands of those who are able to run a business and take the necessary initiatives and risks to make it succeed, then so-called nomenklatura privatization may not be so terrible. If the central aim is to ensure a 'fair' allocation of privatized property across the population, then such a solution is certainly not appropriate, even if sweetened with an element of voucher-based privatization. However, even this argument may be beside the point in the medium term, since once shares are tradable they will almost certainly be concentrated into larger blocks of effective owners within a fairly short period.

In light of the above, what can be said about the political economy of privatization in Ukraine? Perhaps the main point is that for many large firms, strong interest groups have proved able to delay or block privatization. These are mostly the firms with the strongest links to the Russian Federation in the past, those that still see their future in a possible renewal of such links. In contrast, firms that are already privatized are more likely to see their future either in the Ukrainian home market or in non-CIS markets, and in either case the need for restructuring and modernizing investment is more readily accepted. These firms must—to a large extent—be those in which effective blocking coalitions were unable to form, or if formed were unable to resist governmental and state property fund pressures to proceed. Unfortunately, the so far unstable macroeconomic environment in Ukraine and the weak commitment of the parliament to market reform makes it difficult even for those firms favoring privatization to benefit greatly from their preference. For all firms, but especially the larger ones, privatization must be perceived as very risky and potentially reversible, and in certain political conditions this could be very uncomfortable for those who supported privatization initially.

Hence it is useful to think about ways of designing privatization programs to avoid this type of dilemma. For instance, privatization by sale to a foreign buyer has a clear lock-in effect that should help to deter future reversals; this may be one reason such an approach was so strongly favored in Hungary, for instance. Another possibility is to ensure that the new constitution includes provisions enshrining the right to undertake private economic activity and the inviolability of private property, provisions that should be especially difficult to touch by means of constitutional amendments. But in Ukraine neither of these privatization safeguards is in place, nor is there even political agreement as to their overwhelming importance. As result, privatization in Ukraine may well continue within a rather insecure legal and institutional framework, reflecting the relative strengths of the relevant political actors.

Competition Policy

The first Ukrainian law on the control of monopoly and the promotion of competition was passed in early 1992 and formally came into effect in early 1993. Although the Antimonopoly Committee (AMC) law itself, specifying AMC powers, organization, staffing, and so on, was not formally passed in parliament until late 1993, its chairman was already appointed in 1992. Local offices of the AMC were established by August 1995. The AMC central administration has about 250 staff. There are twenty-seven regional offices covering twenty-four oblasts, Kyiv, Crimea, and Sevastopol, with a total staff of about eight hundred. The AMC is responsible to parliament and reports annually.

According to the law (Article 3), the main tasks of the AMC are: (1) preparation of antimonopoly legislation; (2) protection of the interests of enterprises and consumers; and (3) promotion of honest and fair competition in markets. It is also responsible for the program of demonopolization, involving decentralization of management, liquidation of barriers to entry, stimulation of entry, splitting up state-owned enterprises (SOEs) into smaller units, and the liquidation of state monopoly units.

At this early stage of the AMC's work, its powers have apparently not been used very extensively. Decree 135 of the Cabinet of Ministers on antimonopoly regulation covers all monopoly enterprises (market share greater than 35 percent) and natural monopolies, big monopolies (market share greater than 70 percent), and enterprises that violate antimonopoly law.[17] The decree also establishes marginal prices and profits that can be set by relevant sector ministries or the Ministry of Economy and approved by the AMC. The AMC approves arrangements and procedures and compiles lists of firms subject to different types of control. The result is an AMC of very broad scope and is inclined to be very interventionist as compared to similar agencies in the rest of Eastern Europe. In Ukraine's present situation, the AMC needed to be more active than it would be in more market-type economies, according to senior AMC officials.

The AMC needs no formal request before it can act, since it can initiate actions on its own. It has approved a list of national-level monopolies: 470 enterprises and associations, comprising about 5,000 enterprises in all. At regional/local levels there are about 1,300 monopolies, comprising about 7,000 enterprises. Mergers also are under AMC control, and fixed criteria have been established for a merger to come under AMC supervision: at least $8.2 million total assets and at least $18.9 million total sales. The combined market share of the proposed merged companies would also be taken into account.

The AMC is concerned to break down barriers to entry that result either from the actions of other enterprises or from state regulation. There is much indirect regulation of entry via licensing, state orders and contracts, and so on. Hence the AMC wants to reduce the list of goods subject to such controls. To protect their local markets, regional authorities also commonly try to stop goods from moving to another region in Ukraine; this type of behavior needs to be halted but in practice the pressures to operate such controls are very strong. The underlying problem is clearly one of pricing, since it is unclear why firms should refuse to supply the local market if the prices there were set sensibly in relation to available prices elsewhere. But Ukrainian officials seem not to see it as a problem of pricing at all, and their instinct is still to impose quantitative controls on product flows, as they would naturally have done under central planning. Moreover, even if they did accept the pricing interpretation, it is more than likely that they themselves would wish to regulate the relevant prices by imposing margin controls, maximum rates of profit on sales, or even directly fixed prices.

What this reveals is a conception of the market that was quite widespread under the conditions of central planning. This conception has two aspects. First, in situations where some prices in local markets are controlled, firms seeking to increase profits may well (perfectly rationally) choose to supply some markets and not others. Officials concerned about the lack of supply to certain districts might then intervene by instructing local firms not to 'export' their produce. Officials concerned about employment in local firms whose markets are being taken over by firms from other districts might respond by trying to ban or limit 'imports.' No one is likely to respond by proposing the decontrol of prices, by inaction (officials have to be seen to be doing 'something'!), by allowing some firms to shut down, or by leaving firms free to buy and sell wherever they wish. Second, even if prices are not controlled directly, they can be controlled indirectly via tax concessions or even by means of subsidies. Again, officials will try to protect local business whenever they can.

There is no recognition here of the general point that market processes frequently work fine when left to themselves, and that the outcomes of market processes often have desirable efficiency properties. There could be two sets of reasons as to why this line of argument might be rather less than compelling under Ukrainian conditions. One group of reasons essentially observes that markets are not only about the efficient allocation of resources, but also about the distribution and redistribution of economic power through allocating various types of property rights. Thus officials who apparently 'do not understand' the market may understand perfectly well that market processes involve redistribution that may not be to their advantage: officials themselves lose power, workers may be displaced from their jobs, some 'reasonable' demands may not be met, and so on. For the most part, the early beneficiaries of market reforms are not those who are in the most favorable positions in the status quo ante.

The second group of reasons has to do with the Ukrainian institutional structure. When we talk of market processes, we take it for granted that in response to a disequilibrium in the market there will be entry and exit by firms, changes in output by existing firms, and changes in the ruling prices to bring about a new equilibrium. But it may be that under Ukrainian conditions such adjustments could not be relied upon. For instance, social resistance may prevent exit (bankruptcy), regulatory and legal failures may inhibit or prevent new entry (not to mention criminal action to preserve local monopolies), and popular pressure may prevent local prices from rising high enough to overcome these barriers and stimulate adjustment.

Hence officials might justify their intervention by claiming that market processes simply cannot work, and at times this may indeed be so. This implies that the real task for the AMC is more complex and wide-ranging than was outlined above, since obviously it must work to find ways of overcoming these nonmarket factors that prevent markets from functioning well. However, the real significance of this point is not wholly clear, since we do not have firm evidence on the extent of nonmarket barriers to market functioning in Ukraine; this could be a useful field for further investigation.

Summary and Conclusions

To sum up, the contradictory nature of the Ukrainian experience of transition so far can be accounted for by conflict between the different institutions in the political system due to contrasting interests and ideologies, the exercise of influence by dominant interest and lobby groups, and a lack of understanding of the principles of transition. In addition, we find an air of caution about forging into the unknown—in particular, a fear of and unwillingness to incur social costs, even in the short run; the development of contradictory economic models, which conflict in many ways with the requirements of transition; and a weak system of laws, which has attracted gross violations and of contempt for the rule of law.

It can be seen that there has been little continuity in Ukraine's reform program, as witnessed by constant disruptions to the privatization program and the climate of hesitancy and suspicion apparent in the move toward a market economy. In the years ahead Ukraine's economic reform program is likely to continue to be impeded by the presence of political, institutional, and ideological obstacles. Ukraine appears to be experiencing great difficulty in eradicating the old type of state control thinking implicit in Soviet communism; the legacy of central planning remains very strong.

The contradictions that appear in Ukraine's approach to transition—retaining some features of the command economy, a large continuing role of the state in the economy, and preserving the monopoly status of some firms—are not really so surprising. Despite the fact there has been plenty of advice from the West on how to move to a market system, such a process must inevitably take some time. The Ukrainians, like many East Europeans, still lack the necessary experience and knowledge to make them familiar with the operation of a market system, and acquiring such skill and know-how cannot be a quick and rapid task. We should also acknowledge that the state does have an important role to play in transition—in creating market structures and encouraging industrial development. But, of course, its role has to be limited and must not be allowed to develop into excessive intervention. The economy should be influenced largely by the market—not by the state.

Notes

This paper was prepared with the support of ESRC Research Grant No. R000/23/5650, for which the authors are grateful. Some of the information reported in the paper is drawn from interviews with officials and academics during two visits to Ukraine, in November 1995 and March 1996, respectively. The authors are grateful to Taras Kuzio and other participants in the University of Birmingham conference "Soviet to Independent Ukraine: A Troubled Transformation" (June 1996) for their helpful comments on earlier drafts of this paper. Remaining errors are the responsibility of the authors.

1. For a general discussion of the standard transition 'package,' see Richard Portes, "Introduction," in *European Economy, Special Edition No. 2* (Brussels: European Commission, 1991), pp. 1–17.

2. For an assessment of reform progress in various countries, as measured by a selection of country-level transition indicators, see EBRD, *Transition Report* (London: EBRD, 1995), Table 2.1. Paul Hare and Tanya Normak, in "Estimating the Transition Impact of EBRD Projects" (London: EBRD, 1996), present these indicators for both 1994 and 1995, from which it can be seen that while progress continued in the more advanced countries of the region, Ukraine advanced relatively little.

3. Interviews by the authors with officials and academics in Ukraine, autumn 1995. The presence of monopolies might explain an initial burst of inflation following price liberalization, but they do not explain its persistence.

4. Interviews held in Kyiv in 1995 and 1996.

5. This culminated in the president's sacking of Marchuk on 27 May 1995; see the announcement in *The Guardian,* 28 May 1996.

6. For the text of the agreement, see *Holos Ukrainy,* 10 June 1995.

7. An example of a strong lobby is the Ukrainian League of Industrialists and Entrepreneurs, based in eastern Ukraine, which is essentially a lobby of directors of formerly large state-owned enterprises; the lobby has links with other directors in former Soviet-bloc countries. Surprisingly, however, the leadership of the league now appears to be very supportive of market reforms.

8. However, the effect of this legislation was undermined by the presumption that if the government wanted to exceed the legal borrowing limit, it would be able to borrow more from the commercial banks.

9. As an example of this, the Ministry of Coal did not discourage miners' strikes demanding higher pay, since it saw them as strengthening the case for increased subsidies.

10. The World Bank/IMF view, however, is that stabilization is now in sight.

11. For an intriguing analysis of the political economy of reforms, based on a study of many countries, see Dani Rodrik, "Understanding Economic Policy Reform," *Journal of Economic Literature,* vol. 34, no. 1 (March 1996), pp. 9–41. On the Ukrainian case, see John Tedstrom, "Ukraine: A Crash Course in Economic Transition," *Comparative Economic Studies,* vol. 37, no. 4 (Winter 1995), pp. 49–67.

12. The point also, of course, highlights the need for extensive training in market economy methods and practices, as is being done through some of the IMF and World Bank assistance going to Ukraine and through such EU programs as TACIS.

13. In 1993 out of 200 private sector firms surveyed, about 50 percent of their activities were in the shadow economy. An effective system of civil law, comprising

contracts and company laws, will have to be established and effectively implemented in order to allow private firms to operate in a suitable market environment.

14. For a general review of privatization issues in Central and eastern Europe, see Saul Estrin, *Privatization in Central and Eastern Europe* (London: Longman, 1994).

15. The monthly average wage in 1996 was only around eighty dollars at the official exchange rate.

16. In one interview conducted by the authors in Ukraine it was pointed out that the Russian state property fund had reported to Ukraine that Russian privatization was a 'disaster,' with falling output, collapsing firms, falling employment, and so on. However, Ukraine has all these problems with far less privatization to 'blame' for them.

17. Other forms of antimonopoly control are not under the AMC; for example, local authorities control local products such as bread, city transport, and so on. See Saul Estrin and Martin Cave, eds., *Competition and Competition Policy: A Comparative Analysis of Central and Eastern Europe* (London: Pinter, 1993), and Russell Pittman, "Competition Policy in Ukraine and the United States: The Ukrainian Competition Law and the American Experience," PERU White Paper No. 95–002 (Kyiv: Project on Economic Reform in Ukraine, 1995).

11

Ukraine's Economy: Strategic Issues for Successful Recovery

John E. Tedstrom

Some two years after embarking on its program of 'radical' economic reform, Ukraine's economy continues to hang in the balance. Although there can be no doubt that Ukraine's reformers—under the leadership of President Leonid Kuchma—have made significant progress, much remains to be done. And although recent successes at reform suggest that Ukraine and its leaders have the wherewithal to effectively design and implement a reform agenda, it is not clear that in practice the country as a whole has the will to push ahead fast enough to gain the type of momentum that will allow them to meet their goals of becoming a modern, efficient economy based in part on private property and guided by market principles.

The stakes inherent in Ukraine's success are high. It is a country with considerable political, economic, and military potential. It has a long and complicated relationship with Eurasia's largest power, Russia. It is nestled between progressive reforming countries in Central Europe and countries that so far have refused to shake loose the Soviet yoke (Belarus), have done so partially (Russia), or are suffering from internal and even cross-border instability (Russia, Georgia, Moldova, etc.). Ukraine can either languish in the post-Soviet morass as it tries to find some illusory 'third way' to stability and prosperity, or it can take bold and decisive steps toward a more modern political-economic system. As key Western countries look east, well aware of Ukraine's difficult past, they are simultaneously hopeful about its future and skeptical about its present. How to make the transition from the difficult present to a brighter future is the challenge Ukraine's leaders, and those in the West who would provide assistance, must meet.

As Ukraine begins its third year of transformation, three components of its economic reform agenda stand out as critical for the longer run. The first of these components might be called the 'macro mission.' The Macro Mission refers to the necessity to stabilize finances, decontrol markets, and grow the private economy. Without progress on these fronts, economic recovery in Ukraine—a critical element of the long-term transformation—is out of the question. Second, Ukraine must move resolutely to consolidate its position in the regional economic space, particularly vis-à-vis Russia. Ukraine must reduce its dependence on Russia for a number of reasons. Most important among these is the fact that reforms in Russia are far from solidified, the fact that Russia's integration agenda with other Commonwealth of Independent States (CIS) states will be costly and could jeopardize the fragile financial equilibrium that has been achieved, and because if Russia grows stronger while Ukraine languishes, the strategic balance of power, now roughly equal, will shift decidedly in Russia's favor. The third economic challenge is to integrate Ukraine with more modern, growth-oriented countries in the global marketplace. Integration will bring capital and competition, both necessary elements in a successful long-term growth strategy. Before examining these three strategic lines of economic reform, a review of recent trends in economic performance and reform is necessary to set the stage and describe Ukraine's initial conditions.

Recent Economic Performance

When assessing Ukraine's economic performance since independence, one can divide the country's experience into two distinct periods. The first period, from December 1991 through June 1994, is the period of denial. It was during this time that Ukraine failed to design, let alone implement, a serious reform agenda. Some progress was made during this period in liberalizing parts of the economy. But these efforts were meager and generally ineffectual because they were done in a vacuum. Ukraine amassed large debts—both domestic and foreign—and failed to attract foreign investors. Living standards deteriorated for the bulk of the population, even as an underground economy began to flourish and increasingly divert resources to economic criminals. Output was falling while inflation achieved near-hyper levels. Table 11.1, depicts the official record on economic performance.

As the data in Table 11.1 suggest, Ukraine's economic crisis was both profound, resulting in strong negative trends in economic indicators, and pervasive, with virtually no sector of the economy being spared. This deep and widespread depression had three critical ramifications. First, the community of Western governments and international financial organizations all but ignored Ukraine.[1] Second, Ukraine's relations with Russia deterio-

Table 11.1

Ukraine: Basic Economic Indicators, 1990–1995

	1990	1991	1992	1993	1994	1995[a]
GDP	−2.4	−13.5	−16.8	−14.2	−23.0	−12.8
Gross Industrial Output	−0.1	−4.8	−6.4	−7.6	−27.7	−11.0
Gross Agricultural Output	−3.7	−13.2	−8.3	1.5	17.0	−2.0
Consumer Goods Production	5.8	−5.1	−9.4	−15.3	−26.7	
Capital Investment	1.9	−7.1	−36.9	−10.3	−25.0	−20.0
% Monthly change in CPI			33.5	47.1	14.4	9.6
Nonagricultural Privatization[b]	—	—	30.0	3,585.0	11,552.0	16,265.0
Private Farms[c]	—	—	292.3	558.2	699.7	780.0

Source: European Centre for Macroeconomic Analysis of Ukraine and the Ministry of Economics of Ukraine, *Ukrainian Economic Trends,*–various issues.

Notes:

[a]Author's estimates.

[b]Number of private enterprises.

[c]Thousand of hectares privatized.

rated because it simultaneously became more dependent on Russia economically while it was trying to establish itself as an independent nation-state. Third, dissatisfaction with economic performance contributed to the country's incumbent president, Leonid Kravchuk, losing to his former prime minister, Kuchma, in presidential elections in June 1994.

Kuchma moved quickly to impose a comprehensive reform agenda, focusing first and foremost on macroeconomic stability. The results in terms of economic performance have been both positive and expected. Inflation has dropped from a high of over 70 percent per month in November 1994 to much more tolerable levels, generally below 12 percent per month since March 1995 and about 5 percent or less in the second half of 1996. Output has continued to decline, though data for the first quarter of 1996 indicate that even in the official economy the reforms have succeeded in slowing and in some cases arresting the trend of month-after-month decreases in production. One troubling sign is that the services sector has not blossomed as it has in many other transition economies. But even here, there are indications that positive changes are afoot. The banking sector is consolidating itself after several banks faced bankruptcy due to large holdings of under- (or non-) performing loans. Another persisting problem is that investment rates remain low—too low to contribute substantially to economic recovery.

Beyond these issues, it is worth noting that Ukraine's economy is a good deal larger, and is likely performing a good deal better, than official statis-

Table 11.2

Output of Energy, by Source, March 1996 and First Quarter 1996
(percentage growth over period)

	2/96	3/95	I/95	I/94 to I/95
Electricity	3.2	0.2	0.1	−0.8
Oil	4.2	−0.9	0.1	−3.0
Natural gas	6.5	2.7	3.7	−3.3
Coal	16.4	−15.1	−18.5	−13.9
Coking coal	17.9	−11.3	−16.0	−21.6

Source: Ministry of Statistics, Ukraine, cited in *Okno v Ukrainu,* 18 April 1996.

tics would indicate. Although there is no way to produce a reliable estimate of the size of the shadow economy, knowledgeable Ukrainian and Western scholars put it at as much as 40 to 60 percent of the total economy. One piece of evidence that is particularly convincing is data on production of energy sources, especially electricity. As Table 11.2 shows, these data all indicate better performance in the energy sector than in the economy as a whole. When compared to the performance in energy-intensive industries, the discrepancy is even greater. These discrepancies point to the likelihood that official statistics underreport economic activity.[2]

A key goal in the next stage of reforms must be to bring the shadow economy out into the open so that its value added can be distributed more efficiently among all consumers and producers.

The Reform Agenda

Since taking office, President Kuchma has pursued a course of 'shock therapy' modeled loosely on the Polish, Czech, and Russian versions. Like those countries' reforms, Ukraine's program consists of three main pillars: macroeconomic stabilization, privatization, and liberalization. Although the Kuchma record on implementing these reforms is not perfect, many of the key elements of a successful transformation program are now in place, and new market institutions, relations, and forces are beginning to come to life. Moreover, when conservative political forces attempt to stall or turn back reform measures, President Kuchma has demonstrated that he is willing, at least sometimes, to override their objections.[3]

After suffering some three years under near-hyper inflation, imposing macroeconomic stability in Ukraine was one of Kuchma's first-order objectives upon taking office. He introduced important changes in fiscal and

Figure 11.1. M2 and CPI Indexes for Ukraine

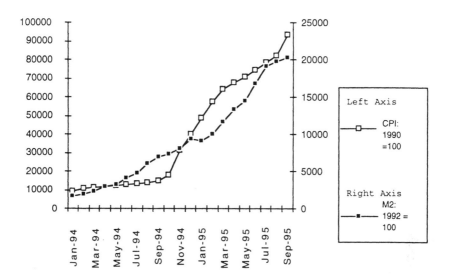

monetary policy alike, though the government's commitment to these measures has come and gone over the last two years. The results point clearly to the fact that Ukraine is not a unique economic system, but that economic agents operating in it respond to economic stimuli in the same way that those in every other economy do. When officials in Kyiv refrain from budget-busting spending habits and keep tight hold of the money supply, inflation slows to impressively low levels and international assistance flows. In late 1995 and early 1996, in particular, Ukrainian officials seemed to be bending to pressure from agricultural and industrial interests. In response, the IMF canceled its standby loan until Ukraine returned to a more responsible policy path. It was not until April and May of 1996 that Ukraine passed a budget for 1996 that was acceptable to the IMF in terms of its income and expenditure flows and in the overall level of deficit. The IMF negotiated a new loan, and in May and June Ukraine qualified for $100 million trenches.

As noted above, the Kuchma administration also moved quickly to improve the government's monetary policy, but this proved a particularly difficult challenge. Figure 11.1 shows that there was little control over monetary policy through early 1995, and clearly shows the strong relationship between M^2 (money supply) and inflation in Ukraine. After allowing significant increases in money emissions in mid-1995, Ukraine's central bank has made a determined effort to control the money supply, contributing to the overall deceleration of inflation.

Table 11.3

Ukraine: The Pace of Privatization, 1992–1995

	Privatized enterprises[a]	Used privatization accounts (thousands)	Privatized apartments (thousands)	Private farms	Land area of private farms (thousands of hectares)
1992	30	5	0.0	14,681	292.3
1993	3,585	728	902.8	27,739	558.2
1994	11,552	7,106	1,812.3	31,983	699.7
1994–1[b]	5,442	1,503	1,218.3	29,666	620.5
1994–2	8,402	2,873	1,448.0	30,895	657.5
1994–3	10,214	4,883	1,620.1	31,325	675.0
1994–4	11,552	7,106	1,812.3	31,983	699.7
1995–1	12,802	11,186	1,989.1	33,040	728.9
1995–2	14,957	15,600	2,122.8	33,746	757.0
1995–3	19,800	21,228	2,236.3	34,149	773.0

Source: European Center for Macroeconomic Analysis of Ukraine and the Ministry of Economics of Ukraine, *Ukrainian Economic Trends*, October 1995.

Notes:

[a]This includes both small scale and the mass privatization of medium and large enterprises in the nonfarm sectors.

[b]Refers to quarters.

Privatizing the large, loss-making state sector of the economy is also a necessary measure for successful reform. Through 1995, the best that could be said about Ukraine's attempt at privatization was that it was better than that of Belarus. Since late 1995, however, the number of large and small businesses privatized has increased significantly, and there are indications that a renewed commitment to privatization at the highest levels is responsible. Still, there are many obstacles for privatizing firms to navigate, including political impediments from the Supreme Rada and from some local and regional leaders. Table 11.3 shows in detail the pace and structure of the privatization experience in Ukraine through late 1995. For virtually every period covered in Table 11.3, privatization targets were unfulfilled, and where growth existed at all, it was sluggish. It should be noted, however, that these data do not cover the de novo creation of completely new firms, which is sometimes referred to as "organic" privatization. Since many new firms are not officially registered, the real importance of the de novo private sector will in any case be underestimated.

In the first half of 1996, data indicate that the pace of privatization accelerated somewhat. In January, a total of 1,709 enterprises were privatized, including 1,388 small firms and 313 large firms. In February, the last month for which we have concrete data, the number of privatized enterprises grew significantly, to 2,002 (1,702 small enterprises, 285 large enterprises). The leading regions for privatization were L'viv (408 privatized enterprises in January–February 1996) and Donets'k (316 privatized enterprises in January–February 1996). Dnipropetrovs'k, Odesa, and Kyiv are also showing relatively strong privatization results.[4]

Ukraine has made its best progress in liberalizing the various sectors of its economy, though as argued in the concluding section of this chapter, more needs to be done. Studies by World Bank economist Daniel Kaufmann and others have measured the degree of 'administrative control' in Ukraine and have found a significant improvement, that is, a decrease in administrative control, since 1992.[5] These studies measure exchange rate distortion, foreign exchange allocation distortion, export restriction, domestic trade, retail price controls, and wholesale price controls. Since the first quarter of 1992, when the overall administrative control index stood at 79, it has fallen to less than 25.[6] The most progress was made in retail price liberalization and foreign exchange liberalization. Less impressive have been efforts to liberalize export restrictions.

Relations with Russia

Ukraine's relations with Russia are complicated and multifaceted, and a full discussion of even the economic dimensions of this relationship is far beyond the scope of this chapter. A key issue is to what degree should Ukraine attempt to shift its economic relations away from Russia. Currently, Russia provides the largest market for Ukrainian goods and services, and as of 1996, that market is likely to be a growing one. On the other hand, Ukraine has expressed a desire, encouraged by the United States and other Western nations, to become part of the larger European system of markets, political institutions, and security arrangements. Political and economic change in Russia is not predictable now, nor is it likely to become so in the near future. Thus Ukraine needs to worry about the timing of any shift from Russia as well as the magnitude and exact nature of the shift. Perhaps foremost in everyone's mind in the context of economic strategy are the politics and economics of the energy interdependence of the two countries, and in fact this issue is likely to help define the overall Ukrainian-Russian relationship for many years to come.

The Russian-Ukrainian energy interdependence is intricately complex. On the one hand, Ukraine is a consumer of Russian energy (mostly oil and natural gas), and has been and will be somewhat vulnerable to Russian political-economic pressure on these points. On the other hand, Russia's leverage over Ukraine in this regard is limited because, at least for the time being, Ukraine controls a large share of the energy transportation system between Russia and lucrative markets in Western Europe. The Druzhba pipeline, for example, carries Russian oil to Western European consumers. The oil that flows through the Druzhba pipeline accounts for some 40 percent of Russia's total oil exports. Complicating this delicate balance is the fact that economic power and decision making in the energy sectors of both countries have begun to devolve significantly away from the central government to private and semiprivate enterprises and conglomerates. In some cases, these new concerns actually take the lead in negotiating various facets of Russian foreign economic policy toward Ukraine.[7]

Russia is making moves to lessen its reliance on pipelines that cross Ukraine by developing port facilities, negotiating deals with countries outside the CIS, and, most important, working with Belarus to construct various alternative pipelines across its territory.[8] There are also Russo-Belarusian plans to cooperate on new oil refinery capacity. This would lessen Russia's reliance on refinery capacity in Ukraine and increase its ability to reach important customers in Central and Western Europe without dealing with Ukraine.

Although all of these alternatives are years off, Russia clearly sees its interests lying in a diversification of its energy relationships inside and outside the CIS. Ukraine would thus be well advised to move now to lessen its own dependence on Russian oil and gas so as to maintain the rough balance of power that now exists in this facet of the relationship. In contrast to Russia's plans to work with Belarus, Ukraine is best advised to reduce energy consumption per unit of GDP by imposing competition and hard budget constraints (which would, of course, be desirable anyway on efficiency grounds regardless of the source of Ukraine's energy; it has moved in this direction already, though state subsidies still support inefficient energy users) and attract Western capital investment and joint venture partners to help develop its energy production and distribution capacities. In fact, Ukraine's energy economy represents one of the more attractive sectors for foreign direct investment, as the following section points out.

Integrating into the Global Economy

In light of the above discussion concerning Ukraine's close economic ties, indeed its lingering economic dependence on Russia and the CIS, it is useful to return to first principles before addressing some of the specifics of economic integration. In this vein we will discuss both trade and investment with an eye toward understanding their roles in the overall transition process and will enumerate some general policy options, some of which Ukraine has flirted with, that would promote its integration with the West.[9]

Under centrally planned economic systems the domestic economy was separate from those parts of the state sector that were involved in international economic activity. For this reason, many reformers, including those in the former Soviet Union, turned to liberalizing their foreign economic systems early on in the transition process. It is important to understand, however, that liberalizing the foreign trade and investment regimes of a formerly centrally planned economy is an integral part of the overall transition process, and cannot be pursued successfully on its own. Liberalization of foreign trade and investment is linked to the rest of the reform agenda in the following ways:

- Increased trade/investment promotes domestic price adjustment;
- Increased trade/investment increases domestic competition;
- Increased trade/investment promotes economic restructuring.

These three effects of liberalized trade and investment regimes are obviously closely connected to and interdependent with sound monetary and fiscal policy, antimonopoly policies, and privatization and corporatization efforts, respectively. Thus, it is not enough simply to disband old Soviet-era institutions and policies. Rather, private firms, flexible prices, and other key attributes of an enabling entrepreneurial environment must be in place if the new trade and investment regimes are to have their full, desired effect.[10]

Currently, foreign trade statistics indicate that Ukraine is enjoying significant growth in both imports and exports. Foreign investment, on the other hand continues to flag. The main impediments to increased foreign investment in Ukraine are:

- perceptions of political instability;
- signals that Ukraine's commitment to market reforms is weak;
- an unclear and often unstable body of business law;
- an opaque and uncompetitive tax regime;
- lack of confidence in the property rights regime in Ukraine, especially as it pertains to foreigners.

In contrast, one need only point to the success of the Czech Republic during 1995–1996. In that time it has attracted considerable amounts of foreign direct investment due largely to its political and economic stability and its investor-friendly business climate.

Ukraine, given its geographical proximity to growing economies in Central Europe and a potentially large and dynamic market in Russia, is well positioned to serve as a key transit point for East-West trade and as a regional hub for foreign direct investors. Before progress along these lines can be expected, however, Ukraine must improve its infrastructure, though it can and should do this with foreign assistance and, where possible, private foreign investment. First, Ukraine should increase its road, rail, and airport capacities that link the country with the emerging markets in Central Europe, in particular Poland and Hungary. Second, the telecommunications system in Ukraine needs to be modernized. These two sectors—transportation and communications—are both critical for future economic growth and are prime targets for foreign investors.[11]

A second area that is ripe for investment is agriculture and the agricultural-industrial sector. In the past, some Western companies have pursued a 'drop and run' strategy of simply delivering shiny new tractors to Ukrainian farmers, who proceeded to let them sit in open fields until they rusted. The appropriate strategy for Ukraine's agricultural sector is a more comprehensive and coherent one that would include importing capital goods, using new farming techniques, implementing modern financial management practices, and so on. Addressing the entire agroindustrial *system* in Ukraine means that agriculture and attendant industries will rebound, generating returns for consumers, farmers, and investors alike.

The energy sector is another possible candidate for future investment, though the opportunities are not likely to be as easily realized as in other sectors. Recently, Ukrainian scientists discovered new reserves of oil off the Black Sea shelf, but Ukraine lacks both the technology and the capital to exploit these deposits. An important issue to be resolved in this area is ownership of oil and gas deposits in the Black Sea. A likely scenario is the further development of multilateral investment activities that have tended to prove complicated and frustrating for Western partners. The Ukrainian coal industry is undergoing a massive restructuring, mostly a downsizing, but there are likely to be needs for Western technologies and capital there as well. Finally, there is a need for foreign investment in modernizing the natural gas distribution system (getting gas to consumers and measuring their consumption) and in improving the natural gas transportation system (modernizing pipelines, compressor stations, and the like).

Other possibilities for foreign direct investment include environmental protection and remediation, water management, and urban transport. Significantly, most of these projects are supportable through programs managed by USAID, OPIC, EBRD, World Bank, IFC, and other international financial institutions. By developing more of the key attributes of an investor-

and trade-friendly economy, Ukraine is likely to find not only private sector interest, but international support for these projects as well.

One myth that Ukraine should avoid pursuing is that the military-industrial legacy it inherited from the Soviet Union will generate significant revenues from the international arms market. Some reports indicate that President Kuchma is personally overseeing the development of Ukraine's arms export capability and that plans are for Ukrainian arms exports to total some U.S.$10 billion by the year 2000.[12] There are at least two major problems with this strategy. First, the global arms market is small and shrinking, and the countries that would buy Ukrainian arms are not particularly wealthy, though some, like Pakistan, do have considerable arms import desires. Second, Ukraine faces a major competitor in Russia. Most, if not all, of Ukraine's arms exports will be standard Soviet-design items that Russia also produces and markets abroad.[13]

Challenges for the Future

Ukraine faces some distinct choices as it charts its course into the twenty-first century. Although it is impossible to lay out all the possible policy paths Ukrainian leaders can pursue, it is possible to examine, in light of the preceding analysis, the two principal choices: a strong commitment to economic reform, and a more modest, 'Ukraine is special' approach. A full and permanent collapse of the reform effort, though theoretically possible, is not at all likely. It is impossible to construct these two approaches fully, but some of their basic characteristics will be familiar to those who have watched the transition experiences of Poland, Hungary, the Czech Republic, and Russia. And even if many of the subtleties are missing, the two hypothetical scenarios serve to orient our thinking along general policy lines.

Weak Reform Scenario

A weak reform scenario for Ukraine focuses on macroeconomic stability but does not tackle other important questions such as liberalization, privatization, and restructuring. Essentially, efforts would be made to sustain the political-economic situation as of 1996–1997. The primary reason that the focus of the weak scenario is on macro stability is that Ukraine has already seen the benefits of lowering inflation, in terms of economic performance, political support for reforms, and international economic and financial support.

Importantly, a weak reform scenario neglects the foreign sector: Ukraine would maintain, roughly, its current level and composition of imports and exports with both the CIS and the West, and foreign economic activity would not generate either the kind of export revenues needed to finance a robust import agenda or the scale of current account deficit that could accommodate a large and inward resource transfer, for example, through inward foreign investment.

Under the weak reform scenario, many of the current state enterprises are neither restructured nor privatized. They continue to carry the bulk of the country's social services portfolio, and they continue to operate at a loss. There are virtually no efficiency gains from microeconomic reform. The growth of the private sector is sluggish but positive, and would likely bring only modest positive results.

Another characteristic of the weak reform scenario is that government is not restructured. First, because the state sector of the economy remains large and largely unreformed, its burden on the budget remains large. Public spending would remain relatively large and skewed toward the 'national economy' and social services accounts. Second, the government payroll itself would be a large and nontrivial budget item. The social safety net would continue without reforms, passing out meager amounts of assistance to large numbers of Ukrainians, few of whom notice its impact on their daily lives. All of this would combine to limit the scope for private investment.

Finally, we should expect that the shadow economy in Ukraine would grow under this scenario. On one hand, this sector of the economy would provide economic opportunity and welfare to a growing number of people abandoned by the official economy. On the other hand, this economy would not, in the end, contribute to overall economic development in the longer run. The government would be deprived of critical tax revenues, consumers would have few or no rights, the risk to investors would carry a premium, and entrepreneurs would funnel money to the Mafia, where it could well get lost in numbered bank accounts abroad.

An unfortunate but inevitable result of such a scenario would be a sharp decline in the amount of economic support Ukraine receives from the West. This contraction of outside assistance would further limit Ukraine's ability to service debt and undertake important restructuring projects. In the end, it is likely that Ukraine would be compelled to increase its formal political, economic, and security ties with Russia, especially if the Russian economy begins to grow, as many expect.

An Ambitious Reform Scenario

A policy agenda that is committed to fundamental reforms and restructuring the Ukrainian economy would look similar to the reform paths that other successful transition economies have pursued. The only key difference is that Ukrainians need to worry about the high degree of concentration of their foreign economic relations with Russia.[14] As noted above, reorienting Ukraine's trade among CIS and non-CIS partners would be a delicate balancing act, primarily because of the economic boost Ukraine is likely to enjoy due to economic stabilization and recovery in Russia. At the same time, however, in order to earn hard-currency revenues and eventually attract hard-currency investments on a meaningful scale, Ukraine must begin to focus its attention on its economic relations with the West. Given the partial success at reform that Ukraine has thus far achieved, an ambitious reform agenda would include the following key initiatives.

Stabilization Measures

World Bank studies have shown that without sustained success in controlling inflation, economic recovery remains elusive. Not only do high and variable rates of inflation confound government policy makers, but they inhibit private and foreign investment and distort markets. As noted above, the IMF had a difficult time ensuring Ukraine would commit itself to a reasonable budget deficit target for 1996. In the end, we see in the first-quarter statistics for 1996 that austere monetary and fiscal policies have paid off with low monthly inflation rates. During 1996–1997, the government faced pressures to pay back wages and other arrears, to increase subsidies to industry, and to increase credit limits to unrealistic levels. Under the ambitious reform agenda, Ukraine would:

- reduce subsidies to state enterprises across the board, especially to loss-making firms;
- resist increasing credit limits for state enterprises;
- move quickly to improve tax collection by reducing marginal tax rates, simplifying the tax code, and improving the tax collection bureaucracy;
- improve the state's capacity to finance the budget deficit through noninflationary means, i.e., sovereign debt;
- reduce the size of the government payroll at all levels of government (this is also a good way to weed out bureaucrats who do not support reform);
- strengthen the financial sector of the economy by stabilizing banking regulations and closing all remaining failing banks;
- devote considerably more attention to the development of the country's stock market, and not impeding private efforts to do so, e.g., through improved share registry and custody arrangements.

Privatization and Structural Reform

Although privatization and structural reform are usually treated separately in transitioning economies, the policies are intimately intertwined and are usefully thought of as two parts of the same problem. Under the ambitious reform scenario, Ukraine would accelerate its efforts to privatize industrial and agricultural assets. This will require more than just improved laws on privatization. It will require serious efforts to create the appropriate environment for entrepreneurial activities. An improved tax regime, as discussed above, is characteristic of such an environment, as are reliable, stable business laws. More specifically, an ambitious reform agenda would:

- support privatization by shifting part of the funds formerly used to subsidize the state sector to privatization programs;
- simplify the privatization red tape, encouraging average Ukrainians to more fully participate in the privatization program;
- simplify the process for new business start-ups;
- institute a new process for setting values for privatizing enterprises, one that is market-oriented and would result in lower prices for these enterprises;
- take a radical approach to reforming regional and local regulations and laws so as to create an encouraging environment for private business activities;
- divest state enterprises of their social safety net functions;
- focus on resuscitating the energy sector, accelerating the program to close loss-making coal mines and enacting a legal framework that encourages competition and foreign investment in oil, gas, and coal production and transportation.

Liberalization

Ukraine has made most progress in liberalizing both its domestic and foreign economic activities, but more needs to be done. Enough has been done to show results, but further progress will mean real, though temporary, economic and social discomfort. The ambitious reform agenda would:

- move steadily to remove remaining domestic price controls and subsidies;
- pursue the final stage of foreign economic liberalization resolutely, including reducing remaining export and import restrictions and resisting the temptation to increase 'protectionist' measures.

Social Support

Perhaps the key indicator that Ukraine is serious about reform will be the emergence of a serious social safety net. Until such a support system is put into place, real reform is unlikely due simply to political realities. The ambitious reform agenda would:

- liberalize the labor market to improve labor mobility so as to reduce the need for state support of the underemployed;
- target social support resources to a smaller group of the neediest people so that the assistance makes a difference;
- raise the retirement age;
- make the financial health of these programs a priority.

This type of ambitious reform agenda, following on Ukraine's experience with reform since late 1994, would produce positive results in the near term. The main engine of growth is likely to be exports, both to Russia and to other CIS states as well as to the West. If this concentration on exports was accompanied by responsible fiscal and monetary policy, it would not be unreasonable to expect the economic decline to bottom out in 1997 and real economic growth to begin as soon as 1998. If efforts are made to liberalize the economy and bring the shadow economy into the light, growth from 1998 could be robust.

Any attempt to model a national economy, let alone one in transition, is bound to produce questionable results. There is no reason to believe, however, that Ukraine could not achieve the same type of growth as other European countries in transition if strong reforms are implemented now. This would mean real growth on the order of 6 percent per annum by the year 2000, and annual inflation down to something like 10 percent. Consumption per capita would also increase, and should parallel the experience of Poland, though with something of a lag. To insist that Ukraine is unique and is therefore not capable of meeting this challenge is demeaning and underestimates its citizens' abilities.

Ukraine has made considerable progress on some of the issues raised here but has fallen short on most. It has been seen that its economy responds normally to economic stimuli. It has been seen that Western governments and international financial institutions respond generously and productively when a country makes a good-faith effort to get its economics right. These are all strong arguments in favor of pursuing an ambitious reform agenda, one that holds the best hope for Ukraine to become a solid anchor in the European and global marketplaces.

Notes

The views expressed here are the author's own and not necessarily those of the RAND Corporation or its sponsors. The author thanks Professor Philip Hanson, Deputy Director, Centre for Russian and East European Studies, University of Birmingham, for his comments on an earlier draft.

1. Ukraine was ignored for three main reasons. In terms of overall importance, the first reason was that until Ukraine made progress on denuclearization, Kyiv's dialogues with other governments were limited to that issue. Second, because the West already had significant exposure in Eurasia, most governments were reluctant to invest in a country not clearly on the road to reform. Third, some countries, the United States included, de facto pursued a 'Russia first' policy agenda.

2. A similar discrepancy between electricity usage and reported levels of overall economic activity has been seen in Russia. Many of the same incentives to underreport output operate there, but there is relatively little scope for underreporting the output of electricity. Of the numerous incentives for individuals and enterprises to underreport economic activity, the main one is to avoid paying taxes. A culture of tax evasion has already begun to emerge in Ukraine; this is a difficult problem to correct once it becomes established.

3. An example of this is Kuchma's veto of a controversial legislative bill on advertising. The bill, passed by parliament in March 1996, stipulated a 15 percent tax on advertising and banned all tobacco and alcohol advertisements. Another example is his sacking of former Prime Minister Yevhen Marchuk in May 1996.

4. Council of Advisors to the Presidium of the Parliament of Ukraine, *Update on Ukraine,* January, February, and March 1996.

5. See Daniel Kaufmann, "Economic Reform 'Correction' in Ukraine? Myth and Reality," unpublished paper, 29 September 1995. His findings are discussed in more detail in John E. Tedstrom, *Ukraine's Economy at Risk,* MR-752.0–RC (Santa Monica, RAND Corporation, 1996), pp. 25–29.

6. In mid-1995, it stood at 24.9, but there has been marked improvement since then.

7. Lukoil, in particular, negotiated the development of the oil deposits in the Caspian Sea. Gasprom has played an increasingly large role in similar negotiations.

8. The most ambitious option is the Yamal pipeline, which would carry gas from the Yamal Peninsula across Russia and through Belarus to consumers in Poland and Germany. In the best of circumstances this pipeline is likely to be a long time in the making.

9. Space constraints preclude a discussion of the other side of the problem, i.e., the West's economic opening to Ukraine.

10. The importance of competition policy should be understood here as applying also to the foreign investors themselves. Sweetheart deals in which a foreign firm agrees to invest under conditions that rule out effective competition from other companies—foreign or domestic—are often sought by major Western firms. Although in the short term these arrangements are an important source of capital, their long-term impacts are likely to be less beneficial.

11. According to the Czech National Bank, some 53 percent of foreign direct investment in the Czech Republic in 1995 was concentrated in these two sectors.

12. *Izvestia,* 16 April 1996.

13. A third issue is that several of the traditional customers for Soviet weaponry are pariah regimes such as those of Iraq and Libya, against which new international export controls arrangements are directed.

14. The example of Estonia, whose 'dependence' on Russia in 1990–1991 appeared to be a great deal larger than that of Ukraine, has shown that such dependence can indeed be rapidly reduced. The radical character of Estonian economic reforms is relevant here, although Estonia's special constituency of Western supporting nations (especially the Scandinavian countries) is unfortunately something that Ukraine cannot reproduce.

Foreign and Defense Policies

Introduction

Roy Allison

The debate on Ukrainian security policy and the best means to reinforce national identity has underlined the geopolitical reality that Ukraine's heritage is at once Eastern and Western European. The current momentum toward the integration of Ukraine into European structures is undoubtedly strong and politically justified. But it is complicated by uncertainty over how far the country could or should form a bridge to Russia, or project a form of positive neutrality, and by the wish to avoid a new line of division emerging in Europe on Ukraine's eastern borders, which would give rise to new insecurities.

The two chapters in this section explore the complications and paradoxes that confront Ukrainian security policy decision making in these circumstances. In Chapter 12, Taras Kuzio describes how the East Slavic conundrum—the historical legacy of deformed national identities that still trouble Ukraine, Russia, and Belarus—helps to explain differences in their state of national consciousness and their attitudes to interstate integration processes after the collapse of the USSR. Ukraine's view of the Commonwealth of Independent States (CIS) as a temporary, if necessary, mechanism for a 'civilized divorce' is at the heart of its lukewarm response to CIS-level initiatives. By contrast, the Russian legacy of empire that preceded efforts to build a Russian nation-state predisposes Russian leaders to view supranational bodies such as the CIS as a means to project influence or control over former Soviet lands, including Ukraine. This fusing of Russian (post-Soviet and imperial) and Soviet identity prevents Russian public opinion from coming to terms with Ukrainian independence on the psychological level, or, prior to 1997, to seek legal codification of Ukraine's borders.

Ukrainian alarm over Russian ambitions and Russian hopes for Slavic integration have been stimulated in particular by the treaty of April 1996 forming the Russian-Belarusian Community of Sovereign States. Kuzio observes that this treaty offers strategic benefits for Russia, yet he recognizes that its economic clauses are utopian because of the divergent economic reform processes of the two states. The treaty destroys any Ukrainian or Belarusian nationalist dream of forming an anti-Russian cordon sanitaire through a Baltic–

Black Sea axis. But in any case, this idea would risk a harsh Russian reaction in a period of imminent NATO enlargement eastward. It remains to be seen if the uncertain benefits for Russia of integration efforts with Belarus may dampen Russian hopes for the development of supranational relations with Ukraine.

In Chapter 13, James Sherr highlights the need to understand the domestic determinants of Ukrainian security policy, which are influenced but not driven by the proximity of preponderant Russian power. Instead of emphasizing ethnic divisions, he points to the connections between lawful authority, a sound economy, and the political viability of the country. To hold effective power, President Leonid Kuchma requires the support of both old and new elites, from the east and the west of the country, from both sides of the political spectrum; support of Ukrainian statehood and suspicions of Russian state policy need not be accompanied by anti-Russian sentiment. Ukraine is more directly challenged by economic issues than by ethnic vulnerability.

These domestic challenges could reduce Ukrainian resistance to the reintegration schemes of Russian Eurasians. The fact that even Russian democrats are unreconciled to Ukraine's long-term independence dictates the need, in Sherr's opinion, for a prolonged and complex struggle with Russia. Sherr describes stages of evolution in Russian policy since December 1991, but it is a policy that has continued to combine an attempt at political, economic, and strategic outreach in the CIS region (in Sherr's words, 'revanche') with weakness. The lack of proper accountability in Russian power structures and their links with business interests (such Russian and Ukrainian interests are often meshed together) raise specific concerns. Against this background Russian-led CIS economic integration plans need to be carefully analyzed, as do bilateral economic proposals; debt-for-equity links in the energy sector or the creation of Ukrainian-Russian financial-industrial groups have larger policy implications for interstate relations.

The question of how far Western states can or should seek to reinforce Ukrainian statehood for strategic reasons has remained controversial. This is further complicated at present. Sherr points to the keen Ukrainian commitment to NATO Partnership for Peace exercises but also to its anxiety about NATO enlargement. Kuchma's goal of balancing some kind of strategic partnership with Russia with a policy of military nonalignment may be unsustainable if NATO proceeds to enlarge rapidly. This explains Ukrainian proposals to transform NATO into the nucleus for a future all-European security system. To avert unmanageable Russian pressures on Ukraine, Sherr suggests, any enlargement should be slow and carefully defined, perhaps involving restraints in Central Europe. Sherr recognizes the dualism in Ukraine's policy of simultaneous military nonalignment and growing cooperation with NATO, driven by the need to avoid confrontation with Russia.

12

National Identity and Foreign Policy: The East Slavic Conundrum

Taras Kuzio

Russian mentality does not accept an independent Ukraine. Democratic feelings end on the Russian-Ukrainian border.
—Ukrainian Foreign Minister Hennadiy Udovenko[1]

I don't say that tomorrow we should unite politically (with Russia) and off we go, or as the saying goes, get wed and into bed.
—Belarusian President Alyaksandr Lukashenka[2]

The legacies of history inherited by all three members of the East Slavic conundrum—Ukraine, Russia and Belarus—produced deformed national identities that shaped the direction in which nation and state building and security policies in all three states evolved after the disintegration of the former USSR. The divergent development of all three states was a direct outgrowth of their troubled legacies. Russian national identity was subsumed within both a tsarist and Soviet identity, a factor that defined its preference for union with other states and inability to accept the right of Belarusians and Ukrainians to a separate existence outside the East Slavic conundrum. In Russian eyes all three east Slavic peoples are branches of the one *Rus'kiy narod,* whose 'natural' state of affairs is unity under Russian leadership.[3] Meanwhile, this inheritance is compounded by the profound national identity crisis affecting Russians themselves in the aftermath of the disintegration of the former USSR. Russians are therefore in the 'Ottoman stage of national identity,' adjusting their horizons to the 'unnatural' borders of the Russian Federation.[4]

Belarusian national consciousness was already sufficiently weak to make it practically inevitable that when compounded by other weaknesses it inherited, the country would step backward from independence to the status of a quasi state.[5] This, in turn, reinforced Russia's perception of the east Slavic conundrum as somehow 'Russian' and placed pressure upon Ukraine to conform and follow in the Belarusian path. Russian government leaders have pointed to the fact that "Russians coming to Belarus do not consider themselves citizens of a foreign state. The same is true of Belarusian migrants in Russia."[6]

Ukraine, in contrast to Belarus, possessed more favorable factors for the development of nation and state building, but it could not fully break away from the Commonwealth of Independent States (CIS) or Russia.[7] Kyiv therefore chose a midway option of only participation in the CIS (not legal membership) with one foot in Europe and the other in Eurasia.[8] Nevertheless, Ukraine's strategic foreign policy agenda remains based on the idea of a 'return to Europe.'[9] The domestic debate within Ukraine is therefore not with regard to whether Ukraine should or should not 'return to Europe,' but whether this should be undertaken with *or* without Russia.

This chapter surveys developments in the east Slavic conundrum between the early 1990s and the aftermath of the Russian presidential elections in the second half of 1996. It argues that history has gone full circle: the Gorbachev-Yeltsin Union of Sovereign States (SSG) was finally installed by Yeltsin and Lukashenka five years after it was first mooted in the form of the Community of Sovereign Republics (SSR), which was renamed the Union of Sovereign Republics in April 1997.

Toward a Union of Sovereign States (SSG)

Events in all three east Slavic states proved to be very different in the last few years of the former USSR's existence. By 1990–1991 the former Soviet states could be divided into four groups, a pattern that has largely persisted within the CIS.

The first group consisted of countries with very highly developed national consciousness and state-making traditions, such as Georgia, Armenia, Lithuania, Latvia, and Estonia. These states proclaimed their independence quite early and elected nationalist presidents and parliaments. In the case of the three Baltic states, the fact that they were not parties to the 1922 Union Treaty and that their incorporation within the USSR was not recognized de jure by the West meant that their independence was recognized as early as September 1991, without any need to hold referendums (a condition leveled at Ukraine by the West). Georgia only reluctantly joined the CIS in 1993 due to economic crisis and separatist revolts. Armenia increasingly came to perceive Russia as the lesser of two evils in comparison to neighboring Turkey, in particular after Russia began to covertly support the Armenian separatist enclave of Nagorno-Karabakh in Azerbaijan.

The second group of countries consisted of those, such as Ukraine, Moldova, and Azerbaijan, whose national consciousness remained relatively high (but not as high as in the first group of countries). Nationalists who were elected to power, as in Moldova and Azerbaijan, proved short-lived and were removed through either the ballot box or a coup d'etat (or a combination of the two). One of the outcomes of the nationalists' term in office was its impact upon interethnic relations within those countries, which turned sour in the Transdnister and Nagorno-Karabakh regions. In Ukraine national consciousness was not sufficiently high to elect a nationalist president in either 1991 or 1994; like Moldova and Azerbaijan after their brief flirtations with nationalism, Ukraine elected national communist leaders who grew out of the divisions that sprang up within its Communist Party during 1990–1991.

The third group of countries included the four Central Asian states (Kyrgyzstan, Uzbekistan, Turkmenistan, and Tajikistan), Kazakhstan, and Belarus. These six countries had played minor roles within the dissident movements of the Brezhnev era, possessed low national consciousness, and had entrenched Communist Party leadership that had not divided along 'national' and 'imperial' lines.[10] They played largely passive roles in the disintegration of the USSR. But since the breakup of the Soviet Union even this group of countries has divided into two. Those that see the salvation of their sovereignty and territorial integrity and/or the resolution of their economic crises through close integration with Russia include Kazakhstan, Tajikistan, Kyrgyzstan, and Belarus. In contrast, Uzbekistan and Turkmenistan, due primarily to being better endowed with natural resources and/or stronger national identities, moved in to the second group of countries in terms of their attitude toward the CIS.[11]

Russia remained different to the rest of the former Soviet republics. It was the only Soviet state not to declare independence from the USSR, and it declared itself the successor state of the Soviet Union. The June 1990 Declaration of Sovereignty is therefore celebrated as Russia's 'independence day.' Prior to the August 1991 coup, President Boris Yeltsin sought allies from among the other republican leaderships in his conflict with Soviet President Mikhail Gorbachev. The failed putsch and banning of the Communist Party in August 1991 ensured Yeltsin's victory over Gorbachev and a change in strategy by the former, who no longer advised the republics and autonomous republics "to take as much sovereignty as you could use." Between August and November 1991 Yeltsin and Gorbachev were allied, working to secure the new Union Treaty for a 'revived union,' which would have consisted of a confederal Union of Sovereign States (SSG).[12]

The CIS, created at the 7–8 December 1991 Belaia Pushcha meeting of the leaders of the east Slavic conundrum, ended any need that Yeltsin still had for Gorbachev. With a 90 percent endorsement for Ukrainian independence, newly elected President Leonid Kravchuk rejected Gorbachev's 're-vived union,' which meant that the USSR was doomed. But Yeltsin clearly saw the CIS as something similar to the confederal Union of Sovereign States—although minus the Soviet center. Russian democrats did not cry over the disintegration of the former USSR, believing that it would be eventually replaced by a new CIS confederation with Russia as the new center.[13] Viewed in this light, it is little wonder that Yeltsin's moves in this direction since 1993 have been supported by the majority of Russian political parties and elites. This was reflected in the overwhelming vote by the State Duma (320–8) in favor of ratification of the SSR treaty with Belarus on 5 April 1996. The Duma also heavily ratified the reworked Belarusian-Russian treaty in June 1997 by a vote of 363–2 (with 19 abstentions). Clearly, opposition to Russian-Belarusian integration and a future union is minimal, restricted as it is to Democratic Russia and the reformist media (e.g., NTV). Even Yabloko backed economic integration along the lines of the October 1991 Economic Union drawn up by Grigorii Yavlinsky. The remainder of the political spectrum (including Our Home Is Russia, the All-Russian Women's Political Movement, and economic lobbies) backed integration/union with Belarus. Sixty-two percent of Russians themselves supported the Russian-Belarusian treaty; of these, 43 percent were in favor of the merging of both countries into a single state and another 41 percent were supportive of a federation embracing both countries.

In contrast, Ukraine regarded the CIS as more a means of achieving a 'civilized divorce.' The CIS would be something similar to the European Union, Kravchuk hoped, as well as reassure Western governments about continued joint control over former Soviet nuclear weapons. Belarus initially leaned toward Ukraine's position but over time was progressively pulled back into the third group of countries, which sought closer ties with Russia.

Russia and Ukraine: Twin Brothers?

The Myth of Russian Nationalism

Russian nationalists as a political force who supported the separation of the territories of Greater Russia from the tsarist Russian Empire[14] or that of the

Russian Federation from the former USSR into an independent nation-state have represented a small but courageous minority. Few Russian dissidents during the Brezhnev era supported a step so radical as the independence of the Russian Federation from the USSR.[15] Of those that did, such as the writer Alexander Solzhenitsyn, this did not mean separation from the east Slavic conundrum or Kazakhstan (where, according to the 1989 Soviet census, over 50 percent of the population were Russian-speakers). Out of a sample of 802 arrested 'nationalists' in the Brezhnev era only 36 were Russians, 5 fewer than the number of Latvians and proportionately fewer than the Moldovans. The Russian figure of 36 could be halved even further if we discounted members of the All-Russian Social-Christian Union, who never called for the disintegration of the USSR or the Russian Federation's separation from it. No Russian movement for self-determination from the USSR existed (unlike in Ukraine, the Baltics, and the Transcaucasus).[16]

No Russian political movement during the last years of the former USSR supported the independence of the Russian Federation and the disintegration of the Soviet state. No major Russian political parties since the disintegration of the former USSR have called for the secession of the Russian Federation from the CIS. In contrast, in all of the non-Russian CIS member states, political parties on the center-right and radical right demand their countries' withdrawal from the CIS, while those reformist parties that support CIS membership usually restrict this to the economic spheres (see Table A12.1, Appendix, p. 239). The only parties in the non-Russian states which are in favor of full integration are those on the radical left.

A Confused Russian National Identity

Why is Russia therefore so different from the other member states of the CIS? Indeed, within what borders do Russians perceive their psychological understanding of 'Russia' to exist?

In contrast to nation-state building and national identity formation in Western Europe, which largely preceded the creation of empires, in Russia these processes occurred simultaneously. It has always therefore become difficult to define where 'Russia' begins and where it ends. This confusion is clearly seen in the four images of 'Russia' that Russians hold:[17]

- Kyivan Rus'
- Vladimir Suzdal and Muscovy
- St. Petersburg Russia (a 'younger brother' of the West trying to catch up with, and rejoin, 'Europe')
- Eurasian (cradle of the imperial state idea, where the Mongol empire was rebuilt from the West; Europe is rebuffed in favor of Asia)

The Kyivan Rus', St. Petersburg, and Eurasian images of Russia all include within the Russian patrimony the east Slavic states of Belarus and Ukraine. These two territories are not somehow different, like Catholic Lithuania or Muslim Tajikistan, but are 'Rus'ian,' part of the east Slavic conundrum. In the words of the former State Duma speaker Ivan Rybkin, "The countries which have a common origin, must have not only a common past but also a common present and future."[18]

Russia's confused national identity has profound implications for the other two members of the east Slavic conundrum, Belarus and Ukraine, who are all 'peoples of one blood' *(edinokrovnye)*. Even Russian liberals could not accept the breakup of the east Slavic conundrum, the former Soviet and CIS core states.[19] In the Brezhnev era, these three states were slated to be fused as the core of the newly defined 'Soviet people,' which would spread to the remainder of the former USSR. Russification of the Ukrainians and Belarusians was therefore stepped up to merge them into a pan–east Slavic bloc. Their identities were further subsumed within a *Rus'kiy* identity that denied them any historical past or future existence except in union with Russia.

Ukrainian independence was therefore a 'temporary' phenomenon, as former Russian ambassador to Ukraine Leonid Smolyakov believed.[20] It was 'artificial,' in that its existence was possible only due, on the one hand, to national communists, preserving their rule by becoming nationalists while, on the other, the West was propping it up. Ukrainian independence, especially if it withdrew from the CIS, could only be at the expense of losing its eastern and southern territories, which would inevitably, in Russian eyes, clamor to 'rejoin' Russia.[21] This analysis stemmed from the widespread Russian view that "Ukraine is a fragile, artificial, heterogeneous ethno-political formation lacking any real chances of the formation of its own statehood," Andranik Migranian, a member of the Presidential Council, wrote.[22] Solzhenitsyn, who wanted the Russian Federation to reject empire in favor of an east Slavic state that included Kazakhstan, also suggested that if Ukraine refused to join this state, its eastern and southern territories should be allowed to secede to Russia.[23]

These views are regularly found in Russian opinion polls. One opinion poll, for example, found that three quarters of Russians believed that they and Ukrainians were the same nation and should unite into one state with Belarus and Kazakhstan.[24] Other polls, conducted five years after the disintegration of the former USSR, show that the overwhelming majority of Russians still believe that Ukrainians are not a separate ethnic group (it goes without saying that this is true to an even greater extent for their attitudes toward Belarusians). "Ukraine is not like a nation. Russia and Ukraine will be one state in the future," Stanislaw Cherkashin, a twenty-four-year-old Russian banker, said while on a trip to Kyiv.[25] "The Russian man in the street is more confused than anyone. In general, he cannot believe that beyond the Kursk bridge is not our land now. You only hear: 'But we are one people ... and Kyiv is the Mother of Russian cities,' " one Russian author explained.[26]

In regular surveys since early 1992 of Ukrainian and Russian attitudes toward each other, the Moscow-based Public Opinion Foundation found the following results:[27]

- Russians could not accept Ukrainian independence.
- Russians could not accept that Ukraine was no longer a part of 'Russia.'
- Russians could not accept Ukraine as a political equal to the Russian Federation.
- One in two Russians would back the secession of the Crimea.

Over time Russian national identity has increasingly distanced its understanding of 'Russia' from the former USSR while increasingly falling back upon the image of 'Russia' as the east Slavic conundrum of Kyivan Rus'. During Yeltsin's inauguration as Russia's newly reelected president in July 1996 Vladimir Zhirinovsky, leader of the Russian Liberal Democrats, proposed to President Leonid Kuchma that they re-create the Kyivan Rus' state—even if this meant that its capital would be in Kyiv. Whereas 70.2 percent of Russians looked to closer relations with Ukraine, only 42.3 percent looked to Kazakhstan and even fewer (0.5 percent) to Tajikistan.[28] As this tendency continues, pressure will therefore grow on Ukraine to fall into line with Belarus into a unified east Slavic conundrum (as Belarus actually did after Yeltsin's reelection).

Grappling with the Loss of Empire

Russia still remains confused about its Soviet inheritance. Ukraine has regularly sparred with Russia over its unilateral monopolization of all former Soviet assets.[29] Russia appropriated the positive aspects of the Soviet inheritance (the World War II victory, Soviet foreign assets, and Soviet financial reserves) while attempting to distance itself from the negative side of Soviet rule (the invasion of the Baltic states in 1939, the deportation of entire nations from their homelands, etc.). Is this dual-track policy feasible? "If the world permits Russia to claim the international property of the USSR, then it ought to require that Russia also assume the social and economic burden of the former colonizer as well."[30]

Russia can no longer distance itself from its Soviet inheritance; after all, the former USSR was as much 'Russian' as it was Soviet. In inheriting the think tanks, diplomats, media, high echelons of the power ministries, and other top-heavy institutions of the former USSR, Russia also inherited the psychology and world outlook of the personnel that had manned these institutions. Russian national identity was an extension of Soviet identity; the two were interwoven until 1990–1991, when Yeltsin's desire for power brought him into conflict with the Soviet center and Russia, for the first time, created its own institutions and republican Communist Party.[31] The end of the Soviet empire brought forward a sense of angst, a crisis of Russian national identity similar to that experienced by France after the collapse of its empire in North Africa.[32]

Russian security policy toward the Near Abroad has therefore largely replicated the former USSR's relationship to Central Europe within the CIS, described as Russia's 'exclusive zone of strategic interests' (the CIS military command grew out of that of the Warsaw Pact headquarters in Moscow).[33] Russia's attitude to NATO enlargement is largely grounded in the Cold War rhetoric of the 1950s. Meanwhile, the Russian general staff see 'Russian territory' as synonymous with the former Soviet Union. Russia is therefore opposed to NATO's expanding 'up to its borders' when the only area where Russia borders a potential new NATO member is in the Kalingrad region.[34] In attempting to speak against the enlargement of NATO 'up to its borders,' Russia is, in effect, attempting to speak on behalf of the former USSR by limiting the sovereignty of former Soviet states such as Ukraine to have any say on this question. Ukraine actually borders two new NATO members but does *not* oppose NATO enlargement. After the signing of the Russian-NATO charter in July 1997, the Russian leadership warned that it would tear up this agreement if NATO expanded into the former USSR, a threat that, in effect, attempted to 'Finlandize' these non-Russian successor states.

The CIS: From 'Civilized Divorce' to New Empire

As pointed out earlier in this chapter, Russia perceives CIS integration in a very different light than does Ukraine. The Russian leadership always supported the transformation of the CIS into a confederation, with Russia 'naturally' playing the leading role.[35] In Russian eyes, strengthening the CIS and strengthening Russian statehood are mutually interdependent policies that would help the revival of Russia as a 'great power.' For Russia, therefore, the CIS is like a corset holding together the Russian state; if the CIS were allowed to disintegrate, this would pave the way for border disputes. "Today, the strength of the CIS is not a movement toward an empire, but perhaps the only opportunity to avoid the overall disintegration of statehood for the larger part of the former USSR," one Russian author believes. "Preservation and, if possible, strengthening of the commonwealth is the only civilized way of constructing each of the constituent states."[36]

In contrast to Russia, Ukraine views the CIS as an important mechanism to help smooth its economic transition and as a glorified place for "talking shop"—nothing more. Ukraine sees the CIS as propping up its statehood during the difficult early period of nation and state building. The disintegration of the former USSR is therefore regarded as beneficial because it has allowed Ukrainian national identity to grow in an independent state. If Ukrainian national consciousness had been as high as that in the first group of former Soviet countries outlined earlier in this chapter, its attitude toward the CIS would have been equally as disparaging. Participation in the CIS—a halfway station between full membership and withdrawal—suits Ukraine in its current stage of nation and state building. Whereas Russia believes that the CIS has a glorious long-term future and plans accordingly, Ukraine utilizes the CIS in the short term to help it overcome its inherited structural, national, and regional deficiencies. Ukrainian foreign policy is therefore now described as 'cooperation with the CIS—integration with Europe.'[37]

Russia's Eurasian statist-realist security policies, which replaced the liberal internationalism of Gorbachev's 'common European home' in 1993, are a major stumbling block to improving relations with the CIS states and especially with the east Slavic conundrum.[38] Russia's policy of demanding that the CIS be its exclusive sphere of influence is seen as the only way in which to revive Russia as a 'great power.' Ukraine and Belarus play a key role in this scenario. In addition, Russia is offering only the status of satellite—not equality—to the other members of the CIS, using as its reference point U.S. relations with Latin America. This neo-imperialism aims not to militarily reconquer CIS states but to penetrate them economically and thereby gain political influence with the help of forward military bases. Russia should encourage, the Council on Foreign and Defense Policy argued, "unlimited access to Ukraine's market of goods, services and capital and the creation of an effective military-political alliance."[39]

Karaganov, a leading ideologist of this new brand of Russian neo-imperialism, outlined this policy as it applies to Ukraine:

> The best that the advocates of Ukrainian statehood can hope for is the preservation of a politically independent but really (economically) semidependent state. This is not the worst option for Russia either. Given this model of

relations with Ukraine and other CIS states, we can turn from a milk cow into a state delivered from the burden of the empire, but retaining many advantages of its previous geostrategic and, so to speak, geoeconomic position.[40]

In other words, Russian advocates of this new brand of neo-imperialism would like to reap the benefits of empire without accepting the responsibilities. They back the retention of Russian hegemony over the Near Abroad—not full dominion over their internal affairs.

Russian and French attitudes toward their respective Near Abroad are similar. In the United Kingdom, anticolonial groups actively campaigned for Britain's withdrawal from empire, which was later facilitated by Lancaster House conferences. Anticolonial movements of this sort never existed in France or the Russian Federation. Meanwhile, both France and the former USSR adopted policies of assimilation toward their dependencies. Russia and France both attempted to re-create spheres of influence in their respective Near Abroads through 'flag independence'—signing treaties of cooperation seeking to preserve hegemony and forward military bases.

The ending of a land empire presents far greater obstacles to the former imperial center than that of a sea empire, especially vis-à-vis the east Slavic conundrum, which was always perceived as a natural extension of the Russian patrimony. In both France and Russia decolonization nearly led to civil war; in Russia the postimperial psychological climate may not even be conducive to reform.[41]

Ukraine and Russia both approach their relations from different perspectives. For Russians, the key question regarding Ukraine is, "Where will Ukraine go—to the East or to the West? Whom does it support and to whom will it belong?" For Ukrainians the key question is, Will Russia build relations with it on equal terms and the legal recognition of its borders? For Russians this issue was irrelevant. At the sixth Russian-Ukrainian conference held in Kyiv in late 1995, "the Moscow intelligentsia did not even mention that issue. According to them, strategic partnership amounts to two states' unanimous attitude toward a third state."[42] In Russia's eyes, therefore, Belarus—not Ukraine—adopted the right attitude to relations between both countries, and this led to the normalization of relations between them (on Moscow's terms). The transformation of Belarus into a quasi state has made the normalization of Ukrainian-Russian relations more difficult. It is little wonder that Yeltsin failed to travel to Ukraine to sign an interstate treaty three days after putting his name to the agreement to sign the SSR treaty with Belarus in April 1996. The SSR treaty was Russia's preference, not the interstate treaty proposed by Ukraine that would have established relations between Russia and Ukraine as two equal subjects of international law. Only with the threat of NATO enlargement looming did the Russians panic and decide to visit Kyiv in May 1997 to sign the same draft treaty prepared by their governments over two years earlier and rejected by Yeltsin at the time. In other words, Russia signed the interstate treaty only when it was in its strategic interests to do so, fearing that Ukraine might be 'lost' forever to a pro-European, Westward-leaning foreign policy and NATO after the July 1997 Madrid summit.

Prior to May 1997 the failure to convince Russia to treat Ukraine as an equal partner and Russia's continued refusal to legally recognize their joint border forced Ukraine to look westward in search of strategic partners.[43] Ukraine therefore decided it was more profitable to be strategic partners with Poland, the United Kingdom, Germany, and the United States than with a Russian Federation that had very different ideas as to the content of any such partnership. Belarus might be returning to Eurasia, but Ukraine had decided to travel in the opposite direction and 'return to Europe.'[44] In a nutshell, Ukrainian-Russian relations could not have been normalized, as "Ukraine is inevitably struggling for equality with Russia. Russia is inevitably struggling for a great power position in the former USSR."[45]

Despite the signing of the interstate treaty, Russia's growing assertiveness within the CIS, whose capital was moved to Moscow in 1998, will remain of deep concern to the Ukrainian leadership. In Kyiv's eyes, the Russian presidential decree 'The Strategic Course of Russia towards the CIS States' (September 1995) reflected its disinterest in seeing the CIS as a means of achieving equal and mutually beneficial relations. In the view of the Ukrainian Foreign Ministry:

> Russia has no intention to build its relations with CIS countries in line with international law, nor to respect the principles of territorial integrity, sovereignty and non-interference in domestic affairs. . . . The integration proclaimed as useful and necessary in Yeltsin's decree . . . in fact means undermining the CIS countries' sovereignty, subordinating their activity to Russia's interests and restoring the centralized superpower.[46]

During the June 1996 Russian presidential elections President Yeltsin repeated his calls for a close union with Belarus, Kazakhstan, and Ukraine in his annual address on national security to the State Duma. Although Ukrainian officials rejected the proposal and blamed it on election rhetoric, Yeltsin was merely outlining long-held Russian strategic policy vis-à-vis the east Slavic conundrum. Similarly, Yeltsin's letter to Belarusian President Lukashenka in January 1997 agreeing to a unification of both countries could not be solely explained as a response to NATO enlargement.

Yeltsin's support for unification has far deeper underlying reasons and reflects Russia's ambivalent national identity.

Legally Codified or Transparent Borders?

Russia has no disputed borders with Belarus; these have been resolved by the creation of the SSR. With Ukraine the situation was more complicated. Yeltsin's press secretary, Pavel Voshchanov, challenged Ukraine's borders immediately after it declared independence on 24 August 1991.[47] Russia had argued ever since that the borders of the CIS member states inherited from the former USSR were to be respected by Moscow only if the states remained members of the CIS. Russian Foreign Minister Yevgenii Primakov does not believe that the Helsinki principles apply to these 'internal' CIS borders. Moscow supported separatist enclaves within Moldova, Georgia, and Azerbaijan to force them to join the CIS; Russia then offered to support the territorial integrity of these three states (that is, no longer back their separatist enclaves) in return for permanent military basing rights.

Russia also supports a policy of dividing borders into two categories: transparent 'internal' CIS borders and jointly guarded 'external' CIS borders. This policy, rejected by Ukraine out of hand, has been supported by Belarus, Armenia, Georgia, Turkmenistan, and Tajikistan.[48] Ukraine signed interstate treaties with all of its neighbors recognizing current frontiers, something it only accomplished with the Russian Federation in May 1997. Belarus did not raise border problems with Ukraine or Russia, but did raise this question with Poland and Lithuania. Russia has threatened to encourage Belarus to demand the return of territory in Lithuania, including the capital city, Vilnius, if Lithuania joins NATO.

Transparent 'internal' CIS borders remove the need for their ratification in interstate treaties, something that Ukraine has long demanded and which had been one of the factors holding up Yeltsin's visit to Kyiv to sign the interstate treaty. With a purely administrative function, these transparent 'internal' CIS frontiers would resemble those of the Soviet era, prolonging and reinforcing the deep confusion within Russian national identity of where 'Russia' ends and whether it is synonymous with the former USSR. Belarus agreed to these proposals, while Ukraine did not. Russians actually presented the matter in a different manner to Ukrainians: "Really, do we need a border with Ukraine? After all, we have managed to come to an agreement with Belarus. We believe that many Russians pose the questions in just this way."[49]

Russia found it very difficult to accept Ukrainian demands for the legal codification of their border. Eastern and southern Ukraine, together with the

Crimea and the 'City of Russian Glory' (Sevastopol), lie outside the core of historic Ukraine. To Russians, the Donbas, 'New Russia,' and Crimea are as much 'Russian' as they are Ukrainian. Konstantin Zatulin, former chairman of the State Duma on CIS Affairs and currently director of the Institute of the New Abroad, complained about this Ukrainian "interest only in the recognition by Russia of borders that never existed in history, of a state that never existed in history."[50] Russia finds it difficult to perceive Ukraine and Belarus as 'foreign' countries. They are treated as 'internal' problems, a part of Russian domestic politics. In Russia's eyes, therefore, their desire for union of the east Slavic conundrum cannot be described as 'imperialism.' Indeed, a State Duma draft resolution in June 1996 attracted nearly two hundred votes in favor of the annexation of eastern and southern Ukraine, Crimea, and northern Kazakhstan to Russia. Consequently, Russia believes that one should not apply the same diplomatic rules to Belarus and Ukraine, for example on borders, as one would to other countries.

Russian and Ukrainian border problems reflect their different attitudes toward nation and state building. Russia's support for transforming the CIS into a confederation removes the need for legally codified borders. In contrast, Ukrainian nation and state building regards the legal codification of its borders as part of the development of its new state structure—as central a component of a new state as armed forces, the national flag, and a national airline.[51]

Ukraine regards Russia's recognition of its borders as confirmation that it has come to terms with its independence.[52] In contrast, Russia had always looked at this problem from a different angle, the press service of the Ukrainian Border Troops believed:

> The fact is that there have been no proposals from Russia whatsoever regarding talks on the legal formulation of the common border during the four years of the modern history of our state. Meanwhile, from the moment that she proclaimed her independence, Ukraine has been constantly interested in such talks.[53]

The Community/Union of Sovereign States

On 2 April 1996 Russia and Belarus signed a treaty establishing a Community of Sovereign Republics (known by its unfortunate Russian abbreviation of SSR) in an elaborate ceremony in the Kremlin that was blessed by Patriarch Aleksey II of the Russian Orthodox Church and which combined Soviet and Russian nationalist rhetoric and symbols. Henceforth, April 2 would be celebrated as the 'Day of People's' Unity holiday in both countries.

Why did President Yeltsin attempt to co-opt this nationalist agenda and what does it tell us about likely developments within the east Slavic conundrum?

The State Duma Backs a Revived USSR

Two weeks prior to the creation of the Community of Sovereign Republics (SSR), the State Duma adopted by wide margins two resolutions denouncing the disintegration of the former USSR and the creation of the CIS as well as recognizing the continued legal validity of the 17 March 1991 referendum, which produced a Soviet-wide majority in favor of a 'revived union.' These resolutions were in turn denounced throughout the former USSR—except by Belarusian President Lukashenka.

Clearly, Lukashenka would have preferred to have Russian communist leader Gennadii Zyuganov—not Yeltsin—in the Russian presidential chair. Lukashenka has often boasted how he was the sole member of the Belarusian parliament who voted against the disintegration of the former USSR and the creation of the CIS in December 1991. The SSR, therefore, is an unclear body caught between the designs of a Soviet revivalist and a Russian leadership that would like to see the CIS transformed into a union resembling the Russian-dominated Union of Sovereign States that both Yeltsin and Gorbachev jointly backed between August and November 1991.

SSR Backed by State Duma

The SSR was created due to pressure from the State Duma and its mid-March 1996 resolutions. Zyuganov triumphantly proclaimed, "One can believe that the Russian executive power carries out the Duma's decisions on accelerating integration between the former Soviet republics rather energetically."[54] Zhirinovsky, leader of the Liberal Democratic Party of Russia (LDPR), was not slow to claim credit, either: "The signing of the treaty on the creation of the union of Russia and Belarus is the implementation of the program of the LDPR," he said.[55]

The SSR treaty was ratified by an overwhelming majority of the State Duma (320–8), with even reformist factions such as Yabloko backing it. Perhaps on this occasion at least, the Russian parliament and president were not out of step with one another's policies—a reflection of the Russian elite policy consensus toward Ukraine and the CIS. As pointed out earlier, many Russian democrats had always supported the transformation of the CIS into a confederation under Russia's rightful leadership. The exceptions to this were in a distinct minority by 1997 (e.g., Russia's Choice and the Economic Freedom Party). Viktor Chernomyrdin's Our Home Is Russia

Party has always been an enthusiastic supporter of the union with Belarus. The Russian government, led by Prime Minister Chernomyrdin, had worked together with the Communist Party to prepare the documents for the April 1997 second stage of the unification process.

Ukrainian and Belarusian democrats and reformers remain confused that Russian democrats and Russia's ostensibly proreform government are supporting the Lukashenka regime. As one Ukrainian newspaper commentator wrote: "The fact that in order to 'expand its territory' Russia is ready to close its eyes on the encroachment of the human rights and freedoms and on Belarus's economic backwardness demonstrates precisely the Kremlin's genuine aim: an intention to revive the Russian empire at any cost."[56]

The SSR

The SSR brings few, if any, economic benefits to Russia, as the Belarusian market is too small. Anyway, the Customs Union treaty signed by Belarus, Russia, Kazakhstan, and Kyrgyzstan on 29 March 1996 provided the best forum for economic integration through customs and payments unions. Full unification of Belarus and Russia, along German lines, would be too costly for Russia. Yet Belarus is clearly hoping that the creation of the SSR will lead to subsidies from Russia, especially in the form of cheap energy, 90 percent of which Belarus imports from Russia. Belarusian President Lukashenka has convinced his countrymen that these subsides will be far higher than the assistance offered by the IMF. Russia, though, is under IMF pressure to raise the prices of energy supplied to its domestic consumers to world levels. Is it really therefore feasible for Russia to do this and continue to sell subsidized energy to Belarus? Nevertheless, despite the Russian Central Bank's opposition to any unification of Belarus and Russia on grounds of cost, Russia has written off $1.2 billion in Belarusian energy debts.

For Russia, the creation of the SSR has only two advantages—strategic and electoral. Clearly, with the majority of the Russian population holding the view that the disintegration of the former USSR was a negative phenomenon, Yeltsin hoped the creation of the SSR would help him obtain additional votes in the June 1996 presidential elections. In this respect, both Zyuganov and Zhirinovsky were right to accuse Yeltsin of having stolen their policies, as they also propagated such an idea during the 1996 presidential elections.

The maintenance of a Belarusian quasi state does have important strategic considerations. Like Georgia and Kazakhstan, Belarus is an important strategic ally on one of Russia's vulnerable flanks. It has allowed the stationing of Russian military bases on its territory and Russian border troops and customs officers four-hundred kilometers west of Russia, on the Belarusian-Polish border. Belarus was an important Russian ally in Moscow's campaign against the expansion of NATO, allowing two-pronged pressure to be exerted upon Poland (in both the Kaliningrad and the Belarusian sectors). The SSR treaty calls for coordinated foreign policy and joint use of military infrastructures. The maintenance of a Belarusian quasi state also puts two-pronged pressure upon Ukraine, from both Belarus and the Russian base and separatist enclave in Moldova. It also effectively destroyed any Ukrainian or Belarusian nationalist dream of creating an anti-Russian cordon sanitaire through a Baltic–Black Sea axis.

An Amorphous SSR

Yet the treaty creating the SSR is full of contradictions that may make it unworkable. It calls for a synchronization of economic reform, which is difficult to imagine. How is Russia, which launched reforms in 1992, to coordinate reforms with a country that has no reform program and whose leader supports a state-planned economy? Nevertheless, Lukashenka is adamant that "we have found ourselves in this situation not because we conducted no reforms, but because our economy is to a great extent dependent, and this fact is coupled with total political dependency."[57] Indeed, the entire concept of the SSR is illusory:

> Everything seems to be simple enough—a symbolic border marker was ceremoniously removed—Russian raw materials and fuels will flow towards Belarus at internal prices, and from the opposite direction, tractors and machine tools will return. But how will the two economies, given their different legislatures, state structures and private sectors integrate in practical terms?[58]

One thing is clear, though. Lukashenka clearly sees the SSR as a means of avoiding—not introducing—reform within Belarus. Because of the differing objectives of Lukashenka and Yeltsin, it is also not clear what the SSR is, or is meant to become, in the future. Yeltsin himself seems unclear on whether the SSR is a confederation and whether it will lead to a new federal union. "We can say more definitely that our goal is maybe unity, after deep integration," Yeltsin said.[59] When asked if he was against a new federal union, Yeltsin replied, "Of course not. We share the same attitudes." On another occasion, though, he backtracked: "This will not under any circumstances be a treaty to create one state with Belarus, there has been a mistake in this respect,"[60] adding, "We are not talking about creating a new country."[61]

Lukashenka has other ideas. He clearly perceives the SSR as the stepping-stone to a new federal union (communist or otherwise). The period 1996–1997 was set aside as a transition period toward this united state (although he also is still unclear on whether it will be a confederation or a federation). This new state will possess a joint budget, constitution, and monetary and fiscal system; it will have unified taxation, social welfare, and legal systems. In addition, Belarus will operate coordinated military and foreign policies with Russia and offered to host Russian nuclear weapons if NATO expands eastward.

The signing of the SSR treaty was backed by the establishment of supranational structures, including a Supreme Soviet (of both presidents, prime ministers, and parliaments), an Interparliamentary Assembly, and an Integration Executive Committee (of both prime ministers). The creation of similar supranational structures in the CIS has long been opposed by all of its non-Russian members—except Belarus. It is highly unlikely, therefore, that other CIS member states will sign on to the SSR treaty, as the two founding members clearly hoped. Even 'pro-Russian' CIS member states (e.g., Armenia and Kazakhstan) have refused to join the SSR or new union because it means a step back from nation and state building. Nevertheless, the Russian and Belarusian leaderships remain convinced that sooner or later Armenia and Ukraine will join.

Conclusion

The sources for the diverging post-Soviet nation and state building policies among the east Slavic conundrum can be found in the Soviet era and, in Russia's case, even in the tsarist period of history. All three east Slavic countries inherited specific problems along with national identities that were deformed to a greater or lesser degree; these conditioned the range of policy options that were available to their respective elites in the post-Soviet era. In the Ukrainian case, it inherited relatively favorable factors, allowing it to pursue a determined course toward constructing an independent state. Belarus was less fortunate and its short-term options are more limited, perhaps only to playing the role of a quasi state of Russia.

The legacies of external domination and totalitarianism for Ukraine and Belarus also determined the range of security policies that could be adopted by both countries. Ukrainian national consciousness was higher than in Belarus—but both were not as high as in the Transcaucasus and the Baltic states. Ukraine is therefore caught in a security trap—it can neither leave the CIS nor fully commit itself to full CIS integration. Ukraine's attitude to the CIS has therefore remained fixed in the short term, seeing the CIS as a means to reap economic benefits while encouraging a stable geopolitical environment that will facilitate its nation and state building. Ukraine has asserted this attitude by refusing to sign the CIS charter, opposing the creation of supranational structures and the adoption of CIS symbols, and joining CIS structures only as a participant with observer status (not as a legal member).

Russian political thought in the twentieth century has never proposed nation and state building in 'Russia' as a separate state. This would be difficult anyway, as one would have to first define where 'Russia' began and where it ended. Russian national identity grew simultaneously with the growth of a land-based empire; separating 'Russia' from the empire is difficult if not impossible for most Russians, and it is certainly not desired.[62] This confusion as to what constitutes 'Russia' is particularly poignant when reference is made to Belarus and Ukraine, whose right to separate independent status is regarded as a quaint but temporary aberration. The full normalization of relations between Ukraine and Russia is made all the more hazy by the fact that both the Russian and the Ukrainian nations are in a process of creation; therefore, their national identities are also hazy.[63] The normalization of Ukrainian-Russian relations is more a medium-term development. As a comparison, the breakthrough in Polish-Ukrainian relations in 1997 that has led to their full normalization, despite centuries of bitterness and conflict, came about only as a consequence of Ukrainian-Polish dialogue that began in the late 1940s in the diasporas and then in the 1980s in Poland. In other words, normalization of Polish-Ukrainian relations took decades. Why should we expect that Russian-Ukrainian relations will take any less time?

Russian political thought usually confuses 'Russia' with either the borders of the former USSR or the CIS (or both), and rarely confines its geographical spread to the Russian Federation alone. The preferred option for Russian political parties—even those of a democratic orientation—is to strive to transform the CIS into a confederation. Both Gorbachev and Yeltsin supported the creation of a confederal Union of Sovereign States, and Yeltsin clearly saw the CIS as the embodiment of this union—with the exception that the Soviet center would be replaced by Russia. The CIS would be openly controlled by Russia, and not as in the former Soviet era, where Russian dominance was camouflaged by Soviet nationality policies. The creation of the confederal Belarusian-Russian Community/Union of Sovereign Republics is therefore a logical progression for Russia, a step supported by the majority of Russian political parties, its elites, and its parliamentary factions.

In contrast, the reaction of the former Soviet states to the March 1996 resolutions of the State Duma on reviving the former USSR clearly showed that only one of them—Belarus—supported the re-creation of a new federal 'union.' The ruling elites of 13 of the 15 former Soviet states, including Ukraine, have strong vested interests (political, economic, financial, nationalistic, and other) in maintaining their independence. None—apart from the Belarusian president—supported the creation of a new federal union with supranational structures. Although the Yeltsin leadership sharply condemned the State Duma's resolutions, it nevertheless also attempted to co-opt the policies of Yeltsin's nationalist and communist foes by supporting the creation of the Belarusian-Russian union, the status and future direction of which are uncertain.

President Kuchma, unlike President Lukashenka, supported Yeltsin during the 1996 presidential elections (Lukashenka would have preferred to see a victory by Zyuganov, the communist candidate). But Kuchma's preference was really for the Yeltsin of 1990–1992—not the Yeltsin of post-1993. Events since Yeltsin's reelection have only served to confirm the consensus within Russian elites over their attitudes and policies toward the east Slavic conundrum and the CIS (tactics and strategies aside). In the post-Yeltsin era the two leading contenders for the Russian presidential chair—Aleksandr Lebed and Zyuganov—will merely reinforce the Russian elite consensus that Ukraine should also be maintained as a Belarus-style quasi state.

APPENDIX

Table A12.1a.

Native Language Preferences in Ukraine and Belarus

Censuses	1970	1979	1989
Ukraine[1]			
Ukrainian %	69.39	66.12	66.3
Russian %	28.12	31.15	31.3
Belarus[2]			
Belarusian %	90.1	83.40	80.2
Russian %	9.8	16.40	19.7

Notes and Sources:

[1]Ann Sheehy, "Census Results Reflect Gains of Russian Language in the Ukraine," *Radio Liberty Research*, RL 14/80, 7 January 1980; Neil Melvin, *Russians Beyond Russia: The Politics of National Identity* (London: Royal Institute of International Affairs and Pinter, 1995), p. 87.

[2]Paul Kolstoe, *Russians in the Former Soviet Republics* (London: Hurst and Co., 1995), p. 167.

Table A12.1b.

Votes for independence

	Belarus	Ukraine	Russia
Parliamentary votes for independence	256:0	346:2	N/A
Referendum on independence	N/A	90.3%	N/A

Table A12.2

Attitude of Ukrainian Political Parties to the CIS

Revived USSR and/or CIS military/political/economic bloc	Neutrality/non–bloc status and CIS economic cooperation	Membership of NATO and/or anti-Russian Baltic–Black Sea axis, nonparticipation in the CIS
Communist Party and faction*	Constitutional Democratic Party	Republican Party*
Party Slavic Unity	Green Party	Rukh Party and Faction*
Civic Congress	People's Democratic Party	Democratic Party
Socialist Party and Faction*	Social Democratic Party	Peasant Democratic Party
Peasant Party and Faction	Inter-Regional Bloc Reforms	Christian Democratic Party
	Liberal Party	Congress Ukrainian Nationalists
	New Ukraine	Reform Parliamentary faction
	Agrarian Party	Ukrainian National Assembly
	Centrist Parliamentary Factions (Unity/ Constitutional Center/Inter-Regional Deputies Group/Social-Market Choice)	State Independence for Ukraine

*Represent the four largest political parties in Ukraine.

Table A12.3

The (Belarusian-Russian) Community of Sovereign Republics (SSR)

Administrative Structure:
- Supreme Council (presidents, prime ministers, parliamentary speakers)
- Parliamentary Assembly (members of both parliaments)
- Executive Committee (chaired by prime ministers to carry out decisions of the Supreme and the Parliamentary Assembly)
- Administrative location: Russian presidential building

Aims:
- Coordinate foreign policy
- Coordinate military policy
- Use military infrastructures on each other's territory
- Joint protection of CIS 'external borders'
- Work toward a joint constitution
- Synchronize economic reforms
- Joint use of industrial facilities
- Give individuals in each country the right to buy property in the other state
- Harmonization of legislation
- Joint customs services
- Common energy and transportation systems
- Unification of budget systems
- A common currency

Notes

1. Speech to the Royal Institute of International Affairs, 13 December 1995.

2. Russian NTV, 1 October 1995.

3. See Stephen D. Shenfield, "Alternative Conceptions of Russian State Security and Their Implications for Russian Attitudes towards Ukraine," *The Harriman Review,* vol. 9, nos. 1–2 (Spring 1996), pp. 142–147.

4. Anatoly M. Khazanov, *After the USSR: Ethnicity, Nationalism, and Politics in the Commonwealth of Independent States* (Madison: University of Wisconsin Press, 1995), p. 239.

5. See Taras Kuzio and Marc Nordberg, "Nation and State Building, Historical Legacies and National Identities in Belarus and Ukraine," *Canadian Review of Studies in Nationalism,* vol. 26, nos. 1–2 (forthcoming).

6. Comments by Russian Deputy Prime Minister Valeriy Serov in the *Russian Executive and Legislative Newsletter,* 6 January 1997. Gennadiy Seleznev, Russian State Duma speaker, also said, "The fact that we have ceased to be foreign with regard to each other is another important result of our movement towards each other" (*Rabochaia tribuna,* 14 March 1997).

7. See T. Kuzio, "National Identity in Independent Ukraine: An Identity in Transition," *Nationalism and Ethnic Politics,* vol. 2, no. 4 (Winter 1996), pp. 582–608 and T. Kuzio, *Ukraine: State and Nation Buildin* (London and New York: Routledge,1998).

8. See T. Kuzio, "The Domestic Sources of Ukrainian Foreign Policy," paper presented to the conference "Towards a New Ukraine 1: Ukraine and the New World Order," University of Ottawa, 23 March 1997.

9. See T. Kuzio, " 'Return to Europe': Ukraine's Strategic Foreign Policy Agenda,"

paper presented to the conference "What Security, Which Europe? Belarus, Ukraine, Moldova," College of Europe, Warsaw, 26 April 1997.

10. The most authoritative Western study of Soviet dissent had no chapter on Belarus and not a single reference to Belarus in its index. The chapters on 'Movements for Self-Determination' covered only Ukraine, the three Baltic states, Georgia, and Armenia. See Ludmilla Alexeyeva, *Soviet Dissent: Contemporary Movements for Nationalist, Religious and Human Rights* (Middletown, CT: Wesleyan University Press, 1985).

11. In August 1996 Uzbekistan and Ukraine signed a communique to coordinate their policies toward the CIS. Uzbekistan opposed the creation of CIS supranational structures and has refused to join the CIS Customs Union and the Interparliamentary Assembly. Both countries supported Yeltsin's replacement as chairman of the CIS Council of Heads of State, a position that is meant to rotate among member states but has been held since its inception by Russia.

12. These events are surveyed in Roman Laba, "How Yeltsin's Exploitation of Ethnic Nationalism Brought Down an Empire," *Transition,* vol. 2, no. 1 (12 January 1996)

13. Alexander Rahr wrote that Yeltsin's aim "is to make Russia the core of a restructured Union by swallowing the center and placing himself at the head of the process of building it" ("Changes in the El'tsin-Gorbachev Relationship," *Report on the USSR,* vol. 3. no. 36 [6 September 1991], p. 35).

14. See Anna Procyk, *Russian Nationalism and Ukraine: The Nationality Policy of the Volunteer Army during the Civil War* (Edmonton and Toronto: Canadian Institute of Ukrainian Studies, 1995). Procyk points out that no Russian political party supported the right of non-Russians to secede. The Whites, who opposed federalism and separatism, were dominated by the liberal-leaning People's Freedom Party (pp. 13 and 172). "Viewing the White movement as basically a drive for the salvation of the unity of the state is the key to understanding the VA's (Volunteer Army) nationality policy," the author argued (p. 11).

15. See Chapter 11, "The Myth of Russian Nationalism," in Alexander J. Motyl, *Sovietology, Rationality, Nationality: Coming to Grips with Nationalism in the USSR* (New York: Columbia University Press, 1990), pp. 161–173. Russian imperial nationalism was tolerated in the former USSR because it reinforced Russian myths of hegemony. See Kenneth C. Farmer, *Ukrainian Nationalism in the Post-Stalin Era: Myth, Symbols and Ideology in Soviet Nationality Policy* (The Hague: Martinus Nijhoff, 1980), p. 115.

16. Alexeyeva, *Soviet Dissent.*

17. Ladis K.D. Kristoff, "The Russian Image of Russia: An Applied Study in Geopolitical Methodology," in Charles A. Fisher, ed., *Essays in Political Geography* (London: Methuen, 1968), pp. 345–387.

18. Reuters, 27 July 1994.

19. Andrei Kortunov, "Russia, the 'Near Abroad' and the West," in Gail W. Lapidus, ed., *The New Russia: Troubled Transformation* (Boulder, CO: Westview Press, 1995), pp. 150, 160. Vladimir Lukin, a member of Yabloko and former Russian ambassador to the United States, was instrumental in opening up the Crimean question in the Russian parliament (*Komsomol'skaia Pravda,* 22 January 1992). Borys Fedorov, former Russian finance minister; Konstantin Zatulin, head of the Institute of the New Abroad and member of the Congress of Russian Communities as well as an 'admirer of empire;' and Sergei Shakhrai, leader of the Party of Unity and Accord, all regularly talk of the need to facilitate the reunion of the east Slavic conundrum (*Nezavisimaia gazeta,* 24 March 1995). The views of the main Russian political parties toward Ukraine were aired on the popular *Pisliamova* television program on Ukrainian Television, Channel 1, 26 November 1995.

20. *Financial Times,* 7 May 1991.

21. This argument is used in both the draft military doctrine (*Segodnia,* 20 October

1995) and the document "Vozroditsia li Soiuz? Budushchee Postsovetskogo Prostranstva," prepared by the Council on Foreign and Defense Policy (*Nezavisimaia gazeta,* 23 May 1996).

22. *Nezavisimaia gazeta,* 18 January 1994.

23. See his letter to then Russian Ambassador to the United States Vladimir Lukin (*Moscow News,* no. 11, 1993). Solzhenitsyn refused to accept Ukraine's right to exist as an independent state but agreed that Chechnya, with its northern regions removed, should be allowed to secede (*Vechirnyi Kyiv,* 16 September 1995).

24. *The Christian Science Monitor,* 21 July 1994; *The Ukrainian Weekly,* 9 October 1994. See also Roman Laba, "The Russian-Ukrainian Conflict: State, Nation and Identity," *European Security,* vol. 4, no. 3 (Autumn 1995), p. 477.

25. *Central European Economic Review,* April 1995.

26. *Nezavisimaia gazeta,* 17 January 1996.

27. Igor Kliamkin, "Russian Statehood, the CIS, and the Problem of Security," in Leon Aron and Kenneth M. Jensen, eds., *The Emergence of Russian Foreign Policy* (Washington, DC: United States Institute of Peace Press, 1994), pp. 111–112.

28. In May 1996 Russia appointed Yury Dubinin, one of its most experienced diplomats, to the post of Ukrainian Ambassador. Dubinin had been special ambassador for negotiations with Ukraine since 1992 and will retain his deputy foreign minister post. The Council on Foreign and Defense Policy in its document "Strategy for Russia (2)" argued that Ukraine is "the most serious long-term external challenge to Russian security and domestic stability" (*Nezavisimaia gazeta,* 27 May 1994).

29. Kravchuk argued that "one state has no right to inherit everything produced by all the nations of the former Union" (Mykola Shpakovaty, ed., *L. Kravchuk, Our Goal— A Free Ukraine* [Kyiv: Globus, 1993], p. 29).

30. Martha Brill Olcott, "Soviet Nationality Studies between Past and Future," in Daniel Orlovsky, ed., *Beyond Soviet Studies* (Washington, DC: Woodrow Wilson Center Press and the John Hopkins University Press, 1995), p. 142.

31. Carol Barner-Barry and Cynthia A. Hody, *The Politics of Change: The Transformation of the Former Soviet Union* (New York: St. Martin's Press, 1995), p. 100.

32. See Antony Clayton, *The End of Empire,* no. F47 (Cambereley: Conflict Studies Research Center, May 1995).

33. Dmytro Vydrin and Dmytro Tabachnyk, *Ukraina na porozi XXI stolittia. Politychnyi aspekt* (Kyiv: Lybid, 1995), p. 68.

34. See T. Kuzio, "NATO Enlargement: The View from the East," *European Security,* vol. 6, no. 2 (Summer 1997), pp. 48–62 and "Ukraine and the Expansion of NATO," *Jane's Intelligence Review,* vol. 7, no. 9 (September 1995).

35. Kravchuk always thought that Yeltsin regarded the CIS as a temporary stepping stone to a new union with a new president and Russia as the leading country (see his interview in *Kyivska Pravda,* 7 July 1995). Maybe Kravchuk is right; after all, the CIS capital moves to Moscow in 1998. "Russia simply wants to be recognized as a central player in the space between Europe and the Far East. Any attempts to deny Russia this role would be futile and counterproductive," the deputy editor of *Moscow News* warned (*The Wall Street Journal,* 28 September 1994). This was, of course, a far cry from the Yeltsin of 1990–1991, who said, "The Russian state, having chosen democracy and freedom, will never be an empire; it will be an equal among equals" (Moscow Central Television, 3 September 1991).

36. Kliamkin, "Russian Statehood, the CIS, and the Problem of Security," p. 109.

37. Oleksandr Kupchyshyn, head of the Ukrainian Ministry of Foreign Affairs Department for European Regional Cooperation, "Spivrobytnytsvo-z SND, intehratsiya-z Yevropoiu," *Polityka i Chas,* no. 7, 1996, pp. 13–16.

38. On this question see S. Neil MacFarlane, "Russian Conceptions of Europe," *Post-Soviet Affairs,* vol. 10, no. 3 (July–September 1994), pp. 234–269.

39. "Strategiia dlia Rossiia (2)," *Nezavisimaia gazeta,* 27 May 1994.

40. *Moscow News,* 8–14 April 1994. Karaganov is also the leading force behind the Council on Foreign and Defense Policy, the semi-independent think tank that was co-opted by President Yeltsin in December 1995, and an author of the Institute of Europe, Russian Academy of Science's "Four Variants of Russian Policy to Ukraine" (*Vechirnyi Kyiv,* 12 May 1992). See also the views of the Russian Scientific Fund, which called for a tough line on negotiations over Crimea and the Black Sea Fleet (*Literaturna Ukraina,* 14 May 1993).

41. Clayton, *The End of Empire,* p. 19.

42. *Zerkalo Nedeli,* 11–17 November 1995.

43. T. Kuzio, "Russia Still Threat to Ukraine's Stability," *The Wall Street Journal Europe,* 7 November 1996.

44. See T. Kuzio, "A Friend in Need: Kiev Woos Washington," *The World Today,* vol. 52, no. 4 (April 1996), pp. 96–98, and "A Way with Words: Keeping Kiev Secure," *The World Today,* vol. 52, no. 12 (December 1996), pp. 317–319.

45. *Holos Ukrainy,* 5 July 1994.

46. *Nezavisimost',* 4 October 1995.

47. *Robitnycha hazeta,* 27 August 1991.

48. Article 9 of the Belarusian constitution does describe its territory as "unified and inalienable:" "The territory of the Republic of Belarus is the natural condition of the existence and spatial limit of the self-determination of the people and the basis of their well-being and the sovereignty of the Republic of Belarus" (*Sovetskaia Belarossiia,* 30 March 1994).

49. *Granitsa Rossii,* no. 41 (December 1995), p. 2.

50. K. Zatulin, "Nastupil moment istyny v otnosheniiakh Moskvy i Kyiva," *Nezavisimaia gazeta,* 1–7 April 1995.

51. Yury Porokhniavyi, "Problema Kordoniv Ukrainy," *Nova Polityka,* November–December 1995, p. 43. For historical background on Ukraine's borders, see V.D. Boiechko, O.M. Hanzha, and V.I. Zakharchuk, "Kordony Ukrainy: istoriya ta problemy formuvannia (1917–1940rr.)," *Ukrainskyi Istorychnyi Zhurnal,* no. 1 (1992), pp. 56–77, and V. Boiechko, O. Hanzha, and Borys Zakharchuk, *Kordoniv Ukrainy: Istorychna retrospektyva ta suchasnyi stan* (Kyiv: Osnovy, 1994).

52. Angela Stent, "Ukraine's Fate," *World Policy Journal,* vol. 11, no. 3 (Fall 1994), p. 83.

53. *Narodna Armiya,* 13 December 1995.

54. Interfax news agency, 24 March 1996.

55. *Ekho Moskvy,* 23 March 1996.

56. *Vseukrainskiye vedomosti,* 22 April 1997.

57. Belarusian Radio, 27 March 1996.

58. *Moscow News,* 2–8 June 1995.

59. Reuters, 28 February 1996.

60. UPI, 25 March 1996.

61. Reuters, 25 March 1996.

62. Russia has to come to terms with the legacy of communism and empire. See R. Szporluk, "After Empire: What?" *Daedalus,* vol. 123, no. 3 (Summer 1994), p. 35.

63. Orest Subtelny, "Russocentrism, Regionalism, and the Political Culture of Ukraine," in Vladimir Tismaneanu, ed, *Political Culture and Civil Society in Russia and the New States of Eurasia, The International Politics of Eurasia,* Volume 7 (Armonk, NY: M.E. Sharpe, 1995), p. 189.

13

Ukrainian Security Policy:
The Relationship between
Domestic and External Factors

James Sherr

After his accession to power in July 1994, Ukraine's president, Leonid
Kuchma, introduced a Bismarckian approach to policy that was not only
ambitious but urgent. Although Kuchma's predecessor, Leonid Kravchuk,
had begun to convince key Western powers that Ukraine's future affected
their own interests, three years of independence[1] had done little to dislodge
the widespread prejudice that Ukraine was a geographical expression rather
than a nation and that its second 'experiment' in independence in this century would fail like the first.[2] Strictly speaking, this state of affairs called
for a dual policy rather than a 'balanced' policy on Kuchma's part, for in
the absence of positive Western interest in Ukraine (thanks to the nuclear
issue, there was no deficiency of *negative* interest) there were no counter-
vailing forces to balance. Instead, circumstances demanded nothing less
than a comprehensive effort to reshape the country's geopolitical environment and, by coordinated but asymmetric means, secure long-term, mutually beneficial, and mutually reinforcing relationships with both Russia and
the West.[3]

Two years after that event, most would agree that the dual policy has
produced impressive results—in fact astonishing ones for a country that
lacks the economic and institutional resources that Bismarck took for
granted. Today the West not only acknowledges but openly proclaims that a
stable, independent Ukraine acts as a 'pivot' in European security, and since
early 1994 it has gradually begun to match proclamations with deeds.[4]
Ukraine's relationship with Russia, once menacing, is now merely unsatis-

factory. Viewed from this perspective, the adoption of the Ukrainian constitution on 28 June 1996 and the orderly introduction of a new currency, the
hyrvnia, on 2 September are measures rightly symbolizing the fact that, in
Kuchma's words, "the transitional period in the self-determination of the
state is over."[5]

For all this, Ukraine's future is not ensured, and its greatest trials may
still lie ahead of it. Albeit unconventional, this judgment is only prudent, for
only the most prescient or credulous would argue that *Russia's* future is
ensured. In a benign international environment, the power vacuum at the
top of the Russian state—a vacuum that emerged months before the elections of June–July 1996—might prove less harmful to Ukraine than many
fear and, to the contrary, might well contribute to the consolidation of
Ukraine's position in Europe. The problem is that, by definition, vacuums
are supposed to be filled, and where Russia is concerned, Ukrainians find
themselves looking *à touts azimuths* at a political elite temperamentally
unreconciled to Ukrainians 'living apart.' Moreover, as Western elites are
finally discovering, that problem is being aggravated by the process of
NATO enlargement, a process whose outcome became almost certain once
strategic and geopolitical reservations were trumped by the issue of Western credibility.

Ukraine's internal difficulties provide further grounds for apprehension.
These difficulties have vastly less to do with 'ethnic divisions' than with an
unbreakable but unfavorable connection between lawful authority, a sound
economy, and the political viability of the country. In its own terms, the
combating of inflation (which in 1997 was only 10.1 percent a month) was
a formidable achievement, and it was entirely right that Western lending
institutions made it the litmus test for the loans and grants they have be-
stowed. But if Ukraine is not to find itself perpetually dependent upon
Russia, dependent upon others to pay Russia, and powerless to develop its
own formidable resources, the struggle to be waged against bureaucratic
and criminal power will be no less hard than that already waged against
fiscal and monetary profligacy. Lack of progress in this struggle has become Ukraine's greatest obstacle to meeting the strategic challenge of becoming a "full member of the European family of civilized nations."[6]
Ukraine's highest officials openly warn that this struggle is getting no better; privately, several of them express the fear that Ukraine is losing it.

Domestic Constraints and Imperatives

There is no great controversy in stating that Kuchma's policy is dictated by
internal constraints as well as by external, geopolitical ones. In the elections

of June–July 1994, Kuchma's overwhelming support in the six easternmost oblasts (regions) and amongst the left generally was based upon a platform advocating greater economic closeness to Russia. Yet many of these forces—the industrial workforce and much of the industrial and agro-industrial ex-nomenklatura—opposed what for Kuchma is the prerequisite to such closeness: radical economic reform (and privatization) and the creation of a strong state under an effective presidential regime. Those who were better disposed toward the latter objectives—the western oblasts and the political right—would convert this support into support for Kuchma only if he could persuade them that he was a *national* leader and not, in his own derisory phrase, 'a vassal of Russia.' Without a critical mass of support from old and new elites, from East and West and from left and right, Kuchma would at best hold office instead of power.

Yet it is the cultural factor that most strongly dictates Ukraine's adherence to a dual course. It is now fashionable in some quarters to downplay the geographical divisions that tempted Russians in 1991 to boast that Ukraine was a 'doomed state' without a coherent national identity. Today, Russian pronouncements are more guarded than they were. Nevertheless, the fact that central Ukraine did not become part of a Russian state until 1793–1796 and that the five oblasts of western Ukraine did not do so until 1939–1940 does constrain how national identity is perceived and must constrain how independence is defined. Less important than the fact that ethnic Russians constitute 22 percent of the population are the facts that, depending on which estimate is accepted, between 15 and 50 percent of Ukrainian citizens (by definition, a large proportion of them ethnic Ukrainians) speak Russian as a first language and that a majority have Russian spouses or relations.[7] For once, in speaking of the 'Russian factor,' Russian nationalists might understate the truth.

Yet they also misrepresent it. For the majority of Ukrainian citizens, there is no inhibition about being wary of or even hostile to *rossiiskoe gosudarstvo,* the Russian *state*. To this majority, the shelling of the Russian parliament, the war in Chechnya, and Russian entanglements in Central Asia and the Caucasus are reason enough to be as far removed from that state as possible and to 'live in a normal country.' But, with the exception of the inhabitants of the five western oblasts, this majority will be deeply discomfited by the suggestion that they must be anti-*Russian* in order to be Ukrainian or to defend Ukrainian statehood. Whilst this cultural reality does not necessarily dictate equidistance between Russia and the West, it adds to other pressures to match movement in one direction with movement in the other.

The presentation of this cultural ambivalence as an 'ethnic problem' is at best a tailoring of the truth. Whilst the growing volume of opinion polling reveals divergent generational and regional sentiments about Ukraine's course,[8] it does not show ethnic Russians holding sharply different views from ethnic Ukrainians of the same generation, region, or economic status.[9] The one significant exception, the Autonomous Republic of Crimea, would seem to prove the rule, for what distinguishes Crimea from other parts of Ukraine is not simply the fact that 70 percent of its inhabitants are ethnic Russian, but that close to 90 percent of these Russians immigrated to Crimea after the Second World War.[10]

If the cultural and historical inheritance of Ukraine is a given that must be respected, the institutional inheritance of Ukraine is a given that must be overcome if Ukraine is to transform its independence into a source of strength. At the most general level, Ukraine, like other post-Soviet states, has emerged from a 'command-administrative' system that deprived its opponents not only of power, but of the competence and self-confidence to govern. There as elsewhere, no 'normal' system of authority was capable of filling the gap once the 'deformed' Soviet system collapsed, with the result that many power structures (in industry, agriculture, the armed forces, and security services) became more opaque to outsiders and more capable of obstructing political masters in 'democratic' conditions than they were before.

But whereas in Russia the economic anarchy of late 1991 gave radicals the moment they needed to change the economic mechanism, economic incentives and the economic interests of many of these power structures, Ukraine's radicals had no such moment. Indeed, Ukraine had few such radicals: first, because the brain trust of economic reform was based in Moscow, where most of them wished to remain; second, because the ruthless exuberance of Russia's radicals—who have a long tradition of declaring war on the present—is quite foreign to the 'traditional system of people's values' in Ukraine.[11] The consequences are twofold. Economic shocks have been introduced more gradually, more humanely, and less cynically than in Russia.[12] Paradoxically, yet for this reason, five years after the Soviet collapse, signs of breakdown remain more conspicuous than signs of transformation.[13]

Despite its tradeoffs, Ukraine has not been spared the macroeconomic ills of its less temperate neighbor: 'pseudo money,' the distribution of budget revenues that, in the president's words, "do not exist";[14] real money (now estimated at 43 percent) circulating outside the banking system and tax net;[15] and, not coincidentally, wage debts in the state budgetary sector totalling $1.8 billion. It is no accident that these ills concentrate in sectors most vital to and most resistant to reform—notably, the country's strategically important energy sector, where (as in Russia) funds earmarked for wages and reconstruction frequently end up diverted by local authorities and, with or without their connivance, in criminal hands.[16]

If these are also Russia's problems, then why should they increase Ukraine's vulnerability to Russia? Two contrasts are inescapable. First, despite its privations, Russia remains a net energy exporter and, to this day, the source of over 50 percent of Ukraine's energy requirements.[17] Whilst several of Russia's regions suffer an energy deficit, it is Ukraine as a whole that suffers a deficit. The greater contrast is one of relative peril. The worst-case outcome of the Russian debt crisis is insurrection and disintegration, and, if imaginations are pushed to an extreme, the support of both by 'foreign powers.' But these foreign powers cannot threaten the existence of the Russian state, nor by definition can they reabsorb it. On the other hand, there is no shortage of prominent Russians wishing to reabsorb Ukraine in whole or in part and willing to use energy and other levers to this end. Moreover, official Russian actions have demonstrated the linkages between vulnerability and threats to independence more than once. True as this is, the prospect of Ukraine's reabsorption by Russia (with the possible exception of Sevastopol) becomes more remote, if not outlandish, as time passes. But that does not diminish the risk that Ukraine could be destabilized by Russia or resubordinated to it whilst remaining nominally sovereign. If sovereignty means 'freedom to choose,' Ukraine's long-term sovereignty is still open to question.[18]

Russian Policy

Kuchma is convinced that Ukraine will have no chance of remaining independent without a 'special partnership' with Russia, that is, without Russian *consent.* Equally, he believes that there will be no chance of securing Russian consent unless Ukraine has strong ties with the West, and unless the West displays a strong stake in an independent Ukraine. This Janus-like policy is dictated not only by the weakness of Ukraine and the attitude of the West, but also by the 'reality of Russia.' In the perception of Ukrainians, this reality is not defined simply by Russia's relative power, but by an imperial outlook which, under the banner of Russian great power, is being repackaged and revived.

But what is the Russian perception—and what do terms like 'imperial' mean in a country like Russia, where state and empire have developed coterminously and alongside one another? Many Russians who favor reintegration with Ukraine do so not because they are imperial in outlook, but because in *their* outlook, Ukraine is part of Russia. Indeed, it is often the Russians who are most in opposition to the classically and stridently imperial policies of the Russian 'Eurasians' who put the greatest premium on reintegration with Ukraine, because they deem it essential not only to Russian power in Europe, but to Russia's 'European' character. To invert the distinction above, such integrationists might pursue a course avowedly hostile to Ukrainian statehood, but they do not see themselves as anti-Ukrainian. Nevertheless, if even Russian 'democrats' are unreconciled to Ukraine's long-term independence, Ukrainians must reconcile themselves to a prolonged and complex struggle with Russia.

The necessity for this struggle is only compounded by the nature of the Russian state. In the West, the distinction between Mikhail Gorbachev, the proponent of Soviet 'renewal,' and Yeltsin, the champion of 'Russia's rebirth,' long obscured two core problems: the fact that the Russian Federation was itself a multinational and potentially fragmentable state, and the unlikelihood that this state, however defined, would remain a status quo power within the former USSR.[19] For when in history had a Russian state existed within these post-1991 borders: borders that appeared artificial not only to the proponents of a 'greater Russia' but (as Chechnya's secession showed) to the proponents of a smaller one? By what principle—historical, demographic, economic, or strategic—could they be considered sacrosanct? It is neither surprising that, as early as August 1991 (the month in which Ukraine's Supreme Council [Verkhovna Rada] declared independence), both Yeltsin and his then foreign minister, Andrei Kozyrev, called for border revisions, nor that Yeltsin warned in December 1991 that "if Ukraine refuses to join the new *union* [the CIS], we will be on opposite sides of the barricade."

By the end of 1991, Russian policy makers were beginning to discern a connection between three variables: the viability of the multinational Russian Federation, the strength of 'integration processes' in the former USSR (the so-called Near Abroad), and the standing of Russia in the West. It was Kozyrev's recognition of this connection that prompted him to describe Russia as a country that was 'doomed' [*obrechena*] to be a great power. But exactly how should these variables be linked, and where should the priorities lie? Since late 1991, it is possible to identify three broad stages in Russian policy.[20]

During the first stage, December 1991 to autumn 1992, the Russian foreign policy establishment focused almost exclusively on the West. Toward the newly independent states, policy exhibited high levels of disorientation and 'multivoicedness' *(mnogogolosie)* that did great injury to Russian-Ukrainian relations. During this period, Russian officials (Russia's ambassador to Ukraine, no less) proclaimed that Ukraine's independence was a 'transitional phenomenon'; prominent centrists (e.g., Vladimir Lukin) demanded a 'strong line,' including threats to sever supplies to Ukrainian industry, transfer armed forces to Russian jurisdiction, and exercise effective sovereignty over Crimea; and liberal democratic think tanks toyed with models of 'loose' and 'tight' hegemony.[21]

Yet the actual policy accompanying these statements, studies, and recommendations was one of malign neglect. For this neglect, the team of Egor Gaidar, Gennadii Burbulis, and Kozyrev had three good reasons: first, the absolute primacy of Russia's economic reform; second, the absolute primacy of Western assistance, which was deemed essential to reform *and* to strengthening Russia's influence over its neighbors; third, they were historic optimists who comforted themselves with the thought that 'there is a logic that will bring the republics back our way'—and which required little intervention from them. So, in this formative period, whilst keeping their priorities firmly fixed on the Far Abroad, even democrats displayed a disturbing cast of mind with regard to the newly independent states. An article published by *Moskovskie Novosti* in mid-1992 revealed not only what distinguished liberals from their harder opponents but also what connected them to the attitudes of the past:

> Russian domination is an inevitability. The whole question is at what price. One can't become a great power using the methods of the tsarist or communist regimes. Those times are over! We thus need to learn civilized and neo-colonialist ways of influencing others. . . . The term 'neo-colonialist,' unless used for vulgar propaganda purposes, merely amounts to present-day relations between strong and weak countries. The biological uniformity—the strong subordinate the weak—is still valid in world politics with the inexorability of world gravitational laws. The novelty of this colonialism consists in the fact that the forms and methods of subordination have changed.[22]

The second stage—and the reversal of the 'primacy of the West'—began in October 1992, when Boris Yeltsin reproached the Ministry of Foreign Affairs for its 'unbalanced' foreign policy and its neglect of the 'Near Abroad.' Rivalries between power centers remained intense and continued to inhibit coordination. Nevertheless, the pronouncements of institutional rivals revealed an increasing consensus over core principles. By 1994, it was hard not to discern that:

- under the banner of ending the 'romantic embrace with the West,' the 'Near' and 'Far Abroad' had been reversed in Russian priorities;
- 'great power' and geopolitical terms of reference were supplanting those of liberal universalism (when Yeltsin stated that "ideological confrontation has been replaced by a struggle for spheres of influence in geopolitics," he was articulating what was already taken for granted);[23]
- energy, capital, and money were emerging as tools of influence and leverage in the former Soviet Union.

By this time, the dust had settled, and the 'reasoned nationalists' now dominated policy.

Despite several crises—not least the October 1993 storming of parliament—and many more tribulations, 'reasoned nationalists' established and retained a hold on policy. They were, according to their own description, 'pragmatists' who recognized the necessity of 'limited partnership' with the West, who understood the perils of altering borders and—at least where Ukraine and the Baltic states were concerned—of using military force. Nevertheless, they believed that 'integration'—resubordination by any name—was a 'law-governed' process, to be pursued over the long term, by pressure as well as by persuasion. As then head of Russia's Foreign Intelligence Service (*Sluzhba Vneshnei Razvedki*), Yevgenii Primakov supervised the publication of a report that provided the most authoritative statement of these views. In keeping with 'international norms,' the report declared the sovereignty of the newly independent states to be 'irreversible', whilst also demanding that key areas of sovereignty should be 'delegated.'[24] As in Soviet times, Primakov underscored the 'objective character' of Moscow's policy—then class struggle, now integration—and the 'hopelessness' of resisting it.

When Primakov replaced Kozyrev as Foreign Minister in January 1996 he promptly restated the 'balanced' priorities originally set out by Boris Yeltsin in October 1992: developing Russia's cohesion, strengthening 'centripetal' processes in the Near Abroad, and (only third); promoting 'equal' partnership with the West.[25] The appointment raised expectations not only that the marginalization of the Ministry of Foreign Affairs (MFA) would be reversed, but that policy would once again transcend politics.[26]

Instead, for entirely unrelated reasons, *mnogogolisie* has evolved in the opposite direction: toward a vacuum of policy. The first of these reasons was the triumph of the communists in the elections to the Federal Assembly of December 1995; a triumph that between January and July 1996 shifted the regime's focus to its own survival and brought foreign policy to a standstill. The second reason was the way chosen by the regime to secure survival: the suborning of key opponents and critics, including Aleksandr Lebed, Igor Rodionov, Sergei Glaz'ev, and Aman Tuleev, and their incorporation into prominent foreign policy positions. The third and most recent reason has been the incapacitation of Boris Yeltsin himself.

Dialectics of Weakness

To greater or lesser degree, all three stages cited above expose an incongruity between the spirit of *ressentiment* and the absence of authority that would give it effect. This combination of Russian revanche and debility has burdened Ukraine with two forms of Russian pressure, which must be withstood simultaneously.

The more conventional of the two is pressure from Moscow to adhere to the course that Belarusian President Alyaksandr Lukashenka has eagerly chosen: a course that would transform the CIS from a loose, variegated structure into a Russian-dominated, supranational entity. In the minds of some Ukrainians, the combination of Russia's weakness and diplomatic skill means that the pressure can be surreptitious enough to avoid a European crisis, not to say a Western response.

The more complex pressure arises from the unhealthy autonomy of Russian power structures and of cliques inside them. When the political environment is relatively benign, the penalty of such autonomy is not only, in Horbulin's words, that "it is hard to know who to work with," but that issues are never settled: decisions are difficult to take and, once taken, easy to disregard (a pattern that, over the Black Sea Fleet, has acquired a dreary predictability). As Markian Bilynskyi observes, the reality is that

> short-term horizons and the general subordination of policy to politics become the norm, while the very importance of defining ties with Ukraine means that paradoxically the issue is never fully addressed because . . . no one is eager to assume responsibility. The lack of a coherent policy means that Ukraine has become something of a 'grab-bag' that the Russian political leadership dips into for political rather than policy reasons.[27]

But if the political environment provided Russians with an incentive not only to 'take responsibility' but act, then a genuine danger might arise: the danger that Russian power structures, marching separately and fighting together, would not only put pressure on Ukraine, but unleash forces that escaped the control of both states.[28]

In an economically dissatisfied country, three factors give potency to this worry. The first and most obvious of these is the long-standing discord between Ukraine's president and its parliament, the Supreme Council. Fraught, tumultuous, and exhausting as this discord has been, the two major hurdles to the establishment of a strong presidential system—the 8 June 1995 constitutional agreement and the adoption of the Ukrainian constitution on 28 June 1996—were cleared without the bloodshed that accompanied the establishment of a presidential system in Russia.[29]

The discord has also been manageable, thanks to the divisions within the parliament itself. Within the left bloc, only around two thirds of the communists (KPU) have favored the restoration of the USSR. Whilst sharing the KPU's economic aims, the socialists (SPU) and the Peasant Party (SelPU) have been consistently committed to an independent Ukraine and, hence, to Kuchma's policy of equidistance between Russia and the West. In contrast, the national democratic bloc (principally Rukh) has never accepted Kuchma's premise that 'Ukraine cannot exist without Russia.' Nevertheless, Rukh shares Kuchma's views on economic reform and acquiesces in his foreign policy because it has brought relative security to Ukraine.

This matrix of alignments, always susceptible to presidential manipulation, has become more favorable of late thanks to two further permutations. The lesser of these was the division of the hitherto Agrarian parliament faction into a rump, antireformist group entitled the Peasant Party and the slightly larger Agrarians for Reform. The latter, like the former, was dominated by collective and state farm chairmen, but had become persuaded of the advantages of reforms. The more stunning development was the decision of twenty-eight communist deputies to break ranks and vote for the constitution: a view widely regarded as showing 'who is in favor of the state.'[30] This defection, led by the chairman of the Rada's Foreign and CIS Affairs Commission, Borys Oliynyk, not only signifies the emergence of a communist faction on the central European pattern, but has transformed parliament from a potential threat into a bulwark of current political order. In addition, a third of the communist parliament faction agreed to take the oath of loyalty, as demanded by the Ukrainian constitution.

Nevertheless, the success of Kuchma's own 'balanced' policies will continue to depend on his ability to unbalance his rivals and, more important, achieve results. With or without Russian pressure, common ground between the moderate right and the nationally minded left would vanish if 'social harmony' broke down in Ukraine.

Second is the activity of Russian 'special services' on Ukrainian soil. In his last interview as its director, Yevgenii Primakov asserted that the Foreign Intelligence Service (SVR) used 'all possible means' to facilitate 'reintegration processes' in the 'former Soviet Union.'[31] Although the assertion merely confirmed what Ukrainians knew, it was still noteworthy not only as an admission that the SVR defies Russian Federation law (which bars its activity in CIS states), but as an admission that the Soviet tradition of 'active measures'—promoting 'processes' rather than gathering intelligence—continues to guide the activity of this service. Yet the full dimension of the problem is that Ukraine falls within the 'direction' of at least five other Russian services: the Federal Security Service (FSB),[32] the Federal Agency for Government Communications and Information (FAPSI), Russian Federation border troops (which maintain a separate intelligence directorate), the Chief Intelligence Directorate of the General Staff (GRU), and, quite distinct from the GRU, the military Counterintelligence Directorate (nominally subordinate to the FSB, but virtually autonomous in practice).

The third factor is business. In Ukraine as well as Russia, it is an open secret that power structures have business interests: interests that create informal, sub rosa relationships operating alongside open and official ones. What is more, Russian and Ukrainian business interests are often intertwined. The alleged connections between two senior ministers of the Ukrainian government and Russian business interests in the energy and defense complexes have naturally raised questions as to whether national interests will necessarily benefit from the 'reform' of these complexes. It is largely with such concerns in mind that, at substantial economic cost to Ukraine, three-thousand 'strategic' industries are closed to foreign investment.[33] Where business, trade union militancy, and strategic assets are combined—as they were in the February and July 1996 Donets'k miners' strikes—even moderate figures in the government are quick to warn that the country 'could lose independence.'[34] Today, despite such warnings, Russian involvement is feared rather than officially alleged. But in a country where such strikes, in the words of former Prime Minister Yevhen Marchuk, could "result in a disruption of ties between government structures, the executive structures as a whole," little imagination is required to see the harm that Russia could cause if it set out to cause it.[35]

Ukraine and the CIS

With his characteristic determination to show 'balance' in foreign policy, Kuchma has stated more than once that "the main place in the system of Ukrainian foreign policy priorities is occupied and will always be occupied by the CIS countries and by Russia in particular."[36] A skeptic might observe that these 'priorities' are demonstrated by Ukraine's refusal to join the CIS Customs Union (March 1992), the CIS Interparliamentary Assembly, or the Tashkent Treaty on Collective Security (May 1992), to sign the CIS Charter (January 1993); or to proceed beyond associate membership in the Economic Union (September 1993). The priority, in sum, lies in resisting Russian attempts to transform the CIS from an interstate *(me'gosudarstvennakh)* into a supranational *(nadgosudarstvennakh)* structure.[37] In his 1996 Independence Day speech, Kuchma set out two main reasons for such resistance:

> Relations [with other states] via Moscow have no future, not only because Russia itself needs investment and technological and technical modernization. . . . The main reason is that state and private foreign structures can sense

very well whether a country is truly independent. If the answer is negative, they will maintain contacts through a neo-metropolis where real power is concentrated.[38]

Other perspectives, not only from the government, but from two thirds of the political spectrum (center-left to right) echo the same themes: not only does CIS integration represent the "accelerated integration of underdeveloped markets"[39] and hence a "guarantee of long-term economic and technological backwardness"[40] but its supranational bodies are designed to promote the political and economic dominance of Russia. As a case in point:

> The agreement on the creation of the Interstate Bank contains a provision according to which accounts between members are settled in rubles issued by the Central Bank of Russia. The bank's free funds are kept in a corresponding account in the Central Bank of Russia. This means that the CIS countries are effectively providing credits for the Russian economy.[41]

Yet whilst Ukraine can draw clear battle lines against the CIS and even win the battles thus defined, it may still fail to remedy its core weakness: its economic vulnerability to Russia. As Professor Filipenko notes:

> Russian economic expansionism is not limited by its monopoly in oil, gas and other natural resources. Economic penetration proceeds with the help of powerful Russian banks, financial and trust companies and industrial corporations. They create joint ventures throughout the CIS, hold stocks in promising enterprises and establish financial-industrial groups.[42]

For the most noteworthy fact is not that Russia has openly linked the rolling over of energy debt to the acquisition of equity in Ukraine's energy transport and refining sectors (e.g., during the August 1993 gas cutoff; one of four) or to strategic concessions (e.g., at Massandra, September 1993), let alone that it has actively promoted the establishment of financial-industrial groups linking the Russian and Ukrainian defense-industrial complexes. More salient is the fact that much Russian investment activity, resisted by a notionally left-wing Supreme Council, is supported by a notionally centrist president.[43] And, he would argue, supported with good reason; for most of the 'strategic' sector of Ukraine's economy might not attract investment capital apart from Russian.[44] For the unreformed sectors of a half-reformed economy, there are only Hobson's choices: an outcome in which Ukraine gains, but Russian economic interests gain more, or an outcome in which Russia loses, because investment is barred, and Ukraine loses even more. It is therefore no cliché that, over the long term, "the achievement of genuine independence is impossible without fundamental social transformations within Ukraine."[45]

Western Support and Ukrainian Anxieties

Belatedly but steadily, the Western powers have come to recognize the strategic importance of Ukraine. Precisely because the United Kingdom has played a more positive role than most, the sober verdict of the Ukrainian Ministry of Foreign Affairs—shortly after the visit of Britain's foreign secretary in autumn 1995—is indicative of Ukraine's reservations about the West as a whole:

> Britain has not yet formed a clear, well thought out concept of relations with Ukraine. The policies of John Major's government were in fact being formulated from week to week, which means they had no consistency. Ukrainian policy still is in a formative stage, affected by the stance of NATO allies and by the so-called Russia factor. . . . [Nevertheless] Ukraine is now being viewed separately from Russia, often together with the Baltic countries and, in general, the attitude of British government circles to Ukraine may be briefly described as reserved but positive.[46]

'Reserved but positive' is simply not enough to convince knowledgeable Ukrainians that they can put all of their eggs in the Western basket. Burbulis's maxim of 1991, 'The West will not take them,' has great resonance. Ukrainians well understand what their neighbors in central Europe do not fully grasp: that the post–Cold War West is politically unwilling and psychologically unable to make choices between Central–Eastern Europe and Russia. Because Kuchma knows that the West will not make a choice, he is determined not to give them one. Therefore, just as internal stability and Western support are seen as the precondition for securing friendly relations with Russia, so friendly relations with Russia are seen as the precondition for drawing closer to the West. The 'art of the possible' could not be better understood.

Where relations with NATO are concerned, these ambivalences are never far from the surface. On the one hand, as the first state of the former Soviet Union to accede to NATO's Partnership for Peace (PfP, 8 February 1994), Ukraine has found these relations to be unusually warm. Ukraine has consistently declared that NATO is a 'guarantor of stability in Europe' and has done its utmost to participate in every NATO/PfP aspect open to it (including over 100 PfP exercises) and launch a good many initiatives of its own.[47] But this enthusiasm toward NATO is not matched by enthusiasm toward NATO enlargement. Since the election of President Kuchma in July 1994, Ukraine has consistently pursued two aims that offset its ties to NATO: 'strategic partnership' with Russia[48] and a policy of military nonalignment *(nevmeshatel'stvo)*.[49] Far from masking significant disagreements in official circles, the three aims dictate a nuanced and consistent policy toward NATO enlargement.

- 'In principle,' Ukraine has no objection about 'possible' NATO enlargement. 'Nobody has the right to veto any country's inherent right' to membership.
- The 'no vetoes' principle, however, does not imply that enlargement should be implemented without 'due regard' for the security concerns of 'other interested countries.' Moreover, NATO should commit itself to an 'evolutionary process' of transformation from 'a collective defense' to a 'collective security' institution.[50]
- Ukraine seeks to remain a nonaligned state but is determined not to find itself in a gray zone between hostile military groupings. Kuchma has warned that 'Ukraine will never be able to remain outside the blocs' under these conditions.

Taken as a whole, these pronouncements betray much anxiety about NATO enlargement; anxiety that on at least one occasion produced a sharp public exchange between Ukrainian and Polish officials.[51] Anxiety is assuredly great when the process of enlargement seems to be governed by the interests of Central European but not East European states, when NATO scrutinizes the 'suitability' and 'contribution' of new members rather than the vulnerabilities of states excluded, and when it proceeds on the basis of 'commitments' and a schedule rather than a calculus of likely consequences. Ukrainians can be forgiven for perceiving that enlargement is proceeding according to political considerations rather than geopolitical ones.

The most salient geopolitical fact is that Russia is unlikely to reemerge as the dominant factor in Central or southeastern Europe unless it reincorporates Ukraine into a Russian empire. This fact does not undermine the West's arguments for enlarging NATO, which are compelling in Central Europe given residual anxieties about Germany, lack of confidence about the irreversibility of change, and the equation widely drawn between NATO membership and membership in the West. But as Ukrainians are the first to realize, the Eastern dimension of enlargement is another matter. Had events conspired to produce a postcommunist Soviet Union in 1991, there would be a power vacuum in Central Europe, and NATO might have to fill it. Today, there is no Soviet Union, only Russia, and instead of a power vacuum in Central Europe, there is only a vacuum of confidence.

Not so, however, in Ukraine. Ukrainians believe that the Russian pressures they manage today might become unmanageable on the morrow of NATO's enlargement. Given the geopolitical premises that dominate Russian thinking, Ukrainians understand the logic (if also the falsity) of the Russian charge that NATO's eastward expansion would be an 'offensive' step and a major geopolitical change demanding compensatory steps on Russia's part. The question is not whether such aspirations are enunciated or even 'decreed' (as Yeltsin set out to do in September 1995), but how they might be realized. Were NATO's enlargement to lead, in former Russian Defense Minister Pavel Grachev's words, to the "domination of strongarm tactics'—either by the Russian state leadership or by 'power ministries' inside it—then the consequences could be dire, whether the tactics succeeded or failed. With an abundance of precedents in the Caucasus and Central Asia to point to, some Ukrainian officials privately state that in such a case, Ukraine would need to forestall disaster by taking the first steps back to Russia itself.

The first, but most problematic, would be measures already advocated by President Kuchma and Foreign Minister Hennadiy Udovenko to transform NATO into a "nucleus for a future all-European security system that would encompass other mutually complementary, interlocking institutions." Russians, however, stand little chance of being impressed by such measures unless they divest NATO of its two core attributes: its 'bloc' character (which limits membership to countries with shared geopolitical interests) and its military structures (without which it cannot guarantee what it guarantees). So neutered, NATO would no longer be a 'guarantor of stability in Europe,' but a mechanism without a master.

The second would be a policy that exploited the deterrent potential of enlargement. In practice, NATO would undertake not to move east unless Russia moved west. To be effective, the corollary of such an undertaking would require equal emphasis (and rigorous preparation): the certainty of rapid enlargement if Ukraine or the Baltic states was menaced. In such an eventuality, Russia would surely be the loser, for it would then confront not NATO's 'transformation' but a classic projection of Western power and the reconstitution, from a position of strength, of an anti-Russian front in Europe. This policy would introduce what is sorely lacking in East-West relations: clarity. In the absence of a Western defense of Ukraine, NATO would offer protection through deterrence. It would also offer Central Europeans the prospect of a form of integration and Westernization, on the Swedish or Austrian model, that would not transform them into front-line states. But whatever its merits, this deterrent proposal is roundly opposed, especially in Poland, by rank-and-file political elites who view NATO membership as a transcendental cause, rather than a means to an end, and who fear, perhaps correctly, that rejection could produce the 'loss' of Central Europe.[52]

In the absence of political will to overcome this problem, the least perilous course would be a policy of slow and carefully defined enlargement. NATO's members would commit themselves to the admission of Poland, the Czech Republic, and Hungary and would specify a maximum but sufficient time scale needed to implement complementary measures. First, Ukraine must be helped 'to stand on its own feet' and overcome internal weaknesses that traditionally have provided inducement to Russian 'active measures' and mischief. As a nuclear power, Russia will always have the means to threaten Ukraine, but it should lose the ability to undermine Ukraine without grave risk to itself. Second, NATO would need time to assure Russia that it is amenable to restraints in Central Europe (as it was in Norway and Denmark), that it is open to appropriate revision of arms treaties, and that it seeks 'equal partnership,' not to speak of collaboration, wherever interests coincide. But Russia should be left in no doubt that its relationship with Ukraine will have a decisive impact on its relationship with NATO and on its own future.

Conclusion

Stimulated by and yet defying its own vulnerabilities, Ukraine has transformed the geopolitical environment in which it operates. The Western powers, whilst impressed by Ukraine's effort to 'determine its own course,' are even more impressed by the consequences that would ensue were Ukraine to fail. Indeed, one could say that Ukraine's view of NATO—as an important factor of stability in Europe—now resembles the view that key actors in NATO hold about an independent Ukraine: that it is a pivot of European security. When it is realized how nuclear anarchy and ethnic strife had so recently persuaded many of these actors that stability was *threatened* by Ukraine's independence, it should be obvious that a transformation of Western thinking—at least at the official level—has occurred. Whatever this transformation says about the West, it is a commentary on the dedication of Ukraine's political elite and, more important, on the self-discipline and national consciousness of the country as a whole.

It would be unduly bold to suggest that this national self-discipline and consciousness has produced an equivalent transformation in the attitude of Russia. Nevertheless, the fact of Ukrainian statehood has had two important effects. First and most predictably, it has inspired a search for indirect means to undo the fact, or at least alter it so as to make dependence rather than independence the norm in Russo-Ukrainian relations. But it has also bred grudging acceptance of Ukrainian statehood, its international legitimacy, and the importance that the West attaches to it. Unless and until this grudging acceptance becomes gracious acceptance, Russia will constitute a major and pervasive security problem for Ukraine. But the verdict must be that time has been working in Ukraine's favor. It is therefore tempting to conclude that it will continue to do so.

Like several more classical temptations, this one is best resisted. In political struggles as in war, everything depends upon how time is used. In terms of political victories in Kyiv, and in terms of international relationships, there is every reason to proclaim that the 'transitional period in the development of the state is over.' But in the terms that matter most to Ukraine's citizens, state building has hardly begun. The adoption of the constitution was an important victory, but it will prove to be a hollow victory so long as significant powers in regions and localities are able to treat laws and contracts as 'scraps of paper.' To many, statehood will have hazy, artificial, or even cynical connotations until economic order exists, is seen to exist, and is seen to benefit ordinary people.

Today, there is as great a probability that statehood will erode as there is that it will consolidate. The external and internal enemies of Ukraine both understand Clausewitz's dictum: "It is impossible to obtain possession of a great country with European civilization otherwise than by aid of internal division." The twist is not simply that Ukraine's greatness is still open to question, but that its divisions could be exploited by an equally divided Russia. Far from diminishing risks, Russia's fragmentation only increases the possibility that pressure could produce anarchy in the post-Soviet space.

The challenge for Ukraine is not to be mesmerized by its own international success: not to allow the 'virtual reality' of European and transatlantic relationships to divert attention from the less glamorous battles that must be fought and won. Today Ukraine has an avid, almost obsessive interest in joining the 'structures' of Europe's emerging 'security architecture.' But in the absence of defenses (still unreformed) and alliances (still rejected), even Europe's 'harder' security structures could turn out to be fair-weather friends. The obsession about 'integrating with European structures' also makes it easy to forget that the real challenge is to integrate with 'Europe.' To be sure, there is ample reason to welcome Ukraine's admission to the Central European Initiative despite the fact that its founders "did not really regard Ukraine as a central European country."[53] But the fact is that Ukraine was admitted *despite* this perception, and its triumph may be largely symbolic. Similarly, the June 1994 Partnership and Cooperation Agreement with the European Union offers encouragement, incentives, and (once it is ratified) benefits; but the agreement will not bring Ukraine's economy up to European standards. Indeed, the agreement was concluded only because of a related agreement to exempt more retrograde, 'sensitive' areas of Ukraine's economy—which account for two thirds of Ukraine's exports—from these benefits. As the record of antidumping disputes and trade discrimination against Ukraine shows, Western business will continue to treat Ukraine as a nonmarket economy until there are real transformations in the way goods are produced and services delivered.[54]

Difficult as it is to say to people who have achieved much and withstood more, threats to Ukraine and its 'freedom to choose' have not disappeared. Today, the greatest inducement to such threats comes not from Western fickleness or even NATO enlargement but, as Kuchma has warned, from "expecting someone other than ourselves to deliver our coveted freedom and wealth."[55] If that expectation disappears, a sound Ukraine will not only be an important 'factor of stability' in Europe, it will also become the principle guarantor of its own integrity. The danger is that an infirm Ukraine, like nineteenth-century Ottoman Turkey, will become a fault line in the international system and a guarantor of great power mischief, intrigue, and discord. Today at least there is reason to hope that international uncertainty will again provide the incentive for Ukrainians to remedy their infirmities and disappoint those who would attempt to exploit them.

Notes

1. Although most scholars date Ukraine's independence from the independence referendum of 1 December 1991, Ukrainians tend to give more significance to the Verkhovna Rada's Declaration of Independence of 24 August of that year.

2. But the Ukrainian People's Republic, formed in November 1917, had few moments of peace. Displaced by the scarcely independent, German-sponsored Hetmanate after the Treaty of Brest-Litovsk, the republic was reestablished in December 1918, whereupon it found itself almost immediately invaded by Bolshevik troops and, by the spring of 1919, White Russian armies as well. In practice, the republic had effectively dissolved several months before Bolshevik authority was established in December 1919.

3. For diplomatic reasons, it is doubtless wise to stress symmetry rather than asymmetry, for which reason Ukraine officially pursues a 'balanced' (ravnovesnyi) policy between east and west.

4. 'Pivot' is the official British term for the role that Ukraine performs in the emerging structure of European security.

5. Leonid Kuchma, Independence Day speech, 23 August 1996 (Uriadovyi Kurier, 29 August 1996).

6. Volodymyr Horbulin, secretary of the National Security and Defense Council (and in the eyes of many, the second most powerful person in the government), "Ukraine's Place in Today's Europe," Politics and the Times (journal of the Foreign Ministry of Ukraine), October–December 1995, pp. 15.

7. Only after the 1989 education law did it become mandatory for all schools in the country to teach the Ukrainian language until age seventeen. Yet the reform merely

signified that Ukrainian would be taught as an obligatory second language, not that it would become the language of instruction. With the exception of a few schools in each oblast (in some eastern oblasts, no more than one or two), history, mathematics, and sciences were taught in Russian, and in a large number of schools throughout Ukraine, this is still the case.

8. As a case in point, a March 1995 Democratic Initiates poll demonstrated that 55 percent of citizens aged between 18–29 wanted Ukraine to adopt an unambiguously pro-Western course, whereas only 33 percent of those in the 30–55 age group agreed.

9. A Democratic Initiatives poll of Kyiv residents conducted at a high point of disillusionment, January 1995, revealed 62 percent of ethnic Ukrainians and 58 percent of ethnic Russians firmly in favor of independence; on the other hand, 16 percent of Ukrainians and only 10 percent of Russians pronounced themselves against it.

10. Moreover, as Natalia Belitser points out, "although [Crimea's] population makes up merely a tiny part of Ukraine (some 5 percent), 53,000 members of the Crimean Communist Party constitute over half of all communists in Ukraine." *Visnyk: The Ukrainian Center of Human Rights Herald,* no. 2, 1995.

11. The full quotation from Kuchma's Independence Day speech is: "The traditional system of our people's values plays the role of a kind of safety valve which prevents conflicts occurring" (*Uriadovyi Kurier,* 29 August 1996).

12. One need only contrast the Russian currency reform of 1993, implemented by stealth and at considerable cost to millions of ordinary citizens, with the elaborate efforts taken to ensure that the replacement of the *karbovanets* by the *hryvnia* was "honest, transparent, open and non-confiscatory" (Deputy Prime Minister Viktor Pynzenyk on Ukrainian radio, 26 August 1996—one of several detailed briefings to the public about the change).

13. In the worm's-eye view of the author, traveling through the east and south-east of Ukraine in the summer of 1996, economic conditions seemed reminiscent of Russia in 1993—irreversible, but heading in no certain direction.

14. In July 1996, the hidden budget deficit was estimated at *Kv* 1,700,000 billion, or almost $10 billion.

15. The currency reform, which obliged citizens to exchange *karbovantsi* for *hryvnyi* over a two-week period, unexpectedly revealed $10 billion that had not been accounted for existing outside the banking system.

16. According to former Prime Minister Yevhen Marchuk, "The coal industry's structure, organization *and economic management* remain the same as they were in the former Soviet Union. It was not the industry of an independent state, and not an industry working in a market economy, but part of the Soviet Union's coal industry." One reason for the February 1996 strike "was that money allocated for the coal industry often went to managers' favored mines" (Radio Ukraine World Service, 8 February 1996, in *Summary of World Broadcasts,* 12 February 1996). By July 1996 it was commonplace to blame that month's ten-day coal strike (and the 16 July assassination attempt on then Prime Minister Pavlo Lazarenko) on the 'struggle between Donets'k and Dnipropetrovs'k mafia clans.' By the same token, it seems hardly coincidental that the fifteen-day February 1996 miners' strikes coincided with the conclusion of an agreement with the EBRD to restructure the mining industry or that the July strikes coincided with the Rada's ratification of that agreement.

17. Though this is notoriously difficult to estimate. Russia provides Ukraine with about 90 percent of its oil and 60 percent of its gas, though it has no easy way of cutting supplies of the latter without cutting supplies to its customers in Central Europe. Ukraine is also able to siphon Russian gas transiting its territory.

18. The distinction between notional and actual sovereignty is doubtless what prompted this ponderous passage in Kuchma's Independence Day speech: "A sign of sovereignty is a country's ability to *develop its own course,* acceptable to the majority of its population, whereby external factors and influences are taken into consideration as long as they do not radically change this course, and the effect of internal factors and forces prevails over that of external ones. Therefore, independence is *freedom to choose* one of the possibilities, predetermined by society's internal forces, its interests and needs" (emphasis added) (*Uriadovyi Kurier,* 29 August 1996).

19. The state's official designation, the Russian Federation, was adopted in March 1992.

20. For a more detailed analysis, see James Sherr, *Russia Returns to Europe* (Camberley: Conflict Studies Research Center [hereafter CSRC], May 1994); John Lough, *The Place of Russia's "Near Abroad"* (Camberley: CSRC, January 1993); and John Lough, *Defining Russia's Role in the "Near Abroad"* (Camberley: CSRC, April 1993).

21. For a concise survey of carly centrist and 'liberal-democratic' approaches, see Alexander Goncharenko, *Ukrainian-Russian Relations: An Unequal Partnership* (London: Royal United Services Institute, 1995), pp. 4–19.

22. M. Shmelev, "Za nashu i vashu metropoliiu," *Moskovskie Novosti,* no. 4, 1992.

23. In a closed speech to senior staffs of the Foreign Intelligence Service (SVR), 27 April 1994.

24. 'Russia and the CIS: Does the Western Position Need Correction?' *Rossisskaia gazeta,* 22 September 1994.

25. "Zapis' press-konferentsii Ministra Inostrannikh del' Rossii Y.M. Primakova," 12 January 1996.

26. By the autumn of 1995, this marginalization was obvious to all. Following the 21 November Dayton accords, Russian participation in the future IFOR was negotiated directly between Grachev and U.S. Defense Secretary William Perry, without MFA involvement. Like the rest of the MFA, Russia's ambassador to Brussels and NATO, Vitaliy Churkin, had no knowledge of the contents of Grachev's 28 November 1995 speech at NATO headquarters until he heard it.

27. Markian Bilynskyj, *Update on Ukraine* (newsletter of the U.S.-Ukraine Foundation), 26 September 1996.

28. Lebed's boldness over Chechnya demonstrates that, even today, there are incentives to take responsibility.

29. Whilst granting the *Verkhovna Rada* important powers of lawmaking, appointment, and monitoring, the constitution affords the president the power to issue 'decrees and directives' and the power of veto (Article 106), which can only be overturned by a majority of two thirds (Article 94). "The right to legislative initiative . . . belongs to the President of Ukraine, the National Deputies of Ukraine, the Cabinet of Ministers of Ukraine and the National Bank of Ukraine" (Article 93).

30. Out of 420 elected deputies, 83 did not vote for the Constitution (voted against, were absent from parliament, or abstained).

31. *Komsomol'skaia Pravda,* 26 December 1995.

32. The law of 12 April 1995, "On the Bodies of the Federal Security Service of the Russian Federation," gives the FSB "the right to conduct intelligence operations on the territories of foreign countries": a right that its former director, Sergey Stepashin, admitted "simply brings us into line with what we have been doing in the past year." His admission was not surprising given Yeltsin's injunction in 1994 that the service's "extensive possibilities must be effectively used in the defense of Russians both in this country and abroad."

33. An estimate (as the Ukrainian list is unpublished) supplied by the European Bank for Reconstruction and Development on 15 June 1995.

34. Horbulin on 17 July 1996 (*Summary of World Broadcasts,* 19 July 1996).

35. Marchuk on Radio Ukraine World Service, 8 February 1996 (*Summary of World Broadcasts,* 12 February 1996).

36. Cited by ITAR-TASS news agency, 23 August 1996 (*Summary of World Broadcasts,* 24 August, 1996).

37. In Udovenko's formula, the aim is 'cooperation' as opposed to 'integration.' As expressed by Ivan Zayets, deputy chairman of the Verkhovna Rada's Foreign Affairs Commission, Ukraine opposes the 'institutionalization' of cooperation.

38. Kuchma, in *Uriadovyi Kurier,* 29 August 1996.

39. Horbulin, "Ukraine's Place in Today's Europe."

40. Anton Filipenko (professor of international relations at the Taras Shevchenko Kyiv State University), "The CIS Economic Union: Pros and Cons," *Politics and the Times,* October–December, 1995, p. 60.

41. Ibid., p. 60.

42. Ibid., p. 60.

43. It was Kuchma's decree, "On the Creation of Financial-Industrial Groups," vetoed by the Verkhovna Rada, that provided Russia with the opportunity to create the controversial International Aircraft Engines group, amalgamating 140,000 Russian and 75,000 Ukrainian employees.

44. In the Donbas, it is even debatable how much Russian capital can be attracted. This reluctance to be saddled with the Donbas may explain why Russians have done little to exploit instability there.

45. Horbulin, "Ukraine's Place in Today's Europe."

46. Foreign Minister Hennadiy Udovenko after his return from Moscow in early August 1996. When, during the same month, Ukraine's then naval commander in chief, Admiral Volodymyr Bezkorovaynyy, claimed that there were "no problems" between the fleet, but "it is politicicans who are trying to foist them," he earned a stinging rebuke from the Russian Black Sea Fleet commander, Admiral Viktor Kravchenko, who accused him of trying to 'reverse the negotiating process' (*Nezavisimaia gazeta,* 13 August 1996).

47. Rear Admiral Aleksey Aladkin, deputy commander of the Black Sea Fleet, 14 February 1996.

48. The term, however, is less significant than it appears. 'Strategic partnership' is the term that officially describes Ukraine's relationship with many of its neighbors. What is especially significant, therefore, is not that Russia is termed a 'strategic partner,' but that the United States, United Kingdom, Germany and Poland are also so designated.

49. A word wrongly translated as 'neutrality': a term that does not accord with the activeness of Ukraine's policy and which might encourage Russia to demand Ukrainian silence on key international questions.

50. H. Udovenko, "European Stability and NATO Enlargement," *NATO Review,* November 1995.

51. At a 7 October 1995 press conference during the visit of the speaker of the Polish Sejm to Kyiv, then Prime Minister Marchuk urged that Poland be 'very careful' about joining NATO. When Zych, the Polish speaker, replied that Poland would 'not retreat,' Foreign Minister Udovenko declared, "Ukraine must regard relations with Russia as its main foreign policy priority. . . . While Poland is a fully independent country, Ukraine still has to fight for its independence" (*Summary of World Broadcasts,* 9 October 1995).

52. For a fuller outline of this proposal, see James Sherr, "After the Cold War: The Search for a New Security System," *European Security,* vol. 4, no. 4 (Winter 1995), pp. 571–583.

53. F. Stephen Larrabee, "Ukraine's Balancing Act," *Survival,* vol. 38, no. 2 (Summer 1996), pp. 155–156.

54. For an effective presentation of Ukraine's point of view on these disputes, see Volodymyr Konovalov, "Why is Ukraine Being Accused of Dumping?" *Politics and Times,* October–December 1995, pp. 52–57.

55. Kuchma, in *Uriadovyi Kurier,* 29 August 1996.

Bibliography of Selected Secondary Sources on Contemporary Ukraine

Books and Monographs (General)

D'Anieri, Paul, *Economic Interdependence in Ukrainian-Russian Relations* (New York: State University of New York Press, 1998).

Drohobycky, Maria, ed., *Crimea: Dynamics, Challenges, and Prospects* (Lanham, MD and London: Rowman and Littlefield Publishers and The American Association for the Advancement of Science, 1995).

Garnett, Sherman W., *Keystone in the Arch: Ukraine in the Emerging Security Environment of Central and Eastern Europe* (Washington, DC: Carnegie Endowment for International Peace, 1997).

Goncharenko, Alexander, *Ukrainian-Russian Relations: An Unequal Partnership. RUSI Whitehall Paper 32* (London: Royal United Services Institute, 1995).

Ham, Peter van, *Ukraine, Russia and European Security: Implications for Western Policy, Chaillot Papers No. 13* (Paris: Institute for Security Studies, West European Union, February 1994).

Jaworsky, John, *The Military-Strategic Significance of Recent Developments in Ukraine, Operational Research and Analysis, Directorate of Strategic Analysis, Project Report No. 645* (Ottawa: Department of National Defence, August 1993).

———, *Ukraine: Stability and Instability, McNair Paper 42* (Washington, DC: Institute for National Strategic Studies, National Defense University, August 1995).

Kis, Theofil I., *Nationhood, Statehood and the International Status of the Ukrainian SSR/Ukraine: University of Ottawa Ukrainian Studies, Occasional Papers No. 1* (Ottawa: University of Ottawa Press, 1989).

Kisersky, Leonid, Michael C. Soussanm, and Daniel L. Cruise, *Security in Eastern Europe: The Case of Ukraine* (Providence, RI: The Center for Foreign Policy Development of the Thomas J. Watson Institute for International Studies, Brown University, 1994).

Kravchuk, Robert, *Ukrainian Politics, Economics and Governance, 1991–96* (New York: St. Martin's Press, forthcoming).

Kuzio, Taras, *Ukraine. The Unfinished Revolution. European Security Studies 16* (London: Institute for European Defence and Strategic Studies, 1992).

———, *Ukraine-Crimea-Russia: Triangle of Conflict. Conflict Studies 267* (London: Research Institute for the Study of Conflict and Terrorism, 1994).

———, *Ukraine. Back from the Brink. European Security Studies 23* (London: Institute for European Defence and Strategic Studies, 1995).

———, *Ukrainian Security Policy. Washington Paper 167* (Washington, DC: The Center for Strategic and International Studies and Praeger, 1995).

————, *Ukraine under Kuchma. Political Reform, Economic Transformation and Security Policy in Independent Ukraine* (London: Macmillan and New York: St. Martin's Press, 1997).

————, *Ukraine: State and Nation Building*. Studies of Societies in Transition Series (London and New York: Routledge, forthcoming).

———— and Andrew Wilson, *Ukraine: Perestroika to Independence* (London: Macmillan, and New York: St. Martin's Press and Edmonton: Canadian Institute for Ukrainian Studies, 1994).

Matseiko, Youri, and Steven E. Miller, eds., *Safeguarding Ukraine's Security: Dilemmas and Options* (Cambridge: MIT Press, forthcoming)

Motyl, Alexander J., *Dilemmas of Independence. Ukraine after Totalitarianism* (New York: Council on Foreign Relations, 1993).

Nahaylo, Bohdan, *The Ukrainian Resurgence* (London: Hurst, 1998).

Wilson, Andrew, *Ukrainian Nationalism in the 1990s. A Minority Faith* (Cambridge: Cambridge University Press, 1997).

Articles

Part A. Nation and State Building

Arel, Dominique, "Voting Behaviour in the Ukrainian Parliament—The Language Factor," in Thomas F. Remington, ed., *Parliaments in Transition: The New Legislative Politics in the Former USSR and Eastern Europe* (Boulder, Colorado: Westview Press, 1994), pp. 125–158.

————, "Language Politics in Independent Ukraine: Towards One or Two State Languages?" *Nationalities Papers*, vol. 23, no. 3 (September 1995), pp. 597–622.

————, "Ukraine—The Temptation of the Nationalising State," in Vladimir Tismaneanu, ed., *Political Culture and Civil Society in Russia and the New States of Eurasia. The International Politics of Eurasia, Volume 7* (Armonk, NY, and London: M.E. Sharpe, 1995), pp. 157–188.

————, "A Lurking Cascade of Assimilation in Kiev?" *Post-Soviet Affairs*, vol. 12, no. 1 (January-March 1996), pp. 73–90.

Barrington, Lowell, "The Domestic and International Consequences of Citizenship in the Soviet Successor States," *Europe-Asia Studies*, vol. 47, no. 5 (July 1995), pp. 731–763.

Furtado, Charles F., "Nationalism and Foreign Policy in Ukraine," *Political Science Quarterly*, vol. 109, no. 1 (Spring 1994), pp. 81–104.

Hagen, Mark von, "Does Ukraine Have a History?" *Slavic Review*, vol. 54, no. 3 (Fall 1995), pp. 658–673.

Hague, Judy, Rose Aidan, and Marko Bojcun, "Rebuilding Ukraine's Hollow State: Developing a Democratic Public Service in Ukraine," *Public Administration and Development*, vol. 15, no. 4 (October 1995), pp. 417–433.

Kohut, Zenon E., "History as a Battleground: Russian-Ukrainian Relations and Historical Consciousness in Contemporary Ukraine," in S. Frederick Starr, ed., *The Legacy of History in Russia and the New States of Eurasia. The International Politics of Eurasia, Volume 1* (Armonk, NY, and London: M.E. Sharpe, 1994), pp. 123–146.

Markus, Ustina, "The Bilingualism Question in Belarus and Ukraine," *Transition*, vol. 2, no. 24 (29 November 1996).

Motyl, Alexander J., "Structural Constraints and Starting Points: The Logic of Systematic Change in Ukraine and Russia," *Comparative Politics,* vol. 29, no. 4 (July 1997), pp. 433–447.

Petheridge-Hernandez, Patricia, and Rosalind Latiner Raby, "Twentieth-Century Transformations in Catalonia and the Ukraine: Ethnic Implications in Education," *Comparative Education Review,* vol. 37, no. 1 (February 1993), pp. 31–49.

Plokhy, Serhii M, "Historical Debates and Territorial Claims: Cossack Mythology in the Russian-Ukrainian Border Dispute," in S. Frederick Starr, ed., *The Legacy of History in Russia and the New States of Eurasia: The International Politics of Eurasia, Volume 1* (Armonk, NY, and London: M.E. Sharpe, 1994), pp. 147–170.

———, "The History of a 'Non-Historical' Nation: Notes on the Nature and Current Problems of Ukrainian Historiography," *Slavic Review,* vol. 54, no. 3 (Fall 1995), pp. 709–716.

Prizel, Ilya, "The Influence of Ethnicity on Foreign Policy: The Case of Ukraine," in Roman Szporluk, ed., *National Identity and Ethnicity in Russia and the New States of Eurasia. The International Politics of Eurasia: Volume 2* (Armonk, NY, and London: M.E. Sharpe, 1994), pp. 103–128.

———, "Ukraine's Foreign Policy as an Instrument of Nation Building," in John W. Blaney, ed., *The Successor States to the USSR* (Washington, DC: Congressional Quarterly Inc., 1995), pp. 196–207.

Prymak, Thomas, "Hrushevsky and the Ukraine's 'Lost' History," *History Today,* vol. 39, no. 1 (January 1989).

Saunders, David, "What Makes a Nation a Nation? Ukrainians since 1600," *Ethnic Groups,* vol. 10 (1993), pp. 101–124.

Shevchuk, I. Yuri, "Citzenship in Ukraine: A Western Perspective," in *State and Nation Building in East Central Europe. Contemporary Perspectives,* John S. Micgiel, ed. (New York: Institute on East Central Europe, Columbia University, 1996), pp. 351–369.

Shved, V'iacheslav, "The Conceptual Approaches of Ukrainian Political Parties to Ethno-Political Problems in Independent Ukraine," *Journal of Ukrainian Studies,* vol. 19, no. 2 (Winter 1994), pp. 69–84.

Solchanyk, Roman, "The Politics of Language in Ukraine," *RFE/RL Research Report,* vol. 2, no. 10 (5 March 1993).

Subtelny, Orest, "The Current State of Ukrainian Historiography," *Journal of Ukrainian Studies,* vol. 18, nos. 1–2 (Summer-Winter 1993), pp. 33–54.

———, "Imperial Disintegration and Nation-State Formation: The Case of Ukraine," in *The Successor States to the USSR,* J.W. Blaney, ed. (Washington, DC: Congressional Quarterly Inc., 1995), pp. 184–195.

Szporluk, Roman, "Nation-Building in Ukraine: Problems and Prospects," in *The Successor States to the USSR,* J.W. Blaney, ed. (Washington, DC: Congressional Quarterly Inc., 1995), pp. 173–183.

———, "Ukraine: From an Imperial Periphery to a Sovereign State," *Daedalus,* vol. 126, no. 3 (Summer 1997), pp. 85–120.

Torbakov, Igor, "Historiography and Modern Nation-Building," *Transition,* vol. 2, no. 18 (6 September 1996).

Wilson, Andrew, "The Donbas between Ukraine and Russia: The Use of History in Political Disputes," *Journal of Contemporary History,* vol. 30, no. 2 (April 1995), pp. 265–289.

———, "Myths of National History in Belarus and Ukraine," in Geoffrey Hosking and George Schopflin, eds., *Myths and Nationhood* (London: Hurst, 1997), pp. 182–197.

Zviglyanich, Volodymyr, "Ethnic Economics: Is a Ukrainian Economic Model Possible?" *Ukraine Business Review,* vol. 4, nos. 1–2 (December 1995–January 1996), pp. 1–4.

Part B. National Identity and Regionalism

Aarrevaard, Timo, "Ukrainian Cities: Weak Soviets and Strong Mayors," *The Journal of Post Communist Studies and Transition Politics,* vol. 10, no. 4 (December 1994), pp. 55–70.

Arel, D., and Valentyn Khmelko, "The Russian Factor and Territorial Polarization in Ukraine," *The Harriman Review,* vol. 9, nos. 1–2 (March 1996), pp. 81–91.

Birch, Sarah, and Ihor Zinko, "The Dilemma of Regionalism," *Transition,* vol. 2, no. 22 (1 November 1996).

Boukhalov, Oleksandr, and Serguei Ivannikov, "Ukrainian Local Politics After Independence," *The Annals, The American Academy of Political and Social Science,* vol. 540 (July 1995), pp. 126–136.

Bremmer, Ian, "Ethnic Issues in Crimea," *RFE/RL Research Report,* vol. 2, no. 18 (30 April 1993).

———, "The Politics of Ethnicity: Russians in the New Ukraine," *Europe-Asia Studies,* vol. 46, no. 2 (March-April 1994), pp. 261–283.

Bukkvoll, Tor, "A Fall from Grace for Crimean Separatists," *Transition,* vol. 1, no. 21 (17 November 1995).

Burant, Stephen R., "Foreign Policy and National Identity: A Comparison of Ukraine and Belarus," *Europe-Asia Studies,* vol. 47, no. 7 (November 1995), pp. 1125–1144.

Golovakha, Evgenii, Natalia Panina, and Nikolai Churilov, "Russians in Ukraine," in Vladimir Shlapentokh, Munir Sendich, and Emil Payin, eds., *The New Russian Diaspora: Russian Minorities in the Former Soviet Repubics* (Armonk, NY: M.E. Sharpe, 1994), pp. 59–71.

Hesli, V., "Public Support for the Devolution of Power in Ukraine: Regional Patterns," *Europe-Asia Studies,* vol. 47, no. 1 (January-February 1995), pp. 91–121.

Jung, Monika, "The Donbas Factor in the Ukrainian Elections," *RFE/RL Research Report,* vol. 3, no. 12 (25 March 1994).

Kolstoe, Paul, *Russians in the Former Soviet Republics* (London: Hurst and Company, 1995), chapter 7, "The Eye of the Whirlwind: Belarus and Ukraine," pp. 166–199.

Kuzio, Taras, "The Crimea and European Security," *European Security,* vol. 3, no. 4 (Winter 1994), pp. 734–774.

———, "National Identity in Independent Ukraine: An Identity in Transition," *Nationalism and Ethnic Politics,* vol. 2, no. 4 (Winter 1996), pp. 582–608.

Laba, Roman, "The Russian-Ukrainian Conflict: State Nation and Identity," *European Security,* vol. 4, no. 3 (Autumn 1995), pp. 457–487.

Marples, David R., and David F. Duke, "Ukraine, Russia and the Question of Crimea," *Nationalities Papers,* vol. 23, no. 2 (June 1995), pp. 261–289.

Melvin, Neil, *Russians beyond Russia: The Politics of National Identity. Chatham House Papers* (London: Royal Institute for International Affairs, 1995), Chapter 5, "Russians, Regionalism and Ethnicity in Ukraine," pp. 78–99.

Meyer, David J., "Why Have Donbas Russians Not Ethnically Mobilized Like Crimean Russians Have? An Institutional/Demographic Approach," in John S. Micgiel, ed., *State and Nation Building in East Central Europe: Contemporary Perspectives* (New York; Institute on East Central Europe, Columbia University, 1996), pp. 317–330.

Molchanov, Mikhail A., "Borders of Identity: Ukraine's Political and Cultural Significance for Russia," *Canadian Slavonic Papers,* vol. XXXVIII, nos. 1–2 (March-June 1996), pp. 177–193.

Panina, Natal´ya, "Interethnic Relations and Ethnic Tolerance in Ukraine. An In-depth Analytical Report," in *Post-Soviet Puzzles: Mapping the Political Economy of the Former Soviet Union.* K. Segbers and S. De Spiegeleire, eds. *The Emancipation of Society as a Reaction to Systematic Change: Survival, Adaptation to New Rules and Ethnopolitical Conflicts, Volume IV* (Baden-Baden: Nomos Verlagsgesellschaft/Stiftung Wissenschaft und Politik, 1995), pp. 101–122.

Pirie, Paul S., "National Identity and Politics in Southern and Eastern Ukraine," *Europe-Asia Studies*, vol. 48, no. 7 (November 1996), pp. 1076–1104.

Ryabchuk, M., "Two Ukraines?" *East European Reporter*, vol. 5, no. 4 (July-August 1992).

Resler, Tamara J., "Dilemmas of Democratisation: Safeguarding Minorities in Russia, Ukraine and Lithuania," *Europe-Asia Studies*, vol. 49, no. 1 (January 1997), pp. 89–106.

Sasse, Gwendolyn, "The Crimean Issue," *The Journal of Communist Studies and Transition Politics*, vol. 12, no. 1 (March 1996), pp. 83–100.

Smith, Graham, and Andrew Wilson, "Rethinking Russia's Post-Soviet Diaspora: The Potential for Political Mobilisation in Eastern Ukraine and North-east Estonia," *Europe-Asia Studies*, vol. 49, no. 5 (July 1997), pp. 845–864.

Solchanyk, Roman, "The Politics of State Building: Centre-Periphery Relations in Post-Soviet Ukraine," *Europe-Asia Studies*, vol. 46, no. 1 (January-February 1994), pp. 47–68.

Stewart, Susan, "Ukraine's Policy toward Its Ethnic Minorities," *RFE/RL Research Report*, vol. 2, no. 36 (10 September 1993).

Wilson, Andrew, "The Growing Challenge to Kiev from the Donbas," *RFE/RL Resarch Report*, vol. 2, no. 33 (20 August 1993).

———, "Crimea's Political Cauldron," *RFE/RL Research Report*, vol. 2, no. 45 (12 November 1993).

Part C. Politics and Civil Society

Arel, Dominique, and Andrew Wilson, "The Ukrainian Parliamentary Elections," *RFE/RL Research Report*, vol. 3, no. 26 (1 July 1994).

———, "Ukraine under Kuchma: Back to 'Eurasia'?" *RFE/RL Research Report*, vol. 3, no. 32 (19 August 1994).

Aslund, Anders, "Eurasia Letter: Ukraine's Turnaround," *Foreign Policy*, no. 100 (Fall 1995), pp. 125–143.

Birch, S., "The Ukrainian Parliamentary and Presidential Elections of 1994," *Electoral Studies*, vol. 14, no. 1 (March 1995), pp. 93–99.

———, "Electoral Behaviour in Western Ukraine in National Elections and Referendums, 1989–1991," *Europe-Asia Studies*, vol. 47, no. 7 (November 1995), pp. 1145–1176.

Bojcun, Marko, "The Ukrainian Parliamentary Elections in March-April 1994," *Europe-Asia Studies*, vol. 47, no. 2 (March-April 1995), pp. 229–249.

———, "Ukraine Under Kuchma," *Labour Focus on Eastern Europe*, no. 52 (Autumn 1995), pp. 70–83.

Chudowsky, Victor, "The Ukrainian Party System," in John S. Micgiel, ed., *State and Nation Building in East Central Europe: Contemporary Perspectives* (New York: Institute for East Central Europe, Columbia University, 1996), pp. 305–321.

Kubicek, Paul, "Delegative Democracy in Russia and Ukraine," *Communist and Post-Communist Studies*, vol. 27, no. 4 (December 1994), pp. 423–441.

———, "Dynamics of Contemporary Ukrainian Nationalism: Empire-Breaking to State Building," *Canadian Review of Studies in Nationalism*, XXIII, nos. 1–2 (1996), pp. 39–50.

————, "Variations on a Corporatist Theme: Interest Associations in Post-Soviet Ukraine and Russia," *Europe-Asia Studies,* vol. 48, no. 1 (January 1996b), pp. 27–46.

Kuzio, Taras, "The Multi-Party System in Ukraine on the Eve of Elections,"*Government and Opposition,* vol. 29, no. 1 (Winter 1994), pp. 109–127.

————, "Ukrainian Nationalism," *Journal of Area Studies,* no. 4, 1994, pp. 79–95.

————, "Ukraine since the Elections: From Romanticism to Pragmatism," *Jane's Intelligence Review,* vol. 4, no. 12 (December 1994).

————, "The 1994 Parliamentary Elections in Ukraine," *The Journal of Communist Studies and Transition Politics,* vol. 11, no. 4 (December 1995), pp. 335–361.

————, "Kravchuk to Kuchma: The 1994 Presidential Elections in Ukraine 1994," *The Journal of Communist Studies and Transition Politics,* vol. 12, no. 2 (June 1996), pp. 117–144.

————, "Radical Nationalist Parties and Movements in Contemporary Ukraine Before and after Independence: The Right and Its Politics, 1989–1994," *Nationalities Papers,* vol. 25, no. 2 (June 1997), pp. 211–242.

Lapychak, Christina, "Media Independence is Still Alien to Ukraine's Political Culture," *Transition,* vol. 1, no. 18 (6 October 1995).

————, "Playing the Patronage Game in Ukraine," *Transition,* vol. 2, no. 21 (18 October 1996).

———— and Ustina Markus, "Ukraine's Continuing Evolution," *Transition,* vol. 3, no. 2 (7 February 1997).

Markov, Ihor, "The Role of the President in the Ukrainian Political System," *RFE/RL Research Report,* vol. 2, no. 48 (3 December 1993).

Markus, Ustina, "Ukraine: Stability and Political Turnover," *Transition* (15 February 1995).

Marples, David R., " 'After the Putsch': Prospects for Independent Ukraine," *Nationalities Papers,* XXI, no. 2 (Fall 1993), pp. 35–46.

————, "Ukraine after the Presidential Elections," *RFE/RL Research Report,* vol. 3, no. 31 (12 August 1994).

Martyniuk, Jaroslaw, "The Demographics of Party Support in Ukraine," *RFE/RL Research Report,* vol. 2, no. 48 (3 December 1993).

————, "The Shifting Political Landscape," *Transition,* vol. 1, no. 13 (28 July 1995).

Miller, Arthur H., Vicki L. Hesli, and William M. Reisinger, "Comparing Citizen and Elite Belief Systems in Post-Soviet Russia and Ukraine," *Public Opinion Quarterly,* vol. 59, no. 1 (Spring 1995), pp. 1–40.

Motyl, Alexander J., "The Conceptual President: Leonid Kravchuk and the Politics of Surrealism," in Timothy J. Colton and Robert C. Tucker, eds., *Patterns in Post-Soviet Leadership. The John Olin Critical Series* (Boulder and Oxford: Westview Press, 1995), pp. 103–121.

————, and Bohdan Krawchenko, "Ukraine: From Empire to Statehood," in Ian Bremmer and Ray Taras, eds., *New States, New Politics: Building the Post-Soviet Nations* (Cambridge: Cambridge University Press, 1997), pp. 235–275.

Mroz, Edwin John, and Oleksandr Pavliuk, "Ukraine: Europe's Linchpin," *Foreign Affairs,* vol. 75, no. 3 (May-June 1996), pp. 52–62.

Potichnyj, Peter J., "The Referendum and Presidential Elections in Ukraine," *Canadian Slavonic Papers,* vol. 33, no. 2 (June 1991), pp. 123–138.

Prisiajniuok, Oxana, "The State of Civil Society in Independent Ukraine," *Journal of Ukrainian Studies,* vol. 20, nos. 1–2 (Summer-Winter 1995), pp. 161–176.

Prizel, I., "Ukraine between Proto-democracy and 'Soft' Authoritarianism," in Karen Dawisha and Bruce Parrott, eds., *Democratic Changes and Authoritarian Reactions in Russia, Ukraine, Belarus and Moldova* (Cambridge: Cambridge University Press, 1997), pp. 330–369.

Reisinger, William, Arthur H. Miller, Vicki L. Hesli, and Kristen Hill Maher, "Political Values in Russia, Ukraine and Lithuania: Sources and Implications for Democracy," *British Journal of Political Science,* vol. 24, part 2 (1994), pp. 183–223.

Riabchouk, M., "Between Civil Society and the New Etatism: Democracy in the Making and State Building in Ukraine," in Michael D. Kennedy, ed., *Envisioning Eastern Europe. Postcommunist Cultural Studies* (Ann Arbor, MI: The University of Michigan Press, 1994), pp. 125–148.

Sochor, Zenovia A., "Political Culture and Foreign Policy: Elections in Ukraine 1994," in Vladimir Tismaneanu, ed., *Political Culture and Civil Society in Russia and the New States of Eurasia: The International Politics of Eurasia, Volume 7* (Armonk, NY, and London: M.E. Sharpe, 1995), pp. 208–226.

———, "From Liberalization to Post-Communism: The Role of the Communist Party in Ukraine," *Journal of Ukrainian Studies,* vol. 21, nos. 1–2 (Summer-Winter 1996), pp. 147–164.

Solchanyk, R., "Crimea's Presidential Election," *RFE/RL Research Report,* vol. 3, no. 11 (18 March 1994).

———, "Ukraine: The Politics of Reform," *Problems of Post-Communism,* vol. 42, no. 6 (November-December 1995), pp. 46–51.

Stent, Angela, "Ukraine's Fate," *World Policy Journal,* vol. X1, no. 3 (Fall 1994), pp. 83–87.

Wasylyk, Myron, "Ukraine Prepares for Parliamentary Elections," *RFE./RL Research Report,* vol. 3, no. 5 (4 February 1994).

———, "Ukraine on the Eve of Elections," *RFE/RL Research Report,* vol. 3, no. 12 (25 March 1994).

Wilson A., "The Elections in Crimea," *RFE/RL Research Report,* vol. 3, nos. 25 and 26 (24 June and 1 July1994).

———, "Parties and Presidents in Ukraine and Crimea, 1994," *The Journal of Communist Studies and Transition Politics,* vol. 11, no. 4 (December 1995), pp. 362–371.

——— and Artur Bilous, "Political Parties in Ukraine," *Europe-Asia Studies,* vol. 45, no. 4 (1993), pp. 693–703.

Part D. Economics and Society

Boss, Helen, "Ukraine: Better, but Not Good Enough," in Leon Podkaminer et al., eds,, *Transition Economies: Economic Development in 1995 and Outlook for 1996 and 1997, no. 225* (Vienna: The Vienna Institute for Comparative Economic Studies [WIIW]), February 1996), pp. 103–110.

———, and Peter Havlik, "Slavic (Dis)union: Consequences for Russia, Belarus and Ukraine," *Economics of Transition,* vol. 2, no. 2 (June 1994), pp. 233–254.

Chandler, Andrea, "State Building and Social Obligations in Post-Communist Systems: Assessing Change in Russia and Ukraine," *Canadian Slavonic Papers,* vol. XXXVIII, nos. 1–2 (March-June 1996), pp. 1–21.

Crowley, Stephen, "Between Class and Nation: Worker Politics in the New Ukraine," *Communist and Post-Communist Studies,* vol. 28, no. 1 (March 1995), pp. 43–69.

Dabrowski, Marek, "The Ukrainian Way to Hyperinflation," *Communist Economies and Economic Transformation,* vol. 6, no. 2 (June 1994), pp. 115–137.

——— and Rafal Antczak, "Economic Transition in Russia, Ukraine and Belarus: A Comparative Perspective," in Bartlomiej Kaminski, ed., *Economic Transition in Rus-*

sia and the New States of Eurasia. The International Politics of Eurasia, Volume 8 (Armonk, NY: M.E. Sharpe, 1996), pp. 42–80.

Havrylyshyn, Oleh, "Ukraine's Economic Crisis: An Extreme vVersion of Post-Soviet Trauma," *Ukraine Business Review,* vol. 2, no. 1 (February 1994), pp. 5–13.

———, "How Patriarchs and Rent-Seekers Are Hijacking the Transition to a Market Economy," *Perspectives on Contemporary Ukraine,* vol. 2, no. 3 (May-June 1995).

———, Marcus Miller, and William Perrandin, "Deficits, Inflation and the Political Economy of Ukraine," *Economic Policy,* no. 19 (December 1994), pp. 354–402.

Johnson, Simon, and Oleg Ustenko, "Ukraine Slips into Hyperinflation," *RFE/RL Research Report,* vol. 2, no. 26 (25 June 1993).

Kaufmann, Daniel, "Market Liberalization in Ukraine: To Regain a Lost Pillar of Economic Reform," *Transition,* vol. 5, no. 7 (7 September 1994), pp. 1–3.

———, "Diminishing Returns to Administrative Controls and the Emergence of the Unofficial Economy," *Economic Policy,* vol., no. 19 (December 1994), pp. 51–69.

Kistersky, Leonid, "Economic Reasons for the Political Crisis in Ukraine," *Brown Journal of Foreign Affairs,* vol. 1, no. 1 (Winter 1993–1994), pp. 171–176.

Kramer, Mark, "Blue-collar Workers and the Post-Communist Transitions in Poland, Russia and Ukraine," *Communist and Post-Communist Studies,* vol. 28, no. 1 (March 1995), pp. 3–11.

Krasnov, Gregory V., and Josef C. Brada, "Implicit Subsidies in Russian-Ukrainian Energy Trade," *Europe-Asia Studies,* vol. 49, no. 5 (July 1997), pp. 825–843).

Kuzio, Taras, "Economic Reform Surges Ahead," *Ukraine Business Review,* vol. 3, no. 8 (May 1995), pp. 3–11.

———, "After the Shock the Therapy," *Transition,* vol. 1, no. 13 (28 July 1995).

———, "Organised Crime and Corruption in Ukraine," *Jane's Intelligence Review,* vol. 9, no. 1 (January 1997), pp. 10–13.

Lapychak, C., "Agricultural Reform in Ukraine," *Transition,* vol. 1, no. 22 (1 December 1995).

Marples, D., "Ukraine, Belarus and the Energy Dilemma," *RFE/RL Research Report,* vol. 2, no. 27 (2 July 1993).

Martyniuk, Jaroslaw, and Ustina Markus, "Attitudes Prove to be a Major Obstacle in Economic Reform," *Transition,* vol. 2, no. 18 (6 September 1996).

Miller, William L., Tatyana Koshechkina, and Ase Grodeland, "How Citizens Cope with Postcommunist Officials: Evidence from Focus Group Discussions in Ukraine and the Czech Republic," *Political Studies,* vol. XLV, no. 3 (Special Issue, 1997), pp. 597–625.

Pleines, Heiko, "Ukraine's Organized Crime Is an Enduring Soviet Legacy," *Transition,* vol. 2, no. 5 (8 March 1996).

Rhodes, Mark, "Divisiveness and Doubt over Economic Reform," *Transition,* vol. 1, no. 6 (28 April 1995).

Rick, Simon, "Workers and Independence in Divided Ukraine," *Labour Focus on Eastern Europe,* no. 49 (Autumn 1994), pp. 18–34.

Rose, Richard, "Adaptation, Resilience, and Destitution. Alternative Responses to Transition in Ukraine," *Problems of Post-Communism,* vol. 42, no. 6 (November-December 1995), pp. 52–61.

Rosefielde, Steven, "Ukraine's Economic Recovery Potential to the Year 2000," *Journal of Ukrainian Studies,* vol. 21, nos. 1–2 (Summer-Winter 1996), pp. 165–190.

Sekarev, A., "Ukraine's Crisis on the Basis of Vague Economic Policy," *Problems of Economic Transition,* vol. 37, no. 9 (1995), pp. 40–56.

De Simone, Francisco Nadal, "Ukraine's New Currency and the Unstable Ruble Currency Area," *Communist Economies and Economic Transformation,* vol. 6, no. 1 (1994), pp. 99–112.

Smolansky, Oles M., "Ukraine's Quest for Independence: The Fuel Factor," *Europe-Asia Studies,* vol. 47, no. 1 (January-February 1995), pp. 67–90.

Tedstrom, John, "Ukraine: A Crash Course in Economic Transformation," *Comparative Economic Studies,* vol. 37, no. 4 (Winter 1996), pp. 49–67.

Varfolomeyev, O., "Rival 'Clans' Mix Business, Politics, and Murder," *Transition,* vol. 3, no. 6 (4 April 1997).

Whitlock, Erik, "Ukrainian-Russian Trade: The Economics of Dependency," *RFE/RL Research Report,* vol. 2, no. 43 (29 October 1993).

Zviglyanich, Volodymyr, "Public Perceptions of Economic Reform," *Transition,* vol. 1, no. 13 (28 July 1995).

Part E. Foreign and Defense Policies

D'Anieri, P., "Interdependence and Sovereignty in the Ukrainian-Russian Relationship," *European Security,* vol. 4, no. 4 (Winter 1995), pp. 603–621.

————, "Dilemmas of Interdependence. Autonomy, Prosperity, and Sovereignty in Ukraine's Russia Policy," *Problems of Post-Communism* (January-February 1997), pp. 16–25.

Baev, Pavel, and Tor Bukkvol, "Ukraine's Army under Civilian Rule," *Jane's Intelligence Review,* vol. 8, no. 1 (January 1996).

Blank, Stephen, "Russia, Ukraine and European Security," *European Security,* vol. 3, no. 1 (Spring 1994), pp. 182–207.

Brzezinski, Ian, "Polish-Ukrainian Relations: Europe's Neglected Strategic Axis," *Survival,* vol. 35, no. 3 (Autumn 1993), pp. 26–37.

Bukkvoll, Tor, "Ukraine and NATO: The Politics of Soft Cooperation," *Security Dialogue,* vol. 28, no. 3 (September 1997), pp. 363–374.

Crow, Susan, "Russian Parliament Asserts Control over Sevastopol," *RFE/RL Research Report,* vol. 2, no. 31 (30 July 1993).

Duncan, Andrew, "Ukraine's Forces Find That Change Is Good," *Jane's Intelligence Review,* vol. 9, no. 4 (April 1997).

Ellis, Jason, "The 'Ukraine Dilemma' and U.S. Foreign Policy," *European Security,* vol. 3, no. 2 (Summer 1994), pp. 251–280.

Foye, Stephen, "Civil-Military Tension in Ukraine," *RFE/RL Research Report,* vol. 3, no. 25 (18 June 1993).

Garnett, S.W., "The Sources and Conduct of Ukrainian Nuclear Policy," in George Quester, ed., *The Nuclear Challenge in Russia and the New States of Eurasia. The International Politics of Eurasia, Volume 6* (Armonk, NY, and London: M.E. Sharpe, 1996), pp. 125–151.

Izmalkov, Valerii, "Ukraine and Her Armed Forces: The Conditions and Process for Their Creation, Character, Structure and Military Doctrine," *European Security,* vol. 2, no. 2 (Summer 1993), pp. 279–319.

Kincade, William H., and Natalie Melnyczuk, "Eurasia Letter: Unneighborly Neighbors," *Foreign Policy,* no. 94 (Spring 1994), pp. 84–104.

Kulinich, Nikolai A., "Ukraine in the New Geopolitical Environment: Issues of Regional and Subregional Security," in Adeed Dawisha, ed., *The Making of Foreign Policy in Russia and the New States of Eurasia. The International Politics of Eurasia, Volume 4* (Armonk, NY, and London: M.E. Sharpe, 1995), pp. 113–140.

Kuzio, Taras, "Ukraine—A New Military Power?" *Jane's Intelligence Review,* vol. 4, no. 2 (February 1992).

————, "The Security Service of Ukraine—A Transformed Ukrainian KGB?" *Jane's Intelligence Review,* vol. 5, no. 3 (March 1993).

————, "Nuclear Weapons and Military Policy in Independent Ukraine," *Harriman Institute Forum,* vol. 6, no. 9 (May 1993).

————, "The Ukrainian National Guard," *Jane's Intelligence Review,* vol. 5, no. 5 (May 1993).

————, "Ukraine and Its Future Security," *Jane's Intelligence Review,* vol. 4, no. 12 (December 1993).

————, "From Pariah to Partner. Ukraine and Nuclear Weapons," *Jane's Intelligence Review,* vol. 5, no. 5 (May 1994).

————, "Ukraine and the Expansion of NATO," *Jane's Intelligence Review,* vol. 7, no. 9 (September 1995).

————, "Civil-Military Relations in Ukraine, 1989–1991," *Armed Forces and Society,* vol. 22, no. 1 (Fall 1995), pp. 25–49.

————, "Ukrainian Civil-Military Relations and the Military Impact of the Ukrainian Economic Crisis," in Bruce Parrott, ed., *State Building and Military Power in Russia and the New States of Eurasia: The International Politics of Eurasia, Volume 5* (Armonk, NY: M.E. Sharpe, 1995), pp. 157–192.

————, "A Friend in Need: Kiev Woos Washington," *The World Today,* vol. 52, no. 4 (April 1996), pp. 96–98.

————, "The Organization of Ukraine's Forces," *Jane's Intelligence Review,* vol. 8, no. 6 (June 1996).

————, "Crisis and reform in Ukraine," Parts 1 and 2, *Jane's Intelligence Review,* vol. 8, nos. 10 and 11 (October and November 1996).

————, "The Baltics, Ukraine and the Path to NATO," *Jane's Intelligence Review,* vol. 9, no. 7 (July 1997).

————, "A Way with Words: Keeping Kiev Secure," *The World Today,* vol. 52, no. 12 (December 1996), pp. 317–319.

————, "Ukraine and the Yugoslav Conflict," *Nationalities Papers,* vol. 25, no. 3 (September 1997), pp. 587–600.

Larrabee, F. Stephen, "Ukraine's Balancing Act," *Survival,* vol. 38, no. 2 (Summer 1996), pp. 143–165.

Lepingwell, John W.R., "The Black Sea Fleet Agreement: Progress or Empty Promises?" *RFE/RL Research Report,* vol. 3, no. 28 (9 July 1993).

————, "The Trilateral Agreement on Nuclear Weapons," *RFE/RL Research Report,* vol. 3, no. 4 (28 January 1994).

————, "Ukraine, Russia and Nuclear Weapons: A Chronology," *RFE/RL Research Report,* vol. 3, no. 4 (28 January 1994).

Lester, Jeremy, "Russian Political Attitudes to Ukrainian Independence," *The Journal of Post Communist Studies and Transition Politics,* vol. 10, no. 2 (June 1994), pp. 193–233.

Markus, Ustina, "Ukrainian-Chinese Relations: Slow but Steady Progress," *RFE/Rl Research Report,* vol. 2, no. 45 (12 November 1993).

————, "The Ukrainian Navy and the Black Sea Fleet," *RFE/RL Research Report,* vol. 3, no. 18 (6 May 1994).

————, "Foreign Policy as a Security Tool," *Transition,* vol. 1, no. 13 (28 July 1995).

————, "To Counterbalance Russian Power, China Leans toward Ukraine," *Transition,* vol. 1, no. 17 (22 September 1995).

————, "Belarus, Ukraine Take Opposite Views," *Transition,* vol. 2, no. 23 (15 November 1996).

Morrison, John, "Pereyaslav and After: The Russian-Ukrainian Relationship," *International Affairs,* vol. 69, no. 4 (October 1993), pp. 677–704.

Nahaylo, Bohdan, "Ukraine and Moldova: The View from Kiev," *RFE/RL Research Report,* vol. 1, no. 18 (1 May 1992).
———, "The Shaping of Ukrainian Attitudes toward Nuclear Arms," *RFE/RL Research Report,* vol. 2, no. 8 (19 February 1993).
———, "The Massandra Summit: Questions and Implications," *RFE/RL Research Report,* vol. 2, no. 37 (17 September 1993).
Oliynyk, Stephen D. (Colonel), "Emerging Post-Soviet Armies: The Case of the Ukraine," *Military Review,* vol. LXXIV, no. 3 (March 1994), pp. 5–18.
Pavliuk, Oleksandr, "Ukrainian-Polish Relations: A Pillar of Regional Stability?" in *The Effects of Enlargement on Bilateral Relations in Central and Eastern Europe* (Paris: Institute for Security Studies, Western European Union, June 1997), pp. 43–62.
———, "Ukraine and Regional Cooperation in Central and Eastern Europe," *Security Dialogue,* vol. 28, no. 3 (September 1997), pp. 347–362.
Pedchenko, Volodymyr, "Ukraine's Delicate Balancing Act," *Transitions,* vol. 4, no. 1 (June 1997).
Popadiuk, Roman, "Ukraine: The Security Fulcrum of Europe," *Strategic Forum,* no. 69 (April 1996), pp. 1–4.
Reisch, A.A., "Hungarian-Ukrainian Relations Continue to Develop," *RE/RL Research Report,* vol. 3, no. 16 (16 April 1993).
Rumer, Eugene B., "Eurasia Letter: Will Ukraine Return to Russia?" *Foreign Policy,* no. 96 (Fall 1994), pp. 129–144, and no. 97 (Winter 1994–1995), pp. 178–181.
Rutland, Peter, "Search for Stability," *Transition,* vol. 1, no. 10 (23 June 1995).
Sherr, James, "Russia-Ukraine *Rapprochement?* The Black Sea Fleet Accords," *Survival,* vol. 39, no. 3 (Autumn 1997), pp. 33–50.
Socor, Vladimir, "Annexation of Bessarabia and Northern Bukovina Condemned by Romania," RL 256/91, *Report on the USSR,* vol. 3, no. 29 (19 July 1991).
———, "Demirel Asserts Turkish Interests in Ukraine and Moldova," *RFE/RL Research Report,* vol. 3, no. 31 (12 August 1994).
Solchanyk, Roman, "Ukraine, the (Former) Center, Russia and 'Russia,' " *Studies in Comparative Communism,* vol. XXV, no. 1 (March 1992), pp. 31–45.
———, "The Crimean Imbroglio: Kiev and Moscow," *RFE/RL Research Report,* vol. 1, no. 40 (9 October 1992).
———, "Ukraine and the CIS: A Troubled Relationship," *RFE/RL Research Report,* vol. 2, no. 7 (12 February 1993).
———, "Ukraine's Search for Security," *RFE/RL Research Report,* vol. 2, no. 21 (21 May 1993).
———, "Russia, Ukraine and the Imperial Legacy," *Post-Soviet Affairs,* vol. 9, no. 4 (October-December 1993), pp. 337–365.
Strekal, Oleh, "The New Secret Service," *Transition,* vol. 1, no. 10 (23 June 1995).
Udovenko, Hennadiy, "European Stability and NATO Enlargement: Ukraine's Perspective," *NATO Review,* no. 6 (November 1995), pp. 15–18.
Umbach, Frank, "The Security of an Independent Ukraine," *Jane's Intelligence Review,* vol. 5, no. 3 (March 1994).
Zaloga, Steven, "Armed Forces in Ukraine," *Jane's Intelligence Review,* vol. 4, no. 3 (March 1992).

Index